W9-CDP-077

MONEY and the NATION STATE

Independent Studies in Political Economy

THE ACADEMY IN CRISIS
The Political Economy of Higher Education
Edited by John W. Sommer
Foreword by Nathan Glazer

MONEY AND THE NATION STATE
The Financial Revolution, Government,
and the World Monetary System
Edited by Kevin Dowd and
Richard Timberlake

PRIVATE RIGHTS & PUBLIC ILLUSIONS
Tibor R. Machan
Foreword by Nicholas Rescher

TAXING CHOICE
The Predatory Politics of
Fiscal Discrimination
Edited by William F. Shughart II
Foreword by Paul W. McCracken

MONEY and the NATION STATE

The Financial Revolution, Government and the World Monetary System

Edited by Kevin Dowd & Richard H. Timberlake, Jr.

Foreword by Merton H. Miller

Transaction Publishers
New Brunswick (U.S.A.) and London (U.K.)

Copyright © 1998 by The Independent Institute, Oakland, Calif.

This book is printed on acid-free paper that meets the American National Standard for Permanence of Paper for Printed Library Materials.

Library of Congress Catalog Number: 97-40091
ISBN: 1-56000-302-2 (cloth); 1-56000-930-6 (paper)
Printed in the United States of America

Library of Congress Cataloging-in-Publication Data

Dowd, Kevin.
Money and the nation state : the financial revolution, government, and the world monetary system / Kevin Dowd and Richard H. Timberlake ; with a foreword by Merton H. Miller.
    p. cm.
Includes bibliographical references and index.
ISBN 1-56000-302-2 (cloth : alk. paper). — ISBN 1-56000-930-6 (pbk. : alk. paper)
1. Money—History. 2. International finance—History. 3. National state. 4. Financial institutions—State supervision. I. Timberlake, Richard H. II. Title.
HG220.A2D69 1997
332.4—dc21   97-40091
                                                              CIP

The INDEPENDENT INSTITUTE

THE INDEPENDENT INSTITUTE is a non-profit, scholarly research and educational organization that sponsors comprehensive studies of the political economy of critical social and economic problems.

The politicization of decision-making in society has too often confined public debate to the narrow reconsideration of existing policies. Given the prevailing influence of partisan interests, little social innovation has occurred. In order to understand both the nature of and possible solutions to major public issues, the Independent Institute's program adheres to the highest standards of independent inquiry and is pursued regardless of prevailing political or social biases and conventions. The resulting studies are widely distributed as books and other publications, and are publicly debated through numerous conference and media programs.

Through this uncommon independence, depth, and clarity, the Independent Institute pushes at the frontiers of our knowledge, redefines the debate over public issues, and fosters new and effective directions for government reform.

Contents

III. Foundations for Monetary and Banking Reform

Foreword

Merton H. Miller

Economic events have a way of catching up with tired economic orthodoxies. The fixed-exchange rate orthodoxy of the 1940s and 1950s was eventually undermined by the overproduction of U.S. dollars in the 1960s. The post–Bretton Woods, floating rate orthodoxy that succeeded it in the early 1970s eroded steadily during the 1980s in the face of turbulence in the foreign exchange markets and led, in Europe at least, to a new, single-currency orthodoxy. The disastrous European Monetary Union debacle of October 1992 has in turn discredited that orthodoxy, while many questions the U.S. academic establishment considered long settled have been reopened by the collapse of the Mexican peso (but not the Argentine peso) in December 1994.

The crumbling of tired orthodoxies can lead not only to bitter disputes over current policy decisions but lead also to equally contentious reinterpretations of the critical historical episodes that give rise to those orthodoxies. Of the many such defining historical episodes revisited by the authors in this excellent and very timely volume, few such episodes have played a greater role in shaping the accepted wisdom than the British decision in 1925 to return to the prewar value of the pound.

To Keynesians, that decision was a massive act of folly, as argued so vehemently at the time by Keynes himself in his polemic, *The Economic Consequences of Mr. Churchill.* Churchill, then Chancellor of the Exchequer, though not an economist, surely knew that price and wage inflation during the Great War would make the pound at its prewar parity seem overvalued relative to the dollar and would create a competitiveness problem for the traditional British export industries. But he also knew that Britain would lose its role as the world's banker unless the pound could maintain its reputation as a safe and stable long-run store of value come what may, war or no war. For the pound to be maintainable at its prewar value, however, the British wage level would also have to be restored eventually to its prewar value—adjusted, of course, for the modest improvements in productivity that had taken place over the interval. What Churchill failed to realize, alas, was that any chance the wage level might adjust was lost once his well-intentioned unemployment dole had set a floor under nominal wage rates.

Keynes understood, as well as Churchill, that British competitiveness could be sustained only by lowering British real wages. But why do it, he asked, by the socially divisive tactic of using depression and unemployment to force nominal wages down? Why not lower real wages the easy way—by keeping nominal wages steady and using monetary expansion (and exchange rate devaluation) to raise domestic prices? This "don't lower the river, raise the bridge" line of argument, so characteristic of Keynes, turned up again ten years later as the central policy theme in *The General Theory*. It has been invoked over and over again in every devaluation crisis right up to Italy in 1992 and Mexico in 1994. The official view in Washington today, and among most U.S. academics, is that the Mexican disaster could easily have been avoided with a "modest" devaluation of the "overvalued" Mexican peso in the spring or summer of 1994.

To the authors in this volume, the case for devaluation was never as simple as the Keynesian orthodoxy made it appear either in Mexico in 1994 or Britain in 1925. Workers can be fooled by rising prices for a while, but sooner or later they will catch on (or their spouses will tell them, as Abba Lerner, himself an early Keynesian, once confessed). And then you're right back to where you were before the devaluation, only a good deal poorer and with the government's credibility destroyed.

But let there be no mistake: no single-minded new orthodoxy about devaluations is being expounded here. The authors, though clearly preferring free markets to the dubious performance of central banking and government "management" of monetary affairs, feel free to disagree among themselves in their interpretations of key events, empirical evidence on devaluations, and a variety of other monetary issues. But they do so in ways that should command the full attention of all who seek deeper understanding and solutions to the serious financial problems we face. *Money and the Nation State* provides the essential framework for those willing to return to first principles in thinking about the role of monetary arrangements in economic life. A careful reconsideration of today's failed monetary orthodoxies is clearly overdue, and this book contributes significantly toward that reassessment.

Introduction

Kevin Dowd and Richard H. Timberlake

A large and growing number of observers recognize that monetary and banking problems in the world today arise, not so much from the failure of this or that individual or policy, but from more deep-seated reasons that lie within the institutional structure. While individuals clearly make mistakes and legislatures make bad laws, the institutions from which decisions and laws emanate are the critical factors that determine the efficacy of social operations and the value of social decisions. Unless the present institutional structure changes, we are not likely to get stable solutions to today's most serious monetary and financial problems: ongoing and often erratic inflation and serious banking instability.

The chapters in this book examine the history of modern monetary and banking arrangements, some of the major monetary and banking problems, and several options for meaningful reform. To a greater or lesser extent, all the essays incorporate the view that what really matters is institutional structure. The common theme is that the history of current arrangements is less the history of "great men" than the history of man-made institutions society has inherited—specifically, central banks and the legal and regulatory frameworks that accompany them. The faults of this or that chairman of the Federal Reserve System, for example, or the faults of this or that president of the United States, have less significance than the incentives and expectations that present-day institutional structures offer to the individuals who operate or deal with them. Similarly, meaningful reform is not so much a question of getting the "right man" for the job—appointing a better Federal Reserve chairman, for example—as it is the task of changing the environment within which any Federal Reserve chairman must work.

The chapters in this book also emphasize two other related points. First, they stress the impact of political interference on the workings of monetary and financial institutions. Much of the banking structure that

1

society has inherited has resulted from politicians operating by means of government fiat or through misguided legislation. These human designers have often operated for their own ends rather than for any broader "social welfare." They set up central banks to provide cheap loans with which to fight unpopular wars; they abolished the gold standard because they wanted more inflation than the gold standard would provide, all the while advertising their "commitment" to sound money.

Not surprisingly, a common theme in these papers is that many problems arise because these politically generated structures have proven to be inappropriate to the real needs of the individuals and groups they allegedly were meant to serve. Many of today's problems arise from the way in which the extra-constitutional political process has impinged on the financial system.

The second point emphasized by this book is the multifaceted role of monetary nationalism. Monetary policy is usually framed in a context where it cannot help but be influenced by the priorities of national governments. A decision on whether or not to defend an exchange rate is usually taken, or at least influenced, by a national government with its own political agenda. So, too, are decisions whether to join an exchange rate system, whether to pass a legal tender law, and whether to establish a system of deposit insurance. In short, monetary policy is almost always politicized. It has become a means to further central government objectives. The alternative is a monetary system, constitutionally prescribed, that would operate under the rule of law.

History of the International Monetary System

The chapters of the book fall naturally into three groupings. The first section focuses on historical issues and, in particular, the history of the international monetary system. Chapter one examines the evolution of the state's monetary monopoly from ancient times to the present. As David Glasner notes, the history of money is virtually the history of the state's debasement, depreciation, and devaluation of the currency. The state has usually acted for its own ends with relatively little concern for the general public's welfare. The state's common motive has been to raise revenue, normally in circumstances in which it wished to wage war and where alternative forms of revenue-raising were politically and technically difficult or just inconvenient. These abuses of state power provoked much outcry. Yet, while many sincere statesmen criticized particular instances of abuse, they only infrequently challenged the state monetary monopolies that initiated and perpetrated such abuses.

Even more surprising is the fact that state money monopolies have received relatively little challenge from the economics profession, a group that embraces, almost as an article of faith, the belief that monopoly is an evil. This lack of challenge might be more understandable if the production of money was logically or empirically a natural monopoly with only one producer arising under conditions of free entry. Far from being a natural monopoly needing the aegis of the state, however, money arose spontaneously in many lands, always originating in the private sector with no help from the state. Only when money's productivity as an economic item became apparent did the state enter the picture, and then only as an exploiter of, never as a contributor to, money's utility.

Glasner enhances this picture. He suggests that the state established a monopoly over the production of money because such a monopoly was vital to state security. In the ancient world the state's power to tax was rudimentary, and a state that allowed private mints to operate was vulnerable to takeover by the mint owners. Political power was often captured by the individual or group able to finance the most mercenaries. The owner of a private mint was in a particularly favorable position to raise his own army to carry out an expedient coup d'état.

Even if governments of the day did not monopolize the production of money—and they often did—a state monopoly would often arise anyway because the owner of the mint would take over the state and be anxious to protect himself from a similar coup by another mint owner. Ownership of a mint gave a government a source of emergency funds often crucial in assuring its survival in a crisis such as fighting off an invader. States with their own monopoly mints thus had a better chance to survive political emergencies than states without.

Though the institution of a government monetary monopoly was rarely questioned, there were repeated attempts to restrain the government's monetary powers to prevent abuse. A commodity standard, such as the bimetallic standard or the gold standard, was one such means to limit the state's excesses. But these institutions enjoyed only temporary success; they were not tamper-proof. Governments could always find ways to evade the limitations.

The most successful period for commodity standards was the nineteenth century, when most major governments adopted gold or bimetallic standards. Nonetheless, the relative success of those standards in maintaining a high degree of price-level stability was something of an historical anomaly. Glasner argues that such arrangements only worked, to the extent they did, because governments were willing to go along with them for self-serving reasons. Governments desired stable prices in peacetime, not so much because they hallowed the principle of price-level stability, but because the maintenance of peacetime price stability increased the ex-post levies they could get out of their subjects in a wartime emergency! Since wars were unpredictable, private individuals would normally operate on the assumptions that the monetary regime would not change gears and that prices would remain reasonably stable. When wars did break out, convertibility was abandoned and the government or its pet bank(s) inflated the currency on the pretext that the emergency required it. A good example was the Civil War period in the United States, when the federal (Northern) government abandoned gold convertibility of the currency and embarked on greenback inflation to help finance the war, but much the same thing happened in many other countries at different times.

While Glasner focuses on the minting privilege and seignorage revenues from monarchies in earlier times, Frank van Dun in chapter two examines the relationship between political sovereignty, on the one hand, and the issue of fiat paper money and central banking prerogatives on the other. He notes that Adam Smith did not include monetary manipulation in his list of the duties and perquisites of the sovereign. Most modern economists, however, have fallen under the influence of political and legal arguments that accept the legitimacy of the state's alleged monetary sovereignty, the state's powers to specify what shall be legal tender, and the state's right to create a central bank. Van Dun's chapter focuses on the development of these political and legal concepts and their influence on the political and financial milieu.

Perhaps the critical issue is where does sovereignty reside. The doctrine of sovereignty has its roots in Roman law as interpreted in the Justinian Code, but modern notions of sovereignty date from the work of writers such as Jean Bodin, Thomas Hobbes, and Jean-Jacques Rousseau. These writers saw sovereignty as the prerogative of the state—perhaps its defining attribute. Sovereignty, therefore, played an important role in providing modern arguments for state power and in giving support to those who held that the state had a legitimate role in the monetary system. Some argued, for example, that the state had a "natural right" [sic] to the seignorage profits from money creation since only the state could give legitimacy to money. The state, therefore, should monopolize the minting industry or the supply of banknotes. Others argued that protecting the integrity of the monetary system was one of the duties of the sovereign—a duty, they implied, the unaided private sector was unable to handle.

The doctrine of sovereignty, when applied to the monetary system, also lent support to arguments for legal tender laws, by which private agents were to be compelled to accept state currency that was worth less than the real value of the contractual debt it cleared. The power to impose legal tender laws contradicted the state's supposed duty to protect and enforce the laws of contract; however, the proponents of legal tender argued that state sovereignty took precedence over private interests and thereby justified what otherwise would have been a violation of contract. In the twentieth century, the doctrine of monetary sovereignty found its extreme expression in Georg Knapp's *State Theory of Money*, which put forward the view that the state not only had sovereignty in monetary affairs but that state fiat gave acceptability to money in the first place! Significantly, some of Knapp's ideas were later picked up and propagated much more widely by John Maynard Keynes.

The next two chapters treat the history of monetary standards, in particular metallic monetary standards. Leland Yeager in chapter three considers the contemporary history of the international monetary system. Present-day monetary arrangements arose from the international gold standard; yet the gold standard has been a relatively recent development. It functioned as the world's monetary standard only for a brief period of time between the early 1870s and 1914. Before then, the international monetary standard was largely bimetallic.

Britain, traditionally on a silver standard, was eased onto a bimetallic standard in 1717 when Sir Isaac Newton, Master of the Mint, recommended the adoption of a mint ratio between gold guineas and silver shillings. The parity chosen made gold cheaper in Britain, relative to silver, than it was elsewhere. Over time silver disappeared except as token coinage; and Britain became de facto, if not de jure, a gold standard country. The Bank of England suspended convertibility in 1797, when the government's demands for credit from the bank made it impossible for the bank to redeem its own notes. Upon resumption of gold convertibility in 1821, the legal fiction of bimetallism was abandoned. Thereafter, the British monetary system was gold-based monometallic.

The United States adopted bimetallism in 1792, but with a world gold-silver price ratio of about 15.5:1. The chosen U.S. ratio meant that gold was undervalued at the mint. Therefore, gold did not come to the mint and the U.S. monetary system functioned as if it were on a silver standard. In 1834 the U.S. gold-silver price ratio was revised to near 16:1. Since the world price ratio remained much as it was before (around 15.6:1), this new ratio put the United States onto an effective gold standard.

In 1861 the federal government of the United States abandoned convertibility to finance the Civil War with issues of paper money. When convertibility was finally restored in 1879, the U.S. system returned, as Britain did in 1821, to a gold standard in name as well as in fact. The period from the 1860s onward also saw a number of other countries reform their monetary standards, most of them eventually adopting a formal gold standard.

The *international* gold standard, in the proper sense of the term, dates primarily from the late nineteenth century to World War I, during which time it functioned reasonably well. However, the financial and monetary upheavals accompanying the war obliterated the gold standard and seriously jeopardized its reestablishment after the armistice.

Murray Rothbard in chapter four details the rather bizarre machinations of the world's major central bankers during the 1920s. Montagu Norman, governor of the Bank of England, and Benjamin Strong, president of the Federal Reserve Bank of New York, tried to structure a "gold standard" in which all the gold would be held by the central banks and would not be used to redeem paper currencies, and under which no corrective adjustments for central bank excesses would occur. Rothbard's account of the relations between the Bank of England and the Fed, and their efforts to counteract the pressures of what would have been routine gold standard adjustments, emphasizes the validity of the maxim that a true gold standard and an activist central bank are incompatible institutions. A nation-state either has one or the other.

In the face of the world financial crisis of 1931, the Bank of England permanently abandoned gold convertibility of the pound sterling. Many other government central banks also abandoned the gold standard, and exchange rates were for the most part left to float for the rest of the decade. As the Second World War drew to a close, the Allies agreed to set up a government-operated, pseudo-gold standard structure. In the postwar era, the Bretton Woods plan provided the basis for a world exchange rate system until the incompatible policies of the major central banks finally brought about its collapse in the early 1970s.

The next chapter by Richard Timberlake focuses on a different aspect of the history of the gold standard. In the late nineteenth and early twentieth centuries, many governments set up central banks and initiated legal tender paper money systems that encroached on the adjustment procedures of the earlier self-regulating commodity-money standards. The constitutional rule of law in monetary affairs began to give way to the discretionary rule of men.

The roots of this transition are seen in the early history of metallic standards. For reasons discussed in chapter two, states had earlier assumed the monopoly of minting coins and certifying their face value. Yet, they could never for long resist the temptation to debase or otherwise devalue their own coins in order to extract seignorage revenue from the private sector.

The state thus developed a Jekyll and Hyde character. The state as Dr. Jekyll issued coins and certified their content, a task that it insisted on doing itself but which would have been done by the private sector if it were allowed the opportunity. Then the state as Mr. Hyde would debase its own currency for essentially political ends. The appearance of constitutionally restrained governments in the seventeenth and eighteenth centuries initiated a growing demand for rule-based monetary standards to facilitate both international and domestic trade. By the early nineteenth century Dr. Jekyll seemed to be very much in ascendancy. Most countries were on gold or bimetallic standards that provided a reasonable degree of price stability. Prices would sometimes rise gently when gold was discovered, as they did after the strikes of gold in Australia and California in the late 1840s, but prices would also fall slightly in other periods. Over the long haul the price level was remarkably stable. Money prices in Britain in 1914, for example, were very close to what they had been ninety-nine years earlier at the time of the Battle of Waterloo!

Yet, even as commodity-based monetary standards were reaching their operational zenith, statist sentiment had already begun to undermine them by setting up central banks. Judicial activism was also instrumental in providing legal tender apologias for government issues of fiat currency.

The development of legal tender money and central banking had only a limited impact as long as most countries remained on the gold standard. When widespread convertibility was temporarily abandoned in 1914 and permanently in the early 1930s, these subsidiary institutions became dominant. Once the statutory or constitutional link between the value of the currency and a quantity of gold was broken, no restraints could prevent government-sponsored central banks from issuing whatever money they wished. Court-sanctioned legal tender laws compelled private agents to accept the depreciated paper of these central banks as full payment for previously contracted debts. The undisciplined fiat standard replaced the earlier gold standard, and the vagaries of the political process now determined the value of the currency. In the United States and in many other countries private holdings of gold held and used for monetary purposes were outlawed altogether in the 1930s. The ancient monopoly rights of state coinage issues and debasement reappeared as legislatures gave central banks monopoly powers to issue paper money and depreciate it without limit.

Modern Money and Central Banking

The second part of this book explores various aspects of modern monetary systems and central banking. Thomas Cargill in chapter six examines U.S. financial policy since the collapse of the Bretton Woods system in the early 1970s. Cargill argues that U.S. financial policy in the years before the collapse operated on the assumption that financial markets were inherently unstable. Financial policy in those years was designed to limit market forces by a variety of domestic legal restrictions. The failure of such policies to insulate domestic markets coincided with the collapse of Bretton Woods, when American authorities had to grant market forces a larger role in both domestic and foreign exchange markets. "Deregulation" of one sort or another became fashionable.

Cargill makes three general observations about this deregulation process. First, he notes that U.S. policy has generally been reactive rather than constructive. Deregulation became an accepted principle only after market innovations had rendered earlier governmental attempts to control the system an obvious failure. In many ways, deregulatory measures, such as the Depository Institutions Deregulation and Monetary Control Act of 1980, merely ratified what already had been achieved by market participants in the 1970s. Far from unleashing market forces by deregulating them, deregulatory measures were often little more than attempts by legislators and regulators to accommodate current market realities.

Second, Cargill shows that the commitment of U.S. legislators and regulators to enhance the role of competitive forces in the U.S. domestic financial system is far from complete. They never have had a consistent vision of deregulation, and their acceptance of deregulation such as it is has been slow, partial, and grudging.

Third, Cargill demonstrates that the process of deregulation that has already taken place is still very incomplete. Large areas of the U.S. financial system remain either regulated or are still suffering from the effects of previous regulatory policies. Furthermore, the reforms that have taken place have often been ineffective. Despite repeated reforms, for example, the thrift industry still remains a mess, and to a lesser extent the same can be said of much of the rest of the banking system. The high cost of the thrift bailout, the insolvency of the thrift industry, and the weakened condition of the financial services industry in general all attest to the failure of regulatory reform to undo the web of financial regulations that have so crippled the U.S. financial sector.

Chapter seven treats one specific and very important area of financial policy: the use of deposit insurance to protect banks against runs. Genie Short and Kenneth Robinson observe that economists generally agree about the source of U.S. banking problems. Geographic and product restrictions have greatly hampered the ability of banks to compete and have limited their ability to protect themselves by diversifying portfolios and realizing economies of scale. At the same time, the operation of the authorities' financial safety net, consisting of federal deposit insurance and the Federal Reserve's discount window, has further weakened the financial services industry. By protecting banks against runs from depositors, these provisions have encouraged financial institutions to forgo sound policies that would maintain depositor confidence. Depositors know that some federal insurance agency, or perhaps the Federal Reserve, will repay their deposits if their banks default, so they have little reason to care about the soundness of their banks. In the presence of apathetic depositors, many banks take excessive risks they otherwise would avoid. Furthermore, weak banks can remain in business simply by raising their deposit rates to attract more resources, regardless of the losses they may have suffered on their loan books. To make matters worse, banks no longer have the incentive to maintain their capital adequacy. They allow their capital ratios to decline, thereby putting themselves in a position where they are less able to absorb loan losses and still remain solvent.

The causes of these problems are widely accepted, but there is little agreement on what to do about them. Since 1980 Congress has passed five major acts to reform the financial services industry in one way or another, but these measures have so far proven ineffective. Indeed, many observers regard them as little more than cosmetic exercises to give the appearance of something being done.

As in the early 1980s, discussion of U.S. financial reform continues on how to eliminate the legal restrictions that prevent U.S. banks from competing effectively. There is also much concern over how legal restrictions can be removed without aggravating the moral hazard problem that has accompanied government subsidized deposit insurance. Nonetheless, discussions ten years ago and discussions today are noticeably different. Ten years ago, the focus of attention was on whether U.S. policy needed to change the deposit insurance system. Today, it focuses on how to change it without creating a financial crisis in the process.

Short and Robinson argue that effective financial reform in the U.S. requires a major reexamination of the extent to which the deposit insurance system can discipline banks. Deposit insurance was supposed to protect banks against what was perceived as the instability inherent in the industry. However, it has created moral hazard and related problems that have had the effect, over time, of severely weakening the industry at enormous cost to the taxpayer.

Short and Robinson review the history of federal deposit insurance in the United States. They discuss the reasons insurance coverage has gradually risen over the years until virtually all deposits are 100 percent guaranteed. They also discuss the spread of similar guarantees in other countries, arguing that such widespread coverage has played a major role in exacerbating financial instability around the world. They conclude that fundamental changes are needed to allow financial markets to function more freely in order to discipline banks that pursue excessively risky policies or fail to maintain their capital adequacy. Until such reforms are forthcoming, the prospects for a return to financial stability in the United States and elsewhere are not good.

Chapter eight examines another major problem area in the modern world economy—the role of the IMF in promoting destructive policies on its client governments. The IMF has well over $100 billion in resources which it lends out on conditional terms to client governments to help them out of short-term difficulties. In his review of IMF policies, Alan Reynolds asks: What is the nature and effect of the IMF package of economic policy reforms on which it bases its loans? Much Western economic policy presumes superficially that the IMF package works. Agreement to implement the IMF package is often made a condition for other forms of Western aid to client countries, and the "success" of IMF policies has been the principal reason given to Western parliaments and electorates for continuously supplementing IMF resources. Funding the IMF has been part and parcel of Western aid to less developed countries.

The IMF record, however, is remarkably poor. There are no commonly accepted IMF "success stories." Some countries, including many in sub-Saharan Africa and Latin America, have been regular IMF "patients" for decades and still show no signs of recovery. Indeed some—the African ones in particular—have only deteriorated under IMF "care."

Reynolds argues that this poor record is no accident but can be traced directly to the policy reforms that the IMF forces on its reluctant "patients." A typical IMF program features devaluation of the currency, ostensibly to improve the balance of payments; restrictions on the amount of domestic credit to improve inflation performance; specific targets to lower public sector borrowing, thereby reducing domestic credit expansion; and an agreement to remove restrictive trade practices to promote longer-term economic growth. Underlying this package are the views that a current account deficit represents a problem for the country concerned and that devaluation is an effective means of dealing with this problem.

Both views are highly questionable. To say that a country has a current account deficit is to say that it is importing capital. In fact, many poorer countries need large capital imports if their economic growth is to "take off." Capital import restrictions, therefore, prevent the economic growth the IMF claims it is promoting. Even if one accepts a current account deficit as a problem, the available empirical evidence suggests that manipulating the exchange rate by devaluing the currency is not an effective means of reducing the deficit.

The IMF package is also contradictory. While the IMF professes to be concerned about reducing inflation, devaluation of the exchange rate often leads to monetary polices that worsen inflation rather than abate it. Aggravated inflation in turn tends to make more difficult the effort to bring public finances under proper control, especially when inflation has been long-term. Greater inflation also tends to undermine the goal of trade liberalization, thereby deteriorating the economy's future growth prospects. In practice, therefore, the IMF package has often discouraged inflation control. Failure to control inflation has in turn hindered the achievement of economic stabilization, promoted widespread poverty, and prevented the establishment of a solid basis for future growth.

A much better project for IMF promotion would be unqualified stabilization of the price level. The current account deficit should be allowed to grow so as to accommodate capital imports, and trade should be freed. Japan, Korea, and other countries followed this recipe in earlier decades, as did Israel in the 1980s. It has proven very successful. Instead of relying on inflationary devaluations to boost their economies artificially, these countries allowed their current account deficits to get larger—thereby providing economic growth—so that they eventually were able to pay off their debts. Success came from flouting IMF rules, in particular by rejecting its "devaluation theory" and its obsession with the current account deficit.

Reynolds also notes irony in the fact that the IMF was founded not to promote devaluations but to prevent them. Its original purpose was to lend to member governments to enable them to carry out reforms that would prevent the need for currency devaluation. A commitment to avoid devaluation, except in extreme circumstances, was a fundamental principle of the Bretton Woods system. When Bretton Woods collapsed in the early 1970s, the IMF in true bureaucratic fashion sought a new, more activist role to justify its continued existence.

The last chapter in this section, by Robert Keleher, examines recent trends in the financial services industry and alternative policy responses. Perhaps the most important development has been the increasing integration of the world financial services industry. This integration might be seen as a natural consequence of more general economic integration, but it also has been assisted by other factors such as the widespread, though not complete, deregulation of financial markets and the related phenomenon of widespread financial innovation. These developments have significantly reduced artificial or legal barriers to global financial integration. Revolutions in telecommunication and information technology also have notably reduced other barriers.

Many economists have argued that heightened international interdependence severely limits the degree of control that national authorities have on their countries' financial systems. Economists have also recognized the phenomenon of exchange rate "overshooting," and they realize that governments face an increasingly complex economic environment that makes their holistic decision making ever more difficult. The greater interdependency and complexity of the world economy have placed a premium on wider coordination of economic policy making, an issue much discussed in recent years.

Two different views have emerged on this issue. Those still wedded to the Keynesian approach to economic management argue that governments must retain major discretion to "do the right thing," but they also argue that this traditional type of policy making needs to be more coordinated. This view is very much in evidence at the regular G-7 summit meetings where the political managers of the worlds' major economies meet to coordinate their macroeconomic and demand-management policies.

Most economists also subscribe to policies of hands-on control in one form or another. According to this view, international policy coordination implies that national governments should rely less on formulating independent demand-management policies and more on developing a unified demand-management agreement. The underlying idea is that by coordinating their macroeconomic policies, national governments will be less inclined to inflict undesirable "externalities" on each other. When formulating their fiscal policy, for example, the Germans would take into account the impact of their fiscal policy on other countries. Countries considering shifts in monetary policy would acknowledge the possibility that such change might induce exchange rate overshooting that would affect other countries.

The alternative thesis is quite different. It regards information and knowledge as dispersed and the costs of acquiring information so high as to be unrealizable. It concludes that centralized decision makers cannot have the omniscience presumed by the interventionist view. This alternative perspective sees the problem of coordination as ultimately resolved, not by political policy makers coordinating economic policy decisions, but by hundreds of market participants making their own arrangements for economizing resources under simple, acceptable, and recognizable rules of the game. The important role of governments is to carry out whatever structural reforms might be useful in assisting markets to function effectively. Governments are vital for establishing the rules of the game, for enforcing sensible standards for private agents to follow, and for removing obstacles to the free movement of capital, labor, and goods.

Professor Keleher observes that the available empirical evidence of benefits from interventionist policy coordination of the first type is relatively small or nonexistent. The second type of coordination appears to be more effective; one can point to a number of important success stories where it has clearly worked. The lesson for government policy makers is that they should rely less on discretionary macromanagement of the old type and more on rules-based arrangements if they wish to maximize the welfare of their constituent peoples.

Monetary and Banking Reform

The final set of chapters focuses on different proposals for monetary or banking reform. The first paper discusses the public choice aspects of monetary policy. Burdekin, Westbrook, and Willett point out that serious endemic flaws in the control apparatus of the present-day monetary system give it a pronounced inflationary bias. One frequently cited problem is that elected governments typically have an incentive to manipulate the macroeconomy to maximize the incumbent administration's chances of winning the next election. Politicians have a decided preference, for example, to reduce interest rates in order to improve their short-run popularity, regardless of whether such changes can be justified by current recessionary trends in the economy. The use of monetary policy to buy short-term popularity then translates into inflation, despite most politicians' claims that they oppose inflation and prefer price stability.

Since the problem of this inflationary bias arises from the underlying institutional structure, it cannot be dealt with by changing the particular individuals involved, such as firing the chairman of the Federal Reserve. What is needed is institutional reform, and here there are many choices. Some economists advocate the adoption of simple constitutional rules, such as a return to the gold standard, or passage of a law mandating the growth rate of a particular monetary aggregate or the inflation rate.

Burdekin, Westbrook, and Willett are skeptical about the chances of such measures being adopted. They argue that these rules would provoke great opposition, and they question whether the legislature has the political will to implement them. They also question how effective such rules might actually be. The authors therefore focus on more modest reforms that they believe would stand a better chance of obtaining a consensus and would perhaps be easier to implement.

Two possible types of reform come to mind. The first is adoption of a fixed-exchange rate system of one sort or another. This type of reform can come in many packages, ranging from an international gold standard, another Bretton Woods, an arrangement such as the Exchange Rate Mechanism (ERM) of the European Monetary System, or the currency board system discussed by Hanke and Schuler in the last chapter. The argument for fixed exchange rates is that the obligation to maintain the exchange rate imposes a discipline on the domestic central bank to follow the rule, but the authors admit that this discipline is probably weaker than is often supposed. One might add that the discipline will inevitably be ineffective if the national central bank can simply withdraw from the international system at will when the going gets tough. This problem was graphically illustrated by the ERM debacle in September 1992. The authors conclude that a fixed-exchange rate policy has little chance of success. They prefer the alternative of making the central bank more independent.

A strong body of empirical evidence supports the case that the more independent central banks tend to produce lower rates of inflation than those under the aegis of the central executive administration. The authors argue that what matters here is not so much the stated objective of the central bank but its actual independence. The Reserve Bank of Australia, for example, has a duty to stabilize prices; yet it has conspicuously failed to do so. In fact, the Reserve Bank is not independent. As the Australian prime minister stated a few years ago when he was Australian treasurer (in the mode of Louis XIV), "They [the Reserve Bank] do as I say." Institutional arrangements clearly make a difference.

The authors argue that statutes to make the central bank more independent should be at the top of the agenda for monetary reform. Some of us would disagree and argue that monetary reform should abolish or privatize the central bank outright. Any improvement in the current monetary regime, however, is clearly welcome; the reforms advocated by Burdekin, Westbrook, and Willett are a step in the right direction.

The next chapter also takes up the question of monetary policy reform, but in quite a different way. This chapter, by Kevin Dowd, provides a case study of one of the most important attempts to effect institutional change in recent years—the program to establish a monetary union in Europe. While much of the literature on this subject is relatively sympathetic to what European leaders have been trying to do, Dowd condemns it as an ill-thought-out and politically motivated action that will almost certainly do much more harm than good. He argues that this drive to reform must be understood in its historical and, most especially, in its political context.

The balance of power between the major Western European nations has always been precarious, and the emergence of Germany as the economic powerhouse of Western Europe threatens to destroy that balance. The national states that feel threatened by Germany's economic success have devised, therefore, a plan that would erect a federal superstate over German hegemony. Such a superstate also fits in with the desires of many of Europe's political establishments for a mercantilist

European federation big enough to "take on" the United States and Japan. Political factors have encouraged the planners to tout a dubious artificial European "unity." They propose a single European currency and a supranational European central bank as devices to promote and maintain that unity.

The drive towards European monetary union is almost entirely motivated by political factors, not by a sensible discussion of its potential economic merits. The few attempts to defend the program on economic grounds have been little more than ex-post rationalizations to justify decisions taken for altogether different reasons.

The lack of any sensible economic motivation bodes very ill. The Maastricht Treaty tends to be extremely vague and in places self-contradictory. It states that the new European central bank should be committed to the objective of price stability, but it nowhere defines what is meant by price stability. Nor does it specify the means that would ensure achievement of price stability, nor the remedial measures to be taken if the effort is botched. If price stability were not forthcoming under the unified program, European citizens could do little about it.

Many European politicians seem to want the new central bank because they are dissatisfied for political reasons with German monetary conservatism. Their behavior implies that they want more inflation than they are currently getting through the Bundesbank-dominated ERM. This design in promoting the new bank does not sit well with the claim that the bank would be committed to price stability, especially since the German Bundesbank has come closer to price stability than any other monetary agency. One cannot help but feel that the Maastricht Treaty's commitment to price stability is only an insincere facade.

The proposed European central bank would face other serious problems. The Treaty states that the bank should be independent; but its independence would be seriously qualified by the Council of Ministers, which would be able to impose its own norms on the bank. The Council might sign exchange rate agreements with foreign governments, for example, or pursue macroeconomic policies that would de facto compromise the maintenance of price stability. The new central bank might also be called upon to lend to the EC itself or to member governments. By financing such loans, the central bank would create more money than planned, thereby undermining its commitment, such as it is, to price stability. Serious inconsistencies and gaps in the defined powers of the proposed bank and other awkward issues have been left unresolved for reasons of political expediency. In short, many of the most serious problems with the scheme have been evaded. It is most unlikely that it will deliver the benefits its proponents claim.

The last two chapters look further afield. In chapter twelve Lawrence H. White reexamines the phenomenon of monetary nationalism. Hayek wrote in 1937 that the rational choice for monetary reformers was that between full-fledged free banking (a choice that gives no scope for monetary policy as conventionally understood) and a world central bank conducting an international monetary policy. A national central bank pursuing its own policies toward an ostensible national interest falls, as it were, between these two stools. Monetary nationalism was widely practiced in the 1930s following the abandonment of the international gold standard in 1931, but it was then supplanted to some extent by the operation of the Bretton Woods system after the Second World War. Monetary nationalism came back into its own again after the Bretton Woods system collapsed in the early 1970s, and most major countries have practiced it ever since.

Hayek himself expressed a decided preference for monetary internationalism conducted by a world central bank, and this type of view has since found favor with a variety of other prominent economists (e.g., Cooper 1988, McKinnon 1988). The essential weakness of monetary nationalism, as Hayek saw it, was that the criteria for a good monetary policy in a single country in a closed economic system are equally valid for a single country operating in a network of global trade. He compared the choice between a policy of monetary nationalism with a local central bank and a policy of monetary internationalism with a world central bank and came out in favor of the latter. Despite the fact that he acknowledged free banking as a rational option, Hayek paid relatively little attention to its operations as an international institution either in a pure form or mixed (a system in which some countries accepted free banking and some retained their provincial central banks).

In his chapter White suggests that the choice is not just between national and international monetary arrangements. There is also the question of whether a central bank is desirable at all. White argues that any central bank—whether a national central bank or an international one—intrinsically harbors certain compulsions. It presumably will want to target the growth rate of a monetary aggregate or the price of its own liabilities, yet it will also have an obligation to provide lender of last resort services to the rest of the banking system.

The problem, as economists have long recognized, is that these central bank obligations do not sit well together. The central bank's obligation to act as a lender of last resort can derail the commitment to control the quantity or price of its liabilities. Private banks might count on lender of last resort assistance, for example, and get themselves into difficulties that force the central bank to assist them. The central bank's aid to stricken banks would undermine its ability to control the quantity or price of money. It might try to avoid such difficulties by threatening not to provide assistance, but such threats would often not be credible to a politically sophisticated and pragmatic private sector. Since these and other such problems arise with any central bank, the main issue is not whether a central bank should be organized at the national or international level, but whether a central bank should exist at all. The real question is not so much monetary nationalism or monetary internationalism as it is monetary statism or monetary constitutionalism.

The last chapter, by Steve Hanke and Kurt Schuler, examines yet another alternative to central banking—a currency board system in which currency is issued at a fixed rate against a reliable foreign currency with a reserve ratio of 100 percent or greater in some high quality and highly liquid foreign assets. A currency board is much like using the foreign currency itself, except that the profits (seignorage) of issuing domestic currency go to the domestic agency (i.e., the currency board or the government) instead of to a foreign issuer. A domestic currency exists, but the issuing institution has no freedom to pursue its own discretionary policies. The system is therefore fully automatic. The domestic price level, interest rates, inflation rate, and other financial variables are tied down by the fixed exchange rate to the policies pursued by the issuer of the major currency to which the domestic currency is pegged.

Currency boards originally arose to replace free banking. The first one was established in Mauritius in 1849. Many currency boards were subsequently established in other British territories, and less frequently elsewhere in countries such as Argentina, Russia, and the Philippines. Historically, currency boards issued currencies tied to stable foreign currencies such as sterling that were themselves tied to gold. Since the reserves of currency boards were often held in safe places abroad, currency boards could function with certainty and maintain public confidence in their currencies even under very unstable domestic conditions. For example, a currency board in northern Russia was successfully able to issue a sterling-backed currency even in the midst of the Russian civil war.

Currency boards are attractive for a variety of reasons. They have a significant advantage over an "undeveloped" central bank by avoiding the credibility problem. When a novice central bank claims to commit itself to some policy, the private sector often has reason to doubt that the central bank will deliver the promised outcome. This lack of credibility can have real effects, such as higher inflationary expectations, thereby making the central bank's task more difficult.

Currency boards avoid the monetary policy decision-making problems that central banks face because the rules of the currency board give it no authority to pursue an independent policy. In other words, the problems of monetary management do not arise and the task of running the currency board is very simple and straightforward.

Currency boards are also very easy to set up and the principles behind them are easy to understand. They offer an attractive option to governments indulging in high inflation and the various other problems caused by central banking or central planning. They are, however, only as good as the national currency to which they are anchored. If no national central bank is currently pursuing stable monetary policies, the currency board attachment to a stable foreign currency would be impossible.

The implicit mission of these essays is to examine past and current institutional relationships between money and the nation-state. The experiences of the past and present serve as lessons for restructuring monetary institutions to be both more stable and more in keeping with the rule of law and a free society than the institutions we have with us everywhere in the world today. The rule of men and majorities has become dominant in the twentieth century and with catastrophic results. Correcting monetary institutions is just one task for constitutionalists, but it is an important one.

A single book can hardly pretend to cover this monumental task in its entirety. Here, only the most salient excesses of the state are exposed for correction. Implememtation of reforms may seem elusive and politically unrealistic. Nonetheless, alternatives to the current (mis)mananged discretionary systems need constant publicity if any reforms at all are to appear. These essays are offered in that spirit.

References

Cooper, Richard N. 1988. "Toward an International Commodity Standard?" *Cato Journal* 8 (Fall): 315–38.

Hayek, F. A. [1937] 1971. *Monetary Nationalism and International Stability*. Reprint, New York: Augustus M. Kelley.

McKinnon, Ronald I. 1988. "An International Gold Standard without Gold." *Cato Journal* 8 (Fall): 351–73.

I

The History of the Modern
International Monetary System

1

An Evolutionary Theory of the State Monopoly over Money[1]

David Glasner

The history of money virtually coincides with a history of the debasement, depreciation, and devaluation of the currency by the state. Despite the discontent that the sovereign's debasement of the coinage has always provoked, neither the monopoly over coinage that allowed such debasement nor state control over more modern forms of money creation has occasioned any serious challenge to the legal monopoly over money that has permitted the state to depreciate the value of money for its own purposes. Perhaps more surprising is that the legal monopoly has scarcely ever been challenged by economists, a group that embraces, almost as an article of faith, the proposition that monopoly is an evil.

The lack of opposition to the state monopoly over money would be less surprising if the production of money had the properties of a natural monopoly. But if, as I have shown elsewhere (Glasner 1991), there is no technical necessity for money to be produced by a monopolist, let alone by the state, the virtual ubiquity of the state monopoly demands a more satisfying explanation. This paper therefore examines the evolution of the monopoly of the state over money.

I shall argue that a monopoly over money was vital to the security of the state.[2] In the ancient world, when coinage was just beginning and the power to tax was barely developed, states that allowed private mints to operate were vulnerable to takeover by owners of private mints who could raise large sums of money quickly to finance their takeovers. Even after the state strengthened its power to tax, it found control over the mint to be a critical source of emergency revenue in wars against external enemies (Burns 1927).

Although the state monopoly over money has rarely been questioned, repeated attempts have been made to restrain governments in exploiting that monopoly. But periods such as the nineteenth century, when the world, under gold, silver, or bimetallic standards, enjoyed an unusual era of price stability, have been more the exception than the rule. Explaining the evolution of the monopoly over money will also illuminate the reasons for the temporary ascendancy of the gold standard.

In the next two sections, I discuss how the state monopoly over money evolved. In the third section, I use the sovereignty–national-defense argument for the state monopoly to suggest the optimality (for a selfish government) of price stability during peacetime. Since peacetime price stability enlarges the ex-post, wartime capital levy on cash balances and on other fixed nominal liabilities of the state, a problem of time consistency arises. To cope with the time-consistency problem, governments can commit themselves to a contingent monetary rule or invest in a reputation for stable prices (Barro and Gordon 1983; Barro 1983, 1986). The fourth section argues that the growth of democracy and the extension of the franchise complicated the time-consistency problem. The time-consistency problem provides the motivation for a public-choice–theoretic explanation of the evolution of constraints, such as the nineteenth-century gold standard, on the exercise of the state monopoly. I offer some concluding remarks in section five.

The Evolution of Money and the Origins of the State Monopoly

Monetary evolution began long before the state assumed any role in monetary affairs (Burns 1927, Ederer 1964, Menger 1892). Only after a few of the precious metals had evolved to become media of exchange did the state assume a key role. The state never prescribed what money should be, but by minting coins the state did assure the weight and fineness of metals that had already begun to circulate as media of exchange. By reducing the costs of transacting, minted coins could command a premium over unminted metals of equal fineness. Seeking not to improve the monetary system but only to exploit the profit opportunity implicit in this premium, governments extracted the premium as a charge for coining metal at the mint.

Nothing about operating a mint requires the state rather than private enterprise to perform that function.[3] The oldest known coins were struck in Lydia. Since the names on them are not those of any known Lydian sovereigns, it is likely that they were minted privately (Burns 1927, 75). Perhaps the imprimatur of the sovereign gave traders more confidence in the weight and fineness of coins than any private trademark could have. Such confidence, however, would have manifested itself in the market and would have allowed the sovereign's mint to command a larger premium for his coins than competing private mints could for theirs. Technical superiority in the provision of confidence is not a rationale for a state monopoly over coinage.

It is often said that the production of money is a natural monopoly. But the meaning of this assertion is not exactly clear. For the production of a good to be a natural monopoly, the technology must exhibit economies of scale that ensure that the average cost of production is always lower if one firm produces the entire output of an industry than if two or more firms with access to the identical technology divide the output. But even if the state were the lowest-cost producer of money, it would not necessarily enjoy the economies of scale required for the existence of a natural monopoly.

The assertion that money is a natural monopoly is sometimes alleged to follow from the demand-side characteristics of money instead of from its supply-side characteristics (Vaubel 1977). Thus, because it is cheaper to make calculations and execute transactions using just one currency unit rather than several, it is maintained that only one currency unit will survive within a reasonably self-contained economic area. But, as I have argued in another paper (Glasner 1991), the cost savings from trading in only one currency do not imply that the production of money is a natural monopoly. To suggest that it is confuses the gains from standardizing technology with economies of scale. Standardization confers external benefits to consumers at large. It is possible that these benefits cannot be fully internalized by individual producers but could be internalized if production were undertaken by just one firm. But even then, there would be no natural monopoly because the market would accommodate entry by firms adopting the standards set by the monopolist. Just as the gains from standardization did not make IBM a natural monopolist in the computer industry, they do not make the production of dollars a natural monopoly. Competing issuers can (and do) issue distinguishable moneys denominated in dollar units, thereby achieving the gains from standardization without limiting production to a single issuer.

That the state asserted a legal monopoly over the production of money cannot, therefore, be explained by any requirements implied by the technology of producing or using money. A more plausible explanation is that the monopoly was the result of the characteristic quest by the state for sources of revenue. In ancient times, when the state was just beginning to develop its power to tax, a potential source of revenue could be critical to the survival of the sovereign.

But control of the mint did more than provide the ancient state with a source of revenue. Control of the mint enabled owners of private mints to compete for control of the state itself (Burns 1927, 81–83). Minting a large quantity of debased coins might enable a private mint owner to finance an attempt to overthrow an incumbent sovereign. To be sure, such a debasement would violate the mint owner's promises about the content of the coins he was issuing. But upon becoming the sovereign, the owner could avoid any legal liability by annulling his legal obligation to those he had defrauded.

Thus, coinage and tyranny seem to have emerged together, a confluence which is borne out by the experience of the ancient world. Both coinage and tyranny originated in Lydia. Gyges, the Lydian king of the seventh century B.C. to whom the term tyrant was first applied (Durant 1939, 122), is also credited with having made the coinage "the prerogative of the state after he had first used it to obtain supreme power" (Ure 1922, 143).

A similar pattern appears in the Greek world during the seventh and sixth centuries B.C. (known as the Age of Tyrants), when currency developments were most rapid (Burns 1927, 81). The Greek tyrants "were the first men in their various cities to realize the political possibilities of the new conditions created by the introduction of the new coinage and...to a large extent they owed their positions as tyrants to a financial or commercial supremacy which they had already established before they had attained supreme political power in their several states" (Ure 1922, 2). Moreover, "Sparta, the most antityrannical state in Greece, was without a real coinage" (Ure 1922, 14).

Burns (1927, 82–83) suggests that it was the general economic power of the early tyrants rather than their control over the mints specifically that enabled them to seize power. Still, he concludes:

> Having risen to power, the tyrant assumed the monopoly over coining. This step was probably part of a policy aimed at the enhancement of his own power and commercial success and the hindrance of his rivals. He kicked away the ladder by which he had risen lest others might attempt to use it.

Once they monopolized coinage, ancient sovereigns sought to increase the revenue potential of their monopolies by limiting the circulation of coins minted by other states. The Greek city-states, which almost invariably established local monopoly mints, introduced the legal principle of legal tender to reinforce their local monopolies in just this way (Kraay 1964).

Local monopolies required legal protection because, contrary to Gresham's Law, bad moneys do not necessarily drive out good ones. That only happens when, for some reason, it is costly to trade the good money at a premium over the bad money. For example, full-bodied and debased coins were sometimes different denominations of the same money of account defined by a particular state (e.g., a debased one-pound coin and a full-bodied five-pound coin). The relative value of the two coins would be determined independently of their metallic content (Rolnick and Weber 1986). Heavier coins would then disappear from circulation and only the lightweight coins would be exchanged. But when two coins were defined in terms of different moneys of account, their exchange rate could reflect the difference in their metallic content. If one were debased more rapidly than the other, the debasement would show up in the exchange rates. If the public could choose to hold either currency, wealth maximization implies that they would hold the appreciating currency. But this preference would also imply the disappearance of the depreciating currency from trade.

Despite the special legal privileges accorded to local coins, coins often circulated beyond the territory of the governments that minted them (Finley 1973, 166). The circulation of coins minted by foreign mints, and the opportunity of making payments by weighing precious metals as well as by counting coins, constrained the monopoly power of any single government. Only in modern times, when payments in precious metals have ceased, could the state increase the levy on holding its money virtually without limit.[4]

As the apparatus of the state and its power to tax grew stronger,[5] maintaining a monopoly over coinage simply to prevent competition for power within the state became less necessary. Private minting might more safely have been tolerated, especially since complaints about shortages of coins abounded in ancient times (Finley 1973, 166), but the monopoly over coinage was as useful in defending the state against external threats as against internal ones.[6] The monopoly over money is distinguished from monopolies over other goods by the power conferred by the monopoly over money to impose an ex-post tax on certain forms of capital. Debasing the currency can be very lucrative when it is levied unexpectedly. Monopolizing other goods would generate revenue over time, but they would not generate as much revenue on short notice as the monopoly over money via currency debasement.

In the Near East it was not uncommon for the state to monopolize a range of commodities, usually through regulation rather than by direct operation. Only rarely did the Greek city-states do so, but the Hellenistic kings followed the Near Eastern practice as did the Roman emperors. Their motive was always openly fiscal (Finley 1973, 165–66). However, only the coinage was universally monopolized by the state.

It is also significant that attempts to depreciate the coinage were almost always carried out in time of war (Burns 1927, 462–63). Numerous Greek city-states exploited their monopolies over coinage to raise additional funds during wars. It is well known that Athens issued token bronze coins in 406 B.C. to help defray the costs of the Peloponnesian War.[7] Not long afterwards, Timotheus of Athens seems to have used a forced token coinage, which he promised eventually to redeem—an important promise, as we shall see later—to pay his soldiers in the war against the Olinthians.[8] And Dionysius of Syracuse, trying to stave off the Carthaginians, used both depreciation and debasement of the currency to raise funds.[9] After conquering Rhegium, Dionysius called in all coins for counterstamping. He reduced the standard by half and reissued the coins at double their nominal value, keeping half the coins to pay off his outstanding debts, the real value of which he had just reduced by 50 percent. He later debased the currency by issuing tin-plated bronze coins to pass as silver coins. Although his tactics have been deplored, Dionysius did prevent the Carthaginians from sacking Syracuse as they had other Sicilian cities (Burns 1927, 366–69).

Currency debasement in republican Rome was invariably associated with wars. As Burns (1927, 463) observed:

> The first issue of coins was probably made during the Samnite War, the first issues of silver during the Pyrrhic War, a possible reduction of the *as* during the first Punic War, a reduction of both silver and bronze and the issue of silver-plated coins during the second Punic War, and the reduction of the *as* and the reissue of plated coins during the Social War.

Currency debasement became a continuing source of revenue when the Empire went into decline. Why the Republic and the early emperors were able to maintain monetary stability during peacetime while the Empire lapsed into more or less continuous currency depreciation and debasement is an issue I shall come back to in section four.

In his history of Roman money Theodore Mommsen (1860) held that the monopoly over coinage was on a par in Roman law with the power to tax (de Cecco 1985, 811). The prerogative of the sovereign over coinage was preserved after the fall of Rome. In the Middle Ages, however, monarchs were forced to allow prominent noblemen to operate their own mints. Since medieval monarchs were certainly no more tolerant of competition in coinage than the sovereigns of other epochs, the multiplicity of mints was symptomatic of the fragmentation of sovereignty that characterized the Middle Ages. As Miskimin (1984) has shown for fifteenth-century France, one of the main objectives of monarchs during the late Middle Ages, when they began to reassert their sovereign claims against the nobility, was to reclaim control over the coinage.

The close relationship between control over money, sovereignty, and national defense would explain why counterfeiting was treated as a treasonable offense by the Greeks and Romans (Finley 1973, 167), as well as under English law (Blackstone 1979, 4:84; Maitland 1908, 226). This treatment reflected a feeling, engendered by millennia of historical experience, that control of the monetary system cannot be relinquished without compromising the sovereignty and independence of a country.[10]

The Evolution of Banking and the State Monopoly over Money

As money has evolved from its ancient origins as just another commodity, a growing share of all monetary instruments in most countries has been created by banks; and the significance of the monopoly over coinage has correspondingly diminished. Moreover, because banking requires far more business judgment than does minting coins, it was much more difficult technically for governments to operate their own monopoly banks than it was for them to operate monopoly mints. Consequently, the development of banking institutions posed a threat to the existing state monopoly over money. If the benefits from banking and financial intermediation were not to be lost, the state had to cope with the threat without actually suppressing banks.

Banking evolved because it combined two services that proved to be strongly complementary: provision of a medium of exchange and intermediation between ultimate borrowers and lenders. Banks encroached on the monopoly power of the state, because individuals could use less costly banknotes and deposits (from which governments earned no seignorage) instead of having to use coins (from which governments earned seignorage) as media of exchange. Bank money was less costly than coins for several reasons. Holders of deposits often received interest and bore no losses from the wear and tear of coins. They also bore no costs of transporting coins or of protecting them against theft or robbery. And, when making transactions, they could avoid the costs of counting, weighing, and inspecting coins.

By allowing people to avoid the costs of holding coins, banks reduced the demand for coins issued by the state and hence the value of the monopoly over coinage. The tension between the state monopoly over coinage and private banking is manifested in legislation that was frequently enacted to restrict the creation of notes and deposits by banks. In the fifteenth century, for example, hostile legislation in the Low Countries prohibited the payment of bills of exchange by direct transfer from one account to another, causing virtually all banking activity to cease (de Roover 1948, 350–51). In the same century, the municipal government of Barcelona made the municipal Bank of Deposit the sole legal depository of money that was subject to litigation or was being administered by trustees, executors, or guardians. Some private banks were forced into liquidation, and the number of private banks was strictly controlled. In what seems to have been a misguided, predatory, vertical foreclosure of banking services from competitors, the municipal government prohibited private banks from holding deposits at the municipal Bank of Deposit (Usher 1943, 246–50, 309–10).[11]

But other governments understood that private banks could increase the access of the state to sources of credit as well as promote economic development. Instead of trying to suppress banking institutions, many governments extended monopoly privileges to certain banks in exchange for a share of the monopoly profits. As was true of coinage, monopolistic banks were created not to improve the performance of the monetary system but to create a source of revenue for the state.

An excellent example of how the exigencies of wartime finance led to the creation of monopoly in banking is the establishment of the Bank of England in 1694. Overthrown in 1688, James II fled to France where he sought and received the protection of his fellow Catholic, Louis XIV, and the French monarch's support of his effort to recover his throne. After quelling loyalist resistance in Ireland and Scotland in 1690–91 and facing the threat of a Jacobite restoration supported by French arms, the successor to James, William III, was committed to opposing French expansion on the continent. But strongly opposed internally by elements of the Tory aristocracy and the Church of England, William III could not easily secure from Parliament funds to pursue his military objectives. Moreover, his access to private sources of credit was hindered by the memory of the default of Charles II on his debts in 1672.

As an alternative to raising funds from Parliament, William's Whig supporters devised a plan for a bank that could provide financial aid to the throne. Under the plan, Parliament was to grant a corporate charter to a new bank that would be authorized immediately to lend William's government 1,200,000 pounds at 8 percent interest to fight the French. Although few were willing to lend to the King at 8 percent interest, there were many who were willing to acquire stock in a bank with a corporate charter. Such charters could only be granted by a royal grant or an act of Parliament. The corporate form provided access to formal capital markets and thus gave corporations a lower cost of capital than noncorporate firms.[12] Usually, Parliament or the Crown would not grant corporate charters to more than one firm in any industry, so that a charter could, in effect, be sold for the expected present value of the future monopoly profits accruing to the firm because of the charter (Reiffen and Patterson 1990). Thus, the original subscribers to the Bank of England were willing to lend funds to the Crown at only 8 percent, because they correctly anticipated that the bank would earn monopoly profits in the future.[13] The loan would be paid back by funds raised from a duty on tonnage that was to be earmarked specifically for paying off the debt incurred to the bank's stockholders.

How the bank saved William III from disaster has been described by Sir Arthur Feavearyear (1963, 127) as follows:

> Here was where William III had the advantage of Charles II. Charles's credit in 1672 was utterly bad. His paper orders were payable, not on demand, but 18 months hence. He could not have issued notes payable on demand even if people would have accepted them, for he had no reserve. William and his government were themselves in no better position. But the Bank was an institution newly floated in triumph in the face of all opposition. At least half the City of London believed in it. The king's "pay" was bad; but where his tallies would no longer go he could place with ease the Bank's "bills," sealed with the common seal of the corporation, and engraved with the figure of Britannia seated upon a bank of money. Thus the king's immediate difficulties were surmounted by an inflation of credit of the simplest order.

The bank effectively intermediated between the borrowing needs of the government and the countless small savers from whom the government had formerly been required to borrow directly on less favorable terms and thereby solved the problem of the government's poor credit.

And as the leading creditor of the government, the bank was bound to support it against any threat of a Jacobite restoration, which would instantly repudiate all debts incurred by the usurpers and their government. In his *History of England,* Macaulay (1914, 2438–39) vividly described the close connection between the government, the Crown, and the Bank of England in the years following the establishment of the bank.

> Seventeen years after the passing of the Tonnage Bill,…described the situation of the great Company through which the immense wealth of London was constantly circulating. He saw Public Credit on her throne in Grocers' Hall, the Great Charter over her head, the Act of Settlement full in her view. Her touch turned everything to gold. Behind her seat, bags filled with coin were piled to the ceiling. On her right and on her left the floor was hidden by pyramids of guineas. On a sudden the door flies open. The Pretender rushes in, a sponge in one hand, in the other a sword which he shakes at the Act of Settlement. The beautiful Queen sinks down fainting. The spell by which she has turned all things around her into treasure is broken. The money bags shrink like pricked bladders. The piles of gold pieces are turned into bundles of rags or faggots of wooden tallies. The truth which this parable was meant to convey was constantly present to the minds of the rulers of the Bank. So closely was their interest bound up in the interest of the government that the greater the public danger the more ready were they to come to the rescue.

Though it was certainly a remarkable example of the use of banking as a tool of wartime finance, the creation of the Bank of England was not the first such instance. Others can be found in the late Middle Ages and the Renaissance.

Italian bankers in England advanced huge sums to Edward I in the late thirteenth and early fourteenth centuries, enabling Edward, when faced with a Welsh uprising and unrest in Scotland, to raise a much larger army (30,000) than any of his predecessors. Italian bankers also provided financing for the early stages of Edward III's invasion of France in the Hundred Years War (Prestwich 1979, 77–80).

In the fifteenth century Barcelona used its municipal bank as a source of funds in the unsuccessful attempt by Catalonia, of which Barcelona was the chief city, to secede from Spain under the Castilian dynasty. The advances made by the bank were at least a partial cause of the suspension of the convertibility of deposits into specie (Usher 1943, 382–86).

Similarly, in the sixteenth and seventeenth centuries Venice used its private, but tightly regulated, banking system as a tool of war finance (de Roover 1976, 215). For example, around 1520, the Venetian banks helped the Republic finance a war by creating deposits against government debt. The demands of the government for funds were such that convertibility was suspended and bank money, which was recognized as being distinct from coin, depreciated against metallic currency (de Roover 1976, 215; Lane 1937, 205).

The development of monetary institutions in the United States suggests a similar role for the monopoly over money. Private coinage and relatively free entry into banking continued until the Civil War, when the financial obligations of the war were met by issuing inconvertible greenbacks, abolishing private mints, establishing national banks that could issue notes backed by government bonds, and virtually suppressing the note issue of state banks. After the war, when the federal government was beginning to assert a new dominance over the states, it would not surrender the supposedly temporary monopoly over banknotes acquired during the war.

This explanation of the state monopoly over money would imply that free banking is most likely to be allowed and state control over the creation of currency is most likely to be relinquished when the governing authorities have no defense responsibilities. It is therefore noteworthy that four of the main historical instances of free banking—Scotland in the eighteenth and the first half of the nineteenth centuries, the United States before the Civil War, and Canada (Scherer and Clark 1984) and Australia in the nineteenth and early twentieth centuries—occurred because local authorities with minimal defense responsibilities could allow it. In the first two instances, the regimes were terminated by action of central governments that did have defense responsibilities; in the latter two instances, the regimes were terminated as both Canada and Australia assumed increasing political and military independence from Great Britain.

Free banking in the United States was not ended until the Civil War, when the national government needed new revenue sources and desired to limit the sovereign powers of individual states. Nor is it likely that the National Bank Act, which taxed the note issues of state banks out of existence, could have been passed while representatives of Southern states, who were resisting the power of the federal government, remained in Congress.

Before Germany and Italy became unified national states, private banks of issue operated in both countries. One of Bismarck's first acts was to unify the currency under a monopolistic central bank of issue dominated by the government. The freedom of private banks in Italy was only gradually circumscribed, and the Bank of Italy did not gain an exclusive monopoly of issue until 1926 under Mussolini (Fratianni and Spinelli 1984). Sweden, which permitted private note issue until 1897, seems to be an exception in having a political regime responsible for national defense that allowed free banking. But the regime of competitive note issue was terminated there even though the system performed well (Jonung 1984, 363–64; Sandberg 1978, 663–67). The motivation for terminating competitive issue seems to have been the desire of the Swedish government to capture the revenue accruing to the banks from the note issue.

Other governments that have foregone monopolistic control of money supply are the administration in Hong Kong, which has no defense responsibility, and Panama, which, owing to the Panama Canal, was practically created by the United States and has remained almost continuously under the military control of the United States.[14] Moreover, the development of Eurodollars, which are a kind of competitor to domestically produced dollar deposits, took place in Western Europe and the Caribbean islands, which at least since World War II have been partial free riders on American defense expenditures. Since a government has little interest in protecting the currency monopoly of a foreign government, banks operating in the Eurocurrency market have been less regulated in creating deposits denominated in foreign currencies than in creating deposits in their home currencies. Whether there are instances of governments with substantial national defense responsibilities that have foregone monopolistic control over money and, if so, why they did forego such control, are questions meriting further historical inquiry.

Optimal Exploitation of the State Monopoly over Money

The state monopoly over money has been regarded as such a fundamental prerogative of the sovereign that its infringement has been held treasonous under numerous legal systems. No other good has been so universally monopolized by the state. Thus, in contrast to the view that the technical characteristics of a medium of exchange require the supply of money to be monopolized, I have been arguing that the state monopoly over money evolved because it enhanced the power of the sovereign to defend against internal and external threats. But my argument suggests that the monopoly over money is more than just another revenue source that the state has exploited. It also identifies a basic difference between the monopoly over money and other monopolies governments have established.

The difference arises because the monopoly over money can be exploited in two ways. First, the monopoly can generate a flow of seignorage if the state imposes charges at the mint or, equivalently, if it levies an inflation tax on cash balances. If this were the only way the state could exploit the monopoly over money, the incentive for the state to establish a monopoly over money would be no greater than the incentive to establish one over any other commodity. However, the monopoly over money also can be used to effect a one-time wealth transfer to the state from holders of its money and its debt. Since such transfers can be achieved on short notice and may evade the usual restrictions on the imposition of explicit taxes, it enables the sovereign to make extraordinary expenditures quickly in wartime emergencies.[15] This, as I mentioned before, is because the monopoly over money can be used to levy a lump-sum, ex-post tax on the capital of holders of government money and holders of government debt (yielding a return that does not reflect the unanticipated depreciation), while other monopolies can only raise revenue as sales are made over time.

Early analyses of the inflation tax suggested that the optimal inflation rate for a "profit-maximizing" government would be derived analogously to the profit-maximizing price for any monopolist (Bailey 1956; Friedman 1952, 1971). Although formally correct, those analyses overlooked certain crucial issues. First, they ignored the competitive relationship between government currency and interest-bearing deposits created by the banking system. Since the cost of holding non-interest-bearing currency rises along with the inflation rate while the cost of holding interest-bearing deposits is more or less invariant to changes in expected inflation, a competitive banking system constrains the amount of seignorage the government can collect by imposing a steady anticipated inflation. The higher the inflation rate, the greater the incentive to switch from holding non-interest-bearing currency to interest-bearing deposits. This implies that the elasticity of demand for non-interest-bearing currency is more elastic with a competitive banking system than without one. Moreover, even reserve requirements may not prevent substitution from currency to deposits from eroding the tax base if financial innovation enables the financial system to avoid those reserve requirements while providing the public with close substitutes for currency or for deposits subject to reserve requirements.

Second, and more important, the early analyses failed to recognize that a state may prefer collecting seignorage as a one-time emergency transfer to collecting it as a steady stream of revenue over time. Thus, a maximizing government ordinarily would prefer not to inflate at the steady rate implied by the simple inflation-tax model. However, because of the time-inconsistency problem inherent in the preference for a low-inflation policy that facilitates the unexpected imposition of a one-time capital levy, some form of credible commitment to a long-term noninflationary policy is necessary for the preference to be realized (Kydland and Prescott 1977).

And third, there are strong reasons to suppose that an ongoing inflation tax is inherently inefficient. If money provides no direct utility but is held merely because it reduces transactions costs and provides other indirect services, it is an intermediate good for which the optimal tax rate is zero. A positive tax rate causes an inefficient substitution of other inputs in place of monetary services. In other words, the standard exercise in which the profit-maximizing inflation rate corresponds to the point where the money demand curve is unit-elastic is an incorrect application of partial-equilibrium analysis. In a general-equilibrium framework, the cost (measured by potential revenue foregone) of imposing the inflation tax exceeds the revenue generated.[16]

Note, however, that the second, more crucial method of exploiting the state monopoly over money is effective only if it is applied unexpectedly. For if a capital levy is anticipated, people can avoid it by reducing their holdings of forms of capital subject to the tax. Thus, for a government to be able to exploit its monopoly over money in emergencies, it must refrain from doing so at other times, even though the gains from doing so are very large. This is the well-known time-consistency problem. Because the incentive to exploit the monopoly over money is large and ever-present, the sovereign requires a means of creating and fulfilling expectations that the monopoly will not be exploited.

The time-consistency problem has been recognized in some analyses of optimal seignorage from inflation (Calvo 1978; Barro 1983, 1986). Barro, in particular, discusses how a government can create an expectation of low inflation that it can exploit in periods when seignorage has a high marginal value.

Barro (1983) considers two possibilities. One is a commitment by the government to a rule prohibiting inflation. As long as the rule is followed, expectations of low inflation are validated by the government's behavior. But once the rule is broken, expectations of low inflation can no longer be sustained. The other possibility is that the government can invest in a reputation for low inflation by consistently generating low rates of inflation. The reputation allows the government to collect substantial seignorage from its monopoly in periods

when seignorage has a high value. Thereafter, the government can reinvest in its reputation for low inflation by generating unexpectedly
low inflation or unexpected deflation.[17]

In accord with Barro's analysis, one might expect to find that states
seeking to maintain their war-making capacity would reinvest in their
reputation for protecting the value of their currency by restoring the
value of the currency after wartime inflation or debasement. Moreover, the expectation of such a postwar restoration would permit long-
term borrowing at low rates of interest rather than high rates reflecting
the wartime inflation.[18] It is difficult to rationalize such restorations on
other grounds since there seem to be so few economic benefits from
deliberate deflation. Yet, Sir Arthur Feavearyear in his history of the
pound sterling (1963, 12–13), records that between 1100 and 1300
there were seven recoinages designed to eliminate worn, clipped, and
counterfeit coins, whose share of the circulation tended to increase
over time. These recoinages all maintained the same legal standard.
But that meant raising the de facto standard as the metallic content of
coinage was increased. It was the nearly uniform commitment of British monarchs to maintain the purity, if not always the weight, of the
silver pound sterling that made "sterling" an adjective describing anything of the highest standard or quality. The confidence in the pound
sterling built up over centuries enabled Henry VIII, when under foreign attack and with foreign troops fighting on British soil, to successfully use currency debasement on a massive scale to raise the funds
needed to defend his throne. As Feavearyear (1963, 84) put it:

> Henry VIII carries most of the blame for the [debasement]; but if we could forget
> that he certainly began it as a deep-laid scheme in time of peace, we should be
> compelled to point out that he did no more than inflate the currency at a time when
> England was engaged in a serious war, when the country was threatened with
> invasion, when foreign troops actually landed on our shores, and when the Exche-
> quer was empty.

French monarchs, on the other hand, relied heavily on the mint as a
source of revenue and resorted several times to debasement in the fifteenth century. Each debasement was an emergency measure taken
during the Hundred Years War with England and was quickly followed
by a return of the standard nearly to its previous level. None of them,
as Miskimin (1984) has shown, solved the financial problems of the
impecunious French monarchs, as Henry VIII's debasement helped to
do in the next century.[19] The comparison confirms my earlier sugges-

tion that frequent resort to currency debasement undermines the revenue-generating potential of subsequent debasements.

In the Low Countries in the fourteenth and fifteenth centuries, debasements were frequently followed by restorations (*renforcement,* or *retour à la forte monnaie*). Since, as de Roover (1948, 225) observes, the deflationary and recessionary consequences of raising the standard were understood by the Flemish authorities, it is not outlandish to suppose that some sort of national defense rationale was behind their willingness to bear the costs of raising the standard back to its original level.

By increasing their command over resources in wartime, states that invested in the value of their monopoly over money in peacetime improved their chances of surviving in military competition with states that depreciated the value of their monopoly during peacetime. As a consequence, states that either did not maintain a monopoly over money or, by exploiting it for nonmilitary purposes, underinvested in that monopoly tended not to survive in such competition. A form of social evolution has therefore selected the state monopoly over money as a nearly universal political institution. However, contrary to the views of most monetary economists, this institution has little relationship to the technical requirements of a medium of exchange.

The Evolution of Constraints on the State Monopoly over Money

In the preceding section I argued that investing in a reputation for maintaining stable prices (e.g., by making a credible commitment to preserve price stability) is an optimal policy in the sense that a state that does so improves its survival chances. However, a further question arises about what incentives would induce decision makers to make such an investment. One disincentive to such investment is easy to identify: the limited tenure of government decision makers in office and the lack of transferable property rights over assets they create during their tenure. Government decision makers therefore tend to undervalue benefits accruing to their successors and to underinvest in a reputation for maintaining stable prices.

The lack of secure property rights in the control of the state suggests that the inflationary bias of government decision makers may be minimized under an absolute and hereditary monarchy. However, the tendency of absolute and hereditary monarchy to empower incompetent (or underage)[20] monarchs unable or unwilling to follow policies and rules in the state's interest means that a relatively small and homogeneous ruling elite, such as the aristocracy of a city-state, would perhaps be more likely to invest during peacetime in the monopoly over money.

Another disincentive to investment in reputation is that any government can remain in power only by maintaining the support of some coalition of interests. The value of the state monopoly over money, therefore, tends to be dissipated by the competition among potential ruling coalitions to amass the support necessary to retain power. Both of these problems, which are merely aspects of the general problem of inadequate property rights over a common property resource, suggest that governments (especially large democratic ones with diverse populations) invest too little in the value of the monopoly over money (that is, tolerate too much inflation) in peacetime. A stable and secure ruling elite would have less incentive to dissipate the value of the monopoly than would competing coalitions vying to control the state.

The varying incentives here are exemplified by different phases of Roman history. While Rome was still a republic with a restricted citizenship and governed by a small oligarchy, inflation was resorted to only in wartime emergencies. Monetary stability thus was maintained for the first century or so of the Empire. But as competition to become emperor grew more intense, competitors increasingly resorted to inflation to finance obligations they had incurred while soliciting backers (usually from the army and the imperial guard).[21] On the other hand, in Byzantium, where the monarchy was hereditary, the coinage was not debased until 1204.[22]

While currencies were largely metallic, the potential gain from currency debasement was limited: debased coins would eventually circulate at a discount in comparison with full-bodied coins. Moreover, since taxes and other payments due to the sovereign were often fixed in nominal amount, the sovereign was likely to be a net monetary creditor over a not-too-distant time horizon and would therefore have little incentive to create a prolonged inflation.

It could be argued that until the eighteenth century the control of hereditary monarchies and oligarchies over governments was generally secure enough to limit abuse of the monopoly over money, especially when the predominance of metallic coins limited potential gain from currency debasement. But the democratization that began in that century and the shift from metallic to paper and token currencies progressively increased the incentives for government decision makers to exploit the monopoly over money for purposes other than national defense emergencies.

However, the ascendant political attitudes that accompanied the trend toward greater democracy in the eighteenth and nineteenth centuries, especially in Britain, were hostile to the exercise of arbitrary government power. Consequently, the exercise by the state of its monopoly over money was increasingly circumscribed by law and custom. For example, at the insistence of the more doctrinaire Whigs, the Tonnage Bill that established the Bank of England stipulated that the bank could advance no funds to the Crown without authority of Parliament (Macaulay 1914, 2435). And throughout the eighteenth and nineteenth centuries, official discretion over the money supply was sharply limited by various rules that were either explicitly enacted or that came to be regarded as morally and politically binding. The Bank Charter Act of 1844 was an attempt by Parliament to prescribe explicit rules over the creation of money by the Bank of England even as it strengthened the bank's monopoly over money creation in Great Britain. An unfettered monopoly over money was intolerable to political opinion prevailing at that time.

But the more fundamental constraint on the exercise of the monopoly was the gradual acceptance of an obligation to maintain the convertibility of currency into gold or silver at a fixed parity. Although ancient currencies were made of precious metals, the concept of a formal monetary standard was an innovation of the eighteenth and nineteenth centuries. Before 1816 the pound had never been legally defined by Parliament as a specific weight of either gold or silver. From 1717 England had been on a de facto gold standard, but that standard was due to the undervaluation of gold relative to silver at the mint decreed by Sir Isaac Newton, not to a legal definition of the pound in terms of gold. In the far distant past, a pound originally did correspond to a coin containing a pound of silver, but occasional debasements and the gradual loss of weight of coins in circulation led to a permanent disjunction between the formal pound and its original weight (Feavearyear 1963). That the pound was defined for the first time as a weight of gold in 1816 after a suspension of convertibility during the Napoleonic Wars, reflected the desire of Parliament to formalize a legislative rule that would preclude any tampering with the currency.

In his account of the development of British monetary orthodoxy in the nineteenth century, Fetter (1965) emphasizes the extent to which attachment to the gold standard by midcentury became a matter of belief and moral principle rather than a question for political debate or even scientific inquiry. He notes (234–37) that the leading economists and political figures of the period were loathe to raise the issue of the gold standard lest debate over its merits create doubts about continuing adherence to the standard itself. The only alternative to the gold standard seemed to be political tampering with the currency—an alternative they wished to avoid at all costs.

The gold standard was never characterized by any well-defined set of rules. The notion that there were "rules of the game" incumbent on monetary authorities adhering to the gold standard was largely an invention of the post–gold standard era.[23] But a temporary wartime suspension was not considered an abrogation of the gold standard if there was a commitment to restore the prewar parity after the war. If so, the gold standard can be viewed as a contingent rule with an emergency escape clause. To support expectations of future price-level stability, the contingent rule had to include an irrevocable commitment to restore the original parity after the war. The British resumption at the old parity after the Napoleonic Wars and the U.S. resumption at the old parity after the Civil War, despite the resulting serious postwar recessions, indicate how seriously the commitment was regarded. Yeager (1984, 654) has shown that Russian and Austrian advocates of the gold standard late in the nineteenth century recommended the standard precisely because it would improve the credit of the government's paper-money issues in time of war.

If we think of it as compliance with the implicit rules of the gold standard monetary regime or as an investment in reputation, the return by Great Britain in 1925 to the gold standard at the prewar parity is not as senseless as it is usually represented to have been, not only by Keynes ([1925] 1972) and his followers but by such hard-money advocates as Hayek (1976), Mises (1952), and the early Robbins (1934). Like similar instances cited previously, the 1925 decision exemplifies the time-consistency problem. If future expectations are assumed to be independent of that decision, then Keynes et al. were certainly right to condemn the decision for needlessly imposing substantial costs of deflation on Britain for no apparent gain. But if the decision enhanced the government's reputation for fulfilling its solemn commitments, it also enhanced the capacity of the British government to finance future wars.

Recognition of the time-consistency problem may help rationalize the seemingly irrational attachment to the gold standard that Fetter noted with apparent disdain and the seemingly even more irrational attachment to the prewar parity that Keynes scornfully attacked. What, viewed from a narrow perspective, seems to be an irrational commitment may have been a necessary component of a monetary regime that was optimal in the long run.

Conclusion

I have proposed in this paper an evolutionary explanation of the state monopoly over money that views the monopoly as contributing to the security of the state against internal and external threats. Many aspects of monetary history, I have argued, are better explained by this approach than by one that views the monopoly as required by the technology of money creation.

There are, however, some reasons to suspect that the sovereignty–national defense rationale for the state monopoly is less important now than in earlier stages of monetary evolution. Changes in military technology that require heavier peacetime expenditures and the increase in the tax-collecting and borrowing power of the state all seem to have diminished the contribution of the state monopoly to national defense. Moreover, the Keynesian revolution shifted the focus of monetary policy to macroeconomic stabilization, so that the state monopoly is now held to be desirable because it permits a more activist countercyclical policy than would be possible in its absence. Challenges to the monopoly over money in advanced countries would now be less likely to be resisted on the ground that to abolish the monopoly would infringe on the sovereign power of the state and more likely to be resisted on the ground that to abolish it would deprive the government of an essential tool for promoting high employment and economic growth.

Whether the monopoly over money indeed helps to achieve those goals is a question for a much different inquiry from the one I have conducted in this paper. But there is little reason to suppose that those concerns had anything to do with the evolution of the monopoly over money in the past. Since there seems to be no technical reason inherent in the nature of a medium of exchange that would have necessitated a monopoly over money, the defense-sovereignty explanation I have proposed here seems to be a more plausible explanation for the monopoly than any other yet proposed.

Notes

1. This chapter is a further development of ideas contained in the first two chapters of Glasner (1989).

2. This hypothesis was suggested to me by Earl Thompson. See Thompson (1974, 1979) for attempts to use a national defense hypothesis to rationalize seeming inefficiencies in the tax code and the protection of certain industries against foreign competition. A full application of his national defense theory to monetary institutions is presented in Thompson (1997).

3. Private mints operated in the United States until they were prohibited during the Civil War.

4. Transactors, of course, could still resort to precious metals as a means of payment. However, precious metals have long since ceased to function as media of exchange. Resorting to precious metals as a means of payment would, in a modern economy, be virtually to resort to barter exchange.

5. Indeed, the power to tax helped the state increase its monopoly power over the coinage by allowing the state to declare that only coins from its own mint would be accepted in payment of taxes (Kraay 1964).

6. Other commodities or activities were occasionally monopolized by the state in ancient times. It was understood that such monopolies could be sources of revenue to the state, but not until the later Roman Empire did monopolization seem to have been widely introduced as a revenue source for the state. No enterprise other than coinage seems to have been universally monopolized by the state in ancient times. Nor does it seem that private producers of possibly strategic commodities were considered a threat to the state.

7. The issue of copper coins elicited perhaps the earliest statement of Gresham's Law when Aristophanes complained in the *Frogs,* "in our Republic bad citizens are preferred to good, just as bad money circulates while good money disappears." It seems that the quantity of copper coins was not sufficiently restricted to prevent a depreciation of copper coins in relation to silver (Burns, 289–90).

8. The author of the pseudo-Aristotelian *Economica* described the episode as follows:

   > Timotheus the Athenian, when he was at war with the Olynthians, and in need of money, struck a bronze coinage and distributed it to his soldiers. When they protested, he told them that the merchants and the retailers would all sell their goods on the same terms as before. He told the merchants if they received bronze money to use it again to buy the commodities sent in for sale from the country and anything brought in as plunder, and said that if they brought him any bronze money they had left over they should receive silver for it. (II, 2)

9. The distinction here between depreciation and debasement is that the former openly reduces the weight of the coin while preserving its fineness, while the latter surreptitiously reduces the fineness while maintaining the weight. Depreciation presumably causes a more or less immediate adjustment in prices, while debasement only does so gradually as the public learns of the reduced metallic content of the coins.

10. The abortive 1983 proposal for monetary reform by the Israeli finance minister, Yoram Aridor, illustrates the strength of this feeling. The proposal, immediately identified as the Aridor Plan, was to make the shekel fully convertible into the dollar at a fixed parity and to make all contractual liabilities, including tax liabilities, payable in dollars or the stipulated dollar value. The plan, therefore, envisioned virtually complete dollarization of the economy. Despite the far-reaching de facto dollarization that had been achieved, the Aridor plan was denounced immediately by all segments of Israeli opinion. Although it is likely that Israel had exceeded even the short-run, profit-maximizing rate of inflation, so that the

contribution of the monopoly over money to national defense had been to a large extent exhausted, the typical response to the Aridor plan was the comment of a right-wing, nationalist politician suggesting that, if the plan were implemented, Israel might as well begin flying the American flag and adopt the "Star-Spangled Banner" as its national anthem. (*New York Times*, 14 October 1983, p. A4).

11. See Reiffen and Kleit (1990), who explain why the vertical foreclosure of an essential input for downstream competitors is generally not a profit-maximizing strategy for a monopolist over a unique facility.

12. The original charter did not formally grant the bank any monopolistic privileges aside from its corporate charter. Subsequent legislation, however, did restrict the business of banking to partnerships with no more than six partners, which was responsible for the characteristic undercapitalization and instability of English country banks. Banks in Scotland were not prohibited from adopting a corporate form, which allowed Scottish banks to expand to an efficient size and to avoid widespread failures.

13. The incentive for subscribers was described as follows by Sir Arthur Feavearyear (1963, 125):

> There is no doubt that the intention from the commencement was that the Bank should do an ordinary banking business, that is to say, that it should receive deposits and create a credit currency. It cannot be made too plain that it was the Bank and not the original subscribers to the Bank who lent the money to the king. Most of these would not have been attracted by the offer of 8 percent. They were attracted by the opportunity which the foundation of the first joint-stock bank in England provided of taking a hand in the business of banking, a business which in the last fifty years had raised up more junior clerks and scriveners to be wealthy alderman than had any other in treble the time.

14. Interestingly, the lack of a domestic currency left Panama vulnerable to an attack by the United States on the Panamanian banking system when the United States began its attempts to topple the Panamanian military dictator because of his alleged involvement in the drug trade.

15. A similar view was taken by R. J. Ederer (1964, 105–106). As he put it:

> Another decisive factor was the rise of national states which took place in about the period when monetary evolution passed from the state-issued to the bank-issued money era. Medieval princes who hoped to survive the realignment of political powers, which was then taking place, had to rely upon mercenary soldiers to a large extent and upon expensive cannon and ammunition. The more successful ones became kings of emergent national states. It so happened that when this struggle for supremacy took place, warfare methods underwent a decided revolution. With the arrival of gunpowder, the legendary knight in shining armor became obsolete, and warfare became a far more costly proposition than it had ever been before. Small wonder that the ambitious nobles of the day used debasement of their currencies to levy hidden taxes on their subjects. In doing this they did nothing which modern states do not chronically resort to in times of national peril. Hence they continued to guard jealously the power of issue which helped them to attain their dominant positions. This power and the power to debase coins came to be looked upon as the surest marks of sovereignty. Seignorage became a prime source of revenue.

Also see Ronald W. Batchelder and Herman Freudenberger (1983), who use changes in military technology to explain the transformation of European political entities in the sixteenth century, and L. Aurenheimer (1974), who makes the crucial distinction between the seignorage the government can earn from a fully anticipated inflation and the seignorage it can extract from an unanticipated one.

16. It is only the greater speed with which the inflation tax generates revenue that makes it preferable in emergencies to other less distorting taxes. As an ongoing revenue source, it is probably highly inefficient.

17. Barro's discussion is consistent with either a pure fiat currency that the government can issue at will or with a commodity or convertible currency whose par value the government can determine. He provides no reason why a government might use convertibility to create expectations of stable prices. Barro's theoretical account of the gold standard (1979) suggests that, analytically, he views the gold standard as a kind of quantitative limitation on the monetary base.

18. The importance of the expectation of postwar deflation for a resort to inflation to be a successful strategy of wartime finance has been emphasized by Earl Thompson in a forthcoming book (1994).

19. Bordo (1986, 343–44) suggests that Miskimin may have been too categorical in denying that the repeated debasements by the French monarchs earned no seignorage. The main point remains that repeated debasements, even when followed by restorations of the standard, would be anticipated by the public and hence rendered far less effective than an unanticipated debasement.

20. When underage monarchs assume the throne, regents rule on their behalf. Such situations are obviously extreme instances of principle-agency problems.

21. See Gibbon's account of the brief and unhappy reign of Didano Julianus, a Roman Senator who purchased the support of the Praetorian guard and was elected emperor after the assassination of his predecessor.

22. Whether any conclusion can be drawn from the absence of debasement in Byzantium is perhaps questionable since Mommsen (1860) argues that, as a part of his monetary reform, Constantine decreed that all payments in gold coin be made according to weight. Once coins no longer carried a premium over their metallic content, there was little opportunity for profitably depreciating or debasing the coinage (de Cecco 1985, 812–13).

23. By "rules of the game" I mean a much broader (and probably disjoint) set of rules than Bloomfield (1959) discussed in his study of "the rules of the game" under the gold standard.

References

Aurenheimer, Leonardo. 1974. "The Honest Government's Guide to the Revenue from the Creation of Money." *Journal of Political Economy* 82(3): 598–606.

Bailey, Martin J. 1956. "The Welfare Cost of Inflationary Finance." *Journal of Political Economy* 64(2): 93–110.

Barro, Robert J. 1979. "Money and the Price Level under the Gold Standard." *Economic Journal* 89(1): 13–33.

———. 1983. "Inflationary Finance Under Discretion and Rules." *Canadian Journal of Economics* 16(1): 1–16.

———. 1986. "Reputation in a Model of Monetary Policy with Incomplete Information." *Journal of Monetary Economics* 17(1): 3–20.

Barro, Robert J., and David B. Gordon. 1983. "Rules, Discretion and Reputation in a Model of Monetary Policy." *Journal of Monetary Economics* 12(1): 101–21.

Batchelder, Ronald W., and Herman Freudenberger. 1983. "On the Rational Origins of the Modern Centralized State." *Explorations in Economic History*, 20(1): 1–13.

Blackstone, William. [1776] 1979. *Commentaries on the Laws of England.* Chicago: University of Chicago Press.

Bloomfield, Arthur I. 1959. *Monetary Policy under the International Gold Standard.* New York: Federal Reserve Bank.

Bordo, Michael D. 1986. "Money, Deflation and Seigniorage in the Fifteenth Century: A Review Essay." *Journal of Monetary Economics* 18(3): 337–46.

Burns, Arthur R. 1927. *Money and Monetary Policy in Early Times.* New York: Alfred K. Knopf.

Cagan, Phillip. 1956. "The Monetary Dynamics of Hyperinflation." In *Studies in the Quantity Theory of Money,* edited by Milton Friedman, 25–117. Chicago: University of Chicago Press.

Calvo, Guillermo. 1978. "Optimal Seigniorage from Money Creation: An Analysis in Terms of the Optimal Balance of Payments Deficit Problem." *Journal of Monetary Economics* 4(3): 503–17.

de Cecco, Marcelo. 1985. "Monetary Theory and Roman History." *Journal of Economic History* 45(4): 809–22.

de Roover, Raymond. 1948. *Money, Credit, and Banking in Mediaeval Bruges.* Cambridge, MA.: The Mediaeval Academy.

—————. 1976. "New Interpretations in Banking History." Chapter 5 in R. de Roover, *Business, Banking, and Economic Thought in the Middle Ages and Early Modern Europe.* Chicago: University of Chicago Press.

Durant, Will. 1939. *The Story of Civilization: Our Greek Heritage.* New York: Simon and Shuster.

Ederer, Rupert J. 1964. *The Evolution of Money.* Washington, DC: Public Affairs Press.

Feavearyear, Arthur 1963. *The Pound Sterling.* Oxford: Clarendon Press.

Fetter, Frank W. 1965. *The Development of British Monetary Orthodoxy 1797–1873.* Cambridge, MA: Harvard University Press.

Finley, Moses I. 1973. *The Ancient Economy.* Berkeley: University of California Press.

Fratianni, Michele, and Franco Spinelli. 1984. "Italy in the Gold Standard Period, 1861–1914." In *A Retrospective on the Classical Gold Standard, 1821–1931,* edited by Michael D. Bordo and Anna J. Schwartz, 405–41. Chicago: University of Chicago Press.

Friedman, Milton. 1952. "Discussion of the Inflationary Gap." In Milton Friedman, *Essays in Positive Economics,* 251–62. Chicago: University of Chicago Press.

—————. 1971. "Government Revenue from Money Creation." *Journal of Political Economy* 79(3): 846–56.

Glasner, David. 1989. *Free Banking and Monetary Reform.* New York: Cambridge University Press.

—————. 1991. "How Natural Is the State Monopoly over Money?" (Manuscript).

Hayek, F. A. 1976. *A Tiger by the Tail.* London: Institute for Economic Affairs.

Jonung, Lars. 1984. "Swedish Experience under the Classical Gold Standard, 1873–1914." In *A Retrospective on the Classical Gold Standard, 1821–1931,* edited by Michael D. Bordo and Anna J. Schwartz, 361–99. Chicago: University of Chicago Press.

—————. 1986. "The Economics of Private Monies." (Manuscript).

Keynes, J. M. [1925] 1972. *The Economic Consequences of Mr. Churchill.* In *The Collected Writings of John Maynard Keynes,* vol. 9, 207–30. London: Macmillan.

Kraay, C. M. 1964. "Hoards, Small Change, and the Origin of Coinage." *Journal of Hellenic Studies* 84: 76–91.

Kydland, Finn, and Edward C. Prescott. 1977. "Rules Rather Than Discretion: The Inconsistency of Optimal Plans." *Journal of Political Economy* 85(3): 473–92.

Lane, Frederic C. 1937. "Venetian Bankers, 1496–1533: A Study in the Early Stages of Deposit Banking." *Journal of Political Economy* 45(2): 187–206.

Macaulay, Thomas B. 1914. *The History of England.* London: Macmillan.

Maitland, Frederic W. 1908. *The Constitutional History of England.* Cambridge: Cambridge University Press.

Menger, Carl. 1892. "On the Origin of Money." *Economic Journal* 2(3): 239–55.

Mises, Ludwig von. 1952. *The Theory of Money and Credit.* London: Jonathan Cape.

Miskimin, Harry A. 1984. *Money and Power in Fifteenth Century France.* New Haven, CT: Yale University Press.

Mommsen, Theodor. 1860. *Geschicte des Romischen Munzwesens.* Berlin: Weidman.

Prestwich, Michael. 1979. "Italian Merchants in Late Thirteenth and Fourteenth Century England." In *The Dawn of Modern Banking,* 77–104. New Haven, CT: Yale University Press.

Reiffen, David, and Andrew N. Kleit. 1990. "Terminal Railroad Revisited: Foreclosure of an Essential Facility or Simple Horizontal Monopoly?" *Journal of Law and Economics* 33(2): 419–38.

Reiffen, David, and Maggie Patterson. 1990. "The Rise and Retreat of the Market for Joint–Stock Shares Revisited: The Effect of the Bubble Act in Eighteenth Century England." *Journal of Economic History* 50(1): 163–71.

Robbins, Lionel C. 1934. *The Great Depression.* London: Macmillan.

Rolnick, Arthur J., and Warren E. Weber. 1986. "Gresham's Law or Gresham's Fallacy?" *Journal of Political Economy* 94(1): 186–201.

Sandberg, Lars G. 1978. "Banking and Economic Growth in Sweden before World War I." *Journal of Economic History* 38(3): 650–80.

Shearer, Ronald A., and Carolyn Clark. 1984. "Canada and the Interwar Gold Standard, 1920–35: Monetary Policy without a Central Bank." In *A Retrospective on the Classical Gold Standard, 1821–1931,* edited by Michael D. Bordo and Anna J. Schwartz, 277–302. Chicago: University of Chicago Press.

Thompson, Earl A. 1974. "Taxation and National Defense." *Journal of Political Economy* 82(4): 755–82.

———. 1979. "An Economic Basis for the 'National Defense Argument' for Aiding Certain Industries." *Journal of Political Economy* 87(1): 1–36.

———. 1997. "Gold Standard: Causes and Consequences." In *Business Cycles and Depressions: An Encyclopedia,* edited by David Glasner, 267–72. New York: Garland.

Ure, P. N. 1922. *The Origin of Tyranny.* Cambridge: Cambridge University Press.

Usher, Abbot P. 1943. *The Early History of Deposit Banking in Mediterranean Europe.* Cambridge, MA: Harvard University Press.

Vaubel, Roland. 1977. "Free Currency Competition." *Weltwirtschaftliches Archiv* 113(3): 435–61.

Yeager, Leland B. 1984. "The Image of the Gold Standard." In *A Retrospective on the Gold Standard, 1821–1931,* edited by Michael D. Bordo and Anna J. Schwartz, 651–69. Chicago: University of Chicago Press.

2

National Sovereignty and
International Monetary Regimes

Frank van Dun

*The nature and extent of government
power over monetary affairs depends
entirely on the underlying political
relationship between government and
the individual.*

—H. M. HOLZER

Introduction

It is noteworthy that Adam Smith, in his discussion of the duties of
the sovereign ([1776] 1937, Book V, chapter 1), did not include any
which required him to manage the monetary system of the nation. Smith
saw no economic rationale for any such prerogative.[1] Yet economists
of later generations have tended to take its existence for granted; they
have fallen under the spell of political and legal conceptions of money
that led them to accept the legitimacy of legal tender laws, paper money,
and central banking.[2]

Despite the many episodes of monetary instability since the beginning of central banking, economists long looked upon central banks as
necessary elements of any sound monetary system. In fact, most people
tend to look at money and its social functions from a perspective defined
by the existing monetary and financial institutions. This perspective

The author wishes to thank Richard Timberlake, Kevin Dowd, Alex Jettinghof, and
Nico Roos for their comments and editorial assistance. The usual disclaimers apply.

47

reflects basic presuppositions about the legal and political organization of society from which the institutions derive their claims to legitimacy. In this respect the doctrine of national sovereignty should be considered as a significant factor in any explanation of the current monetary arrangements. This paper focuses on the logic of sovereignty, its influence on constitutional interpretation, and its relevance for understanding national monetary policy making.

The principle of national sovereignty has recently become controversial in discussions of future monetary arrangements in the European Community. Two proposals, one for a European central bank and the other for the denationalization of money in the form of free currency competition,[3] confront the claims of national sovereignty head-on, but they do so in very different ways. The one envisages a "transfer of sovereignty" to some newly created institution with monopoly powers backed up by a European political authority. The other transfers sovereignty to the market, in other words, ultimately to all individuals, leaving them free to support the currencies and the banks of their choice.

The *Locus* of Sovereignty

Medieval legal theorists, building upon Roman Law as transmitted to them by the Justinian Code, included coinage or minting among the traditional prerogatives of the king. They presented no specific arguments for this royal monopoly but merely recorded the existence of an old practice and sanctified it in the language of their discipline.[4] The royal prerogatives, or *regalia,* became the cutting edge for the development of a systematic theory of the sovereignty of the king.

The power of the "logic of sovereignty" proved to be immense. Articulated by Jean Bodin (1530–96) as part of a richly textured historical and sociological account of royal power (Bodin [1576] 1962), it was then used by Thomas Hobbes (1588–1679) for his theory of absolute sovereignty (Hobbes [1651] 1909). Both were highly influential in giving definite form to the modern concept of the sovereign state. For them, the state is sovereign only if there is within it some natural or corporate person who can be considered the sovereign of the state.

Eventually, controversies about the *locus* of sovereignty in the state (the king, the parliament, the people) subsided. Sovereignty came to be seen as the attribute of the state itself, regardless of its particular system of government (Raphael 1976, 54–55). Within the state one could make a distinction between the government and the people or society, but sovereignty could be attributed only to their union: the state itself.

A crucial figure in this development was Jean-Jacques Rousseau (1712–78). He objected that earlier theories vested sovereignty in only a part of the state—its ruler. For Rousseau only the people as a whole could be sovereign, otherwise there is always a risk of conflict of interests. But the people had to be considered as a collective entity, not as a mere collection of individuals each of whom had selfish as well as moral (civic) impulses. The people had to be seen as a single corporate person, defined by nothing else than the commitment to the common good of all its members (i.e., citizens). For Rousseau the citizen was not simply an individual human being subject to the authority of the state, but the embodiment of an idea formed by a process of abstraction. The citizen is only "a partial and artificial person" (Rousseau 1762, Book II, chapter 7);[5] he lacks all individuality, because only the common "moral" and not the individual "selfish" components of the human person constitute his essence. In that sense every citizen *qua citizen* is identical with every other; they all have the same general will. The possibility of a conflict of interests is then logically excluded.

Rousseau's sovereign is an abstract person with no biological or historical reality. That was precisely Rousseau's point: he was convinced that he had identified the conditions under which a state *could* be legitimate. It was the task of politics, in particular of "wise" (quasi-divine) legislators, to undertake the difficult attempt to realize those conditions by "changing human nature," that is, by making citizens out of men (ibid).[6] Rousseau's program would then fulfill the Hobbesian program of absolutism. For Hobbes had insisted that people "should receive their motion from the Authority of the Soveraign" (Hobbes 1651, chapter 29, *in fine*), that is, from the law, and from no other source. Rousseau's point was that this could only happen if people completely and spontaneously identified with the law, that is, with the general will, which they have to see as nothing but an expression of their own interests.[7]

An important feature of Rousseau's and later conceptions of state sovereignty was that the distinction between government and society could no longer be interpreted as a distinction between the rulers and the ruled. If every legal action can, merely because of its legality, be traced to the same sovereign source, legal action exemplifies "the seamless web of (collective self-) government." Questions about the *locus* of sovereignty could then be dismissed. The state is sovereign because it is the source of law. As Kelsen summed up: state and law are identical. Thus, the notion of state sovereignty ends up as an absolutist and formal legal positivism: the law is supreme but it can have any content whatsoever (Kelsen 1960). In Kelsen's view, the fundamental distinction is between legal and illegal actions. The echo of Rousseau's dichotomy between man as a natural person and man as a citizen is unmistakable: legal actions, even those of private citizens, are to be ascribed to the law, and so to the state; illegal actions are the proper mark not of the individual *qua citizen* (for the citizen is a creature of the law itself and as such incapable of illegal action) but of the individual as a natural person.

With regard to money this positivistic view led to Knapp's "state theory of money" (Knapp 1905; Bendixen 1908, 1912),[8] which regards money as a mere symbol of legally defined powers delegated by the political sovereign to its legal possessor. Knapp accounted for the existence of an international monetary system by depicting it as a consequence of "imperialism" in which one state imposes its own commercial and monetary regime on the rest of the world.[9]

The Concept of Sovereignty

The Logic of Sovereignty

Greek, Roman, and medieval political thought recognized many attributes of rulers and forms of political organization and domination which were very similar to what the moderns call sovereignty and which were eventually subsumed under the concept. But premodern political thought did not have the concept of the sovereignty of the state (Vincent 1987, 10–16). The crucial consideration is that sovereignty applies primarily to persons, and classical and medieval political thought did not personify forms of political organization or domination. To speak of the state as sovereign is to regard the state as a person. This is the essence of the peculiarly modern notion of the state.[10] It implies that the state is to be considered as a kind of moral agent, with interests and purposes of its own, with rights and duties, a capability to assume responsibilities and obligations, having the right to hold and manage and dispose of its property, and liable for its actions.[11] The personification of the state, first proposed for primarily analytical purposes in Plato's *Republic*,[12] implied a distinction between the government (the head, as the seat of mind and reason) and society (the body, as the seat of matter and desire). The idea of the sovereign state is analogous to the classical notion of the sovereign person, the wise man, who is governed from above by reason, is immune from the passions, and is in complete harmony with the natural and divine laws.[13]

Personification of the state by itself does not imply its sovereignty. Not all persons need be sovereign. To claim that one person *belongs to* another is to deny sovereignty to the former (without necessarily ascribing sovereignty to the latter). For example, a slave is not a sovereign person because he belongs to his master. A created being is not sovereign if he belongs to his Creator.[14] These examples point to the defining characteristic of sovereign persons. A sovereign person is one who belongs to none other. With the help of a few general assumptions and auxiliary definitions (van Dun 1984),[15] this definition leads directly to the commonly accepted attributes of sovereignty.[16]

Semantics

It should be clear that the definition of sovereignty is purely formal; the same logical relations hold regardless of particular semantic interpretations of the terms involved. Catholic political thought does not generally object to the use of the concept of sovereignty as such, but only to the idea that sovereignty can be attributed to any other person than God (Maritain 1951, chapter 2). The common modern view is that states (and perhaps only states) are sovereign persons,[17] while a libertarian would insist that human beings (and perhaps only human beings) are sovereign persons. Using the same logic, differing interpretations thus imply radically different political views.

Today, personification of the state is likely to cause some embarrassment, more in countries such as the United States[18] and the United Kingdom,[19] less on the European continent where there has been a stronger state tradition. Yet even if not explicitly acknowledged, personification continues to underlie a good deal of political speech in ordinary language. That the state has become "impersonal" merely means that it is no longer identified or associated with one particular natural person—the king—or one particular office and its office-holder(s). It does not mean that the state lacks a legal personality as such. In fact, while some proponents of the doctrine of monarchical absolutism valiantly strove to identify the state and the person of the monarch—as in Louis XIV's *L'Etat c'est moi*—most writers even in the absolutist tradition made ample use of the juristic notion of the *persona ficta* to characterize the state as a corporate body with a unity of its own, in other words, as a legal person.

There is perhaps little to object to when the state is characterized as a fictional person, but does it make sense to regard a fictional person as sovereign? The short answer is that it does not. The idea that a fictional person belongs to no other person does not make sense at all, if the members of the corporation are themselves persons,[20] because there is no action it could conceivably undertake without the consent of any member. To ascribe sovereignty to it is pointless fantasy.

Two Concepts of State Sovereignty

In view of practices such as taxation, compulsory military service, and far-reaching regulation of all sorts of activities, state sovereignty can only be justified if one accepts that citizens belong to the state.[21] We may call this the strong concept of state sovereignty. It conflicts with deep-rooted sentiments concerning human freedom and the inviolability of human rights.

It is, however, conceptually possible to reconcile the idea of state sovereignty with that of the sovereignty of individual human beings or citizens: Let both the state and the individual citizens be sovereign persons. Now suppose that there is some collection of things, which belong to the state, such that *nothing* an individual citizen (or anybody else within the borders of the state) can do can fail to affect at least one of these things. Then, by the logic of sovereignty, no such individual within the borders of the state has a right to undertake any action without the consent of the state. This seems sufficient to enable us to continue to speak of state sovereignty and of the preeminence of the state in its relations with citizens and others, even if it is no longer necessary to assume that citizens belong to the state. Thus, we have here a weaker concept of state sovereignty.

I believe Jean Bodin's theory of sovereignty, as put forth in his *Les six livres de la république* ([1576] 1962), is such a theory of sovereignty in a weak sense. This interpretation removes the difficulty (Sabine 1973, 379–82) of reconciling Bodin's insistence both on the absoluteness of the king's sovereignty and on the limitations which the natural and historical constitution of society imposes on his sovereignty—divine and natural law, institutions such as the family and its inviolable private property, and constitutional practices that predate the king's rise from the position of a supreme judge applying the customary law of the land to that of a supreme legislator (i.e., a sovereign in the full sense, the true and unique source of man-made law).

For all his "absolute power," the Bodinian sovereign did not have the right to levy taxes without the consent of the taxpayer, as this power would violate the private property rights of the families that, in our terminology, are the other sovereign persons in the Bodinian state. For Bodin, the several families were the basic units of society. Bodin also denied the king the right to interfere with contracts, and he insisted the king should faithfully keep his contracts with his subjects. Property and contract belonged to the sphere of natural law (Skinner 1978, 284–301). The sovereign king merely took charge of the public domain (roads, woods, etc.) and the public institutions that grew out of the social fabric, to the extent that they could not be claimed by any family as its property or did not rest on explicit and specific consent of identifiable parties.[22]

However, if there was little or nothing a private person could do which did not have repercussions in the public domain, the king's consent became a necessary condition for the legitimacy of most or all actions. In this view, Bodin's reputation as an advocate of "absolute, limitless" sovereignty of the king rests more on his extensive interpretation of the "public sphere" than on any distinction between the nature of the rights of the king and the nature of the rights of his subjects.

Is this weaker version of state sovereignty a plausible notion for legitimizing current state practices? I do not think so. In the first place, it is difficult to determine just what the "public" things are which no citizen can supposedly fail to affect in some relevant way.[23] Then there is the problem of monopoly: one would have to explain just why these things should be thought of as necessarily and exclusively belonging to one "person," the state.[24] Finally, the weak concept of state sovereignty implies that the state should seek the consent of each and every citizen its actions affect—something states are not in the habit of doing.[25]

It is easy to derive even weaker notions of state sovereignty by supposing that there are in fact some, or even a great many, actions available to individual citizens and others which in no way affect the proper domain of the state. At some point even the preeminence of the state will disappear, as the state is more and more submerged within the rights-based order of a community of sovereign persons, without any particular distinction of its own.[26]

Internal and External Aspects of Sovereignty

There is an obvious difference between internal and external aspects of sovereignty. The internal aspect, comprising the relations between the sovereign person and his belongings, presents all the characteristics of absolutism with which we are familiar in political discourses on sovereignty. The sovereign person has an absolute and supreme authority over himself, over every thing and every person that belongs to him, but to no independent person. Within his own domain the sovereign person is the sole source of law; he is fully autonomous, no other persons having the right to force him to obey their will. If, for example, we take the state to be a sovereign person, state sovereignty, as Maritain noted, implies state absolutism: the omnicompetence of the state.[27] Within the state we have an *authority-based order* grounded in the sovereign right of the state to do with its own what it wills.

In its external aspect sovereignty presents an entirely different picture. The sovereign person's rights are limited by the rights of independent persons, especially other sovereign persons.[28] He has no right to do any action that affects the domain of another independent person without the latter's consent. On the other hand, he has the right to give or to refuse his consent whenever independent persons affect his own domain. Among mutually independent persons, in particular among sovereign persons, all interactions must be based on mutual consent. The order that exists among them is *rights-based*, there being no person with the right to compel them to adhere to his own rules. The inviolability of property and freedom of contract, subject only to the limitations imposed by the sovereignty of third parties, are its fundamental normative principles. Self-defence[29] is its rightful method of enforcement, whether exercised individually or on the basis of mutual help and cooperation.

Applied to states, the logic of sovereignty shows us the fundamental structure of classical international law—territorial integrity, noninterference in the internal affairs of other states, the binding force of treaties, the justification for defensive wars.[30] Applied to human beings, it shows the fundamental legal institutions of a system based on the natural rights of individuals: private property, freedom of contract, and personal liability.

Moral and Methodological Aspects

Moral Aspects

With respect to the internal aspects of sovereignty, the sovereignty of the individual natural person means that he has absolute and final authority over himself and over himself alone. The borders are drawn very close around each person, and his range of permissible action is restricted by the existence of other individuals who may or may not give their consent to his request for cooperation in the pursuit of his goals. To the strong individual, natural justice is a confining condition as he is required never to treat another as a mere means, even if he has the power to do so. In this sense the requirement of natural justice corresponds to the Kantian categorical imperative.

While the weak version of state sovereignty (which restricts the direct authority of the state to some "public sphere") is compatible with sovereignty of the individual, the strong version is not. If states are looked upon as sovereign persons in the strong sense, which actions an individual may carry out can only be decided with reference to the will or the law of the sovereign in the state. Legality replaces natural justice.[31] It may well be legal to take from others without their consent, to force them to provide labor services, and so forth.[32] From the perspective of the theory of state sovereignty, no stigma attaches to the peculiar *modus operandi* of government, which is to impose solutions by force or the threat of force against natural persons. The main achievement of the theory of state sovereignty is thus to give the legal exercise of government power a solid basis in the sovereign right of the state: it provides a blanket justification for actions outside the restricted range permitted by natural justice.

Methodological Aspects

Leaving aside the obvious moral questions, acceptance of this legal point of view is less than satisfactory for purposes of analysis. We are forced to separate radically our normative and our causal worldviews. What in a legal analysis would appear as an ultimate agent or decision maker would not be so considered in a causal analysis. In this way the semantics of rights-talk (based on fictional persons) and the semantics of action-talk (based on natural persons) are largely disconnected. The distinction between rightful and other actions becomes, to that extent, a matter to be settled not by reference to any causal reality but by the arbitrary authority of some dominant opinion. Legal science seems to have resigned itself to this state of affairs, as for example, when it is claimed that the object of legal science is legal science itself.[33] It is a discipline that takes its own fabrications for the ultimate reality. It makes law into a closed self-referential category, with no other obvious use than to justify existing power relations by interpreting them as relations among suitably but arbitrarily defined legal persons.[34]

When we are analyzing legal conceptions in the context of real world economic processes, however, it is especially advisable to apply a methodological individualism not only to an analysis of actions but also to an analysis of rights. Just as we assume that individuals are "the ultimate agents of change" (Mises 1966, 18), so we should assume they are the ultimate bearers of sovereign rights. As indicated above, the concept of natural rights can be deduced from the idea that human beings (natural persons) are sovereign persons, that is, separate persons who do not belong to any other. And this idea can be taken to correspond to the view that individuals are capable of independent action.[35] Thus normative and descriptive-explanatory approaches to social phenomena could be methodologically unified.

As a matter of fact, however, the social sciences have often tended to accept the legal view of social processes and to ascribe ultimate causal relevance to the legal persons themselves, at least as far as legal actions are concerned. Macroeconomics is a good example: the state is seen as a causal agent whose actions determine the condition of its own national economy (e.g., the price level, rate of growth, level of employment, and so on). Like the wise man of old, the good state is characterized as fully rational and self-controlled. The legal person, being defined by law, cannot be a source of illegal action. Coupled to the assumption—which became common with the theory of popular sovereignty—that what is legal cannot produce evil consequences,[36] this way of looking at social reality gives a recipe for a systematic bias in social science. Evil consequences have to be traced either to illegal activity or to insufficient legal organization and regulation. The individual, never a source of legality, can only be a source of trouble.

Sovereignty and the Omnicompetent State

To the extent that the theory of state sovereignty was accepted, it accounted for the traditional prerogatives of the king by providing a sufficient ground for their legitimacy. But its logical import could not be restricted to any particular list of activities. In fact, the theory of sovereignty provided a justification for any exercise of the sovereign power of the state. It completely undercut the legal case for any limitation of state power, if not with respect to the form in which state power could be exercised then certainly with respect to its goals or objects.[37]

Over time the insistence on a legal form—on compliance with formal rules of procedure—grew stronger, but so too did the insistence on implied powers,[38] even in states with a formal constitution. Whatever the proper authorities consider to be conducive to an otherwise undefined "public interest" or "common good," is by implication a legitimate activity of government.

In that sense the doctrine of absolutism survived the demise of monarchical absolutism and the rise of the constitutional state. It fostered the idea that constitutional limitations on the government must be seen as auto-limitations imposed by the state itself. The constitutional limitations on the government can be changed or even lifted by constitutional processes—e.g., amendment, interpretation, the declaration of a state of emergency, or even the appeal to a "living constitution," an evolving set of practices and precedents which permit a continual redefinition of the meaning of constitutional texts.[39] The ultimate decision always and inevitably rests with some organ(s) of government. Even when the wisdom of a particular extension of government powers may be questioned, the notion that such an extension is under no circumstances to be permitted should not be expected to survive in the regular processes of constitutional change. The history of the federal government's monetary powers under the American Constitution is as good an example of this process as any.[40]

Legal grounds for an expansion of government authority can always be found, if not in specific constitutional texts or precedents, then in the reading of those texts as containing the constitution of a sovereign state. The appeal to the inherently absolutist notion of sovereignty imparts a systematic pro-government bias to constitutional interpretation.

Leviathan Revisited: Power and Money

The Fiction of Absolutism

The logic of sovereignty only applies to rights, not to effective power. Omnicompetence is not the same as omnipotence. But theories of sovereignty had to conjoin rights and effective power to fulfill their political purpose, which was to strengthen the position of the central authority in the ongoing struggle for power and control. Bodin and Hobbes constructed their theories against a background of civil and religious wars. Following a long tradition going back to Dante and Marsilius of Padua, they looked to the temporal power, the emperor or king, to restore order and peace. Part of the appeal of the argument was its relation to the Christian metaphysics of order: all order is artificial, that is, created by or at least dependent on some authority to whose care it is entrusted (Bodin [1596] 1962; see also Greenleaf 1973). Hobbes took the argument to its absurd[41] but influential conclusion by making the claim that, without the state, life is not worth living. Society cannot exist outside the state, "that *Mortall God*, to which wee owe under the *Immortall God*, our peace and defence" (Hobbes [1651] 1909, chapter 17).[42] Despite his demand that the sovereign should not shackle the economy, Hobbes held fast to the central idea that people "should receive their motion from the Authority of the Soveraign" and from no other source.[43] The sovereign is then placed under the impossible demand to control everything in order to be able to intervene quickly and effectively and to prevent any of the things "that Weaken, or tend to the Dissolution of a Common-wealth" from getting out of hand. But how can the sovereign comply with these demands, unless he can be assured of the loyalty of many others? And who will guard the guardians?

Hobbes' argument was designed to justify absolute, yet effective, power, which is a practical absurdity in a large political society.[44] Absolutism always was much less fact than fiction, even under the reign of Louis XIV of France. The practice of absolutist regimes was, of course, to buy the allegiance of powerful parties (popular men, great cities, corporations, churches), as well as of soldiers and bureaucrats, with money and privileges, and to give in to popular demands when the pressure became too strong—all things Hobbes condemned on theoretical grounds, without being able to suggest a practical alternative. Those things in fact served *not* to concentrate power in the hands of the sovereign, but to dilute it. Against the realities of political power, Hobbes' theory of sovereignty had little to offer but wishful thinking.[45] Keeping government powerful and access to it closed is extremely difficult, even for a nominally absolute monarch.

The need to secure support and the consequent problem of isolating the government from pressures to accommodate particular interests exist in democratic regimes as much as in any other. In fact, formal democracy has tended to exacerbate the problem.[46] In the wake of the demand for universal suffrage came the demand for universal access to the government. Now deemed to serve the people directly, the government could only be responsible by being responsive to the demands made upon it. In modern economic jargon, the government became a "common pool" resource, access to which could in principle be denied to no citizen or group. As the private costs of using government for one's own purposes are not likely to reflect its social costs, economic theory leads us to expect that people will make excessive demands on governmental resources (the means of power and/or the resources these give access to) (Hardin 1982; De Jasay 1985, 1989). As a result, pressure builds up to bring ever more resources into the common pool— e.g., by tax increases or more extensive regulatory powers[47]—or to institute a privatization of sorts of the commons, with special interests achieving some measure of exclusive control over parts of the governmental apparatus and its budget.[48]

Markets and Money

The accommodation of all those interests exposes the government to immense pressure to intervene on their behalf in "spontaneous" social processes, especially in the market. However, the record of government intervention in the market is not a successful one. Simpleminded attempts to merely outlaw undesired effects, such as by regulating behavior or prices, tend, if effective, to create shortages or gluts and to generate complex and largely unpredictable patterns of substitution effects within and without the law. Intervention in the market is one thing, controlling it for specific effects is another. If the government allows a market at all, it must to some extent respect its essential institutions—private property, contract, personal liability—or face the consequences. In other words: its laws must to some extent *simulate* the system of natural justice. It cannot have a market and prohibit people from having wide discretion over a wide range of choices. Unable to predict or monitor the pattern of individual choices, government intervention can only be a source of mostly unintended consequences which it may not approve of, and which may induce it to further interventions.[49]

Moreover, control over society by means of direct regulations—of prices or behavior—is costly to enforce as well as damaging to the creation of taxable wealth. It is here that its monopoly of money is most valuable for the government. By creating money and controlling the ways in which it enters the economic system, the government can buy support for its policies without incurring large enforcement costs. Money creation also has an advantage over other, more explicit, forms of taxation. It clearly benefits some people, while the harm it does is not easily ascribed to government policy. Redistribution of purchasing power does occur because of changes in relative prices, but these take time to manifest themselves. Since the victims of the distributive effect are usually those who are far removed from the point where the new money enters the system, they are more likely to blame the market (rising prices) than the government. Thus, the political aspect of money creation differs from the political aspect of explicit taxation.

Today, with nonredeemable fiat money and central banking firmly in place, governments have ready access to money and credit. But people must be willing to accept a particular money in exchange for goods and services or it will be worth nothing. To enjoy the advantages (revenue) of an inflationary monetary policy, the government must pay attention to the demand for its money. It is likely to do so by cumbersome interventions in order to protect its money.

The value of money is now completely determined by the demand for something the supply of which depends to a large extent on the discretion of the monetary authority. If the public perceived its value as falling and could switch costlessly to readily available substitutes— easily tradable commodities or other assets ("near-moneys") or foreign currencies, the demand would presumably evaporate immediately. To explain continued demand for an inflating currency in the presence of more stable alternatives,[50] one must look for factors which artificially prop up demand and which restrict competition from other foreign or domestic suppliers of money (Vaubel 1986, 927–42). Legal tender laws come under this head, especially if they go to the extreme of requiring all contracts involving money to be denominated in the national currency. So does the government's use of its "economic power": it can easily decide to accept only its own money in payment for services sold to the public. As a rule, the government will not be a successful competitor as a seller on the market for goods and services— that is, not unless it can secure for itself a legal monopoly or some significant cost advantage (such as direct subsidies or not having to pay taxes). Ultimately, the demand for the government's money may have to be propped up by the requirement that it be used for the payment of taxes and transfers.

If the utility for the government of its monetary powers depends on its ability to enforce legal tender laws for payments in general or for payments to the government in particular, it remains true that the supply and demand for money cannot be completely controlled by the state—at least not unless the government wants to forego the benefits of a money-economy altogether (Mises 1971, chapter 8).

The Chimerical National Economy

The preceding discussion of familiar political and economic realities bears directly on the question of the economic significance of the
doctrine of national sovereignty. From the perspective provided by the
logic of sovereignty this significance should be beyond dispute. Ety-
mologically, an economy (from the Greek words *oikos*, house, home,
and *nomos*, rule) is nothing but a well-ordered household. Economics,
in its original meaning, is the art of managing a household. In this
sense it has almost the same meaning as "government," which can also
be used as a synonym for "management"—as in the antiquarian expression "the government of a farm." The basic idea is that of the
authoritative ordering of all the assets (including people) of a household to the pursuit of its purpose. By concentrating all rights over society in the sovereign, that is, by denying the people in that society any
rights opposable to the state, the theory of the sovereign state actually
enshrined this teleological, monocentric conception of the national
economy as an implication of the concept of the state itself.[51] The right
to determine economic activities belongs to the state and has to be
exercised by or under supervision of the government.

The absolutist state can still be imagined to have its own economy,
geared to achieving the overriding goal of strengthening the military
and diplomatic position of the king on the international scene (*Col-
bertisme*). But in a democracy, despite regular nationalistic appeals to
"unity" in the pursuit of "national" goals, legitimate rule depends on
allowing common access to the government, that is, on allowing various groups to pursue their own ends through the channels of the state.
Policy coordination, in the sense of organizing a coherent set of mutually compatible policies, becomes a chimerical undertaking under a
regime of political pluralism within a sovereign state. Without legal
pluralism one cannot rely on the spontaneous coordinating tendencies
of market processes. One must rely on some sort of explicit planning
and budgeting—i.e., on explicit agreements in an atmosphere characterized by strategic bargaining.

Destructive of the liberal conception of a limited government, democratic pluralism also forced a retreat from socialistic thinking, which
saw the central government as a single agent "in charge of the national
economy." One response was to redefine the national economy as a
macroeconomy that the government ought to take care of by means of
its traditional fiscal and monetary prerogatives, without bothering to

intervene directly in market processes or to attempt to engineer policy coordination by explicit agreement. Keynesianism (stressing fiscal policy) and monetarism (stressing monetary policy) were both, I believe, inspired by the desire to restore autonomy to the central level of government, where the pursuit of the common good (defined as "stable economic growth") would supposedly be immune from particular interests. Both doctrines cling to a very traditional vision of government as a single rational and benevolent agent clearly separated from the rest of society, with undisputed authority and a capacity for sustained coherent action in the public interest. Fiscal and monetary policies are seen as auxiliaries, serving no specific fiscal or monetary ends. Their job is to facilitate the implementation of any mix of policies—military, social, industrial, commercial, or whatever—by a macroeconomic attempt at harmonization.[52]

Disappointment with Keynesian fiscal policies led to a greater reliance on monetary macromanagement but not to greater monetary stability. Some monetarists, blaming the discretionary nature of monetary policy making for continued monetary instability, called for a rule or constitution which would oblige the authority to pursue monetary stability as its only goal (Friedman 1987; Buchanan 1982). Whether this is sensible, not just in theory but in practice as well, is debatable. In order to keep its central bank in command of the monetary system, the government should be prepared to stifle in the bud all market processes that might eventually reduce the economic significance of government money, both nationally and internationally.[53] If the government does not relinquish its monopoly over money, it is hard to see how it could effectively resist pressures to make monetary policy once again subservient to nonmonetary goals, or why it should want to resist such pressures, especially when confronted with a crisis.

The Sovereign State in a Global Economy

Political pluralism in conjunction with the formalism of law (which traces all legal actions to the same source) has blurred the distinction between government and society. This blurring has *prima facie* strengthened the case for a nationalistic interpretation of national sovereignty (i.e., of the state as a self-governing individual unit), but the close cooperation between government and special interests may actually have undermined the appeal of nationalism and national sovereignty. A cooperation of that kind is likely to foster an extremely utilitarian perspective on government, as well as political loyalties focused more in the particular group than in the nation as a whole.[54] Yet, national sovereignty has accustomed people in general to the idea that everything that is legal is morally acceptable. They learn to seek their own private ends by legal means, irrespective of whether achieving their ends involves the use of government power to take what belongs to others or to make them comply with imposed rules. What people value is not the source of the power put at their disposal but the power itself—not national sovereignty, but the vast expansion of the range of courses of actions they can legally follow if they make use of state power.

In an international economic system groups within various states might discover they have common interests which can be served most efficiently by an international agency or organization with governmental powers. Alternatively, governments may have a similar incentive to set up inter- or supranational structures. Borders, in open economies, confine governments rather than citizens. To the extent that citizens are free to move, policies may attract or chase away people and capital; and governments have clear incentives to prefer attractive rather than repulsive policies. Only the borders between states, when not successfully sealed off, provide citizens of national states with the opportunity to "vote with their feet," or at least "with their wallets" (Cf. Tiebout 1956; Hirschman 1970).

Migration and capital flight have always been significant factors checking discretionary policies, because they directly threaten the local or national power base. In that sense, national borders are an ultimate safety valve for the citizens. Especially when they are numerous (as is the case when many states coexist in a relatively small area, such as Europe), borders are important elements of the international constitutional order, not the least in respect to the protection of human rights, but also in respect to the creation of wealth.

From the perspective of the politically powerful within the national state, borders severely limit their capacities to impose their will, especially in an age of increased mobility and telecommunications. One solution is to enter into "market-sharing" and other cooperative agreements (cartels) with other governments in order to further diminish the citizens' expected gains from physical or financial emigration.[55] Fiscal and monetary policies provide obvious examples of means by which states can compete for citizens and capital. Given the nature of the fiscal extraction process itself, such fiscal competition would be to the advantage of the (net-)payers of taxes and to the disadvantage of the (net-)recipients of taxes, primarily the political class and its clientele.

Foregoing the benefits of inflation, governments can presumably attract large funds from outside their borders. Significantly, for many years now one of the most effective arguments against inflationary policies, as well as against high taxation and overregulation, has been the need to remain internationally competitive. One should not overlook the possibility that in the areas where governments are more internationally oriented than their citizens, the government's desire to eliminate competitive pressures from abroad is a primary motive.[56]

Either cartels break down, or they evolve into more unified structures. Given the nature of the interests that fuel the attempts to strengthen governmental cartels, it is to be expected that the second alternative is the preferred outcome of those seeking cartelization. It is true that intergovernmental cooperation and coordination tend to restrict the national government's freedom of action; but there are indications that such restrictions, to the extent they are effective, merely reflect a gradual shift of interventionist and discretionary policies to the inter- or supranational level.[57] In fact, the restrictions imposed on them by treaties and supranational governmental institutions may even strengthen the position of the national governments vis-à-vis the national pressure groups, by allowing them to shift responsibility for their policies to the international level.

To assume that national governments in Europe will not give up their national monetary prerogatives because money creation is an important source of revenue, is to overlook the fact that governments (corporate persons) are not causally active agents. The individuals who at any time make up the government and determine its decisions may well feel that the advantage to them of a European central bank outweigh its disadvantage. From their point of view, the loss of discretionary powers on the national level may be compensated by the increased opportunities for access to prestigious and lucrative offices and contacts in the international bureaucracies. Moreover, depending upon the specifics of its charter and prerogatives, such a bank could still be a source of revenue and of discretionary monetary power. It would in any case be far less exposed to the pressures of international competition.

Inevitably, the question has been raised as to where the development of supranational governmental institutions leaves the principle of national sovereignty. Leaving aside for the moment whether this question is as interesting as is sometimes suggested,[58] we may note that the concept of state sovereignty does not appear to be an important obstacle to the emergence of international and supranational governmental agencies. History—even very recent history—shows that the concept is readily adapted to cover new political realities on the national front (changing structures of government) as well as on the international (redrawing borders after wars, conquests, the breakup of empires, etc.). In addition, the identification of state and law has allowed a reformulation of sovereignty theory in terms of the supremacy of the formal lawmaking process itself. This can be applied with equal ease to national and to international and supranational law.

From a legal point of view it may not be very illuminating to talk about "transfers of sovereignty" in connection with the outcome of international negotiations. The doctrine of national sovereignty interprets treaties, when not imposed by force, as an exercise, and not as a limitation or transfer, of sovereignty. International agreements no more involve transfers of sovereignty than do laws that permit individual citizens to engage in actions of a certain kind without prior authorization or licence. From a legal point of view they are no more than "autolimitations"(Stankiewicz 1977, 312). It seems to me, however, that such an interpretation attests to the enduring influence of the old personality theory which lies at the heart of the concept of the sovereign state. An individual person, considered to be sovereign, does not lose his sovereign status by the mere fact of assuming contractual obligations, or empowering another to make certain decisions for him, which he will accept as binding. But it is far from self-evident that this conclusion can be transposed from reasoning about natural persons to an argument about corporate persons, without begging the question whether it makes sense to attribute sovereignty to a *persona ficta* in the first place.

Regardless of such niceties of legal doctrine, we may in fact be witnessing something analogous to the emergence of the strong state sovereignty of the past. At present, national states are still considered to be the basic units of the international order. But there is a growing sense of an international public sphere which needs to be policed under international law. The tendency is to create international or even supranational institutions with sovereign powers over this public sphere. Although the doctrine of noninterference in internal affairs is still defended, an increasing number of exceptions (e.g., human rights) are being contemplated and sometimes used to justify interventions. So far, the emerging "international" sovereigns (such as the UN, EU, IMF, and so on) are sovereign only in a relatively weak sense, but there is no reason to suppose that international power structures will be less able to break through the barrier of national borders than the old sovereign was able to set aside the Bodinian barrier of private property. On the contemporary scene, this process has perhaps advanced further in Europe than elsewhere. Eventually, taxation or some other form of legalized direct intervention, without consent of individual states, will force transition to a concept of strong supranational sovereignty. The logical end-state of this process is a world-state, with a world-government.

Whatever one may think of the appropriateness of talk about the transfer of sovereignty from the national to a supranational level, or of the costs and benefits of such a transfer, surely the more fundamental question lies elsewhere. Supranational sovereignty and national sovereignty are birds of a feather. In both cases there is the same negation of individual sovereignty, the same disregard for natural persons and their natural rights, the same justification of legal takings and legal monopolies and other privileges. International or supranational government is still government. If not dictatorial it will be democratic, and if democratic it will be under high pressure to finance all kinds of political projects by whatever means possible, including manipulation of the money supply. The prospects of an international monetary regime under political control thus present little that is new, or appealing.

Concluding Remarks

Perhaps the increased distance from local or national influences may make it easier for supranational monetary authorities to pursue sound monetary policies, but only if the weakening of international competitive pressures does not tempt the authorities to exploit the far wider range of discretion open to them. The subjects of petty tyrants have always appealed to faraway emperors and kings to deliver them from local abuses of power. Kings and emperors have generally been willing enough to comply with the request, and their willingness to do so is a significant part of the explanation of the rise of national states (Rüstow 1980, 101–06). The transfer of quasi-religious awe from the king to the national parliament to the European Parliament or the United Nations shows a remarkable continuity in the belief that somewhere up there a truly good ruler is waiting to set matters straight. But the bottom-line is that talk about national or supranational sovereignty, with its implicit or explicit references to fictional legal persons, merely serves to mask the realities of political power—regardless of the direction and nature of ongoing processes of state-formation. As Blaise Pascal noted in his *Pensées*, "Unable to fortify justice, we have justified force" (Pascal 1958, part 1, no. 81).

Notes

1. As a cause of the wealth—as opposed to the poverty—of nations, governmental monetary policy apparently had no role to play. The late-scholastic theologians of the sixteenth century had already commented extensively on the ways in which rulers could impoverish whole nations by abusing their monetary prerogatives (e.g., the monopoly of minting). See Chafuen 1986, chapter 5.
2. This despite the fact that central banks were organized and evolved to meet the financial needs of governments. Their primary function has always been political, or fiscal, rather than monetary. See Glasner (1989, 30–35); Dowd (1989).
3. Klein (1974); Hayek (1976, 1978). The argument was taken up by Roland Vaubel, Pascal Salin, and many others. Especially in the United States, there has been a boom in studies on free banking by Murray Rothbard, Lawrence White, Richard Timberlake, George Selgin, and others.
4. "Learned studies of public law (*le droit public*) are often nothing but the history of ancient malpractices" (D'Argenson, quoted by Rousseau 1762, Book I, n. to chapter 2).
5. The "citizen" thus stands in contrast to the individual who exists as a "perfect and solitary whole," that is, as a "physical and independent" being.
6. The idea that the key to a good society was to change human nature, to create a "new man," was to have a fateful impact on political thought and praxis in the nineteenth and twentieth centuries. See, for example, Heller (1988). Rousseau himself, however, cannot easily be blamed for the totalitarian and collectivist excesses against which he warned constantly. His point was that unless the state was constituted by citizens in the true (i.e., his) sense, it could not possibly have legitimacy. But the attempt to change human nature was *not* likely to succeed except under very propitious circumstances (Rousseau 1762, Book II, chapter 10). In any case, Rousseau's *législateur* had no legislative powers (which would have made him the sovereign). Hence, the superhuman or quasi-divine qualities which legislation requires, but which few men are likely to have and fewer would know how to use effectively without having recourse to force. Thus Rousseau's argument in *Du Contrat Social* comes close to a philosophical justification of anarchism: if there is to be a legitimate state, it should be possible to change man from a natural and individual into an artificial and collective being; but as such change is impossible, so is the justification of the state. Substitute "unlikely" for "impossible" and you get the basic presupposition of Rousseau's political philosophy.
7. See also Rousseau (1762, Book II, chapter 12): "a nation can always change its laws, even the best of them; for if the people desire to harm themselves, who has the right to stop them?"
8. Nussbaum (1925) elaborated Knapp's state theory into a "societary theory," mainly to account for the public's occasional repudiation of government money. See Pribram (1983, 237–39).
9. Thus, in Knapp's view, the international gold standard of his day should be seen not merely as a manifestation of British dominance in international trade and of

the preeminence of the City of London as the world's leading financial center (Timberlake 1991, 49, who refers to Cassel 1936 and Bordo 1984), but also and primarily as a manifestation of the acceptance of British legal and political sovereignty by the world's leading trading nations in matters of trade and international payment.

10. The modern concept of the state has been credited to Machiavelli; however, most modern research dates its appearance as late as the sixteenth century. See Hexter (1973); Skinner (1978); Dyson (1980). "There is...a complex and subtle connection between the 'State as the monarch' and the 'State as standing over and above the monarch' and the 'impersonal abstract State'" (Vincent 1987, 65). The same author rightly stresses, "It is also the case that the cohesive unity of the twentieth-century State *is* the direct result of the personal theory [of the sixteenth-century French theorists of absolutism]" (Ibid., 51).

11. It is a small step from the conception of the state as a moral or legal person to the idea that this person is, or is analogous to, a real organism. Hobbes (1651, chapter 24) and Rousseau (1755) made ample use of this analogy, and both saw money as the blood of the social organism.

12. As a political concept Plato's personification of the *polis* was rejected as irrelevant and even pernicious by Aristotle and by most other classical (and medieval) writers. It left no mark on political practice. It should be noted, however, that Plato introduced the concept as a means to investigate the notion of a just man. As R. L. Nettleship (1925, 4) put it, despite its title, we very soon find that *The Republic* is a book of moral rather than political philosophy.

13. Cf. Maritain (1951, n. 48 to chapter 2, with a reference to Thomas Aquinas, *Summa Theologica*, Ia–IIae 96:5).

14. Locke (*Second Treatise,* II: 2, 6) uses this idea to foreclose the possibility of an absolute power (i.e., sovereignty) in human affairs.

15. For a full presentation with proofs of theorems, see my "A Formal Theory of Rights" (1985 unpublished working paper, University of Maastricht). The assumptions upon which the derivations rely are: 1) every person belongs to at least one person; 2) whatever belongs to a person A belongs to person B, if A belongs to B; 3) if an action makes use of a means M then it affects M; 4) for every action, there is some means such that the action makes use of the means; 5) for every means, there is some action such that the action makes use of the means.

16. For example, it can be shown that a sovereign person has authority over his own property (i.e., such things as belong to him and to no independent person) without the consent of any person. Also, that no person has authority over what belongs to a sovereign person without the latter's consent. Now, the fact that a sovereign person has absolute authority over his own property does not by itself mean that he has the right to do with it whatever he likes, for there may be in effect no action available to him which does not also affect something that is not his, but another's, property. He has to consider the rights of independent persons (i.e., persons who do not belong to him, such as other sovereign persons). However, if there is an action available to him that does not affect the property of independent persons, then it can be shown that a sovereign person does have the right to do the action without the consent of any person. If there are persons who belong to a sovereign person (and to no independent person), then the former are under the supreme authority of the latter. The sovereign has the right to determine what they shall do, for example, to command them to obey his will or to lay down the law for them. He also has the right to force or compel them to obey, because he has the right to do to or with them whatever he wants, as long as his actions do not also affect others over whom he has no authority. These state-

ments are all paraphrases of theorems of the formal system referred to in the previous note.

17. In one interpretation, going back to Jean-Jacques Rousseau (1762, Book I, chapter 6), popular and state sovereignty are really the same thing, "the State" and "the People" being but names for the same phenomenon.

18. At the time of the founding of the United States, there was a conscious effort to distinguish the American political system from that of European states. Nevertheless, many Americans have been willing to look upon the United States as one sovereign nation, not just in an international context but also with regard to the internal aspect of sovereignty.

19. In Great Britain the "common-law perspective from the middle ages and the general lack of separation between public and private law, has tended historically...to diminish the significance and function of the State" (Vincent 1987, 11).

20. The problem disappears if the members are not persons. In that case the analogy between a corporate person and a natural person becomes perfect. The natural person also is a composite body, but its parts are not persons. Here again Rousseau (1762, Book I, chapter 7) deserves special mention: only "citizens" are members of the state, natural persons are not. Citizens *are* the state, natural persons *belong* to it. Therefore, force may be used against natural persons in order "to compel them to be free," i.e., to become citizens, sharing indivisibly in the sovereignty of the state.

21. In the *Mémoires for the Dauphin* (1666), Louis XIV of France wrote that "Kings are absolute Lords and by nature have complete and true disposition of all wealth owned by either churchmen or by laymen...according to the general needs of their state." (Quoted in Rowen 1961, 91–92).

22. Bodin was apparently willing to recognize that the king's monopolistic control over the public sphere rested not on law but on force. For Bodin, the state was geographically defined by the reach of the king's power, not by any internal unity. Therefore, the same state could comprise many communities or *cités* and even peoples (nations), all of them with their own customary laws. What interested Bodin was not the foundation of the king's power, but the conditions under which its exercise would be lawful.

23. The problems of defining the "public sphere" are still with us, as is evident in the controversies surrounding the political significance of the theories of "public goods" and "external effects". In the Hobbesian and Rousseauist theories of sovereignty, these problems evaporate: it belongs to the office of the sovereign to draw the line between public and private spheres (Hobbes 1651, chapter 21; Rousseau 1762, Book II, chapter 4).

24. The monopoly question remains at the heart of political philosophy. Nozick (1974) has a complex (and unconvincing) explanation of the emergence of a monopolistic state.

25. One aspect of the problem emerges clearly in Locke's remarks on taxation (*Second Treatise*, sections 139–40). Locke hesitates between an individual's own consent and the consent of the majority.

26. If one reverses the steps of this conceptual exercise, the sequence will mirror the evolution from a chieftain as a ceremonial head and warleader, to a king with various enumerated prerogatives, to the king as supreme judge (the medieval conception of kingship), to the lawful and constitutional king as the supreme lawgiver in some restricted public sphere (Jean Bodin), to the absolute monarch as the supreme lawgiver with respect to all things (Hobbes), and finally to the state as a sovereign corporate person constituted by people in their "corporate

capacity," i.e., *qua citizens* to which people *qua natural persons* belong (Rousseau).

27. I use the word "omnicompetence" rather than "omnipotence" to stress the legal character of the notion under discussion. What the state may legally do is not always physically or politically feasible. Also, an absolutist state need not be totalitarian; although it would have the right to move towards totalitarianism, even if it would be very foolish to do so. Hobbes insisted that, while the sovereign's laws, whatever they are, are necessarily just (i.e., in accord with the sovereign's right), not every law is a good law (Hobbes 1651, chapter 30).

28. Obviously, if only one person is sovereign and there are no persons who are independent of him (e.g., God in some politico-theological systems), then there simply is no external aspect of sovereignty.

29. Self-defence is itself a right based on the sovereign person's right to do with his own what he wills as well as on the no-right of any other persons to interfere with his rights without his consent.

30. Most of the early history of the concept of state sovereignty was concerned only with its internal aspect, that is, with the relations between a sovereign and his subjects. International law got little attention. Consequently, the concept was often criticized because of an alleged incompatibility of state sovereignty and international law. Characteristically, Kelsen (1945, 384) put the problem in the following terms: "The question whether the State is sovereign or not thus coincides with the question whether or not international law is an order superior to national law." Apparently, the incompatibility could only be overcome by subordination! In fact, international law and national law both have their logical foundation in the concept of the sovereignty of the state, and the question of the superiority of the one or the other should therefore not arise. However, when the distinction between an internal authority-based order and an external rights-based order is neglected, and national—i.e., authority-based—law is regarded as paradigmatic, international law will only be recognized as law if it conforms to the pattern of an authority-based system of binding rules. The question of the superiority of either the one or the other authority then becomes inescapable.

31. From Locke to H. L. A. Hart (1961) much has been made of the deficiencies of natural justice and of the remedies for them in the context of the state. However, the question as to why the remedies should be supplied under a system of a territorial monopoly of force (the state) is passed over in silence. See Benson (1989). Before the nationalization of lawmaking and law enforcement under the doctrine of national sovereignty, legal pluralism was the rule rather than the exception (Berman 1983).

32. Hobbes (1642, chapter 6, par. 16) rejects the old doctrine of *mala in se*; only the civil law determines what is a crime.

33. Samuels and Rinkes (1992, chapter 14). It should be noted that Frédéric Bastiat (1801–50) often presented the clash between the worldviews of liberals and socialists in terms of a clash between *économistes* and *juristes*, the former basing their science on the reality of things (natural law) and the latter on conventional rationalizations of existing social relations. See especially his pamphlets *Propriété et loi* and *La Loi* (Bastiat [1848] 1983, 1850).

34. Kelsen (1960) stresses "effectiveness of the legal order" as a presupposition of its validity. However, "effectiveness" has nothing to do with the long-run viability of a social system in terms of human welfare. It refers only to the degree to which the norms of the legal order are obeyed.

35. Spinoza (1665, chapter 20), while generally adhering to an even more absolutist theory of state sovereignty than Hobbes, argued from the impossibility to con-

trol another's thoughts to a natural right to freedom of thought. It is absurd to say that as a being capable of thought one person belongs to another. The argument can be extended to generate a notion of self-ownership, i.e., of individual sovereignty. See Van Dun (1983).

36. Cf. Rousseau's famous dictum (1762, Book II, chapter 3): "The general will is always right." Also Joseph Chamberlain: "Now Government is the organised expression of the wishes and the wants of the people, and under these circumstances let us cease to regard it with suspicion." *Speech at the Eighty Club*, 28 April 1885 in Schultz (1972, 54).

37. This applies only to the internal aspect of state sovereignty. Most theorists, though not Hobbes, accept that a sovereign state has no right to interfere in the internal affairs of other sovereign states.

38. In his 1791 controversy with Jefferson over the constitutionality of a national bank, Alexander Hamilton maintained as a general political principle "that every power vested in Government is in its nature sovereign, and includes by force of the term, a right to employ all the means requisite, and fairly applicable to the attainment of the ends of such power; and which are not precluded by restrictions & exceptions specified in the constitution; or not immoral, or not contrary to the essential ends of political society." *The Papers of Alexander Hamilton* (New York: Columbia University Press, 1965), VIII, 98.

39. Chief Justice John Marshall, relying on Hamilton's opinion (see previous note), defended in *M'Culloch vs. Maryland* (1819) the power of Congress to charter a bank by noting that the principle "was introduced at a very early period of our history, has been recognized by many successive legislatures, and has been acted upon by the judicial department...as a law of undoubted obligation.... An exposition of the constitution, deliberately established by legislative acts, on the faith of which an immense property has been advanced, ought not to be lightly disregarded." Quoted in Beveridge (1919, IV, chapter 6:291).

40. "From 1862 on, law after law and judicial interpretations thereof eroded the monetary norms of the Constitution, until today the U.S. monetary system is the complete antithesis of everything the Founding Fathers prescribed" (Timberlake 1989, 320).

41. The absurdity was first pointed out by Leibniz (1988, 118–19).

42. Deification of the state reached its zenith during the period of "enlightened despotism" (Bluche 1969, 364) and in the nineteenth century with Hegel's influential *Rechtsphilosophie* (Plant 1973, 122–23).

43. "[The Sovereign] hath the use of so much Power and Strength conferred on him, that by terror thereof, he is inabled to forme the wills of them all, to Peace at home, and mutuall ayd against their enemies abroad" (Hobbes 1651, chapter 17). The idea is an old one. It can be found in the *Book of Lord Shang*, one of the extant treatises representing the teachings of the legalist philosophers in ancient China from around the fourth century B.C.

44. This was noted earlier by Etienne de la Boétie (1530–63) in his radical essay on tyranny, *De la servitude volontaire*, an uncompromising investigation of the sources of political power.

45. Rousseau admitted this quite openly. With respect to public finance, he noted: "Especially in this delicate part of the administration, virtue is the only effective instrument.... Let us forget about registers and paper-work, and leave financial matters to trusted hands; there is no other way to ensure trustworthy management" (Rousseau 1755, 85).

46. Rousseau, the champion of popular sovereignty, objected to democracy on principle—the sovereign should be *above* the government not coextensive with it—

as well as for prudential reasons: "There is no government so subject to civil wars and intestine agitations as democratic or popular government.... Were there a people of gods their government would be democratic. So perfect a government is not for men" (1762, Book III, chapter 4).

47. Crises in the provision of what people consider to be public goods (i.e., goods they feel the government should provide) often shift the limits of the politically possible. Wars are the obvious examples (Tilly 1975). For the American case see Higgs (1987).

48. Depending on one's appreciation, one could call this phenomenon the "new pluralism," or the "new feudalism," or the "institutionalization of rent-seeking behavior." Often praised as the perfect antidote to authoritarian, even totalitarian tendencies of states, pluralism has also been criticized as hostile to individual liberty, on the ground that it insufficiently distinguishes between the leaders and managers of associations or corporations, on the one hand, and their members, employees, or consumers, on the other. See McConnell (1966); Lakoff and Rich (1973).

49. Recognizing this, Rousseau formulated "the most important maxim in the matter of financial administration, viz. that it is much more important to avoid expenditures than to increase revenues...," otherwise "government will grow weak, and little will be achieved at great cost" (Rousseau 1755, 85).

50. This condition is necessary to meet the objection, pointed out to me by Kevin Dowd, that continued use could be explained by noting the "external economies" of the use of a particular money: "I use this money because everybody else here does." The problem, it seems to me, is then to explain why everybody else continues to use that particular money. If *other people* do not perceive its value as falling, or if *they* are not aware of the available alternatives, the external economies will be sufficient to induce me to continue to use that money, regardless of other factors. But if the public does perceive the loss of value and is aware of the alternatives, and there are no factors which artificially prop up demand, I cannot see the force of the external economies argument. Does good money drive out bad money on the free market, or doesn't it?

51. The classic discussion of *oikonomeia* is in Aristotle's *The Politics* (Book I), which deals with the problems of managing a household's property, especially its slaves, as well as with those of managing the wealth of a city or state. For Aristotle the concept of *economy* is irrevocably linked to that of *rule* or *government*. Faithful to this classic conception, Rousseau (1755) divided *l'économie générale* into the government of persons and the administration of goods. But it was the German philosopher Johann G. Fichte (1762–1814) who went furthest in deducing the notion of a centrally planned national economy from the premise of a self-sufficient, autonomous (i.e., sovereign) political entity (Fichte 1800).

52. For Rousseau (1755) such macroeconomic manipulation was, understandably, a sign of weakness and moral decay: "a government has reached the final stage of corruption when it has no other power than money."

53. Financial innovations have to be controlled very carefully if the government is to protect its monopoly. Various funds outside the traditional financial system (banks and thrift institutions) have begun to create an alternative system of payments by offering transactions services to depositors. Such developments may in time reduce the use of the government's money in economic transactions, thus to a significant extent depriving the authorities of their monetary power. There is a strong case for the proposition that communication technologies and product differentiation in the financial markets of the world have already outstripped the regulatory powers of the national monetary authorities, while the discretionary

controls imposed by central banks and governments (with respect to exchange rates, often it would seem for fiscal, rather than monetary, reasons) merely serve to create or exacerbate turbulences in financial flows (Stockman 1988; Bovenberg 1989).

54. Both Hobbes and Rousseau warned against pluralism and intermediate organizations that would compete with the state for the loyalties of its members. All the advantages of the state would be lost if diversity and divisiveness replaced its essential unity of purpose and organization (Hobbes 1651, chapter 29; Rousseau 1762, Book II, chapter 3, Book IV, chapter 1).

55. Another solution to this "problem" is to seal off the national economic borders while trying to maintain a strong military position internationally. The internal contradictions of this approach, which has been tried within the socialist bloc, should by now be too evident to require elaboration.

56. These considerations are likely to be rated weightier in small countries, such as Belgium or the Netherlands, than in large countries. While participating as the Belgian minister of finance in the preparation of what was to become the Treaty of Maastricht, Philippe Maystadt repeatedly warned his collegues in the European Community against "the pernicious effects of fiscal competition." In an op-ed piece in *De Standaard* (a Belgian newspaper, June 1992), an influential Belgian economist, Paul van Rompuy, warned against a transfer of fiscal powers from the national Belgian government to the regions (Flanders, Wallonia) by pointing to "the sorry state of public services in the USA," which he attributed to fiscal competition among the states.

57. This is certainly the case in the European Community and in international aid bureaucracies which have spawned large and opaque bureaucratic systems of decision making (Tuft 1989; Hancock 1989).

58. With respect to European monetary unification, it has been asserted that "the main costs arise from the loss of autonomy over domestic monetary policy" (Leigh-Pemberton 1989, 12). But then the main costs of monetary union are assumed to fall exclusively on the politicians and officials who actually exercize that autonomy. It is not clear why their welfare should be the overriding consideration.

References

Bastiat, Frédéric. [1848] 1983. *Propriété et loi*. Paris: Editions de l'Institut Économique de Paris.

———. 1850. *La loi*. First published as a pamphlet in Paris. *The Law*. Irvington-on-Hudson: The Foundation for Economic Education, Inc., 1977.

Bendixen, Friedrich. 1908. *Das Wesen des Geldes*. Leipzig.

———. 1912. *Geld und Kapital*. Leipzig.

Benson, Bruce L. 1989. *The Enterprise of Law*. San Francisco: Pacific Research Institute.

Berman, Harold J. 1983. *Law and Revolution*. Cambridge, MA: Harvard University Press.

Beveridge, Albert J. 1919. *The Life of John Marshall*. Boston: Houghton Miflin Company.

Bluche, François. 1969. *Le despotisme éclairé*. Paris: Fayard.

Bodin, Jean. [1576] 1962. *Les six livres de la république* (*The Six Books of a Commonweal*), edited by Kenneth D. McRae. Cambridge, MA: Harvard University Press).

———. 1596. *Universae Naturae Theatrum*.

Bordo, Michael. 1984. "The Gold Standard: The Traditional Approach." In *A Retrospective on the Classical Gold Standard*, edited by Michael Bordo and Anna J. Schwartz. Chicago: University of Chicago Press.

Bovenberg, A. Lans. 1989. "The Effects of Capital Taxation on International Competitiveness and Trade Flows." *American Economic Review* 79.

Buchanan, James M. 1982. "Predictability: The Criterion of Monetary Constitutions." In *In Search of a Monetary Constitution*, edited by Leland B. Yeager. Cambridge, MA: Harvard University Press.

Cassel, Gustav. 1936. *The Downfall of the Gold Standard.* Oxford: Clarendon Press.

Chafuen, Alejandro A. 1986. *Christians for Freedom: Late-Scholastic Economics.* San Francisco: Ignatius Press.

De Jasay, Anthony. 1985. *The State.* Oxford: Basil Blackwell.

———. 1989. *Social Contract, Free Ride.* Oxford: Clarendon Press.

Dowd, Kevin. 1989. *The State and the Monetary System.* New York: St. Martin's Press.

Dyson, K. H. F. 1980. *The State Tradition in Western Europe: A Study of an Idea and Institution.* Oxford: Martin Robertson.

Fichte, Johann G. 1800. *Der geschlossene Handelsstaat.* Tübingen.

Friedman, Milton. 1987. "Monetary Policy: Tactics versus Strategy." In *The Search for Stable Money*, edited by James A. Dorn and Anna J. Schwartz. Chicago: University of Chicago Press.

Glasner, David. 1989. *Free Banking and Monetary Reform.* New York: Cambridge University Press.

Greenleaf, W. H. 1973. "Bodin and the Idea of Order." In *Jean Bodin: Proceedings of the International Conference on Bodin in Munich*, edited by H. Denzer. Munich: C. H. Beck.

Hancock, Graham. 1989. *Lords of Poverty.* London: Macmillan.

Hardin, Russell. 1982. *Collective Action.* Baltimore: Johns Hopkins University Press.

Hart, H. L. A. 1961. *The Concept of Law.* London: Oxford University Press.

Hayek, Friedrich A. [1976] 1978. *The Denationalisation of Money.* London: Institute for Economic Affairs.

Heller, Mikhail. 1988. *Cogs in the Wheel: The Formation of Soviet Man.* New York: Alfred A. Knopf.

Hexter, J. H. 1973. *The Vision of Politics on the Eve of the Reformation.* London: Allan Lane.

Higgs, Robert. 1987. *Crisis and Leviathan.* New York: Oxford University Press.

Hirschman, A. O. 1970. *Exit, Voice and Loyalty.* Cambridge: Cambridge University Press.

Hobbes, Thomas. [1642] 1983. *De Cive*, edited by Howard Warrender. Oxford: Oxford University Press.

———. [1651] 1909. *Leviathan.* Oxford: Oxford University Press.

Kelsen, Hans. 1945. *General Theory of Law and State.* Cambridge, MA: Harvard University Press

———. 1960. *Reine Rechtslehre.* Vienna, revised edition (*Pure Theory of Law.* Berkeley: University of California Press, 1967).

Klein, Benjamin. 1974. "The Competitive Supply of Money." *Journal of Money, Credit and Banking* 5 (November): 423–53.

Knapp, Georg F. 1905. *Staatliche Theorie des Geldes.* Leipzig.

Lakoff, Sanford A., and Daniel Rich (eds.). 1973. *Private Government: Introductory Readings.* Glenview, IL: Scott, Foresman and Company.

Leibniz, G. 1988. *Caesarinius Fürstenerius.* In *Leibniz: Political Writings*, 2d ed., translated and edited by Patrick Riley. Cambridge: Cambridge University Press.

Leigh-Pemberton, Robin. 1989. *The Future of Monetary Arrangements in Europe.* London: Institute of Economic affairs, Occasional Paper 82.

Locke, John. 1960. *Second Treatise on Government,* edited by Peter Laslett. Cambridge: Cambridge University Press.

Maritain, Jacques. 1951. *Man and the State.* Chicago: University of Chicago Press.

McConnell, Grant. 1966. *Private Power and American Democracy.* New York: Alfred A. Knopf.

Mises, Ludwig. 1966. *Human Action.* Chicago: Henry Regnery.

———. 1971. *The Theory of Money and Credit.* Irvington-on-Hudson, NY: Foundation of Economic Education.

Nettleship, Raymond L. [1901] 1925. *Lectures on Plato's Republic,* edited by Lord Charnwood. London: Macmillan.

Nozick, Robert. 1974. *Anarchy, State, and Utopia.* New York: Basic Books.

Nussbaum, Arthur. [1925] 1950. *Money in the Law.* Brooklyn: Foundation Press.

Pascal, Blaise. 1958. *Les Pensées.* Texte établi par Louis Lafuma. Paris: Le Club du meilleur livre.

Plant, Raymond. 1973. *Hegel.* Bloomington: Indiana University Press.

Pribram, Karl. 1983. *A History of Economic Reasoning.* Baltimore: Johns Hopkins University Press.

Raphael, D. D. 1976. *Problems of Political Philosophy.* London: Macmillan Press.

Rousseau, Jean-Jacques. 1755. *Discours sur l'économie politique.* First published as an article in the 5th volume of the *Encyclopédie. Rousseau: Sur l'économie politique,* edited by Barbara de Negroni. Paris: Flammarion, 1990.

———. 1762. *Du Contrat Social.*

Rowen, H. 1961. "L'Etat c'est moi: Louis XIV and the State." *French Historical Studies* 2.

Rüstow, Alexander. 1980. *Freedom and Domination.* Princeton, NJ: Princeton University Press.

Sabine, George H. 1973. *A History of Political Theory.* 4th ed., rev. by Thomas L. Thorson. Hinsdale, IL: Dryden Press.

Samuels, Geoffrey, and Jac Rinkes. 1992. *Contractual and Non-Contractual Obligations in English Law.* Nijmegen: Ars Aequi Libri.

Schultz, Harold J., ed. 1972. *English Liberalism and the State.* Lexington, MA: D. C. Heath.

Skinner, Quentin. 1978. *The Foundations of Modern Political Thought.* 2 vol. Cambridge: Cambridge University Press.

Smith, Adam. [1776] 1937. *The Wealth of Nations,* edited by Edwin Cannan. New York: The Modern Library.

Spinoza, Benedictus. 1665. *Tractatus Theologico Politicus.*

Stankiewicz, W. J. 1977. "Sovereignty," in *Macropaedia,* vol. 17, *Encyclopaedia Britannica,* 15th edition.

Stockman, Alan C. 1988. "On the Roles of International Financial Markets and Their Relevance for Economic Policy." *Journal of Money, Credit and Banking* 2.

Tiebout, Charles M. 1956. "A Pure Theory of Local Expenditures." *Journal of Political Economy* 64 (October).

Tilly, Charles, ed. 1975. *The Formation of National States in Western Europe.* Princeton, NJ: Princeton University Press.

Timberlake, Richard H. 1989. "The Government's License to Create Money." *Cato Journal* 9 (Fall): 301–21.

———. 1991. *Gold, Greenbacks, and the Constitution.* Berryville, VA: George Edward Durell Foundation.

Tuft, Nigel. 1989. *Europe on the Fiddle: The Common Market Scandal.* London: Helm.

van Dun, Frank. 1983. *Het fundamenteel rechtsbeginsel.* Antwerpen: Kluwer-rechtswetenschappen.

————. 1984. "De logische structuur van het recht," in Boudewijn Bouckaert, et al., *Recht en Criminaliteit. Liber Amicorum Willy Calewaert.* Antwerpen: Kluwer-rechtswetenschappen.

Vaubel, Roland. 1986. "Currency Competition versus Governmental Money Monopolies." *Cato Journal* 5 (Winter).

Vincent, A. 1987. *Theories of the State.* Oxford: Basil Blackwell.

3

From Gold to the Ecu:
The International Monetary System
in Retrospect

Leland B. Yeager

Our present international monetary system evolved from the inter-national gold standard, to which, even nowadays, some reformers would have us return. It is not a standard hallowed by the ages. Although gold and silver coins appeared in ancient times, widespread standardization of money units as weights of gold goes back only to the nineteenth century. Money in medieval Europe was a hodgepodge of gold, silver, and base-metal coins of various degrees of fineness issued by a great variety of national and local rulers and traded at fluctuating rates of exchange. As standardization gained ground, silver was probably a more important monetary metal than gold. Fiat paper currencies were far from unknown, as in Sweden in parts of the eighteenth century and in the American colonies before and during the Revolutionary War.

Great Britain had traditionally been on the silver ("sterling") stan-dard. It eased into a bimetallic system after 1717, when Sir Isaac New-ton, as Master of the Mint, recommended a particular value at which to fix the guinea gold coin in silver shillings. Britain was inflated off its metallic standard, leaving Bank of England notes as irredeemable stan-dard money, from 1797 until 1821. When redeemability was restored, the one-pound gold sovereign, first minted in 1817, became the stan-dard unit.

The United States officially adopted bimetallism with the Coinage Act of 1792. Silver was in fact the dominant metal, as reflected in the very word "dollar," the widely used name for the Spanish piece-of-eight reales, one of various large silver coins that were popular in Europe and that had first been minted in Bohemia in 1519. (The Continental Currency of the American Revolution had been denominated in "Spanish milled dollars.") Silver continued as the effective standard through the operation of Gresham's Law because the 15:1 relation between the values of gold and silver specified by the 1792 law clashed with the 15½:1 bimetallic ratio adopted by France under Napoleon. That discrepancy lasted until the coinage acts of 1834 and 1837 cut the gold content of dollar-denominated coins by 6.2 percent, thus changing the U.S. bimetallic ratio to 16:1, reversing the discrepancy with the outside world, and effectively switching the country from a silver to a gold standard. Legally the system was still bimetallic. From the Revolutionary War until the Civil War (with a partial exception during the War of 1812), the U.S. government issued only coins, no paper money. The issue of banknotes was left to privately owned banks (and, in a few states, to state-owned banks).

Gold discoveries in California and Australia around midcentury tended to cheapen gold relative to silver and, through the operation of Gresham's Law, to turn bimetallic standards into effective gold standards. Some economists worried about a serious loss of the purchasing powers of gold currencies, and the French economist Michel Chevalier even recommended a switch to the silver standard (Jevons [1884] 1964, 101). In 1865 France, Belgium, Switzerland, and Italy—and later Greece—formed the Latin Monetary Union in hopes of promoting international standardization of currencies on a bimetallic basis.

The Civil War in the United States inaugurated a regime of irredeemable paper money that lasted until January 1879. Gold and silver coins were still issued, but they traded at a premium against the greenback dollar, which became the usual monetary unit except in the Pacific Coast states. Meanwhile, laws of 1873 and 1876 discontinued the unrestricted coinage of silver dollars and revoked the limited legal-tender power accorded to the somewhat heavier silver trade dollars. These changes meant that a return to convertibility of paper money would no longer restore bimetallism in the United States; rather, it would establish a gold standard with subsidiary silver coinage.

Around 1873 silver began depreciating against gold on world markets. The newly established German Empire was selling off silver to acquire gold reserves, and silver discoveries in the American West were contributing to its depreciation. The Netherlands and the Scandinavian countries switched from silver to gold standards in the 1870s. The members of the Latin Monetary Union discontinued the free coinage of silver, fearing that the inflow of silver into their mints, which had offered an unlimited market for silver, would inflate their money supplies. Their bimetallism became a "limping" standard, a de facto gold standard. Early in 1879, Austria-Hungary, whose paper gulden had been inflated off its traditional silver standard, saw the quantity of silver formerly defining the gulden sink in value below supposedly equivalent coins and banknotes. Austria and Hungary feared an inflationary inflow of silver into their mints and so closed them to the free coinage of silver. For the next thirteen years the gulden remained a paper currency floating in midair at a higher value, in relation to gold currencies, than the silver-bullion content of coins.

The actions of Germany, Scandinavia, the Netherlands, and the United States (with its return to redeemability in 1879) thus led a widespread move onto the gold standard from the 1870s. Austria-Hungary moved onto a gold standard in 1892, introducing a new unit, the crown, equal to one-half of the old gulden. Its gold content was set in close correspondence to the foreign-exchange quotation of the gulden at the time of transition. (Actually, Austria-Hungary moved onto a gold-*exchange* standard: paper money was not unconditionally redeemable in gold coin, but the Austro-Hungarian Bank stabilized the crown's exchange rate against gold-standard currencies through market interventions.) Russia, by piecemeal steps culminating in 1897, adopted a gold standard at a gold content corresponding to the then prevailing exchange rate of the paper ruble (which, like the gulden, had earlier been a silver unit). After a transitional period of floating from 1893 to 1898, India switched from a silver standard to a gold-exchange standard; official foreign-exchange operations pegged the rupee to sterling.

To judge from parliamentary and academic discussions and pamphlet literature in Austria-Hungary and Russia, the chief motive for moving onto the gold standard was not so much unsatisfactory performance of the earlier monetary system as, rather, one of prestige: the gold standard was considered the most modern monetary system, the one most appropriate for advanced countries (Yeager 1984).

This argument from modernity testifies to the absence of a long tradition behind the gold standard. As a truly international system it prevailed for only a few decades up to 1914; its beginning dates somewhere between 1870 and 1900. The Gold Standard Act of 1900 consolidated the de facto gold standard existing in the United States since 1879. Nevertheless, for about three decades, greenback and then bimetallist agitation had caused real doubt about the durability of the U.S. gold standard, doubt reflected in otherwise surprisingly high interest rates on dollar-denominated bonds (Friedman and Schwartz 1982, 515–17).

In 1914 the major powers shared practically a common currency: exchange rates between their currencies were nearly fixed within the gold points. China was still on silver, and several Latin American currencies still had silver currencies or fluctuating paper currencies. But the major powers seemed firmly set on gold.

The decades just before World War I exhibited greater freedom of trade, capital movements, migration, and travel than ever before, although, with hindsight, historians can detect signs of moves back from near free trade toward protectionism as early as the 1870s. Human freedom and the gold standard appeared to support each other. In two of my favorite passages on monetary history, two otherwise quite dissimilar economists, Benjamin M. Anderson and John Maynard Keynes, waxed lyrical about the personal freedom and the expectations of continued progress that characterized the heyday of the classical gold standard.

> Those who have an adult's recollection and an adult's understanding of the world which preceded the first World War look back upon it with a great nostalgia. There was a sense of security then which has never since existed. Progress was generally taken for granted.... We had had a prolonged period in which decade after decade had seen increasing political freedom, the progressive spread of democratic institutions, the steady lifting of the standard of life for the masses of men....
>
> In financial matters the good faith of governments and central banks was taken for granted.... No country took pride in debasing its currency as a clever financial expedient.
>
> London was the financial center, but there were independent gold standard centers in New York, Berlin, Vienna, Paris, Amsterdam, Switzerland, Japan, and the Scandinavian countries. There were many other countries on the gold standard, with some tendency for the weaker countries to substitute holdings of sterling or other means of getting increased earnings. For their purpose the sterling bill was quite as good as gold.... But, in general, the great countries held their own gold. They relied upon themselves to meet their international obligations in gold. At times of great crisis a country under very heavy pressure would seek international cooperation and international assistance, and would get it—at a steep rate of interest. (Anderson 1949, 3–4, 6)

> What an extraordinary episode in the economic progress of man that age was which came to an end in August 1914! The greater part of the population, it is true, worked hard and lived at a low standard of comfort, yet were, to all appearances, reasonably contented with this lot. But escape was possible, for any man of capacity or character at all exceeding the average, into the middle and upper classes, for whom life offered, at a low cost and with the least trouble, conveniences, comforts and amenities beyond the compass of the richest and most powerful monarchs of other ages. The inhabitant of London could order by telephone, sipping his morning tea in bed, the various products of the whole earth, in such quantity as he might see fit, and reasonably expect their early delivery upon his doorstep; he

could at the same moment and by the same means adventure his wealth in the natural resources and new enterprises of any quarter of the world, and share, without exertion or even trouble, in their prospective fruits and advantages; or he could decide to couple the security of his fortunes with the good faith of the townspeople of any substantial municipality in any continent that fancy or information might recommend. He could secure forthwith, if he wished it, cheap and comfortable means of transit to any country or climate without passport or other formality, could despatch his servant to the neighboring office of a bank for such supply of the precious metals as might seem convenient, and could then proceed abroad to foreign quarters, without knowledge of their religion, language, or customs, bearing coined wealth upon his person, and would consider himself greatly aggrieved and much surprised at the least interference. But, most important of all, he regarded this state of affairs as normal, certain, and permanent, except in the direction of further improvement, and any deviation from it as aberrant, scandalous, and avoidable. The projects and politics of militarism and imperialism, of racial and cultural rivalries, of monopolies, restrictions, and exclusion, which were to play the serpent to this paradise, were little more than the amusements of his daily newspaper, and appeared to exercise almost no influence at all on the ordinary course of social and economic life, the internationalization of which was nearly complete in practice. (Keynes 1920, 10–12)

The Decline of the Gold Standard

Far beyond the realm of mere monetary arrangements, the outbreak of World War I was a watershed in world history, one all the more poignant for the string of avoidable blunders that caused it.[1] Anyway, in the words of Howard S. Ellis, the gold standard has been "dead as a dodo...since the guns of August 1914, since which it has only twitched" (quoted in Hinshaw 1971, 105–06). The word "twitched" refers to efforts to resurrect it after the war.

Exchange rates among major currencies fluctuated until the mid-1920s. Hyperinflations plagued eastern and central Europe. Perhaps the best-chronicled hyperinflation of all time climaxed in Germany in 1923, when stabilization was finally achieved at one new mark for 1 trillion (10^{12}) old marks. (It was not the most extreme inflation, however. My favorite economic statistic is the black-market rate on the dollar at the climax of the Hungarian inflation of 1946—4.6×10^{30} pengös [Nogaro 1949, 119 n. 3, and 120], a figure 10 trillion times as large as the number of *seconds* of estimated time elapsed since the Big Bang at the start of our universe.)

France pulled back from the apparent brink of hyperinflation in July 1926 and eventually stabilized the franc at about one-fifth of its prewar gold parity, a rate that somewhat undervalued the franc and gave the country a comfortable balance-of-payments position for several years. Great Britain returned in May 1925 to the gold standard—no

longer the gold-coin standard, however, but a gold-bullion standard—
at the full prewar parity. In contrast with the new French parity, this
rate turned out to overvalue the pound at least slightly, which made the
balance-of-payments position precarious. Britain was particularly vulnerable to withdrawal of foreign funds deposited or invested in London at short term.

Foreigners held voluminous deposits in London, partly because many
of the smaller countries returned after World War I not to the full gold
standard but to a gold-exchange standard. Under that arrangement, a
country's currency, instead of being redeemable in gold directly, was
tied at a fixed exchange rate to a major currency that was on the gold
standard. This arrangement was widely recommended as a device for
"economizing" on gold by making gold reserves do double duty, serving directly as backing for gold-standard currencies and at one remove
also as backing for gold-exchange-standard currencies. Like the gold-
bullion standard, this arrangement was an attempt—whether conscious
or not—to have the trappings or symbols of the gold standard without
its full restraint on money issues. As such, it contributed to the precari-
ousness of the whole system of the 1920s, aptly described as "pegging
operations on a vast scale" (Brown 1940, 2:805). The systems instituted after both world wars resembled each other in that respect. (A
fuller story of the precarious interwar system would have to bring in
international wrangles over war debts and reparations.)

Foreshadowed by earlier departures of some minor currencies from
the gold standard, an international financial crisis broke out in 1931.
Starting in Austria, a morbidly fascinating international chain reaction
culminated in Britain's departure from the gold standard in September
(Yeager 1976, 339–44). Instead of clinging to gold, most of the British
dominions and colonies, along with some other countries, pegged their
currencies to sterling, thus inaugurating the Sterling Area.

The United States clung to gold for another year and a half, then
allowed the dollar's exchange rate to float from April 1933 through
January 1934. Official transactions manipulated the price of gold upward until, under the Gold Reserve Act of January 1934, President
Roosevelt redefined the dollar in gold at a 41 percent devaluation. Thus
began a thirty-seven-year period during which gold's price was fixed
at $35 an ounce. What was restored was not a full gold standard, how-
ever, but a so-called limited gold-bullion standard. Gold coins were
abolished and, with minor exceptions, private ownership of gold was
forbidden. Redemption in gold bullion was limited to dollars presented
by official foreign holders such as governments and central banks.

A congressional joint resolution of June 1933 abrogated the gold clause. The clause promised payment of bond interest and repayment of principal in dollars "of the present weight and fineness." Before 1933 the clause had been included almost routinely in many private and government issues, and its wording assured bondholders of payment in dollars containing as much gold as the dollar had contained when their bonds were issued. If the gold content of the dollar were to be reduced in the meanwhile, then a bondholder would receive enough additional dollars to make his payment equal in value to the amount of gold originally stipulated. In effect, the clause made gold, not the dollar, the standard of deferred payments.

The congressional resolution set this provision aside. Now a bondholder was to receive only the originally specified number of dollars, regardless of what had happened to the dollar's gold content. Contending that this resolution was unconstitutional, some holders of private and government bonds brought suit to collect what they had been promised. The Supreme Court ruled in February 1935 that abrogating the clause in private bonds was indeed constitutional: private agreements must not infringe Congress's constitutional power to coin money and regulate its value—that is, to define the dollar. A different situation existed with U.S. government bonds: Congress did not have authority to repudiate obligations undertaken by the United States. Partly because their legal briefs were judged deficient in proving actual damages suffered, however, the plaintiffs could not collect the additional dollars they sought.

To forestall more cleverly prepared lawsuits, Congress passed a further law amending the jurisdiction of the federal courts to bar them from hearing additional gold-clause cases. The episode is interesting as an example of the U.S. government quite deliberately repudiating its own solemn promises. Some economists have argued that this action, regrettable as it was, was preferable to the alternative under the exceptional economic conditions of the time. Still, memories of this episode must have affected people's reactions later on, as in the 1960s, when gold-value guarantees on foreign-held dollars were suggested as one way to palliate the developing weakness of the U.S. balance of payments and the dollar.

Despite the Sterling Area depreciations of 1931 and the subsequent depreciations of the dollar and currencies linked to it, France, Switzerland, the Netherlands, Belgium, Italy, and Poland issued a joint statement during the London Economic Conference of July 1933 expressing their intention to maintain the existing gold parities of their currencies.

France in 1935 and 1936 even minted 100-franc gold pieces corresponding to the franc's new gold parity defined by a law of 1928. Further events, to be described below, kept these coins from actually going into circulation.

Amidst world depression and in the face of the depreciations of sterling and the dollar and the currencies that followed them downward, gold currencies became increasingly overvalued. Countries that nevertheless tried to cling to gold suffered balance-of-payments strains and unnecessarily severe domestic depression. Czechoslovakia devalued in 1934, Belgium and Danzig in 1935. Increasing distrust of the French franc's parity showed up in forward discounts reaching 37 or 38 percent annual rates at times in the late summer of 1936.

The franc was suffering from one-way-option bear speculation such as sterling had suffered in 1931 and such as sterling and many other currencies would sometimes suffer under the Bretton Woods system after World War II. (A one-way option means almost a heads-I-win-tails-I-break-even opportunity; for speculators know in which direction any adjustment of a fixed exchange rate will occur, while the worst that could realistically befall them is not a change in the opposite direction but simply no change.) As things worked out, the franc had to be devalued in September 1936 by about 30 percent; devaluations of the Swiss franc and other gold currencies quickly followed. Yet after a few months, the devalued French franc came under renewed bearish pressure.

The U.S., British, and French governments announced the French devaluation of September 1936 along with a Tripartite Monetary Agreement. In it they recognized that exchange rates are matters of common concern. Each participant promised to maintain its own currency's exchange rate against the other two currencies at levels that would not be changed without twenty-four hours' advance notice. This assurance would facilitate cooperation in managing rates. Belgium, the Netherlands, and Switzerland soon adhered to the agreement, which has been widely interpreted as a forerunner of the Bretton Woods agreements of 1944.

The decade of the 1930s brought severely shrunken world trade, "beggar thy neighbor policies" by which governments tried to create jobs at other countries' expense (as by raising tariffs and tightening import restrictions), and unstable exchange rates. Exchange controls were widespread and stringent, most notably in Nazi Germany. Most of these troubles were consequences, however, of the world depression and of the inadequate monetary arrangements and policies that made it so severe. People complained frequently about competitive exchange depreciation, that is, of governments' actions to drive their currencies below their equilibrium values to promote exports and ward off imports. Yet harmful delays in correcting overvaluations were probably at least as common as deliberate undervaluations.

Interwar experience was widely supposed—notably in Ragnar Nurkse's influential *International Currency Experience* (1944)—to teach enduring lessons about the evils of floating exchange rates. Nurkse cites four episodes in particular as horrible examples: the French experience of 1922–26 of floating amidst domestically inflationary conditions; Britain's float for the first several months after being driven off gold in September 1931; the U.S. float in 1933–34; and the French float of June 1937 to May 1938, when the franc, after a second devaluation, was still under bearish pressure. But these were exceptional episodes—periods of transition flanked by exchange-rate pegging and themselves characterized by official manipulations. The most unsatisfactory episodes of the 1930s were not examples of *free* floating.

If the 1930s properly count as the death-throes period of the gold standard, some summary remarks about that system belong here. First, as a generally practiced international system, it was a brief episode in world history, stretching from somewhere between 1870 and 1900 until 1914. Its resurrection after World War I was incomplete and temporary. Second, despite its short-lived influence, the ideology of the gold standard contributed to deflationary monetary policies tragically inappropriate to conditions of the early 1930s (Temin 1989; Eichengreen 1992). As long as they clung to the fixed exchange rates of the gold standard, many countries experienced the clash between the requirements of internal and external balance that would be fully explained only by macroeconomic theories still to be developed. Especially in countries that had suffered severe inflations in the 1920s, fear of inflation conditioned policies, inappropriately, under drastically changed conditions. Third, history shows that a government-managed gold standard does not ensure price-level stability or macroeconomic stability, though the record of government-managed paper moneys has often been worse. Fourth, the historical gold standard was not a self-maintaining system: governments eventually perverted it and finally replaced it with discretionary paper standards. (Remember the U.S. abrogation of the gold clause.) Fifth, what really interferes with commercial and financial transactions, especially international ones, is not lack of official convertibility of currencies into gold but impediments to convertibility in the contemporary sense, that is, government interference with free buying and selling of currencies on the foreign-exchange market. Sixth, the mystique that the gold standard may earlier have possessed— its being esteemed as at once modern, permanent, and ethically obligatory—no longer exists; and such a mystique, once destroyed, can hardly be resurrected.[2]

The Postwar Monetary Order

Monetary experiences during a world war like that of 1939–1945 are so exceptional, with governments dominating and tightly controlling international monetary relations, as hardly to require review here. The conference held at Bretton Woods, New Hampshire, in July 1944 does deserve mention. Postwar international monetary arrangements trace to the charter of the International Monetary Fund (IMF), negotiated there.

The Fund was organized in 1946 and opened for business in the spring of 1947. The philosophy of the Bretton Woods or IMF system supposedly embodies lessons of interwar experience and embraces several points. One is a horror of fluctuating exchange rates. Another endorses freedom of national governments to aim their monetary and fiscal policies at domestic macroeconomic objectives, including full employment, uninhibited by rigid exchange rates. The American negotiators tended to sell the scheme as a return to the essentials of the gold standard, improved in its details, while the British negotiators, notably Lord Keynes, tended to sell it as achieving freedom from the fetters of the gold standard. The IMF philosophy also recognized exchange rates as matters of intergovernmental concern, not to be changed outside specified initial limits without international consultation and approval.

The IMF was supposed to enforce its rules. Each member country was to declare a par value for its currency against either gold or the U.S. dollar and to prevent exchange transactions on its territory at rates further than 1 percent away from the declared parity. Ordinarily, each national authority would enforce these limits by whatever exchange-market transactions of its own proved necessary. (The United States, by exception, fulfilled this obligation by standing ready to buy and sell gold at its official price.) Each country was free to change its exchange rate up to as much as 10 percent away from the initially declared rate, but further changes might be made only after consultation with and approval of the IMF. (As things worked out, several momentous exchange-rate changes were made without the Fund's approval and even without its being notified in advance.) The Fund was required to give its approval if it found the change necessary to correct a "fundamental disequilibrium" (a concept left without precise definition), and the Fund might not withhold approval because of dissatisfaction with a member country's internal policies. In principle the IMF required free convertibility of currencies, that is, their exchangeability for other currencies on unhampered markets, but exceptions were provided. Countries might maintain exchange controls during a "postwar transition period" of unspecified length. Beyond that, countries could maintain—and might even be expected to impose—exchange controls to cope with disruptive capital movements, as distinguished from current-account transactions. (In practice, controlling capital-account but not current-account transactions ultimately proved almost impossible.)

Besides administering these rules, the Fund was charged with helping to finance exchange-rate pegging. A country suffering from balance-of-payments difficulties and weakness of its currency on the market was expected to support its currency—provided this condition was deemed temporary rather than indicative of "fundamental disequilibrium." It would buy its own currency in whatever amounts were necessary to keep its quotation from sinking below the prescribed narrow band, paying with foreign exchange (notably dollars) or gold (readily salable for dollars) drawn from reserves previously accumulated for that purpose. Facing exhaustion of these reserves, a weak-currency country could borrow the necessary additional foreign exchange from the IMF. (Technically, the transaction was called a "purchase," not a borrowing, because the country deposited the counterpart in its own currency of the foreign currency drawn; but as the rules required eventual reversal of the transaction, though with a few exceptions, the transaction was in effect a loan from the IMF.) The IMF was able to make such loans out of a fund of gold and, more important, U.S. dollars and other currencies subscribed by the member countries. The bulk of these contributions took the form of home-currency demand notes that each member could be required to redeem when necessary in actual money. Subsequent arrangements enabled the IMF to supplement the funds obtained from members' subscriptions with funds obtained by special borrowings and with funds created in the form of Special Drawing Rights (described below in the section on the collapse of Bretton Woods).

The Bretton Woods system had no automatic method of balance-of-payments adjustment. It lacked the mechanism inherent in a system of truly fixed exchange rates such as a full-fledged gold standard, namely, the mechanism that would regulate each country's domestic money supply through the currency's link to gold and the country's gain or loss of gold through balance-of-payments surpluses or deficits in a way that tended to correct or forestall those imbalances. Nor did the system employ the mechanism of floating exchange rates, forbidden by the IMF's rules. Rather, it confronted balance-of-payments disequilibriums, particularly deficits, with a mere "breath-holding policy" (Allen 1961): ordinarily a country would simply wait and hope for a payments deficit to go away more or less of its own accord, meanwhile continuing to peg its exchange rate by drawing on its own gold and foreign-exchange reserves and perhaps drawing on the IMF. In exceptional cases the country might try to restrain imports and capital outflows by trade and exchange controls, although controls violated the system's philosophy, or it might devalue its currency in cases of "fundamental disequilibrium." The Bretton Woods system thus held the exchange-rate mechanism of balance-of-payments adjustment in abeyance. Fundamental adjustment to changing conditions was at the mercy of national monetary managers.

In the course of events, exchange-rate adjustments occurred less often than, according to the usual interpretation, the intellectual founders of the IMF system expected. One can plausibly argue that rates exhibited too much rigidity. Circumstances described below apparently discouraged official readiness to make rate adjustments.

Yet many adjustments did occur. The first notable wave of adjustments came with Britain's devaluation of the pound from $4.03 to $2.80 in September 1949, promptly followed by devaluations of most other nondollar currencies. This upheaval invites comparison with the one of almost exactly eighteen years later. Britain devalued again in November 1967, from $2.80 to $2.40, followed on this occasion by far fewer countries than before. After earlier adjustments, France devalued the franc again in 1957, 1958, and 1969. Devaluations were common in high-inflation countries of Latin America, Africa, and Asia. Some upward revaluations, such as Germany's in 1961 and 1969, did occur, but they were much less common than devaluations. One reason is that whereas the finite size of reserves and credits limits the defense of an overvalued currency, no symmetric limit restrains maintaining an undervaluation: the country can simply keep on accumulating external reserves bought with newly created home money, though at the eventual risk of importing inflation. Some exchange-rate adjustments during the collapse of the Bretton Woods system will also be mentioned later on.

At least three reasons explain why exchange rates were not altered to adjust balances of payments as often as originally expected. The first concerns the J-curve effect: it takes time for the price changes caused by an exchange-rate adjustment to affect incentives and responses and so affect balances of payments in the "normal" way. Meanwhile, the sheer arithmetic of the changes, applied to old and sluggishly responding trade patterns, is actually perverse. Working with short-time horizons, governments are naturally reluctant to make moves likely to appear unsuccessful for some time. Second, an exchange-rate adjustment may appear to be a sign of government failure. In particular, political opponents and adversely affected economic interests may point to a devaluation as proof of domestic inflationary blunders. Third, merely the live possibility, not to mention the expectation, of an exchange-rate adjustment flags on one-way-option speculation. If adjustments had become a routine recourse in times of balance-of-payments difficulty, making them seem frequently possible, then speculative capital movements would have torn apart the intended system of even *usually* fixed exchange rates.

For such reasons, the Bretton Woods system turned out to be one of fixed exchange rates punctuated by only infrequent parity adjustments among the major currencies. (A different story applies to the inflation-prone currencies of many smaller countries.) No automatic balance-of-payments adjustments operated, but only a mélange of patchwork expedients.

The Supposed Heyday of the Bretton Woods System

Nowadays it is common (e.g., in editorials of the *Wall Street Journal*) to look back with nostalgia to the supposed heyday of the Bretton Woods system, dating from after the first years of postwar recovery, or perhaps from the end of the Korean War, to around 1970. Prosperity generally prevailed, and the real volume of world trade grew even faster than countries' total real outputs. Several rounds of multilateral negotiations reduced tariff levels. The postwar transition period of exchange controls permitted by the IMF charter eventually came to an end as, around 1958–60, the major countries that had not already done so now made their currencies externally "convertible," that is, freely tradable on the exchange markets.

It seems, therefore, that the Bretton Woods system of fixed but adjustable exchange rates, administered and financially supported by the IMF, was a clear success. This impression could be wrong for at least two reasons.

First, exchange-rate arrangements hardly caused the prosperous times. Instead, prosperity accompanied national full-employment policies that, through monetary and fiscal measures, kept total spending ample to buy the outputs of fully employed economies. Such actual or apparent success could not last forever. Sooner or later people would catch on to "expansionary" policies (as they clearly did in the 1970s) and would respond to high or rising levels of spending more with price and wage increases than with sustained rises in output and employment. But the period of fully catching on can be and apparently was quite long—roughly two decades. Meanwhile, domestic prosperity facilitated tariff reductions and the growth of international trade.

Second, the system was a "disequilibrium system," lacking any "automatic" and continuously operating balance-of-payments adjustments. It was marked early by exchange controls and later by backsliding. After a period of "dollar shortage," palliated by U.S. financial aid to the outside world, chronic balance-of-payments problems shifted to the United States.

Various U.S. controls of the 1960s, notably the Interest Equalization Tax and a ban on private American ownership of gold not only within but even outside the United States, as well as other measures to restrain lending, investing, and travel abroad, exemplify the patchwork measures characteristic of the Bretton Woods system. Calling in 1965 for "voluntary" controls over capital exports, President Johnson sought the effect of momentous legislation without enactment by Congress. Business firms were asked to subordinate profit considerations to the administration's notions of national interest. The program's spurious voluntary character and its inherent vagueness violated sound legal principles and were questionable on grounds of political philosophy. Vagueness and appeals to patriotic volunteering put a premium on compliance with the program's spirit as well as its letter, inhibiting vigorous dissent and democratic debate.

Disequilibrium showed up in crises of one-way-option speculation that periodically swept the system. Besides those mentioned elsewhere in this survey, Great Britain experienced crises in 1947, 1951–52, 1956, 1957, 1961, 1964, 1966, and 1968. Even when the defenders of existing parities do succeed in riding through a crisis, it causes much disruption.

In sum, the Bretton Woods system fulfilled original expectations only briefly, for a few years in the 1960s.

The Collapse of Bretton Woods

The system's collapse stretched out over many years. It was pretty clearly complete by 1 March 1973, but it is hard to say just when it began. One might even argue that the decline started as soon as removal of the controls of the postwar transition period inaugurated the full-fledged system. The switch in the general direction of world disequilibrium—from precariously suppressed payments deficits and currency weakness outside North America (the "dollar shortage") to weakness in the U.S. balance of payments and the dollar—came around 1960, give or take a few years. The early and mid-1960s brought various expedients to shore up the U.S. balance of payments and defend the dollar. They included not only the already mentioned controls but also measures to finance external deficits, such as the government's issue of special bonds denominated in foreign currencies ("Roosa bonds") and creation of a network of swap credits among central banks.

In November 1967, after coping over the years with several crises of bear speculation, Great Britain finally devalued the pound sterling from the $2.80 rate set in 1949 to $2.40. Speculative attention then turned bearishly to the dollar and bullishly to gold. Since 1960–61 the United States and several other governments had been cooperating in the London Gold Pool, feeding gold to the open market when necessary to keep its price from rising appreciably above the official figure of $35 an ounce. In March 1968 the members of the Pool discontinued this effort. A two-tier market was established: gold would continue to trade among governmental and intergovernmental agencies at the old official price, but its open-market price was freed from intervention. Although the U.S. government remained avowedly willing to redeem officially held dollars in gold, in practice various pressures behind the scenes discouraged large-scale redemptions. Late 1968 brought an episode of bear speculation on the French franc and bull speculation on the German mark. The authorities withstood this crisis with emergency and patchwork measures and with no change in official currency parities, a supposed success that brought a congratulatory message from President Johnson to General de Gaulle.

Notable events of 1969 were another franc-mark speculative crisis in May, again temporarily weathered without parity changes, a surprise devaluation of the franc in August, and a temporary float of the mark in September before its upward repegging in October.

In 1970 the United States registered an unprecedentedly large balance-of-payments deficit, nearly $10 billion on the official-settlements basis, reflecting dramatic reversals of short-term capital flows. In June, after floating from 1950 to 1962 and then being pegged for eight years at 92½ U.S. cents, the Canadian dollar was again allowed to float upward against the U.S. dollar.

In 1971 the U.S. official-settlements deficit reached nearly $30 billion, largely reflecting precautionary or speculative transfers of funds out of dollars. U.S. dollar liabilities of kinds that count in the foreign-exchange reserves of their foreign official holders more than doubled: their increase in 1971 alone exceeded their total accumulation throughout all earlier history, even counting in that cumulative amount the 49 percent increase that had already occurred in 1970.

Besides these numbers, 1971 brought momentous events. In early May a speculative stampede out of dollars into several European currencies occurred, resulting in upward floats of the German mark and Dutch guilder, upward revaluations of the Swiss franc and Austrian schilling, and a fuller separation of the commercial and financial foreign-exchange markets in Belgium. Worse than being mere palliatives, these piecemeal adjustments aroused expectations of more to come. One-way-option speculation against the dollar mounted in the summer. The "Nixon shock," so called by the Japanese, came on 15 August. The United States "closed the gold window," dropping all remaining pretense that officially held dollars were still redeemable in gold. Foreign authorities faced the choice of either continuing to peg their currencies against the now purely fiat dollar or else floating or revaluing them. A temporary 10 percent import surcharge was meant to prod other countries to raise their currencies against the dollar. At home, President Nixon imposed a wage and price freeze, which would later thaw into a complicated system of controls.

After four months during which major currencies floated against the dollar, negotiations culminating at the Smithsonian Institution in Washington in December 1971 achieved what President Nixon hailed as "the most significant monetary agreement in the history of the world" (Solomon 1977, 208). Most major currencies were revalued upward against gold, while the dollar was devalued by 8 percent. (The official gold price was raised to $38. By now, however, gold parities had ceased to be operational except as a way of implying the central rates of currencies against each other.) By these Smithsonian adjustments, the central rates became $2.6057 per pound sterling (as against the $2.40 rate set in 1967), 31.0 cents per German mark (as against the 25 cents set in 1961 and 27.3 cents set in 1969), and 308 Japanese yen per dollar (as against the long-standing rate of 360). Furthermore, the Smithsonian agreement widened the permissible ranges of currency fluctuations to 2.25 percent on either side of the central rate from the 1 percent specified in the IMF charter and the 0.75 percent generally practiced.

Supposedly, after a few months' interruption, the Bretton Woods system was now reconstructed on a sounder basis, with new equilibrium central rates set according to econometric calculations. The reconstruction lasted scarcely fourteen months. Already in June 1972 the British pound came under bear speculation and had to be set afloat.

Which particular events triggered the final collapse of early 1973 was almost a matter of accident, but vulnerability to accidents had marked the system all along. Disappointment about delay in the Vietnam settlement was evidently one factor. Others were worries about the federal budget deficit and rapid money-supply growth in the United States, along with the particular timing of the inevitable further easing of wage and price controls. In January a flight of funds from Italy into Switzerland triggered introduction of a floating "financial lira" and an upward float of the Swiss franc, which left other nondollar currencies all the more attractive for speculators fleeing the dollar. On 12 February the United States announced a further devaluation, this time by 10 percent. The now almost meaningless official gold price became $42.22. (Actually, the dollar's new parity was expressed against the IMF's Special Drawing Right, to be explained below.) Japan allowed the yen to float, and Italy allowed the lira to float in its commercial as well as financial market, thus joining Canada, Britain, Ireland, and Switzerland as floaters.

Speculators evidently considered the latest U.S. devaluation inadequate. On 1 March alone the German Bundesbank had to absorb $2.5 billion in support of the dollar against the mark, its most massive intervention ever in a single day. Then it gave up trying. Similar actions affected other major currencies not already floating. When the major European foreign-exchange markets reopened officially on 19 March, after partial suspensions, several European currencies were floating jointly against the dollar. (With varying membership, the European currency "snake" had existed since April 1972. It was to be consolidated in March 1979 into the present European Monetary System.)

Significantly, policymakers did not choose to switch from fixed to floating exchange rates; the recommendations of academic economists are not what prevailed. Instead, after prolonged and vigorous defense, the Bretton Woods system simply collapsed. Meanwhile, the defense effort had entailed massive purchases of dollars around the world as central banks and governments strove to maintain fixed parities and keep their currencies from rising against the dollar. During 1970–72 and the first quarter of 1973, foreign official holders increased their dollar claims of types counting as international reserves by 346 percent. In the process, they created massive amounts of local high-powered money, unintentionally setting the stage for multiple expansions of total money supplies through the operation of fractional-reserve banking. This monetary "explosion" fueled a subsequent severe speedup of price inflation throughout the world. (See *International Financial Statistics*, Ingram 1974, Rabin 1977, and Rabin and Yeager 1982.)

By now the original rationale of the International Monetary Fund— to supervise and help finance a system of fixed but adjustable exchange rates—had vanished. Like all good bureaucrats, however, the staff of the Fund had already been busy devising new functions for themselves. Under decisions made at the Rio de Janeiro meetings of the Fund in September 1967 and the provisions of an amendment to the Fund's charter ratified in the summer of 1969, the Special Drawing Right (SDR) had been created as one device for patching up the decaying system.

The chief rationale for the SDR was that the role of the U.S. dollar as the main component of official foreign-exchange reserves was anomalous. A continuing uptrend in the volumes of world trade and payments, balance-of-payments disequilibriums, and official trading to peg exchange rates required a growing volume of reserves. Continuing growth of dollar reserves required continuing deficits in the U.S. balance of payments; yet these deficits and the attendant buildup of U.S. liquid liabilities to foreigners, especially seen in relation to dwindling U.S. gold reserves, made the position of the dollar seem increasingly precarious and vulnerable to speculation. The system as it had unintentionally evolved, in short, made continuing U.S. payments deficits both necessary and alarming.

The supposed solution was to create a new international reserve asset, the SDR, sometimes nicknamed "paper gold." The IMF could create it out of thin air and distribute it to its members in such amounts as would contribute to a correct total of so-called international liquidity. The United States could then attend to correcting its international deficit without blocking the necessary growth of foreign-held reserves. Furthermore, the SDRs allocated to the United States would supplement its gold reserves and aid in defense of the dollar.

It is unnecessary here to review the complicated rules concerning the issue and employment of SDRs. Suffice it to say that the scheme did not work as intended. Years elapsed between its being first proposed, then adopted, and finally implemented. More or less by coincidence, the first issues of SDRs came just when they were least appropriate, in 1970, 1971, and 1972, when foreign official accumulations of dollars were reversing any supposed shortage of international liquidity into a glut of international—and domestic—liquidity. SDR holdings have never amounted to more than a very small percentage of official reserves anyway.

The SDR has, however, gained some prominence as a unit of account, especially in operations of the IMF itself and in denominating some private loans and bonds. Originally defined by the same quantity of gold then theoretically defining the dollar, the SDR was subsequently redefined in such a way as to avoid any jump in its size at the time of the change. In 1974 it was defined by a basket of sixteen currencies, then simplified in 1981 to a basket of only five. The simplified basket originally consisted of 40 U.S. cents plus specified amounts of the German, Japanese, French, and British currencies. The weights of the five currencies in the basket are periodically adjusted (as of 1996 the U.S. component is 58.2 cents). The SDR is thus defined by national fiat moneys lacking any defined values of their own. Under the current system of floating, the value of the SDR in any particular currency changes from day to day (except for a few minor currencies pegged to it). On 7 March 1997 the SDR was quoted at US$1.3758.

For some time after the events of March 1973, the IMF maintained that floating was only temporary. Its Committee of Twenty labored at devising a return to a system of "stable but adjustable par values." That hope lapsed well before the Second Amendment to the IMF Charter was proposed in 1976 and ratified in 1978. Belatedly, floating became legal. Each member might choose to peg its currency to some other currency or to let it float. The original Bretton Woods requirement that each currency have a declared parity against gold or the U.S. dollar was reversed into an actual ban on gold parities. Further to reduce the monetary role of gold, in 1976 the IMF began a program of disposing of part of its gold stocks, partly by returning gold at the low official price to member governments, partly by selling gold in periodic auctions.

Since general floating began, the scale of IMF operations has actually increased greatly. Instead of serving only to defend fixed exchange rates, its loans go largely to help finance official interventions in the markets for floating currencies. Furthermore, the IMF has from time to time created and reshuffled so-called special "facilities" for loans on specially favorable terms to countries suffering designated troubles, such as burdensomely expensive oil imports or weakened export markets. The IMF has been getting into the foreign-aid business, blurring the originally sharp demarcation between its activities and those of its sister Bretton Woods institution, the World Bank.

Arrangements and Events Since 1973

Although the dollar is floating against the major foreign currencies and although the bulk of world trade takes place at floating rates, the current system is by no means one of universal floating. Many Latin American, African, and Asian currencies still remain pegged to the dollar, although flexibly or adjustably. Several are pegged to the French franc, a few to other currencies, and several to the IMF's SDR. Several floating currencies are subject to official intervention intended to keep them stable against a basket of foreign currencies.

The most notable exception to general floating is—or was—the European Monetary System, which succeeded the similarly intended currency "snake" in 1979. The system's significance was much reduced when its bands of permissible exchange-rate fluctuation were widened after episodes of speculative currency crisis in 1992 and 1993. In any case, its members are the countries of the European Union, although not all participate in its exchange-rate-stabilization mechanism. Each participating member declares a parity for its currency against the European currency unit, the ecu, which is defined by a basket of member currencies. (Besides being an acronym, "ecu" is the name of an old French dollar-sized silver coin.) These ecu parities imply parities of each participating currency against each of the others. Central banks are required to intervene in the markets to keep their bilateral exchange rates from deviating beyond prescribed margins. For short periods, each member central bank makes its own currency available to its partners in amounts necessary for these stabilizing interventions. Since 1994 a European Monetary Institute, succeeding an earlier European Monetary Cooperation Fund, has provided longer-term credits and issued ecus for settling debts arising from these interventions.

The ecu, presumably to be renamed "euro," may serve someday as the basis for the projected European monetary unification. (It now seems unclear whether the participating countries will introduce their common currency on schedule in 1999.) Like the SDR of the International Monetary Fund, the ecu does not yet exist in banknote form and rarely serves as a medium of exchange in private transactions. However, some official and private bonds and loans have been denominated in both of those basket currencies (with payments and repayments taking place in equivalent amounts of national currencies). The ecu has won more acceptance than the SDR in private markets. One apparent reason is that the ecu is a better alternative to or hedge against the U.S. dollar, since the dollar remains outside the ecu basket but is the largest component of the SDR basket.

Resemblances between the ecu and the SDR, along with exchange-rate arrangements, suggest interpreting the European Monetary System (EMS) as a Bretton Woods system in miniature. As one might expect, crises of one-way-option speculation have occurred, and several readjustments of currency parities have been made. One main difference from the Bretton Woods system is that its members have contented themselves with less independence for domestic monetary policy. The German Bundesbank has provided leadership, promoting convergence of national inflation rates at a lower level than would presumably have occurred under free floating. Anyway, this is the reputation that the EMS has enjoyed. It will be interesting to see how it or its successor arrangement performs after the almost complete abolition of controls over trade and capital movements within the European Union.

From the start, the period of worldwide floating, like the Bretton Woods period, has been eventful (though, except within the EMS, without major crises of one-way-option speculation). October 1973 saw the Yom Kippur War between Israel and several Arab states, the Arab oil embargo against the United States and the Netherlands, the awakening of OPEC, and the near-quadrupling of oil prices around the turn of the year 1973–74.

Price inflation in countries around the world also heated up at about the same time; year-over-year rates of price increase reached double-digit levels in 1973 and 1974 (Rabin 1977). Superficial observers blamed the severe inflation of the 1970s on OPEC's predation, on other "real" shocks (even including disappearance of anchovies from off the coast of Peru), and, above all, on the floating of exchange rates and attendant loss of the supposed financial discipline of fixed rates. *Post hoc, ergo propter hoc*. The explanation most in accord with economic theory, well supported by historical evidence, points to the earlier bout of worldwide money-supply inflation tracing to dogged but ultimately futile defense of *fixed* exchange rates. Money-supply inflation raised prices with the usual lag of roughly two years.

Other events include the world recession of 1975, associated with the macroeconomic consequences of the oil price increases, another oil shock in 1979, the sharp depreciation and then recovery of the British pound in 1976, associated with changing expectations of monetary policy and exchange-rate support, and the vicissitudes of the U.S. dollar in 1978 and 1979, culminating in appointment of Paul Volcker as Federal Reserve chairman in hope that he would stop inflation and save the dollar. What turned out in retrospect to be the rather light-hearted "recycling of petrodollars" to finance trade deficits caused by increased oil prices contributed to the international debt problem of third-world countries that reached the headlines in 1982.

More pertinent than further details of this unstable environment in which exchange rates have been fluctuating are some comments on volatility and misalignments. Rates have moved widely, even wildly. "As someone who has always strongly favored floating exchange rates," Milton Friedman admitted that he "did not anticipate the volatility in the foreign exchange markets that we've had" (*New York Times*, 26 December 1985, op-ed page). Bilateral rates have fluctuated 10 and 20 percent over periods of months and sometimes several percent from day to day or even within days. The dollar fell nearly 10 percent against the German mark from early April to early May 1986, climbed 7 percent for three weeks, then dropped 5 percent in a week (*Wall Street Journal [WSJ]*, 9 June 1986, 27). Earlier, between Friday 20 and Monday 23 September 1985, on news of the Plaza agreement concerning market intervention, the dollar plunged by a reported record amount from one business day to the next—by 5.4, 5.3, 5.2, and 5.0 percent against the yen, mark, Swiss franc, and pound sterling, respectively (*WSJ*, 24 September 1985, 3; 26 September 1985, 3). After falling sharply during December 1991, in one week of January 1992 the dollar jumped nearly 8 percent against the mark and other European currencies (*WSJ*, 16 January 1992, C15). Contrary to hopes pinned earlier on development of market institutions and accumulation of experience, rate fluctuations appear not to have been getting milder over time. Again the question arises of how to apportion blame, if any is due, between the markets themselves and the climate of irresponsible and unpredictable government policies in which they operate.

It is an unsettled issue whether official intervention, together with rumors of its being started, altered, or suspended, has made exchange rates less or more volatile on the whole than they otherwise would have been. (Yeager 1976, chapter 14, explains how intervention might increase volatility and surveys episodes in which it apparently did. Gyrations of the British pound in 1976–77 and of the U.S. dollar in 1977–78 further illustrate the influence of official intervention, its suspension, negotiations for international support of a currency, and related rumors, true and false.) In the view of Professor Steve Hanke, chief economist for a commodity- and currency-trading firm, the threat of more central-bank intervention leads to greater market volatility. It raises the risk for currency speculators and forces them to seek greater returns in compensation. "We're getting another set of big players in the market and you never know when they're going to hit the accelerator or slam on the brakes" (*WSJ*, 8 May 1986, 34). The financial press frequently carries stories interpreting day-by-day exchange-rate jumps as responses to news and correct or incorrect rumors about presence, intensification, absence, or diminution of official intervention. Newspaper stories scarcely prove cause and effect, of course. Hard evidence on such matters is elusive. But an economic historian, like a detective (cf. Winks 1970), would be ill-advised to rule out any evidence a priori. Newspaper stories offer clues to the thinking of people in the markets, and their thinking and reactions are bound to affect what happens.

Explanations of exchange-rate volatility, however plausible, do not explain it *away*. How serious its consequences are is not clear. Volatility seems not to have impaired the volume of international trade, or not enough for the effect to be detectable beyond doubt (Aschheim and others, 1987, esp. 433–441). Capital movements have flourished, perhaps excessively in some sense; and foreign-exchange transactions associated with them now vastly overshadow transactions associated with trade in goods and services.

Volatility, some proponents of intervention argue, is a nuisance but not the worst defect of the current float. More serious, they say, are exchange rates "misaligned" with their long-run equilibrium levels or with relative price levels and other "fundamentals" (Williamson 1985; Bank for International Settlements 1986, 150). Misalignments cause alternations of splurge and austerity as a country's currency floats too high and then too low. They distort the allocation of resources between tradable-goods and nontradable-goods industries; they impose unemployment and other costs of otherwise unnecessary interindustry resource shifts; they contribute to inflation through ratchet effects; they breed protectionist measures; and so forth. Such concerns about misalignment form the core of the case for exchange-rate management—for "target zones" and the like.

The most conspicuous case of misalignment was the growing strength of the U.S. dollar up to early 1985. From its low in July 1980 to its peak in February 1985 "the multilateral trade-weighted value of the dollar rose 87 percent in nominal terms and 78 percent in real terms" (U.S. Council of Economic Advisers 1986, 31; other measures show roughly the same degree of nominal appreciation against other currencies on average).

Around the peak, concerted intervention by the Federal Reserve and other central banks worked for a decline in the dollar; and the Plaza Agreement of September 1985 reenforced this interventionist posture. Yet the turnaround and subsequent sharp decline cannot be attributed mainly to intervention. The dollar had risen unsustainably high. By early 1987, official worries focused on its weakness, and the Louvre Accord of February 1987 was intended to restrain its fall. Although the Louvre target zones for exchange rates never were publicly announced, it had become evident by late in the year that the official support of the dollar had collapsed. By the end of 1987 the dollar had fallen to below half of its 1985 peak values against the mark and yen. Thereafter it recovered somewhat, reportedly thanks in part to official intervention; but by late 1991 and early 1992 the dollar was again scoring record lows against the mark.

This is not the place to offer and test explanations of the dollar's rise and fall in the 1980s. Changing influences of and reactions to the U.S. government budget deficit enter into the most prominent conjectures. The size of the exchange-rate swings in comparison with fundamentals such as relative price levels suggest that if the dollar was not massively overvalued at its peak of 1985, it must have been massively undervalued in mid-1980 and again at the end of 1987.

Some free-market champions are inclined to answer the question whether exchange rates have been correct during the period of floating by observing that markets are efficient and take account of all information cost-effectively available. Anyone who knew better than the opinion already reflected in exchange rates was free to profit from such superior knowledge. The rates that did emerge must have been correct.

This interpretation comes dangerously close to tautology, to defining whatever happens on a free market as correct and not subject to second-guessing.

I am willing to employ hindsight. But I press the question: What would the alternative have been to the rate swings actually experienced? Dissatisfaction with one course of events does not imply knowing how and being able to achieve a more satisfactory course. Anyone who argues that the dollar's appreciation to its peak of early 1985 should have been prevented should say *how* and should examine the likely consequences of the measures contemplated. The alternative policies that occur to me do not seem attractive. (I refer, of course, to palliative policies of the usual variety, not to genuine commitment by governments and central banks to currencies of stable purchasing power.)

On the issue of the exchange-rate system, it is superficial to say that we should have kept rates fixed in 1973 and should fix them again now. Prodigious efforts to keep them fixed simply collapsed. More recently, even the Louvre accord for pegging rates loosely within fuzzy and unannounced ranges collapsed within several months. What is the point of saying that something should have been done or should now be done if in fact it could not and cannot be done?

Where Do We Go from Here?

Although my task has been to describe historical developments, I feel entitled to offer some hints about possible reforms.

First, we should be clear about just what is absurd in the existing system. It is not the free determination of prices on the foreign-exchange market (rates are not *freely* flexible anyway). The absurdity consists in what those prices are the prices of. They are the prices of national fiat moneys quoted in each other, each lacking any defined value. At bottom, the unit of account in the United States is whatever value the supply of and demand for cash balances fleetingly accord to a scruffy piece of paper, the dollar bill. The value of each money responds to conjectures about the intentions of the government issuing it and about that government's ability to carry through on good intentions. These conjectures are understandably subject to sharp change.

Ideas for reform along the lines of the European Monetary System and its ecu are popular nowadays. Yet the ecu does not represent a fundamental reform. It is merely a basket of national currencies, each continuing to suffer erosion of its purchasing power for reasons amply illustrated in the entire history of fiat money.

In contrast, the "Eurostable" proposed by Jacques Riboud (1975, 1977) would be a stable unit. The Eurostable would also be a basket of currencies, but the number of units of each currency included in the basket would be periodically adjusted up (or down) in proportion to a price index of its home country. The Eurostable would thus have a stable average purchasing power over the goods and services whose prices entered into calculating the national price indexes employed in adjusting the basket's composition. So conceived, Riboud's Eurostable presupposes the continued existence of national currencies.

The idea underlying the Eurostable might be implemented in a simpler way. Instead of being defined by periodically adjusted amounts of national currencies, a stable unit might be defined *directly* by a basket of goods and services of the kinds and in the amounts appropriate for calculating a wholesale or cost-of-living index.

The issue of money denominated in a new stable unit need not necessarily be entrusted either to a supranational agency or to national governments. Proposals for radical reform can at least stimulate ideas. One promising approach would privatize the monetary system (Greenfield and Yeager 1983; Yeager and Greenfield 1989; Dowd 1989). No longer allowed to issue money, the government would merely designate a new unit of account and promote its general voluntary adoption by using it in its own accounting, taxation, contracting, payments, and other operations. Instead of being defined by government money or by any other particular medium of exchange, the unit would be defined by a bundle of goods and services comprehensive enough for the general level of prices quoted in it to be approximately stable. Private banks would issue notes and checkable deposits, and they might also offer checking privileges against equity mutual funds. The quantities of these media of exchange would accommodate themselves to the demand for them at the price level corresponding to the definition of the unit. Incipient imbalances would trigger corrective arbitrage. This automatic equilibration of demand for and supply of media of exchange at a stable price level would prevent price inflation and major recessions.

Under the discipline of competition, the private issuers of notes and deposits would probably stand ready to redeem them in convenient assets (gold or agreed securities) in amounts having the same total value in bundle-defined units as the denominations of the notes and deposits being redeemed. Most redemptions would probably take place at clearinghouses, where banks acquiring notes issued by or checks drawn on other banks would routinely present them for settlement against their own obligations presented by others. Net balances at the clearinghouse would be settled by transfers of the agreed redemption medium. The necessary calculations and operations would be carried out every business day by professionals. With the proposed reform in effect, ordinary persons would no more need to understand what determined the purchasing power of the unit of account than they needed to understand how the gold standard worked before World War I or than they need to understand Federal Reserve operations and the rest of today's unsatisfactory process of determining the purchasing power of the fiat dollar.

The particular reform just sketched needs no further argument here and no defense against appealing alternatives. It already illustrates what a *fundamental* monetary reform would be, in contrast to superficial tinkering with the arrangements under which undefined national fiat currencies trade against each other. The root absurdity of our existing system will eventually become manifest. How long will the U.S. government, like other governments, remain able to run up debt denominated in an undefined unit and ultimately repayable in nothing more definite than pieces of paper to be printed by itself?

Notes

1. The explanation of the war that invokes the Leninist theory of imperialism, one theme of a course I was assigned to teach at the University of Maryland long ago, seems to me contrary to fact and reason.
2. Credible commitment to gold before World War I "depended on a unique constellation of political and economic factors." The kind of cooperation among central banks that facilitated the system's operation "rested on a specific conjuncture of political, economic, and intellectual circumstances unique to the late-nineteenth and early-twentieth centuries" (Eichengreen 1992, 390–91).

References

Allen, William R. 1961. "The International Monetary Fund and Balance of Payments Adjustment." *Oxford Economic Papers*, n.s., 13 (June): 149–65.

Anderson, Benjamin M. 1949. *Economics and the Public Welfare*. New York: Van Nostrand.

Aschheim, Joseph, Martin J. Bailey, and George S. Tavlas. 1987. "Dollar Variability, the New Protectionism, Trade and Financial Performance." In *The New Protectionist Threat to World Welfare*, edited by D. Salvatore. New York: North-Holland/Elsevier Science Publishing.

Bank for International Settlements. 1986. *Fifty-Sixth Annual Report*. Basel: BIS, June.

Brown, William Adams, Jr. 1940. *The International Gold Standard Reinterpreted*. 2 vols. New York: National Bureau of Economic Research.

Dowd, Kevin. 1989. *The State and the Monetary System*. New York: St. Martin's Press.

Eichengreen, Barry. 1992. *Golden Fetters*. New York: Oxford University Press.

Friedman, Milton, and Anna J. Schwartz. 1982. *Monetary Trends in the United States and the United Kingdom*. Chicago: University of Chicago Press for National Bureau of Economic Research.

Greenfield, Robert L., and Leland B. Yeager. 1983. "A Laissez-Faire Approach to Monetary Stability." *Journal of Money, Credit, and Banking* 15 (August): 302–15.

Hinshaw, Randall, ed. 1971. *The Economics of International Adjustment*. Baltimore: Johns Hopkins Press.

Ingram, James C. 1974. "The Dollar and the International Monetary System: A Retrospective View." *Southern Economic Journal* 40 (April): 531–43.

International Financial Statistics. Washington, DC: International Monetary Fund, various issues.

Jevons, W. Stanley. [1884] 1964. *Investigations in Currency and Finance*. Reprint, New York: Kelley.

Keynes, John Maynard. 1920. *The Economic Consequences of the Peace*. New York: Harcourt, Brace and World.

Nogaro, Bertrand. 1949. *A Short Treatise on Money and Monetary Systems*. London: Staples Press.

Nurkse, Ragnar. 1944. *International Currency Experience*. Princeton, NJ: League of Nations.

Rabin, Alan A. 1977. A Monetary View of the Acceleration of World Inflation, 1973–1974. Ph.D. diss., University of Virginia.

Rabin, Alan A., and Leland B. Yeager. 1982. *Monetary Approaches to the Balance of Payments and Exchange Rates*. Essays in International Finance, no. 148, Princeton University, November.

Riboud, Jacques. 1975. *Une Monnaie pour l'Europe: L'Eurostable*. Paris: Editions de la R.P.P.

———. 1977. Eurostable. *Bulletin du Centre Jouffroy pour la Réflexion Monétaire* (March–April).

Solomon, Robert. 1977. *The International Monetary System, 1945–1976*. New York: Harper & Row.

Temin, Peter. 1989. *Lessons from the Great Depression*. Cambridge, MA: MIT Press.

U.S. Council of Economic Advisers. 1986. *Economic Report of the President Together with the Annual Report of the Council of Economic Advisers*. Washington, DC: Government Printing Office.

Williamson, John. 1985. *The Exchange Rate System*. Rev. ed. Washington, DC: Institute for International Economics.

Winks, Robin W., ed. 1970. *The Historian as Detective*. Colophon edition. New York: Harper and Row.

Yeager, Leland B. 1976. *International Monetary Relations*. 2d ed. New York: Harper & Row.

———. 1984. "The Image of the Gold Standard." In *A Retrospective on the Classical Gold Standard, 1821–1931,* edited by M. D. Bordo and A. J. Schwartz. Chicago: University of Chicago Press for National Bureau of Economic Research.

Yeager, Leland B., and Robert L. Greenfield. 1989. "Can Monetary Disequilibrium Be Eliminated?" *Cato Journal* 9 (Fall): 405–21.

4

The Gold-Exchange Standard
in the Interwar Years

Murray N. Rothbard

Great Britain emerged victorious from its travail in World War I, but its economy, and particularly its currency, lay in shambles. All the warring countries had financed their massive four-year war effort by monetizing their deficits, most of them doubling, tripling, or quadrupling their money supplies, with equivalent impacts upon their prices.[1] The massive influx of government paper money forced these warring governments to go rapidly off the gold standard. The currencies depreciated in terms of gold, but the ongoing relative changes were hard to see due to the exchange controls that prevailed in these economies during World War I. Only the United States, which entered the war two and a-half years after the other countries and hence inflated its currency less, managed to remain de jure on its prewar gold standard. De facto, however, the U.S. barred export of gold during the war, and so was effectively off gold during that period. In March 1919, when foreign exchange markets became free once more, the bad news became evident: while the dollar, again de facto as well as de jure on gold, remained at its prewar par (approximately 1/20 a gold ounce), European fiat paper currencies were significantly depreciated. The once mighty pound sterling, traditionally at (approximately) \$4.86, now sold at approximately \$3.50, and at one point, in February 1920, was down to \$3.20.[2] Here was a 30 to 35 percent depreciation of British sterling from its prewar par.

The editors are grateful for the editorial assistance of Robert Formaini in preparing this chapter for publication.

Europe, both during and after the war, saw its monetary and financial markets broadly affected and transformed by the effects of that war; inflation,[3] depreciation, and exchange rate volatility were the consequences. For the first time since the Napoleonic Wars, commercial markets lacked an international money, a medium of exchange that could be used throughout the trading world. They also lacked the international harmony, monetary stability, and calculability that a generally accepted worldwide money could provide. The entire commercial world went through a period of difficult adjustment after the war as each nation sought both to protect its own interests and to reestablish a workable international system such as had functioned prior to the war's outbreak. Given the ongoing difficulties such a retrenchment imposed, it is not surprising that many looked back with nostalgia to the pre–World War I period as an economic "Eden."

The Classical Gold Standard[4]

The nineteenth-century monetary system has been referred to as the "classical" gold standard. It has become fashionable among many economists to denigrate that system as only existent in the last decades of the nineteenth century and as simply a form of pound-sterling standard, since London was the great financial center during this period. This depiction of gold, however, is faulty and misleading. It is true that London was the major financial center in that period, but the world was scarcely on a pound standard. Active oversight from other great financial centers—Berlin, Paris, Amsterdam, Brussels, New York—insured that gold was truly the standard money throughout the world.[5]

Furthermore, to stress only the few decades before 1914 as the age of the gold standard ignores the fact that gold and silver have been the world's most often chosen monetary metals throughout history. Countries shifted to and from freely fluctuating parallel gold and silver standards in attempts, self-defeating in the long run, to fix the rate of exchange between the two metals ("bimetallism"). The fact that countries shifted from silver and toward gold monometallism in the late nineteenth century should not obscure the fact that gold and silver, for centuries, were the world's moneys, and that previous paper money experiments (the longest during the Napoleonic Wars) were considered to be both ephemeral and disastrously inflationary. Specie standards, whether gold or silver, have been virtually coextensive with the history of civilization.[6]

Under the classical gold standard, most national currencies are defined as a unit of weight of gold and, therefore, the currency is redeemable by its issuer (the government, its central bank, or private issuers) in the defined weight of gold coin. While gold bullion, in the form of large bars, was used for international payment, gold coin could be used in everyday transactions by the general public. For obvious reasons, it is the inherent tendency of every money-issuer to create as much money as he can get away with. But governments, central banks, and private issuers on the gold standard were constrained in their issue of paper or bank deposits by the ultimate necessity of redemption in gold coin. This fact accounts for the often torturous legislation whose purpose, usually, was to prevent such treasury and central bank redemption. Such legislation took the form of legal tender laws, special tax regulations, and central-government operated and regulated fractional reserve systems in general.

As in the familiar Hume-Cantillon international price-specie flow mechanism, an increase of banknotes or deposits beyond the redemptive gold stock increases the supply of money, for example, francs in France. The increase of the supply of francs and incomes in francs leads to (a) an increase in both domestic and foreign spending, hence increasing prices of imports; and (b) a rise in domestic French prices, thereby making domestic goods less competitive abroad and diminishing exports, while making foreign goods more attractive and raising imports. The result is a deficit in the balance of payments, putting pressure upon French banks to supply gold to English, American, or Dutch exporters. In short, since in government fractional reserve central banking, paper and bank notes pyramid as a multiple of gold reserves, this expansion of the already engorged top of the inverted pyramid must be followed by a loss in the apex supporting the swollen liabilities. In addition, clients who are holders of French banknotes or deposits are apt to become increasingly concerned, lose confidence in the viability of the French banks, and hence call on those banks to redeem in gold— thus putting those banks at risk for a devastating bank run. The result was an often panicky and sudden contraction of banknotes, generating a recession to replace the previous inflationary boom and leading to a contraction in notes and deposits, a drop in the French money supply, and a consequent fall in domestic French prices.[7] The balance of payments deficit is reversed, and gold flows back into French coffers. In short, the classical gold standard put a severe limit upon the inherent tendency of monopoly money-issuers to issue money without check.

Britain Faces the Postwar World

At the end of World War I, only the United States dollar remained on the old gold-coin standard, at the 1/20 ounce par.[8] The other powers suffered from national fiat currencies. Suddenly, their currencies were no longer units of weight of gold but legal tender paper notes, such as pound, franc, mark, etc. Their rates depreciated with respect to gold and fluctuated with respect to one another. It was generally agreed that this system was intolerable and that a way must be found to reconstruct the world's monetary system, including restoration of a world money and a universal medium of exchange. At the heart of the European monetary crisis was the British government, which took the lead in trying to solve the problem. In the first place, London had been the major prewar financial center; secondly, Britain dominated the postwar League of Nations and, in particular, its powerful Economic and Financial Committee. Furthermore, though inflated and depreciated, the British pound was still in far better shape than the other major currencies of Europe. The pound sterling in February 1920 was depreciated by 35 percent compared to its 1914 gold par, the French franc was depreciated by 64 percent, the Belgian franc by 62 percent, the Italian lira by 71 percent, and the German mark by 96 percent (Palyi 1972, 38–39). It was clear that Britain was in a position to guide the world to a new postwar monetary order, and the English government eagerly accepted what turned out to be one of the last remnants of its imperial task.

Understandably, the British decided that the postwar system might be successfully replaced by the prewar one; that is, by a return to the old gold standard arrangement. However, at the same time they also decided that they would have to return to gold at the old prewar par of $4.86. Apparently, few economists or statesmen, Keynes being a notable exception, argued at the time for cutting British losses, starting with the real world as it existed in the early 1920s, facing reality, and going back to gold at the realistic, depreciated $3.20 or $3.50 per pound sterling. In view of the enormous difficulties the decision to go back to gold at $4.86 entailed, it is difficult in hindsight to understand why there was so little support for going back to a realistic par or why there was so much drive to go back at the old one.[9] For going back to a pound 30 to 35 percent above the market rate meant that English exports, upon which the country depended to finance its imports, would be priced far above their competitive price in world markets. Coal, cotton textiles, iron, steel, and shipbuilding—specifically—the bulk of the export industries that had generated prewar prosperity, became permanently depressed in the 1920s, with accompanying heavy unemployment. In order to avoid export depression, the British government would have to have been willing to allow a substantial monetary and price deflation to make its goods once more competitive in foreign markets.

In contrast to pre–World War I days, however, British wage rates had been made rigid downward by powerful government support of trade-unionism, and particularly by a massive and extravagant system of national unemployment insurance. Rather than accept a rigorous deflationary policy to accompany its return to gold, the British government therefore insisted on just the opposite: a continuation of monetary inflation and a policy of low interest rates. England would emerge in the postwar world as committed to a monetary policy based on three rigid but mutually self-contradictory axioms: (1) a return to gold; (2) a return to the sharply overvalued pound of $4.86; and (3) a continuation of a policy of inflation (cheap money). Given a program based on such internal self-contradiction, the British government, though they maneuvered on the world monetary scene with brilliant tactical shrewdness, ultimately had to fail in their policies.

Why did the British government insist on returning to gold at the old, overvalued par? Partly it was a vain desire to recapture old glories, to bring back the days when London was the world's financial center. The British government did not seem to realize fully that the United States had emerged from the war as the great creditor nation and also, financially, as the strongest one: financial dominance was moving to New York. To recapture their financial dominance, the British government believed it would have to restore the old, traditional $4.86 pound. Undoubtedly, they also remembered that after two decades of war against the French Revolution and Napoleon, the pound had recovered relatively quickly from its depreciated state, and that the government had been able to restore the pound at its pre-fiat money par. This restoration was made possible by the fact that the post–Napoleonic War pound returned quickly to its prewar par because of a sharp monetary and price deflation that was initiated by the British Treasury through the Bank of England.[10] After the war, the government apparently did not realize that the restoration of the pre–Napoleonic War par had required a policy of deflation and that their newly rigidified war structure could not easily adapt to a deflationary policy. Instead, British policy makers insisted on enjoying the benefits of gold and a highly overvalued pound while, simultaneously, continuing a policy of inflation. Another reason for returning at $4.86 was a desire by the powerful City of London—the financiers who held much of the public debt swollen during the war—to be repaid in pounds that would be worth their old prewar value in terms of gold and purchasing power.

Since the British were now attempting to support more than twice as much money on top of approximately the same gold base as before the war, and the other European countries were suffering from even more inflated currencies, the British and other Europeans complained throughout the 1920s of a gold "shortage," or shortage of "liquidity." These complaints reflected a failure to realize that, on the market, a "shortage" can only be the consequence of an artificially low price of a good. The "gold shortage" of the 1920s reflected the artificially low "price" of gold, that is, the artificially overvalued rate at which pounds— and many other European currencies—returned to gold in the 1920s, and therefore the arbitrarily low rate at which gold was pegged in terms of those currencies.

More particularly, since the pound was pegged at an overvalued rate compared to gold, Britain would tend to suffer in the 1920s from gold flowing out of the country. Or, put another way, the depreciated pound would, in the classic price-specie-flow mechanism, tend to drive gold out of Britain to pay for a deficit in the balance of payments and would put severe contractionary pressure upon the English banking system. But how could Britain, in the postwar world, cleave to these contradictory axioms and yet avoid a disastrous outflow of gold followed by a banking collapse and monetary contraction?

Return to Gold at $4.86: The Cunliffe Committee and After

Britain's postwar course had already been set during the war. In January 1918 the British Treasury and the Ministry of Reconstruction established the Cunliffe Committee, the Committee on Currency and Foreign Exchanges After the War, headed by the venerable Walter Lord Cunliffe, retiring governor of the Bank of England. As early as its first *Interim Report* in the summer of 1918, and confirmed in its *Final Report* the following year, the Cunliffe Committee called, in no uncertain terms, for return to the gold standard at the prewar par. No alternatives were considered (Moggridge 1972, 18; Palyi 1972, 75). This course was confirmed in 1918 by the Bassar-Smith Committee on

Financial Facilities, which was composed largely of representatives of industry and commerce. A minority of bankers, including Sir Brien Cockayne and incoming Governor of the Bank of England Montagu Norman, argued for an immediate return to gold at the old par, but they were overruled by the majority, led by their economic adviser, the distinguished Cambridge economist and chosen successor to Alfred Marshall's professorial chair, Arthur Cecil Pigou.

Pigou argued for postponement of the return, hoping to ease the transition by loans from abroad and, in particular, by inflation in the United States. The hope for U.S. inflation became a continuing theme during the 1920s, since Britain's depreciated pound was causing gold to flow into the United States, a loss which could be staved off, at least in theory, by inflation in the United States. After exchange controls and most other wartime controls were lifted at the end of 1919, Britain, not knowing precisely when to return to gold, passed the Gold and Silver Export Embargo Act in 1920 for a five-year period. The act in effect continued a fiat paper standard until the end of 1925, with an announced intention of returning to gold at that time (Sayers 1970, 86).

The United States and Great Britain both experienced a traditional immediate postwar boom, continuing the wartime inflation in 1919 and 1920, followed by a severe corrective recession and deflation in 1921. The English deflation did not suffice to correct the overvaluation of the pound, since the United States, now the strongest country on gold, had deflated as well. The fact that sterling began to appreciate toward the old par during 1924 misled the British into thinking that the pound would not be overvalued at $4.86. Actually, the appreciation was the result of speculators betting on a nearly sure thing: the pound's return to gold during 1925 at the old $4.86 par.

While prices and wage rates rose together in England during the wartime and postwar inflationary boom, they scarcely fell together. When commodity prices fell sharply in England in 1920 and 1921, wages fell much less and remained well above prewar levels. This rise in real wage rates, bringing about a high level of chronic unemployment, reflected the severe downward wage rigidity in Britain after the war caused by the spread of trade unionism and also by the massive new unemployment insurance program (Palyi 1972, 155; Anderson 1949, 74).

The condition of the English economy, in particular the high rate of unemployment and depression of the export industries during the 1922–24 recovery from the postwar recession, should have given the British pause. From 1851 to 1914, the unemployment rate in Great Britain had hovered consistently around 3 percent; during the boom of 1919–20, it was 2.4 percent. Yet during the postwar "recovery," British unemployment ranged between 9 and 15 percent. It should have been clear that something was very wrong.

It is not surprising that the high unemployment was concentrated in the British export industries. Compared to the prewar year of 1913, most of the domestic economy in Britain was in fairly good shape by 1924. Using 1913 as the base year (=100), real gross domestic product was 92, consumer expenditures were 100, construction was 114, and gross fixed investment was a robust 132. But while real imports were 100 in 1924, real exports were in sickly shape at only 72. Or, in monetary terms, British imports were 111 in 1924, whereas British exports were only 80. In contrast, world exports were 107 compared with 1913.

The sickness of British exports may be seen in the fate of the traditional major export industries during the 1920s. Compared with 1913, iron and steel exports in 1924 were 77.5; cotton textile exports were 65; coal exports were 80; and shipbuilding exports a very low 35. Consequently, Britain was now in debt to such strong countries as the United States, while a creditor to such financially weak countries as France, Russia, and Italy (Moggridge 1972, 28–29).

These data clearly show that the export industries suffered particularly from depression because of the impact of the overvalued pound; and that, furthermore, the depression took the form of permanently high unemployment even in the midst of a general recovery because wage rates were kept rigid downward by trade unions and especially by the massive system of unemployment insurance.[11]

There were several anomalies and paradoxes in the conflicts and discussions over the Cunliffe Committee recommendations from 1918 until the actual return to gold in 1925. The critics of the committee were generally discredited for being ardent inflationists as well as opponents of the old par. These forces included Keynes; the powerful trade association, the Federation of British Industries (F.B.I.); and Sir Reginald McKenna, a wartime chancellor of the exchequer and, after the war, head of the huge Midland Bank. And yet, most of these inflationists and antideflationists, with the exception of Keynes and W. Peter Rylands (the F.B.I. president in 1921), were willing to go along with return to the prewar par. This put the critics of deflation and proponents of cheap money in the curiously contradictory position of being willing to accept return to an overvalued pound, while combatting the logic of that pound—namely, deflation. Thus, McKenna, who positively desired a policy of domestic inflation and cheap money and cared little for exchange rate stability or gold, was willing to go along with the return to gold at $4.86. The F.B.I., which recognized the increasing rigidity of wage costs, was fearful of deflation. Its 1921 president, Peter Rylands, argued forcefully that stability of exchange "is of far greater importance than the re-establishment of any pre-war ratio." He went so far as to advocate a return at the far more sensible rate of $4.00 to the pound:

> We have got accustomed to a relationship...of about four dollars to the pound, and I feel that the interests of the manufacturers would be best served if it could by some means be fixed at four dollars to the pound and remain there for all time.[12]

But apart from Rylands, the other antideflationists were willing to go along with the prewar par. Why? The influential journal, *Round Table,* one of their number, noted the anomaly:

> While there is a very large body of opinion which wants to see the pound sterling again at par with gold, there are very few so far as we know, who publicly advocate in order to secure such a result an actively deflationary policy at this particular moment, leading to a further fall in prices....[13]

There are several answers to this question, all centering around the view that deflationary adjustments resulting from a return to the prewar par would be insignificant. In the first place, there was a confident expectation, echoing the original view of Pigou, that price inflation in the United States would set things right and validate the $4.86 pound. This argument was used in behalf of $4.86 by the *Round Table,* by McKenna, and by McKenna's fellow dissident banker, F. C. Goodenough, chairman of Barlcays Bank. The reasons for that optimism will be further explored below. A second reason already alluded to in this chapter was that the inevitable rise in sterling to par as the return date approached misled many people into believing that the market action was justifying the choice of rate.

A third reason for optimism particularly needs exploring: the British were subtly but crucially changing the rules of the game and returning to a very different and far weaker "gold standard" than had existed before the war. When the British government made its final decision to return to gold at $4.86 in the spring of 1925, Colonel Willey, the head of the F.B.I., was one of the few to register a perceptive warning note:

> (t)he announcement made today...will rapidly bring the pound to parity with the dollar and will...increase the present difficulties of our export trade, which is al-

ready suffering from a greater rise in the value of the pound than is justified by the relative level of sterling and gold prices.[14]

The way was paved for the final decision to return to gold by the Committee on Currency and Bank of England Note Issues, appointed by Chancellor of the Exchequer Philip Snowden on 5 May 1924 at the suggestion of influential Treasury official, Sir Otto Niemeyer. Known as the Chamberlain-Bradbury Committee, it was cochaired by former Chancellor Sir Austen Chamberlain and by Sir John Bradbury, a former member of the old Cunliffe Committee. Also on the new committee were Niemeyer and Professor Pigou of the Cunliffe group. Fortunately, we have a full account of the testimony before the Chamberlain-Bradbury Committee and of the arguments used to induce Chancellor of the Exchequer Churchill to go back to gold the following year.

It is clear from these accounts that the dominant theme was that deflation and export depression could be avoided because of expected rising prices in the United States, which would restore the British export position and avoid an outflow of gold from Britain to the United States. Sir Charles Addis, a member of the Cunliffe Committee and a director of the Bank of England—and the director upon whom Bank Governor Montagu Norman relied most for advice—called for a return to gold during 1925. Addis welcomed any deflation as a necessary sacrifice in order to restore the City of London as the world's financial center. But he too expected a rise in prices in the United States.

After listening to a great deal of testimony, the committee recommended waiting until 1925 so as to allow American prices to rise. Bradbury wrote to Gaspard Farrer, a director of Barclays and member of the Cunliffe Committee, that waiting a bit would be preferred: "Odds are that within the comparatively near future America will allow gold to depreciate to the value of sterling."[15] Pigou stepped in again in early September 1924, reworking an early draft by the committee secretary to make his economist's report. Pigou once more asserted that an increase of U.S. prices was likely, thereby easing the path toward restoration of gold at $4.86 with little need to deflate. Acting on Pigou's recommendation, the Chamberlain-Bradbury Committee in its draft report in October urged a return to $4.86 at the end of 1925, expecting that the alleged gap of 10–12 percent in American and British price levels would be made up in the interim by a rise in American prices.[16]

Even influential Treasury official Ralph Hawtrey—a friend and fellow Cambridge colleague of Keynes, an equally ardent inflationist and critic of gold, and chief architect of the European gold-exchange standard of the 1920s (see below)—favored a return to gold at $4.86 in 1925. He differed in this conclusion from Keynes because he confidently expected a rise in American prices to bear the brunt of the adjustment (Moggridge 1972, 72).

The British Labor government lost the election of 1924 and the Conservatives came into power. After carefully listening to Keynes, McKenna, and other critics, and after holding a now-famous dinner party for the major advocates on 17 March, Winston Churchill, the new chancellor of the exchequer, made the final decision to go back to gold on 20 March. The decision to return to gold at $4.86 put the new gold standard into effect.[17]

It cannot be stressed too strongly that the British decision to return to gold at $4.86 was not made in ignorance of deflationary problems or export depression, but rather it was made in the strong and confident expectation of imminent American inflation. This dominant expectation was clear from the assurances of Sir John Bradbury to Churchill, from the anticipations of even such cautious men as Sir Otto Niemeyer and Montagu Norman, from the optimism of Ralph Hawtrey, and above all in the official Treasury Memorandum attached to the Gold Standard bill of 1925 (Moggridge 1972, 84ff.).[18]

American Support for the Return to Gold at $4.86

The Morgan Connection

Why were the British so confident that American prices would rise sufficiently to support their return to gold at the overinflated $4.86? Because of the power of the new U.S. central bank, the Federal Reserve System, installed in 1914, and because of the close and friendly relationship between the British government, its Bank of England, and the Federal Reserve. The Fed, they were certain, would do what was necessary to help Britain reconstruct the world monetary system.

To understand those expectations, we must explore the Federal Reserve–Bank of England connection, and particularly the crucial tie that bound them together, their mutual relationship with the House of Morgan. The powerful J.P. Morgan & Company took the lead in planning, drafting legislation, and mobilizing the agitations in favor of a Federal Reserve System that brought the dubious benefits of central banking to the United States in 1914. Whatever the publicly stated purposes were for the system, the result was the cartelization of the nation's

banking system, thus enabling all banks to inflate together, centralizing and economizing their reserves, with the Federal Reserve as "lender
of last resort." The Federal Reserve's new monopoly of note issue took
the de facto place of gold as the nation's currency. Not only were the
majority of Federal Reserve Board directors in the Morgan orbit, but
the man who was able to become virtually the absolute ruler of the Fed
from its inception to his death in 1928 was a man who had spent his
entire working life as a leading Morgan banker: Benjamin Strong
(Rothbard 1984, 93–117).

Benjamin Strong was a protégé of the most powerful of the partners
of the House of Morgan after Morgan himself, Henry Pomeroy Davison.
Strong was also a neighbor and close friend of Davison and of two
other top Morgan partners in the then-wealthy New York suburb of
Englewood, New Jersey: Dwight Morrow and Thomas W. Lamont. In
1904 Davison offered Strong the post of secretary of the new Morgan-
created Bankers Trust Company, designed to compete in the burgeon-
ing trust business. So close were Davison and Strong that when Strong's
wife committed suicide after childbirth, Davison took the three surviving Strong children into his home. Strong later married the daughter of
the president of Bankers Trust and rose quickly to the posts of vice-
president and finally president. So highly trusted was Strong in the
Morgan circle that he was brought in to be J. Pierpont Morgan's personal auditor during the Panic of 1907. When a reluctant Strong was
offered the crucial post of Governor of the New York Fed in the new
Federal Reserve System, he was convinced by Davison that he could
run the Fed as "a real central bank...run from New York" (Rothbard
1984, 109; Chandler 1958, 23–41; Chernow 1990, 142–45, 182; Clark
1935, 64–82).

Commercial bankers, as monetary creditors, are generally thought
of as opponents of inflation. Yet this attitude overlooks the banks' position as creators of new money and therefore their position to enjoy
the benefits of issuing new money in advance of prices rising in response. Moreover, inflation acts as a tax upon money held, and money
deposits so taxed are also debts previously incurred by the banks.

The House of Morgan had always enjoyed strong connections with
England. The original Morgan banker, J. Pierpont Morgan's father
Junius, had been a banker in England; and the Morgan's London
branch—Morgan, Grenfell & Company—was headed by the powerful
Edward C. Grenfell, later Lord St. Just. Grenfell's father and grandfa-
ther had been directors of the Bank of England, as well as members of

Parliament, and Grenfell himself had become a director of the Bank of England in 1904. Assisting Grenfell as leading partner at Morgan, Grenfell & Company was his cousin, Vivian Hugh Smith, later Lord Bicester, a personal friend of J. P. Morgan, Jr. Not only was Smith's father a governor of the Bank of England, but he came from the so-called "City Smiths," the most prolific banking family in English history, originating in seventeenth-century banking. Due to the good offices of Grenfell and Smith, J. P. Morgan & Company had been named a fiscal agent of the English Treasury and of the Bank of England before the war. In addition, the House of Morgan had long been closely associated with British and French wars, its London branch having helped England finance the Boer War and its French bank, the Franco-Prussian War of 1870–71.[19]

As soon as war in Europe began, Harry Davison rushed to England and got the House of Morgan a magnificent deal: the monopoly purchaser of all goods and supplies for the British and French in the United States for the duration of the war. In this coup, Davison was aided and abetted by the British ambassador to Washington, Sir Cecil Arthur Spring-Rice, a personal friend of J. P. Morgan, Jr. These war-based purchases eventually amounted to $3 billion, out of which the House of Morgan was able to earn a direct commission of $30 million. In addition, the House of Morgan was able to steer profitable British and French war contracts to those firms which it dominated, such as General Electric, Du Pont, Bethlehem Steel, and United States Steel, or with which it was closely allied, such as the Guggenheims' huge copper companies, Kennecott and American Smelting and Refining.

To pay for these massive purchases, Britain and France were obliged to float huge bond issues in the United States, and they made the Morgans virtually the sole underwriters for these bonds. Thus, the Morgans benefited heavily once more: from the bond issues, as well as from the fees and contracts from war purchases by the Allies.

In this way, the House of Morgan, which had been suffering financially before the outbreak of war, profited hugely from and was deeply committed to, the British and French cause. It is no wonder that the Morgans did their best to maneuver the United States into World War I on the side of the English and French. After the United States entered the war in the spring of 1917, the Fed doubled the money supply by 50 percent to finance the war effort, and the U.S. government took over the task of financing the Allies.[20] Strong was able to take power in the Fed with the help of close cooperation from Secretary of the Treasury

William Gibbs McAdoo after the U.S. entry into the war. McAdoo for the first time made the Fed the sole fiscal agent for the Treasury, abandoning the Independent Treasury system that had required it to deposit and disburse funds only from its own subtreasury vaults. The New York Fed sold nearly half of all Treasury securities offered during the war. It handled most of the Treasury's foreign exchange business and acted as a central depository of funds from other Federal Reserve Banks. Because of this Treasury support, Strong, and the New York Fed emerged from U.S. experience in the war as the dominant force in American finance. McAdoo himself came to Washington as secretary of the treasury after having been befriended and bailed out of his business losses by J. P. Morgan, Jr., and Morgan's closest associates.[21]

Scarcely had Benjamin Strong been appointed when he began to move strongly toward "international central bank cooperation"—a euphemism for coordinated, or cartelized, inflation, since the classical gold standard had no need for such cooperation. In February 1916, Strong sailed to England and worked out an agreement of close collaboration between the New York Fed and the Bank of England, with both central banks maintaining an account with each other and the Bank of England regularly purchasing sterling bills on account for the New York Bank. In his usual direct manner, Strong bluntly told the Federal Reserve Board in Washington that he would go ahead with such an agreement with or without their approval; the FRB then finally decided to endorse the scheme. A similar agreement was made with the Bank of France.[22]

Strong made his agreement with the governor of the Bank of England, Lord Cunliffe, but his most fateful meeting was with the man who was then the bank's deputy governor, Montagu Norman. This meeting proved to be the beginning of the momentous Strong-Norman close friendship and collaboration that was a dominant feature of the international financial world of the 1920s. In 1920 Norman became Governor of the Bank of England, and the two men continued their collaboration, more or less, until Strong's death in 1928.

Montagu Collet Norman was born to banking on both sides of his family. His father was a banker and related to the great banking family of Barings, while his uncle was a partner of Baring Brothers. Norman's mother was the daughter of Mark W. Collet, a partner in the London banking firm of Brown Shipley & Company, the London branch of the great Wall Street banking firm of Brown Brothers. Collet's father had been governor of the Bank of England in the 1880s.

As a young man, Montagu Norman began working at his father's bank and then at Brown Shipley. In the late 1890s Norman worked for three years at the New York office of Brown Brothers, making many Wall Street banking connections, and then he returned to London to become a partner of Brown Shipley.

Intensely secretive, Montagu Norman habitually gave the appearance, in the words of an admiring biographer, "of being engaged in a perpetual conspiracy." A lifelong bachelor, he declared that "the Bank of England is my sole mistress, I think only of her, and I've dedicated my life to her" (Clay 1957, 487; Boyle 1967, 198). Two of Norman's oldest and closest friends were the two main directors of Morgan, Grenfell & Company—Edward Grenfell and, particularly, Vivian Hugh Smith. Smith had buoyed Norman's confidence when the latter had been reluctant to become a director of the Bank of England in 1907. One of Norman's best friends was the wife of Vivian, Lady Sybil. Norman would spend long, platonic weekends with Lady Sybil, and Norman became a godfather to the numerous Smith children.

Strong, who had been divorced by his second wife, and Norman formed a close friendship. While the close personal relations between Strong and Norman were of course highly important for the collaboration that formed the international monetary world of the 1920s, it should not be overlooked that both were intimately bound to the House of Morgan. "Monty Norman," writes a historian of the Morgans, "was a natural denizen of the secretive Morgan world." He continues: "The House of Morgan formed an indispensable part of Norman's strategy for reordering European economies.... Imperial to the core, he (Norman) wanted to preserve London as a financial center and the bank (of England) as arbiter of the world monetary system. Aided by the House of Morgan, he would manage to exercise a power in the 1920s that far out-stripped the meager capital at his disposal." As for Benjamin Strong, he:

> was solidly in the Morgan mold. Hobbled by a regulation that he couldn't lend directly to foreign governments, Strong needed a private bank as his funding vehicle. He turned to the House of Morgan, which benefited incalculably from his patronage. In fact, the Morgan-Strong friendship would mock any notion of the new Federal Reserve System as a curb on private banking power. (Chernow 1990, 244, 246)

Let us now turn specifically to the aid that Benjamin Strong delivered to Great Britain to permit its return to gold at $4.86 in 1925. As we have seen, a key to permit Britain to inflate rather than deflate was to induce the United States to inflate as well. Before the return to gold, the United States was supposed to inflate so as to persuade the exchange markets that $4.86 would be viable and thereby lift the pound from its postwar depreciated state to the $4.86 official figure.

Benjamin Strong and the Fed began their postwar inflationary policy from November 1921 until June 1922, when the Fed tripled its holdings of U.S. government securities and happily discovered that the result was expansion of both bank reserves and the total money supply. Fed authorities hailed the expansion as helping to get the nation out of the 1920–21 recession. Montagu Norman lauded the easy credit in the United States and urged upon Strong a further expansionary fall in interest rates.[23]

During 1922 and 1923, Norman continued his pleas to Strong to expand the money supply further, but Strong temporarily resisted. Instead of rising further toward $4.86, the pound began to fall in the foreign exchange markets in response to Britain's inflationary policies, slipping first to $4.44, and finally reaching $4.34 by mid-1924. Since Strong was ill through much of 1923, the Federal Reserve Board was able to take command during his absence and to sell off most of the Fed's holdings of government securities. Strong returned to his desk in November, however, and by January his rescue of Norman and of British inflationary policy was underway. During 1924, the Fed purchased nearly $500 million in government securities, driving up the U.S. money supply by 8.3 percent during that year.[24]

Strong outlined the reasoning for his inflationary policy in the spring of 1924 to other high U.S. officials. To New York Fed official Pierre Jay, he explained that it was in the U.S. interest to facilitate Britain's earliest possible return to the gold standard and that in order to do so the United States had to inflate, so that its prices were a bit higher than England's and its interest rates a bit lower. At the proper moment, credit inflation, "secret at first," would only be made public "when the pound is fairly close to par." To Secretary of the Treasury Andrew Mellon, Strong explained that, in order to enable Britain to return to gold, the U.S. government would have to bring about a "gradual readjustment" of price levels so as to raise U.S. prices relative to Britain. The higher U.S. prices, added Strong, "can be facilitated by cooperation between the Bank of England and the Federal Reserve System in the maintaining of lower interest rates in this country and higher interest rates in England." Strong declared that "the burden of this readjustment must fall more largely upon us than upon them." Why? Because "it will be difficult politically and socially for the British government and the

Bank of England to force a price liquidation in England beyond what they have already experienced in the face of the fact that their trade is poor and they have a million unemployed people receiving government aid."[25]

Simply put, the American people would have to experience inflation in order to enable the British government to pursue a self-contradictory policy of returning to gold at an overvalued pound, while continuing to inflate at home. In an attempt to ease the British government's return to gold, the New York Fed extended a line of credit for gold, or $200 million, to the Bank of England in early January 1925, bolstered by a similar $100 million line of credit by J.P. Morgan & Company to the British government, a credit instigated by Strong and guaranteed by the Federal Reserve. It must be added that these $300 million credits were warmly approved by Secretary Mellon and unanimously by the Federal Reserve Board (Rothbard 1972, 133; Chandler 1958, 284ff., 308ff., 312ff.; Moggridge 1972, 60–62).

American monetary inflation, backed by the heavy line of credit to Britain, temporarily accomplished its goal. Interest rates on bills in New York were pushed down by 1 1/2 percent by the autumn of 1924, and these interest rates were now below those in Britain. The inflow of gold from Britain was temporarily checked. As Lionel Robbins explains, in mid-1924:

> Matters took a decisive turn. American prices began to rise.... In the foreign exchange markets a return to gold at the old parity was anticipated. The sterling-dollar exchange appreciated from $4.34 to $4.78. In the spring of 1925, therefore, it was thought that the adjustment between sterling and gold prices was sufficiently close to warrant a resumption of gold payments at the old parity. (Robbins 1934, 80; Rothbard 1972, 133; Beckhart 1931, 45)

Just as Montagu Norman was the driving force in England, he himself was being driven by the Morgans in what has been called "their holy cause" of returning England to gold. Edward Grenfell was the Morgan group's figure in London, writing J. P. Morgan, Jr. that "as I have explained to you before, our dear friend Monty works in his own peculiar way. He is masterful and very secretive." In late 1924, when Norman got worried about the coming return to gold, he sailed to New York to have his confidence bolstered by Strong and J. P. Morgan, Jr. Morgan indicated that if Britain faltered on returning to gold, "centuries of goodwill and moral authority would have been squandered."[26]

Benjamin Strong was not the only natural ally of the Morgans in the administrations of the 1920s. Andrew Mellon, powerful tycoon and head of the Mellon interests, including the Mellon National Bank of Pittsburgh and such companies as Gulf Oil, Koppers Company, and ALCOA, was secretary of the treasury for the entire decade. Although there were various groups competing for President Warren Harding's ear, he was closest to the Rockefellers. His secretary of state, Charles Evans Hughes, was a leading Standard Oil attorney and a trustee of the Rockefeller Foundation.[27] Harding's sudden death in August 1923 elevated Vice President Calvin Coolidge to the presidency.

Coolidge has been misleadingly described as a colorless small-town member of a prominent Boston financial family whose members served on the boards of leading Boston banks. One family member, T. Jefferson Coolidge, became prominent in the Morgan-affiliated United Fruit Company of Boston. Throughout his political career Coolidge had two important mentors. One was Massachusetts Republican chairman W. Murray Crane, who served as a director of three powerful Morgan-dominated institutions: the New Haven & Hartford Railroad, AT&T, and the Guaranty Trust Company of New York. The other was Amherst classmate and Morgan partner Dwight Morrow. Morrow began to support Coolidge for president in 1919; and at the Chicago Republican convention of 1920, he and fellow J. P. Morgan & Company partner Thomas Cochran lobbied strenuously, though discreetly, for Coolidge, allowing fellow Amherst graduate and Boston merchant Frank W. Stearns to take the active and visible role.[28]

Furthermore, when Charles Evans Hughes returned to private law practice in the spring of 1925, Coolidge offered Hughes' post to the veteran Wall Street attorney and former Secretary of State and War Elihu Root, who might be called the veteran leader of the "Morgan bar." (Root was at one critical time in Morgan affairs, J. P. Morgan Sr.'s personal attorney.) After Root refused the secretary of state position, Coolidge was forced to settle for a lesser Morgan-connected candidate, Minnesota attorney Frank B. Kellogg.[29] Undersecretary of state for Kellogg was Joseph C. Grew, who had family connections with the Morgans while, in 1927, two highly placed Morgan men were asked to take over relations with troubled Mexico and Nicaragua.[30]

The year 1924 saw the Morgans at the pinnacle of their political power in the United States. President Calvin Coolidge, friend and protégé of Morgan partner Dwight Morrow, was deeply admired by J. P. Morgan, Jr., who saw the president as a rare blend of deep thinker and moralist. Morgan wrote to a friend: "I have never seen any President who gives me just the feeling of confidence in the country and its institutions, and the working out of our problems, than Mr. Coolidge does."

In the other party, the Democratic presidential candidate that year was none other than John W. Davis, senior partner of the Wall Street law firm of Davis, Polk, and Wardwell, and the chief attorney for J. P. Morgan & Company. Davis, a protégé of Harry Davison, was also a personal friend of J. P. Morgan, Jr. Hence, whoever won the 1924 election, the Morgans seemed well positioned to profit (Chernow 1990, 254–55).

The Establishment of the New Gold Standard of the 1920s

Bullion, not Coin

One reason the British were optimistic that they could succeed in their basic maneuver of the 1920s was that they were not really going back to the gold standard at all. They were attempting to clothe themselves in the prestige of gold while trying to avoid its anti-inflationary discipline. They went back, not to the classical gold standard, but to a bowdlerized and essentially sham version of that venerable standard.

Under the old gold standard, the nominal currency, whether issued by government or banks, was redeemable in gold coin at the defined weight. The fact that people were able to redeem in and use gold for their daily transactions kept a strict check on the overissue of paper. But under the new gold standard, British pounds would not be redeemable in gold coin at all but only in "bullion" in the form of bars worth many thousands of pounds. Such a gold standard meant that little gold would be redeemed domestically at all. Gold bars could not circulate for daily transactions. They could be used solely by wealthy international traders.

The decision of the British Cabinet on 20 March 1925 to go back to gold was explicitly predicated on three conditions. First was the attainment of a $300 million credit line from the United States. Second was that the bank rate would not increase upon announcement of the decision, so that there would be no contractionary or anti-inflationary pressure exercised by the Bank of England. Third, and perhaps most important, was that the new standard would be gold bullion and not gold coin. The chancellor of the exchequer would persuade the large "clearing banks" to "use every effort...to discourage the use of gold for internal circulation in this country." The bankers were warned that if they could not provide satisfactory assurances that they would not redeem in gold coin, "It would be necessary to introduce legislation on this point." The Treasury, in short, wanted to avoid "psychologically unfortunate and controversial legislation" barring gold redemption within the country, but at the same time it wanted to guard against the risk of "internal drain" (i.e., redemption in the property to which paper money holders had heretofore been legally entitled) from foreign agents, the "irresponsible" public, or from "sound currency fanatics."[31] The bankers, headed by Reginald McKenna, were of course delighted not to have to redeem in gold coin but wanted legislation to formalize this desired condition.

Finally, the government and the bankers agreed happily that the bankers would not hold gold, or acquire gold coins or bullion for themselves, or for any customers resident in the United Kingdom. The Treasury, for its part, redrafted its banking report to allow for legislation to prevent any internal redemption if necessary and to "enforce" such a ban on the more than willing bankers.

Under the Gold Standard Act of 1925, pounds were convertible into gold, not in coin but in bars of no less than 400 gold ounces with a value equal at the time to about £1646. The new gold standard was not even a full gold bullion standard, since there was to be no redemption at all in gold to British residents. Gold bullion was only due to pound holders outside Great Britain. Britain was now on an "international gold bullion standard" (Moggridge 1972, 79–83).

The purpose of redemption in gold bullion, and only to foreigners, was to take control of the money supply away from the public and to place it in the hands of the government and central bankers, permitting them to pyramid monetary expansion upon the gold centralized in their hands. Asked his advice about returning to gold by the governor of the Bank of Norway, Norman urged that country to return only in gold bars and only for international payments. Norman's reasoning is revealing:

> in Norway the convenience of paper currency is appreciated and confidence in the value of money does not depend upon the existence of gold coin...Demand is rendered more inelastic wherever the principle of gold circulation, for currency or for hoarding, is accepted, and any inelasticity may be dangerous...I do not believe that gold in circulation can safely be regarded as a reserve that can be made available in case of need, and I think that even in times of abundance hoarding is bad, because it weakens the command of the Central Bank over the monetary circulation and hence over the purchasing power of the monetary unit.
>
> For these reasons, I suggest that your best course would be to establish convertiblilty of notes into gold bars only and in amounts which will ensure that the use of monetary gold can be limited, in case of need, to the settlement of international balances. (Clay 1957, 153–54; Palyi 1972, 121–23)[32]

Norway, and indeed all the countries returning to gold, heeded Norman's advice. The way was paved for this development by the fact that, during World War I, the European countries had systematically taken gold coins out of circulation and replaced them with paper notes and deposits. During the 1920s, virtually the only country still on the classical gold coin standard was the United States, which inflated its own currency far less than the other nations of the world.

Despite this tradition, it was still necessary for Norman and the Bank of England to exert considerable pressure to force many European nations to return to gold bullion rather than gold coin. Economic historian William Adams Brown, Jr., writes:

> In some countries the reluctance to adopt the gold bullion standard was so great that some outside pressure was needed to overcome it...(i.e.) strong representations on the part of the Bank of England that such action would be a contribution to the general success of the stabilization effort as a whole. Without the informal pressure...several efforts to return in one step to the full gold standard would undoubtedly have been made. (Brown 1940, I:355)

The Gold Exchange Standard not Gold

The major twist, the major deformation of a genuine gold standard originating with the British government in the 1920s, however, was not the gold bullion standard, unfortunate though that was. The major inflationary camouflage was to return, not to a gold standard, but to a "gold-exchange" standard. Under a gold-exchange standard only one country, in this case Great Britain, was on a gold standard in the sense that its currency was actually redeemable in gold, albeit only gold bullion for foreigners. All other European countries, even though nominally on a gold standard, were actually on a pound-sterling standard. In short, a typical European country would hold as reserves for its currency not gold, but British pounds sterling, in practice bills or deposits payable in sterling at London. Anyone who demanded redemption for the national currency simply received British pounds rather than gold.

The gold-exchange standard, then, cunningly broke the classical gold standard's stringent limits on monetary and credit expansion, not only for the other European countries but also for the base currency of the key country, Great Britain itself. Under the genuine gold standard, inflating the number of pounds in circulation would cause pounds to flow into the hands of other countries, which would demand gold in redemption. Gold would move out of British bank and currency reserves, and pressure would be put on Britain to end its inflation and to contract credit. But under the gold-exchange standard, the process was very different. If Britain inflated the number of pounds in circulation, the result, again, was a deficit in the balance of trade and sterling balances piling up in the accounts of other nations. But now that these nations had been induced to use pounds as their reserves rather than gold, instead of redeeming the pounds in gold, they would inflate and pyramid a multiple of their currency on top of their increased stock of pounds. Thus, instead of checking inflation, a gold-exchange standard encouraged all countries to inflate on top of their increased supply of pounds. Britain, too, was now able to "export" her inflation to other nations without paying a price. Thus, in the name of sound money and a check against inflation, a pseudo-gold standard was instituted, designed to induce a double-inverted pyramid of inflation, all on top of British pounds, the whole process supported by a gold stock that did not dwindle.

Since all other countries were sucked into the inflationary gold-exchange trap, it seemed that the one nation Britain had to worry about was the United States, the only country to continue on a genuine gold standard. That was the reason it became so vitally important for Britain to convince the United States, through the Morgan connection, to go along with this system and to inflate, so that Britain would not lose gold to the United States.[33]

For the other nations of Europe, it became an object of British pressure and maneuvering to induce these countries to return to a gold standard, with several vital provisions: (a) that their currencies be overvalued, so that British exports would not suffer and British imports not be overstimulated—in other words, so that they join Britain in overvaluing their currencies; (b) that each of these countries adopt its own central bank, with the help of Britain, which would inflate their currencies in collaboration with the Bank of England; and (c) that they return not to a genuine gold standard but to a gold-exchange standard, keeping their balances in London and refraining from exercising their legal right to redeem those sterling balances in gold.

In this way, Britain could enjoy for a few years the prestige of going back to gold—at a highly overvalued pound—and yet continue to pursue an inflationary, cheap money. It could inflate pounds and see other countries keep their sterling balances and inflate on top of them; it could induce other countries to go back to gold on overvalued currencies and to inflate their money supplies;[34] and it could try also to prop up its flagging exports by using cheap credit to lend money to European nations so that they could purchase British goods.

Not that every country was supposed to return to gold at the overvalued, prewar par. During the 1920s, this system's operational formula was the following: (a) currencies that had depreciated up to 60 percent from the prewar level (e.g., Great Britain, the Netherlands, and the Scandinavian countries) would return to the prewar par; (b) currencies that had depreciated from 60 to 90 percent (e.g., Belgium, Italy, and France) were to return to gold within that zone, but at a rate substantially above their lowest rate. The French franc, which had depreciated to 240 to the pound due to massive inflation, returned to gold at the doubled rate of 124 francs to the pound. And (c) only those currencies that had been wiped out by devastating hyperinflation (e.g., Austria, Bulgaria, and especially Germany) were allowed to return to gold at a realistic rate, and even they were stabilized above their lowest points. As a result, virtually every European currency suffered, although at different levels of economic discomfort, from the requirement to raise the value of its currency above its true market-determined depreciated level (Palyi 1972, 73–74, 185).

The gold-exchange standard was not created *de novo* by Great Britain in the interwar period. It is true that, prior to 1914, a number of European central banks had held foreign exchange reserves in addition to gold, but these were strictly limited and held as earning assets. They were, after all, privately owned central banks in need of earnings, not instruments of monetary manipulation. In a few cases, particularly where the pyramiding countries were from the third world, they did function as a gold-exchange standard, that is, the third world currencies were pyramided on top of a key country's reserves (pounds or dollars) instead of gold. This system began in India in the late 1870s as an historical accident. The British government's plan was to shift India, which like many third world countries had been on a silver standard, onto a seemingly sound gold standard, mimicking the home imperial nation.

India's reserves in pound sterling balances in London were supposed to be only a temporary transition to gold. But, as seems to happen with so many "official transition periods," the Indian gold-exchange standard lingered on, receiving in the process praise from then India-posted John Maynard Keynes. It was Keynes, when finally leaving the Indian Office for Cambridge, trumpeted the new form of monetary system as a "limping," or imperfect, gold standard but as a "more scientific and economic system," which he termed the Gold-Exchange Standard. As Keynes wrote in February 1910, "It is cheaper to maintain a credit at one of the great financial centers of the world, which can be converted with great readiness to gold when it is required." In a paper delivered to the Royal Economic Society the following year, Keynes proclaimed that out of this new system would evolve "the ideal currency of the future."

Elaborating on this view in his first book in 1913, *Indian Currency and Finance,* Keynes emphasized that the gold-exchange standard was a notable advance because it "economized" on gold internally and internationally, thus allowing greater "elasticity" of money (a longtime euphemism for the ability to expand the supply of credit beyond the constraints imposed by gold) in response to business "needs." Looking beyond India, Keynes prophetically foresaw the traditional gold standard as giving way to a more "scientific" system built upon one or two key reserve centers. "A preference for a tangible reserve currency," Keynes declared optimistically, "is…a relic of a time when governments were less trustworthy in these matters than they are now."[35] He also believed that Britain was the natural center of the newly reformed monetary order. While his book was still in proofs, Keynes was appointed a member of the Royal Commission on Indian Finance and Currency and charged with studying and developing recommendations for the basic institutions of the Indian monetary system. Keynes dominated the commission proceedings, and while he got his way on maintaining the gold-exchange standard, he was not able to convince the commission to adopt a central bank. He did manage, however, to convince the commission to include his book's appendix favoring a state bank in its final report, completed in early 1914.

In his own way, Keynes, as he often did, saw to the heart of things. The issue of the "trust" that can be placed in governmentally controlled financial institutions is precisely the crucial issue. Those who have looked to politically controlled money as some sort of panacea, placing in the bargain their faith in those institutions to do solely what is good for the public as a whole, have been too often rewarded with consequences as bad—and often worse—than the financial situations such institutions were designed ostensibly to correct. While disagreement over the gold standard and historical and theoretical effects of private banking will undoubtedly continue, the empirical record of government manipulations of credit and currency is not contestable.

While Montagu Norman was the field marshal of the gold-exchange standard of the 1920s, its major theoretician was longtime British Treasury official, Ralph Hawtrey. When Hawtrey rose to the position of Director of Financial Inquiries at the Treasury in 1919, he delivered a speech before the British Association on "The Gold Standard." The speech presaged the gold-exchange standard of the 1920s. Hawtrey sought not only a system of stable exchange rates as had existed before the war, but also a monetary system that would stabilize the world purchasing power of gold and, therefore, world price levels. Hawtrey recommended international cooperation to stabilize price levels, and he urged the use of an index number of world prices—a proposal reminiscent of Yale University economist Irving Fisher's 1911 suggestion for a "tabular" gold-exchange standard.[36]

After 1918 this attempt at dual stabilization meant that governments would have to salvage the high postwar price levels from the threat of deflation and, in particular, to alleviate the "shortage" of gold that was, in reality, merely a consequence of the swollen totals of paper currencies then existing in Europe. As economist Eric Davis writes:

> There had been concern in official circles that a return to the Gold Standard would be inhibited by a shortage of gold. Prices were much higher than before the war, and thus if there was a general return to the old parities there might be insufficient gold. Hawtrey picked upon the idea that the Gold Exchange Standard could be widely introduced to economize on the use of gold for monetary purposes. Since countries would hold foreign exchange, much presumably in sterling balances as a substitute for gold, there was a special advantage for Britain; the demand for the pound would be increased at the same time the demand for gold lessened.[37]

The central instrument for imposing the new gold-exchange standard upon Europe was the International Financial Conference called by the League of Nations at Genoa in the spring of 1922. At a previous International Financial Conference at Brussels in September 1920, the League had established a powerful Financial and Economic Committee, which from the beginning was dominated by Montagu Norman through his allies on the committee. The committee head was British Treasury official Sir Basil Blackett; also prominent on the committee were two of Norman's closest associates, Sir Otto Niemeyer and Sir Henry Strakosch. All of these men were ardent price-level stabilizationists. Moreover, Norman's chief adviser in international monetary affairs, Sir Charles S. Addis, was also a dedicated stabilizationist (Rothbard 1972, 161; Einzig 1932, 67,78; Clay 1957, 138; Orde 1990, 105–18).

Prodded by Norman, British Prime Minister Lloyd George successfully urged the British Cabinet in mid-December 1921 to call for a broad economic conference on the postwar reconstruction of Europe, to include discussions of German reparations, Soviet Russian reconstruction, the public debt, and the monetary system. At a meeting of the Allied Supreme Council in Cannes in early January 1922, George persuaded the delegates to propose an all-European economic and financial conference for the reconstruction of Central and Eastern Europe. The British promptly set up an interdepartmental committee on economics and finance to prepare for the conference. Head of the committee was the permanent secretary of the Board of Trade, Sir Sidney Chapman. The aim of the Chapman Committee was to return to a gold standard, restore international credit, and establish cooperation between the various central banks. On 7 March 1922 the Chapman Committee issued its report for a draft agreement, which included currency stabilization, central bank cooperation, and adoption of a gold-exchange rather than a straight gold standard, with each country deciding on the rate at which it would return to gold.

The European economic conference occurred at Genoa from 10 April to 19 May 1922. The conference divided into several commissions, including economic and transportation. The relevant commission for our concerns was the Financial Commission, headed by British Chancellor of the Exchequer Sir Robert Horne. The commission further divided into three subcommissions: credits, exchanges, and currency. Credit resolutions dealt with intergovernmental loans; the subcommission on currency dealt with the international monetary system; and the exchanges subcommission attempted to eliminate exchange controls. The crucial committee, however, was a large Committee of Experts covering all three subcommissions. This committee actually drew up the resolutions finally passed by the conference as a whole. The Committee of Experts was appointed solely by Sir Robert Horne, and it met in London during the early stages of the Genoa Conference. This large committee, consisting of government officials and financial authorities, was headed by the ubiquitous Sir Basil Blackett.

After having "extended discussions" with Montagu Norman, Ralph Hawtrey drew up the Treasury plans for international money and presented them to the Committee of Experts. The Hawtrey plan was reintroduced after a temporary setback and substantially passed, in the form of twelve currency resolutions, by the Financial Commission and then ratified by the plenary of the Genoa Conference (Davis 1981, 219–20, 232; Fink 1984, 158, 232; Silverman 1982, 282ff.). His plan approved by the nations of Europe, Hawtrey became the leading interpreter of the Genoa Resolutions.[38]

The Currency Resolutions of the Genoa Conference, which formed the European monetary system of the 1920s, called for a stable currency value in each country and for the establishment of central banks everywhere: "in countries where there is no central bank of issue one should be established." These central banks, not only in Europe but elsewhere (particularly the United States), should practice "continuous cooperation" in order to bring about and maintain "currency reform." The Genoa Conference suggested an early formal meeting of central banks and an international convention to launch this coordination. The currencies of Europe would be on a common standard and it would be gold.

After expressing a desire for balanced budgets in each nation, the conference declared that some countries would need foreign loans to attain stabilization. Fixing the value of the currency unit in gold was left by the conference to each country. The resolutions that recommended this action were vague on the criteria to be used.

Resolution 9 looked specifically to a new form of gold standard, which would "centralize and coordinate the demand for gold, and so...avoid those wide fluctuations in the purchasing power of gold which might otherwise result from the simultaneous and competitive efforts of a number of countries to secure metallic reserves." Resolution 9 also stated that the point was to economize "the use of gold by maintaining reserves in the form of foreign balances, such, for example, as the gold-exchange standard or an international clearing system."

Resolution 11 spelled out the gold-exchange system in detail, declaring that credit would be regulated not only to keep the various currencies at par "but also with a view of preventing undue fluctuations in the purchasing power of gold." The resolution further stated that "the maintenance of the currency at its gold value must be assured by the provision of an adequate reserve of approved assets, not necessarily gold," adding: "A participating country, in addition to any gold reserve held at home, may maintain in any other participating country reserves of approved assets in the form of bank balances, bills, short-term securities, or other suitable liquid resources." The resolution said, "The ordinary practice of a participating country will be to buy and sell exchange on other participating countries within a prescribed fraction of parity of exchange for its own currency on demand." The *gold* aspect of this scheme was covered in the following clause: "When progress permits, certain of the participating countries (i.e., Great Britain, and the U.S. if it participates) will establish a free market in gold and thus become gold centers." The result, the resolution concluded, is that "the convention will thus be based on a gold exchange standard" (Lawrence 1928, 164).

Ralph Hawtrey's essay on behalf of the Genoa system is instructive in many ways. Most of it is devoted to defending the idea of coordinated central bank action (essentially monetary expansion) to stabilize the price level. Hawtrey asks the crucial question:

> It may be asked, why is any international agreement on the subject of the gold standard necessary at all? When we have once got a currency based on a commodity like gold, why should we not rely on free market conditions, as we did before the war? (Hawtrey 1919, 134–35)

Why indeed? Why could this then new pseudo–gold standard not be like the old? Hawtrey makes it clear that his reason is a phobia about deflation. The paper money stock had multiplied since 1914, and Hawtrey wrote that there "has been a great fall in the commodity value of gold." Even in late 1922, after the price fall of the 1921 recession, the value of the gold dollar is "only two-thirds of what it was before the war." Hence, there was "danger" of a scramble to secure gold and of a contraction of money and prices. But what is so terrible about deflation? Deflation holds no terrors when prices and wages are flexible and free to fall.[39] Here, Hawtrey avoids even mentioning the government policy of wage rigidity and the unemployment insurance system that had changed the economic face of Britain. He simply points to the "notorious…chronic state of depression which prevailed during the spread of the gold standard in the period 1873-96."

Hawtrey was wrong, in the first place, to attribute falling prices during the late nineteenth century to a shift from silver to gold. The falling prices were due to the industrial revolution and the phenomenal advance of productivity. With productivity outpacing the new supply of gold, prices had to fall in terms of gold during that period. Second and more importantly, Hawtrey made the common modern error of identifying falling prices with "depression." In reality, production and living standards were progressing in Britain and the United States during this period as costs fell, so there was no squeeze on profits. The era of falling prices was not a "depression" at all, and was only experienced as such decades later by historians who fail to understand that falling prices have social benefits and do not necessarily coincide with severe economic hardship.[40]

Hawtrey's exegesis virtually concedes that his ideal is to abandon gold altogether and remain with only managed fiat money. Thus, in discussing the key-currency countries, Hawtrey states wistfully, "At the gold centers some gold reserves must be maintained." But if the gold standard becomes worldwide, "if all the gold standard countries adhere to it, gold will nowhere be needed as a means of remittance, and gold will only be withdrawn from the reserves for use as a raw material of industry" (Hawtrey 1919, 136). In short, Hawtrey anticipated the world of the late twentieth century by looking forward to dispensing with gold as a monetary metal altogether and to having the world use fiat paper money exclusively.

Hawtrey concluded his essay by conceding that there was only one defect in the Genoa Resolutions: there was no mention of how long it would take to return to gold. Even the strongest countries, he emphasized, would have to wait until their currencies rose on the exchange market to equal their designated rates. To induce a rise in the pound sterling to meet the high fixed rate, Britain would either have to deflate, or else foreign countries—especially the United States—would have to inflate to correct the international discrepancy. "Further deflation," Hawtrey claimed, "is out of the question." Therefore, the only hope was to "stabilize our currency at its existing purchasing power" and wait for the increased gold supply in the United States to lead to a substantial inflation there (Hawtrey 1919, 147). Like other British leaders, Hawtrey was pinning his faith on an American policy of inflation that would, in the long run, "help Britain."[41]

Many historians have written off the Genoa Conference as a "failure" and dismissed its influence on the international money of the twentieth century. It is true that the formal institutions of central bank cooperation called for at Genoa were not established, largely because of American reluctance. But the critical point is that Genoa triumphed anyway, since Benjamin Strong was willing to perform the same tasks in informal, but highly effective, central bank cooperation to help establish and prop up Britain's pseudo–gold standard. Strong's reluctance stemmed from two sources: an understandable fear that isolationist and antibank sentiment would raise a firestorm against any formal collaboration with European central banks—especially in an America that had reacted against the formal foreign interventionism of the League of Nations. Secondly, Strong actually preferred the full gold standard and was queasy about the inflationary unsoundness of a gold-exchange standard. But his reluctance did not prevent him from collaborating closely in support of his friend Montagu Norman. Their collaboration constituted, in the words of Michael Hogan, an "informal entente."[42] Actually, what Strong preferred was close "key currency" collaboration between, say, the central banks of the United States, England, and

France, rather than to be outvoted at formal international conventions (S. Clarke 1967, 40–41).

In fact, after international commodity prices began to decline in 1926, Norman became more frantic in pursuing formal meetings of central bankers and more insistent on continuing and intensifying the inflationary thrust of the gold-exchange standard. Finally, with the establishment of the Bank for International Settlements at Geneva in 1930, Norman at least succeeded in having regular monthly meetings of central bankers (S. Clarke 1967, 36). Thus, far from Genoa being merely a flash in the pan, the 1922 conference placed its decisive stamp upon the postwar monetary world. In the words of Eric Davis, "the widespread adoption of the Gold Exchange Standard can be seen as the legacy of Genoa" (Davis, 1981, 232–74).

Following the Genoa model, Great Britain, as we have seen, set up the gold-exchange system by returning to its new version of gold in 1925. Other European and non-European nations followed, each at its own pace. By early 1926 some form of gold standard was established, at least de facto, in thirty-one countries. By 1928 forty-three nations were de jure on the gold standard. Of these, even the few allegedly on the gold-bullion standard (such as France) kept most of their reserves in sterling balances in London. The same was true of officially gold coin nations such as the Netherlands. Apart from the United States, the only countries officially remaining on a gold coin basis were minor nations such as Mexico, Colombia, Cuba, and the Union of South Africa (Palyi 1972, 116–17, 107). It should be noted that Norway and Denmark, following the Genoa path of struggling back to gold with a highly overvalued currency, suffered, like Britain, from an export depression throughout the 1920s. Finland, acting on better advice, went back at a realistically devalued rate and thereby avoided chronic depression during this period.[43]

Throughout Europe, Great Britain wielded its control of the Finance Committee of the League of Nations and engineered the stabilization of currencies on a gold-exchange (i.e., a sterling-exchange) standard in Germany, Austria, Hungary, Estonia, Bulgaria, Greece, Belgium, Poland, and Latvia. New central banks were established in the nations that were to become known after World War II as Eastern Europe. These banks were based on reserves in sterling, with British supervisors and directors installed in bank offices (Kooker 1976, 86–90).

Émile Moreau, the shrewd Governor of the Bank of France, recorded his analysis of this British monetary power play in his diary:

England having been the first European country to reestablish a stable and secure money has used that advantage to establish a basis for putting Europe under a veritable financial domination. The Financial Committee (of the League of Nations) at Geneva has been the instrument of that policy. The method consists of forcing every country in monetary difficulty to subject itself to the Committee at Geneva, which the British control. The remedies prescribed always involve the installation in the central bank of a foreign supervisor who is British or designated by the Bank of England, and the deposit of a part of the reserve of the central bank at the Bank of England, which serves both to support the pound and to fortify British influence. To guarantee against possible failure they are careful to secure the cooperation of the Federal Reserve Bank of New York. Moreover, they pass on to America the task of making some of the foreign loans, if they seem too heavy, always retaining the political advantage of these operations.[44]

The Gold-Exchange Standard in Operation, 1926–1929

By the end of 1925 Montagu Norman and the British monetary establishment were seemingly monarch of all they surveyed. Supported in America by Strong and the Morgans, the British government had everything its own way: it had pressured the world to adopt a new form of pseudo–gold standard, with other nations pyramiding money and credit on top of British sterling while the United States, though still on a gold coin standard, was ready to help Britain avoid suffering the consequences of abandoning the discipline of the classical gold standard.

However, it took little time for things to go very wrong. The crucial British export industries, chronically whipsawed between an overvalued pound and rigidly high wage rates kept high by strong, militant unions and widespread unemployment insurance, kept slumping during an era when worldwide trade and exports were expanding. Due to these government policies, unemployment remained high. From 1851 to 1914 the unemployment rate had hovered around 3 percent. From 1921 through 1926 it had averaged 12 percent, and unemployment did little better after the return to gold. In April 1925, when Britain returned to gold, the unemployment rate stood at 10.9 percent. After the return it fluctuated sharply, but always at historically very high levels. Thus, in the year after return, unemployment climbed above 12 percent, fell back to 9 percent, and then jumped to over 14 percent during most of 1926. Unemployment fell back to 9 percent by the summer of 1927, but hovered between 10 and 11 percent for the next two years. In other words, unemployment in Britain during the entire 1920s lingered at severe recession levels (P. Clarke 1990, 177; Palyi 1972, 109).

Most of this unemployment was concentrated in the older, previously dominant, heavily unionized industries in the north of England.

The pattern of the slump in British exports may be seen in some comparative data. If 1924 is set equal to 100, world exports rose to 132 by 1929, while western European exports had similarly risen to 134. United States exports rose to 130. Yet amid this worldwide prosperity, Great Britain lagged far behind, her exports rising only to 109. On the other hand, British imports rose to 113 in the same period.

After the 1929 crash, all exports fell considerably through 1931: world exports to 113, western Europe to 107, and the United States, which had taken the brunt of the 1929 crash, to 91. Yet, while British imports rose slightly from 1929 to 1931 (to 114), its exports fell drastically to 68. This result was due to the combination of an overvalued pound and rigid downward wage rates. The final effects were that, whereas overall 1931 western-European and world exports were considerably higher than in 1924, British exports were sharply lower.

Within categories of British exports there was a sharp and illuminating separation between two sets of industries: the old, unionized export staples in the north, and the newer, relatively nonunion, lower-wage industries in the south of England. These newer industries were able to flourish and provide plentiful employment because they were permitted to hire workers at a lower hourly wage than the industries of the north (Anderson 1949, 166; Moggridge 1972, 117). Some of these industries, such as public utilities, flourished because they were not dependent on exports. But even the exports from these new, relatively nonunionized industries did very well during this period.

Thus, from 1924 to 1928–29 the volume of automobile exports rose by 95 percent, exports of chemical and machinery manufactures rose by 24 percent, and exports of electrical goods by 23 percent. During the 1929–31 recession, exports of these new industries did relatively better than the old: machinery and electrical exports falling to 28 and 22 percent respectively below 1924, while chemical exports fell to only 5 percent below, and automobile exports remained comfortably in 1931 at 26 percent *above* 1924.

On the other hand, the older, staple export industries—the traditional mainstays of British prosperity—fared very badly in both these periods of boom and recession. The nonferrous metal industry rose only slightly by 14 percent by 1928–29 and then fell to 55 percent of its 1924 level in the next two years. In even worse shape were the once mighty cotton and woolen textile industries, the bellwethers of the Industrial Revolution in England. From 1924 to 1929 cotton exports fell by 10 percent, woolens by 20 percent. In the two years to 1931, they plummeted phenomenally: cottons fell to one-half their 1924 level, while woolens fell 54 percent. Remarkably, cotton and woolen exports were, at this point, at their lowest volume since the 1870s. Perhaps the worst problem was in the traditionally prominent export, coal mining. Ominously, coal exports fell 12 percent between 1928–29, slumping, like textiles, in the midst of worldwide prosperity.

So high were British price levels compared to other countries in both of these periods, that Britain's imports rose in every category during boom and recession. Thus, imports of manufactured goods into Britain rose by 32.5 percent between 1924–1929, and then rose another 5 percent until 1931. So costly, too, was the British iron and steel industry that after 1925, the British, for the first time in their history, became *net importers* of iron and steel.

The relative rigidity of wage costs in Britain may be seen by comparing their unit wage costs with the United States, setting 1925 in each country equal to 100. In the United States, as prices fell about 10 percent in response to increased productivity and output, wage rates also declined, falling to 93 in 1928 and to 90 in 1929. Swedish wage rates fell to 88 in 1928, 80 in 1929, and 70 in 1931. In Great Britain, wage rates remained stubbornly high even in the face of falling prices, being 97 in 1928, 95 the following year, and falling to 90 by 1931. In contrast, wholesale prices in England fell by 8 percent in the 1926–27 period and more sharply thereafter (Moggridge 1972, 117–25).

The blindness of British officialdom to the downward rigidity of wage rates was quite remarkable. The powerful deputy controller of finance for the Treasury, Frederick W. Leith-Ross, the major architect of what became known as the "Treasury View," wrote to Hawtrey in early August 1928 in bewilderment at Keynes's claim that wage rates had remained stable since 1925. In view of the substantial decline in prices in those years, wrote Leith-Ross, "I should have thought that the average wage rate showed a substantial decline during the past 4 years." Leith-Ross could only support his view by challenging the wage index as inaccurate, citing his own figures that aggregate payrolls had declined. Leith-Ross did not seem to have realized that that was precisely the problem: keeping wage rates up in the face of declining money demand for labor may indeed lower payrolls, but only by creating unemployment and a reduction in hours worked. By the spring of 1929, Leith-Ross was forced to face reality and conceded the point. At last, Leith-Ross admitted that the problem was rigidity of labor costs:

If our workmen were prepared to accept a reduction of 10 percent in their wages or increase their efficiency by 10 percent, a large proportion of our present unemployment could be overcome. But in fact organized labor is so attached to the maintenance of the present standard of wages and hours of labor that they would prefer that a million workers should remain in idleness and be maintained permanently out of the Employment Fund, than accept any sacrifice. The result is to throw on to the capital and managerial side of industry a far larger reorganization than would be necessary: and until labor is prepared to contribute in large measure to the process of reconstruction, there will inevitably be unemployment.[45]

Leith-Ross might have added that the "preference" for unemployment was made not by the unemployed themselves but by the union leadership on their alleged behalf, a leadership which itself did not have to face the unemployment dole. Moreover, the willingness of the workers to accept this deal might have been very different if there were no generous Employment Fund for them to tap.

It was the highly militant coal miners' union, led by the prominent leftist Aneurin Bevan, that was the first to disseminate doubts about the wisdom of the British return to gold. Not only was coal a highly unionized export industry located in the north of England, but already over-inflated coal mining wages had been given an extra boost during the first Labor government of Ramsay MacDonald in 1924. In addition to high wage rates, the miners' union insisted on numerous cost-raising restrictive and featherbedding practices, some of them resurrected from the defunct post-medieval guilds. These obstructionist tactics helped rigidify the British economy, preventing changes and adaptations of occupation and location, and hampered rationalizing and innovative managerial practices. As Frederick Benham trenchantly pointed out:

employers who wished to make changes had to face the powerful opposition of organized labor. The introduction of new methods, such as the "more looms to a weaver" system, was resisted. Strict lines of demarcation between occupations were maintained in engineering and elsewhere. A plumber could repair a pipe conveying cold water; if it conveyed hot water, he had to call in a hot water engineer. Entry into certain occupations was rendered difficult. A man can become an efficient building operative in a few months, an apprenticeship of four years was required. British railways could not have their labor force as they chose. A host of restrictions, insisted upon by the Trade Unions, made this impossible.[46]

By 1925, the year of the return to gold, the British coal industry faced competition from the rehabilitated, newly modernized and lower-cost coal mines in France, Belgium, and Germany. British coal was no longer competitive, and its exports were slumping badly. The Baldwin government appointed a Royal Commission, headed by Sir Herbert

Samuel, to study the vexed coal question. The Samuel Commission reported in March 1926, urging that miners accept a moderate cut in wages, an increase in working hours at current pay, and suggesting also that a substantial number of miners move to other areas where employment opportunities were greater. This was not the sort of rational solution that would appeal to the spoiled, militant unions, who rejected the proposals and went on strike, precipitating the traumatic and abortive general strike of 1926.

The strike was broken and coal mining wages fell slightly, but the victory for rationality was all to Pyrrhic. Keynes was able to convince the inflationist press magnate, Lord Beaverbrook, that the miners were victims of a Norman-Churchill–international banker conspiracy to profit at the expense of the British working class. But instead of identifying the problem as government inflationism, cheap money, and the gold-bullion–gold-exchange standard in the face of an overvalued pound, Beaverbrook and British public opinion pointed to "hard money" as the villain responsible for recession and unemployment. Instead of tightening the money supply and interest rates in order to preserve its created gold standard, the British government was moved to follow its inclinations still further: to step up its disastrous commitment to inflation and cheap money (Palyi 1972, 102–04).

During the general strike, Britain was forced to import coal from Europe instead of exporting it. In olden times, the large fall in export income would have brought about a severe liquidation of credit, contracting the money supply and lowering prices and wage rates. But the British banks, caught up in the ideology of inflationism, instead expanded credit on a lavish scale; and sterling balances piled up on the European continent. "Instead of a readjustment of prices and costs in England and a breaking up of the rigidities, England by credit expansion held the fort and continued the rigidities" (Anderson 1949, 167).

The large monetary expansion in Britain during 1926 caused gold to flow out of the country, especially to the United States, and sterling balances to accumulate in foreign countries, especially in France. Prior to World War I, Britain would have viewed these developments as a clear signal to contract its money supply; instead, it persisted in monetary expansion, lowering its crucial "Bank Rate" (the Bank of England's discount rate) from 5 to 4 1/2 percent in April 1927. This action further weakened the pound sterling, and Britain lost $11 million in gold during the next two months.

France's important role during the gold-exchange era has served as a convenient scapegoat for British architects of this policy ever since. The historical myth is that France was the spoiler, by returning to gold at an *under*valued franc (pegging the franc first in 1926 and then officially returning to gold two years later) and, consequently, piling up sterling balances and then breaking the gold-exchange system by insisting that Britain redeem in gold. The reality was very different. During World War I and after, France suffered a hyperinflation fueled by massive government deficits. As a result, the French franc, classically set at 19.3 cents under the old gold standard, had plunged to 5 cents in May 1925 and fell to 1.94 cents in late July 1926. By June 1926 Parisian mobs, protesting the runaway inflation and depreciation, surrounded the Chamber of Deputies, threatening violence if former Premier Raymond Poincaré, known as a staunch monetary and fiscal conservative, was not returned to his post. Poincaré was returned to office on 2 July, pledging to cut expenses, balance the budget, and save the franc.

Armed with a popular mandate, Poincaré was prepared to drive through any necessary monetary and fiscal reforms. Poincaré's every instinct urged him to return to gold at the prewar par, a course that would have been disastrous for France, being not only highly deflationary but also saddling French taxpayers with a massive public debt. Furthermore, returning to gold at the prewar par would have left the Bank of France with a very low (8.6 percent) gold-reserve-to-banknotes-in-circulation ratio. Returning at par, of course, would have gladdened the hearts of French bondholders, as well as those of Montagu Norman and the British propertied class. Poincaré was dissuaded from pursuing this policy by the knowledgeable and highly perceptive Émile Moreau, governor of the Bank of France, and also by his deputy governor, the distinguished economist Charles Rist. Moreau and Rist were aware of the chronic export depression and unemployment the British were suffering because of their stubborn insistence on the prewar par. Poincaré was reluctantly persuaded by Moreau and Rist to return to gold at a realistic par.

When Poincaré presented his balanced budget and monetary and financial reform package to Parliament on 2 August 1926, it was adopted quickly. Confidence in the franc dramatically rallied as pessimistic expectations in the franc changed to optimistic ones; and French capital, which understandably had fled massively into foreign currencies, returned to the franc, quickly doubling its value on the foreign exchange market to almost 4 cents by December. To avoid any further rise, the French government quickly stabilized the franc de facto at 3.92 cents on 26 December, and then returned de jure to gold at the same rate on 25 June 1928.[47]

At the end of 1926, while the franc was pegged, France was not yet on a genuine gold standard. De jure, the franc was still set at the prewar par, when one gold ounce had been set at approximately 100 francs. But then, at the new pegged value, the gold ounce—in foreign exchange—was worth 500 francs. Obviously, no one would now deposit gold at a French bank in return for 100 paper francs, thereby wiping out 80 percent of one's assets. Also, the Bank of France (which was a privately owned firm) could not buy gold at the current expensive rate, for fear that the French government might decide, after all, to go back to gold de jure at a higher rate, thereby inflicting a severe loss on its gold holdings. The government, however, did agree to indemnify the bank for any losses it might incur in foreign exchange transactions; in that way, Bank of France stabilization operations could take place only in the foreign exchange market.

The French government and the Bank of France were now committed to pegging the franc at 3.92 cents. At that rate, francs were purchased in a mighty torrent on the foreign exchange market, forcing the Bank of France to keep the franc at 3.92 cents by selling massive quantities of newly issued francs for foreign exchange. In that way, foreign exchange holdings of the Bank of France skyrocketed rapidly, rising from a minuscule sum in the summer of 1926 to no less than $1 billion worth in October of the following year. Most of these balances were in the form of sterling (in bank deposits and short-term bills), which had piled up on the continent during the massive British monetary expansion of 1926 and had by now moved into French hands with the advent of upward speculation in the franc. Against their will, therefore, the French found themselves in the same boat as the rest of Europe: on the gold-exchange or gold-sterling standard.[48]

If France had returned to the old, genuine gold standard at the end of 1926, gold would have flowed out of England to France, forcing contraction in England and forcing the British to raise interest rates. The inflow of gold into France and the increased issue of francs for gold by the Bank of France would also have temporarily lowered interest rates there. As it was, French interest rates were sharply lowered in response to the massive issue of francs, but no contraction or tightening was experienced in England; quite the contrary.[49]

Moreau, Rist, and other Bank of France officials were alert to the dangers of their situation; and they tried to act in lieu of the gold standard by reducing their sterling balances, partly by demanding gold in London and partly by exchanging sterling for dollars in New York.

This situation put considerable pressure upon the pound and caused a drain of gold out of England. In the classical gold standard era, London would have responded by raising the Bank Rate and tightening credit, stemming or even reversing the gold outflow. But the English were committed to an unsound inflationist policy, in stark contrast to the old gold system. And so, Norman tried his best to use muscle to prevent France from exercising its own property rights and redeeming sterling in gold, absurdly urging that sterling was beneficial for France and that they could not have too much sterling. On the other hand, he threatened to go off gold altogether if France persisted—a threat he was to make good four years later. He also invoked the specter of French World War I debts to Britain (Kooker 1976, 100). He tried to get various European central banks to put pressure on the Bank of France not to take gold from London. The Bank of France found that it could sell up to 3 million pounds a day without attracting the angry attention of the Bank of England, but any more sales than that would call forth immediate protest. As one official of the Bank of France said bitterly in 1927, "London is a free gold market, and that means that anybody is free to buy gold in London except the Bank of France" (Anderson 1949, 172–73).

Why did France pile up foreign exchange balances? The anti-French myth was that the franc was undervalued at the new rate of 3.92 cents and that the ensuing export surplus brought foreign exchange balances into France. The facts were precisely the reverse. Before World War I, France traditionally had a deficit in its balance of trade. During the post–World War I inflation, as usually occurs with fiat money, the foreign exchange rate rose more rapidly than domestic prices, since the highly liquid foreign exchange market is particularly quick to anticipate and discount the future. Therefore, during the French hyperinflation, exports were consistently greater than imports.[50] When France pegged the franc to gold at the end of 1926, the balance of trade reversed itself to the original pattern. Thus, in 1928 French exports were only 96.1 percent of imports. On the simplistic trade, or relative purchasing power, criterion, then, we would have to say that the post-1926 franc was "over" rather than "under" valued. Why did gold or foreign exchange not flow out of France? For the same reason as before World War I: the chronic trade deficits were covered by perennial "invisible" net revenues into France, in particular the flourishing tourist trade.

The French, succumbing to both the blandishments and threats of Montagu Norman, were quite cooperative—much against their better judgment. Thus, Norman warned Moreau in December 1927 that if he persisted in trying to redeem sterling in gold, Norman would devalue the pound. In fact, Poincaré prophetically warned Moreau in May 1927 that sterling's position had weakened and that England might all too readily give up on its own gold standard. And when France stabilized the franc de jure at the end of June 1928, foreign exchange constituted 55 percent of the total reserves of the Bank of France (with gold at 45 percent), an extraordinarily high proportion of that in sterling. Furthermore, much of the funds deposited by the Bank of France in London and New York were used for stock market loans and fueled stock speculation. Worse, much of the sterling balances were recycled to repurchase French francs, which continued the accumulation of sterling balances in France. It is no wonder that Melchior Palyi concludes: "it was at Norman's urgent request that the French central bank carried a weak sterling on its back well beyond the limit of what a central bank could reasonably afford to do under the circumstances. No other major central bank took anything like a similar risk (percentage-wise)."[51]

Montagu Norman had neutralized the French, at least temporarily,[52] but what of the United States? The British were counting heavily on America following a policy of monetary expansion so as to keep British gold off American shores. Instead, American prices were falling slowly but steadily during 1925–26 in response to rising American productivity and output. The gold-exchange standard was being endangered by events in America that were beyond Norman's control.

Norman decided to fall back on his trump card, his relationship with Strong. Strong would, Norman hoped, rush to the rescue of Great Britain. After Norman turned for help to his old friend, Strong invited the world's four leading central bankers to a private conference in New York in July 1927. In addition to Norman and Strong, the conference was attended by Deputy Governor Rist of the Bank of France and Hjalmar Schacht, Governor of the German Reichsbank. Strong ran the American side, keeping the Federal Reserve Board in Washington in the dark, and even refusing to let Gates McGarrah, chairman of the board of the Federal Reserve Bank of New York, attend the meeting.

Strong and Norman tried their best to have the four nations embark on a coordinated policy of monetary expansion and easy credit. Rist demurred, although he agreed to help England by buying gold from New York instead of London (i.e., drawing down dollar balances instead of sterling). Strong, in turn, agreed to supply France with gold at a subsidized rate, as cheap as the cost of buying it from England, despite the far higher transportation costs (Rothbard 1972, 141).

Schacht was even more adamant, expressing his alarm at the extent to which bank credit expansion had already gone in England and the United States. The previous year, Schacht had acted on his concerns by reducing his sterling holdings to a minimum and increasing the holdings of gold in the Reichsbank. He told Strong and Norman: "Don't give me a low (interest) rate. Give me a true rate. Give me a true rate, and then I shall know how to keep my house in order."[53] Thereupon, Schacht and Rist sailed for home, leaving Strong and Norman to plan the next round of coordinated monetary expansion themselves. In particular, Strong agreed to embark on a mighty inflationary push in the United States, lowering interest rates and expanding credit—an agreement which Rist, in his memoirs, maintains had already been privately concluded before the four-power conference began. Indeed, Strong gaily told Rist during their meeting that he was going to give "a little *coup de whiskey* to the stock market" (Rist 1955, 1066ff.). Strong also agreed to buy $60 million more of sterling from England to prop up the pound.

Pursuant to the agreement with Norman, the Federal Reserve promptly began its great burst of expansion and cheap credit in the second half of 1927. This period saw the largest rate of increase of bank reserves during the 1920s, mainly due to massive Fed purchases of U.S. government securities and of banker's acceptances, totaling $445 million in the latter half of 1927. Rediscount rates were also lowered, inducing an increase in bills discounted by the Fed. Strong decided to deceive the suspicious regional Federal Reserve Banks by using Kansas City Fed Governor W. J. Bailey as the stalking horse for the rate-cut policy. Instead of the New York Fed initiating the rediscount rate cut from 4 to 3 1/2 percent, Strong talked the trusting Bailey into taking the lead on 29 July, with New York and the other regional Feds following a week or two later. Strong told Bailey that the purpose of the rate cuts was to help the farmers, a theme likely to appeal to Bailey's agricultural region. He did not tell Bailey that the real purpose of the policy was to help England pursue its inflationary gold-exchange policy.

The Chicago Fed, however, balked at lowering its rates, and Strong got the Federal Reserve Board in Washington to force it to do so in September. The isolationist *Chicago Tribune* angrily called for Strong's resignation, charging correctly that discount rates were being lowered in the interests of Great Britain (Anderson 1949, 182–83; Rothbard 1972, 140–42; Beckhart 1931, 67ff.; Clark 1935, 314).

After overseeing the expansion of reserves and hence money in 1927, the New York Fed continued its policy over the next two years by buying heavily in prime commercial bills of foreign countries, bills endorsed by foreign central banks. The purpose was to bolster foreign currencies and to prevent an inflow of gold into the United States. The New York Fed also bought large amounts of sterling bills in 1927 and 1929. The New York Fed frankly described its policy as follows: "We sought to support exchanges by our purchases and thereby not only prevent the withdrawal of further amounts of gold from Europe but also, by improving the position of the foreign exchanges, to enhance or stabilize Europe's power to buy our exports" (Clark 1935, 198).

If Strong was the point man for the monetary expansions of the late 1920s, the Coolidge administration was a willing participant. Pittsburgh industrialist Andrew W. Mellon, Secretary of the Treasury throughout the Republican era of the 1920s, was long allied with Morgan interests. As early as March 1927, Mellon assured everyone that "an abundant supply of easy money" would continue to be available, and he and President Coolidge repeatedly acted as the "capeadores of Wall Street," giving numerous newspaper interviews urging stock prices upward whenever prices seemed to flag. The only sharp critic of Strong's policy within the administration was Secretary of Commerce Herbert C. Hoover,[54] whose recalcitrance was met by Mellon's denouncing his "alarmism" and interference.[55]

The price paid by Strong and his allies for carrying out this policy was small—at least in the short run—because, as Lawrence Clark pointed out, the cheap credit aided especially those speculative financial and investment banking interests with whom Strong was allied—notably, of course, the Morgan complex.[56] The British, as early as mid-1926, knew enough to be appreciative. The influential London journal, *The Banker,* wrote of Strong that "no better friend of England" existed. *The Banker* praised the "energy and skillfulness that he has given to the service of England," and exulted that "his name should be associated with that of Mr. (Walter Hines) Page as a friend of England in her greatest need."[57]

On the other hand, Morgan partner Russell C. Leffingwell was not nearly as sanguine about the Strong-Norman policy of joint credit expansion. When, in the spring of 1929, Leffingwell heard reports that Norman was getting "panicky" about the speculative boom on Wall Street, he impatiently told fellow Morgan partner Thomas W. Lamont, "Monty and Ben sowed the wind. I expect we shall all have to reap the whirlwind.... I think we are going to have a world credit crisis" (Chernow 1990, 313). Benjamin Strong, however, was not destined personally to reap the whirlwind. A sick man, he was not running the Fed throughout 1928, finally dying on 16 October of that year. He was succeeded by his handpicked choice, George L. Harrison, also a Morgan man but lacking the personal charisma and political clout of Strong.

At first, as in 1924, Strong's monetary expansion was temporarily successful in accomplishing Britain's goals. Sterling was strengthened, and the American gold inflow from Britain was sharply reversed, gold then flowing outward. Farm produce prices rose from an index of 100 in 1924 to 110 the following year, slumped back to 100 in 1926 and 99 in 1927, and then jumped to 106 in 1928. Farm and food exports spurted upward; and foreign loans in the United States were stimulated to new heights, reaching a peak in mid-1928. But, once again, the stimulus was only temporary. By the summer of 1928, the pound sterling was sagging again. American farm prices fell slightly in 1929, and agricultural exports fell in the same year. Foreign lending slumped badly, as both domestic and foreign funds poured into the American stock market.

The stock market had already been booming by the time of the fatal injection of credit expansion in the latter half of 1927. The Standard & Poors (S&P) industrial common stock index, which had been 44.4 at the beginning of the 1920s boom in June 1921, had risen to 103.4 by June 1927. S&P rail stocks had risen from 156.0 in June 1921 to 316.2 in 1927, and public utilities from 66.6 to 135.1 in the same period. Dow-Jones industrials had doubled from 95.1 in November 1922 to 195.4 in November 1927. It was at this point that the Fed's expansionary monetary and credit policy ignited the stock market fire. In particular, throughout the 1920s, the Fed deliberately and unwisely stimulated the stock market by keeping the "call rate" (i.e., the interest rate on bank call loans to the stock market) artificially low. Before the establishment of the Federal Reserve System, the call rate had frequently risen far above 100 percent when a stock market boom became severe. Yet, in the historic and virtually runaway stock market boom of 1928–29, the call rate never went above 10 percent. The call rates were controlled at these low levels by the New York Fed, in close collaboration with, and at the advice of, the Money Committee of the New York Stock Exchange (Rothbard 1972, 11b; Clark 1935, 382; Miller 1935).

During 1928 and 1929, the stock market went into overdrive, virtually doubling during these two years. The Dow-Jones industrials hit 376.2 on 29 August 1929, and the S&P index stood at 195.2. (Credit expansion always concentrates its booms in titles to capital, in particular stocks and real estate.) Bank credit propelled a massive real estate boom in the late 1920s in New York City, in Florida, and throughout the country. These included excessive mortgage loans and construction for everything from farms to Manhattan office buildings.[58]

The Federal Reserve authorities, now concerned about the stock market boom, tried feebly to tighten the money supply during 1928 but failed. The Fed's sales of government securities were offset by two factors: (a) the banks shifting their depositors from demand to "time" deposits, which required a much lower rate of reserves and which were really savings deposits redeemable de facto on demand, rather than genuine time loans; and (b) more importantly, the disastrous Fed policy of creating a market in bankers' acceptances, a market which had existed in Europe but not in the United States. The Fed's policy throughout the 1920s was to subsidize and, in effect, create an acceptance market by standing ready to buy any and all acceptances sold by certain favored acceptance houses at an artificially cheap rate. Hence, when bank reserves tightened as the Fed sold securities in 1928, the banks simply shifted to the acceptance market, expanding their reserves by selling acceptances to the Fed. Thus, the Fed's selling of $390 million of securities was partially offset, later during 1928, by the Fed's purchase of nearly $330 million of acceptances.[59] The Fed's maintenance of an easy money policy in 1928 was simplified by adopting the fallacious "qualitativist" view, which was also held by Herbert Hoover, that the Fed could dampen the boom by restricting loans to the stock market while merrily continuing to inflate in the acceptance market.

In addition to pouring in funds through acceptances, the Fed did nothing to tighten its rediscount market. The Fed discounted $450 million of bank bills during the first half of 1928; it finally tightened a bit by raising its rediscount rates from 3 1/2 percent at the beginning of the year to 5 percent in July. After that, it stubbornly refused to raise the rediscount rate any further, keeping it there until the end of the boom. As a result, Fed discounts to banks rose slightly until the end of the boom instead of declining. Furthermore, the Fed failed to sell any more of its hoard of $200 million of government securities after July 1928; instead, it bought some securities on balance during the rest of the year.

Why was Fed policy so supine in late 1928 and in 1929? A crucial reason is that Europe, and particularly England, having lost the benefit of the inflationary impetus by mid-1928, was clamoring against any tighter money in the United States. The easing in late 1928 prevented gold inflows to the United States from England from getting very large. Britain was again losing gold, sterling was again weak, and the United States once again bowed to England's wish to see Europe avoid the consequences of its own inflationary policies.

Another relaxing of stock prices in March spurred Secretary Mellon to call for, and predict, lower interest rates. Again, a weakening of stock prices in late March induced Mellon to make his statement assuring "an abundant supply of easy money which should take care of any contingencies that might arise." Later in the year, President Coolidge made optimistic statements every time the rising stock market fell slightly. Repeatedly, both Coolidge and Mellon announced that the country was in a "new era" of permanent prosperity and permanently rising stock prices. On 16 November the *New York Times* declared that the administration in Washington was the source of most of the bullish news and noted the growing "impression that Washington may be depended upon to furnish a fresh impetus for the stock market." The administration continued emitting bullish statements for the next two years, Coolidge continuing until the very end of his term.[60] A few days before leaving office in March 1929, Coolidge called American prosperity "absolutely sound" and assured everyone that stocks were "cheap at current prices."[61]

The clamor from English economic interests against any tighter money in the United States was driven by England's loss of gold and the pressure on sterling. France, having unwillingly piled up $450 million in sterling by the end of June 1928, was anxious to redeem sterling for gold; it indeed sold $150 million of sterling by mid-1929. In deference to Norman's threats and pleas, however, the Bank of France sold that sterling for dollars rather than for gold in London. Indeed, so cowed was the French government that French sales of sterling in 1929–31 were offset by sterling purchases by a number of minor countries. Norman managed to persuade the Bank of France to sell no more sterling until after a disastrous day in September 1931, when Britain abandoned its own gold-exchange standard and went on to a fiat pound standard (Payli 1972, 187, 194).

Meanwhile, despite the great inflation of money and credit in the United States, the massive increase in the supply of goods in the United States continued to create relative retail price stability with wholesale prices falling from 104.5 (1926=100) in November 1925, to 100 in 1926, and then to 95.2 in June 1929. Consumer price indices in the United States also fell very slightly in the late 1920s. Thus, despite Strong's loose money policies, Norman could not count on price inflation in the United States to bail out his gold-exchange system.

In addition to pleading with the United States to keep expanding credit, Montagu Norman resorted to dubious short-run devices to try to keep gold from flowing to the United States. Thus, during 1928 and 1929, he would sell gold for sterling to raise the sterling rate a bit, in sales timed to coincide with the departure of fast boats from London to New York, thus inducing gold holders to keep the precious metal in London. Such short-run tricks were hardly adequate substitutes for tight money or for raising the bank rate in England, and they weakened long-run confidence in the pound sterling (Anderson 1949, 201).

In March 1929 Herbert Clark Hoover became President of the United States. While not as intimately connected as Calvin Coolidge, Hoover had long been close to Morgan interests. Mellon stayed on as Secretary of the Treasury, with the post of Secretary of State going to a long-time top Wall Street lawyer in the Morgan orbit, Henry L. Stimson, disciple and partner of J. P. Morgan's personal attorney, Elihu Root.[62] Perhaps most important, Hoover's closest though unofficial adviser, whom he regularly consulted three times a week, was Morgan partner Dwight Morrow.[63]

Hoover's method of dealing with the inflationary boom was to try not to tighten the money supply, but to keep bank loans out of the stock market by a jawbone method then called "moral suasion." This, too, was the preferred policy of the new Governor of the Federal Reserve Board in Washington, Roy A. Young. The fallacy was to try to restrict credit to the stock market while keeping it abundant to "legitimate" commerce and industry. Using methods of intimidation of business honed when he was Secretary of Commerce, Hoover attempted to restrain stock loans by New York banks, tried to induce the president of the New York Stock Exchange to curb speculation, and warned leading editors and publishers about the dangers of high stock prices. None of these superficial methods were effective.[64]

Professor Beckhart added another reason for the adoption of the ineffective policy of moral suasion: that the administration had been persuaded to try this tack by Montagu Norman. By June 1929 moral suasion was at last abandoned, but discount rates were still not raised, so that the stock market boom continued even as the economy, in general, was quietly but inexorably turning downward. Secretary Mellon once again trumpeted "unbroken and unbreakable prosperity." In August the Federal Reserve Board finally agreed to raise the rediscount rate to 6 percent, but any tightening effect was more than offset by the Fed's simultaneously lowering its acceptance rate, thereby once again giving an inflationary fillip to the acceptance market. One reason for this resumption of acceptance inflation, after it had previously been reversed in March was, yet again, "another visit of Governor Norman" (Beckhart 1931, 142ff., 127). Thus, Montagu Norman once more was able to lend his final impetus to the boom of the 1920s.

Great Britain also was entering a depression, and yet its inflationary policies resulted in a serious outflow of gold that summer. Norman was able to get a line of credit of $250 million from a New York banking consortium, but the outflow continued through September, much of it to the United States. Continuing to help England, the New York Fed bought large amounts of sterling bills from August through October.

A perceptive epitaph on the qualitative credit politics of 1928–29 was pronounced by A. Wilfred May:

> Once the credit system had become infected with cheap money, it was impossible to cut down particular outlets of this credit without cutting down all credit, because it is impossible to keep different kinds of money separated in watertight compartments. It was impossible to make money scarce for stock-market purposes, while simultaneously keeping it cheap for commercial use.... When Reserve credit was created there was no possible way that its employment could be directed into specific uses, once it had flowed through the commercial banks into the general credit stream. (May 1935, 292–93; Hardy 1932, 124–77; Mogenstern 1930, 2–3; Rothbard 1972, 151–52)

Depression and the End of the
Gold-Sterling-Exchange Standard, 1929–31

The depression that struck the world economy in 1929 could have been met in the same way as the United States, Britain, and other countries had faced the severe contraction of 1920–21, and the way in which all countries met depressions under the classical gold standard. They could have recognized the folly of the preceding monetary expansion boom and accepted the fact that the depression mechanism needed to return to an efficient free market economy. In other words, they could have accepted the liquidation of unsound investments and the liquidation of egregiously unsound banks. They could have accepted the contractionary deflation of money, credit, and prices. If the major world governments had done so, they would, as in the cases, have encountered a depression-adjustment period that would have been severe but mercifully short. Recessions unhampered by government interventions almost invariably work themselves into recovery within a year or so.

But the United States, Britain, and the rest of the world had been seduced by the siren song of cheap money. If bank credit expansion had gotten the world into this mess, then more of the same would be the only way out. Pursuit of this demand-side, proto-Keynesian policy, along with other massive government interventions to prevent price deflation, managed to convert what would probably have been a short, sharp recession into a chronic, lingering stagnation with an unprecedentedly high amount of unemployment that ended only with the coming of World War II (Vedder and Gallaway 1993).

Great Britain tried to depreciate its way out of the recession, as did the United States, despite the claim by some economists that the Federal Reserve deliberately contracted the money supply from 1929–33. Partly, the Fed expanded monetarily to help Britain and partly for its own sake. During the week of the great stock market crash—the final week of October 1929—the Federal Reserve Bank of New York, specifically George Harrison, doubled its holding of government securities and discounted $200 million for member banks. During that one week, the Fed added $300 million to bank reserves, the expansion being generated to prevent stock market liquidation and to permit the New York City banks to take over brokers' loans being liquidated by nonbank lenders. Over the objections of Roy Young of the Federal Reserve Board, Harrison told the New York Stock Exchange, "I am ready to provide all the reserve funds that may be needed" (Chernow 1990, 319). By December, Secretary Mellon issued one of his traditionally optimistic pronouncements that there was "plenty of credit available." President Hoover, addressing a business conference on 5 December, hailed the nation's good fortune in possessing the splendid Federal Reserve System, which had succeeded in saving shaky banks, restored confidence, and made capital more abundant by reducing interest rates.

In early 1930 the Fed launched a massive cheap money program, lowering rediscount rates during the year from 4 1/2 percent to 2 percent, with acceptance rates and call loan rates falling similarly. The Fed purchased $218 million in government securities, increasing total

member bank reserves by over $100 million. The money supply, how-
ever, remained stable and did not increase, due to the bank failures of
late 1930. The inflationists were not satisfied, however. *Business Week*
(then as now a spokesman for "enlightened" pro-interventionist business opinion) claimed in late October that the "deflationists" were "in
the saddle." In contrast, H. Parker Willis, in an editorial in the New
York *Journal of Commerce,* trenchantly pointed out that the easy money
policy of the Fed was actually bringing about the bank failures, because the banks were being encouraged to avoid the painful but necessary process of liquidation. Willis noted that the country was suffering
from frozen and wasteful mal-investments in plants, buildings, and
other capital, and that the depression could only be cured when these
unsound credit positions were liquidated.[65]

In 1930 Montagu Norman got part of his wish to achieve formal
inter–central bank collaboration. Norman was able to push through a
new "central bankers' bank," the Bank for International Settlements
(BIS) meeting regularly at Basle, to provide clearing facilities for German reparations payments and to provide regular facilities for meeting
and cooperation. While Congress forbade the Fed from formally join-
ing the BIS, the New York Fed and Morgan interests worked closely
with the new bank. Indeed, the BIS treated the New York Fed as if it
were the central bank of the United States. Gates W. McGarrah resigned his post as chairman of the board of the New York Fed in
February 1930 to assume the position of president of the new BIS.
Jackson E. Reynolds, a director of the New York Fed, was chairman of
the BIS's first organizing committee. J.P. Morgan & Company
unsurprisingly supplied much of the capital for the BIS. Even though
there was no legislative sanction for U.S. participation in the bank,
Governor George Harrison made a "regular business trip" abroad in
the fall to confer with the other central bankers, while the New York
Fed extended loans to the BIS.

During 1931, many of the European banks, swollen by unsound credit
expansion, faced liquidation. In October 1929 the important Austrian
bank, the Boden-Kredit-Anstalt, was one of those. Instead of allowing
the bank to be liquidated, a group of international financiers, headed
by the Rothschilds and the Morgans, bailed the bank out. The Boden
bank was merged into the older and stronger Oesterreichische-Kredit-
Anstalt, now by far the largest commercial bank in Austria, capital
being provided by an international financial syndicate that included
Morgan and Rothschild. Moreover, the Austrian government guaranteed some of the Boden bank's assets.

Kredit-Anstalt was weakened by the merger and in May 1931 a run occurred on the bank, led by French bankers angered by the announced customs union between Germany and Austria. Despite aid to the Kredit-Anstalt by the Bank of England, Rothschild of Vienna, and the BIS (aided by the New York Fed and other central banks) to a total of over $31 million, and the Austrian government's guarantee of Kredit-Anstalt liabilities up to $150 million, the bank run, once launched, proved irresistible. Austria went off the gold standard and, in effect, declared national bankruptcy in June 1931. At that point, a fierce run began on the German banks, the Bank of International Settlements again trying to shore up Germany's financial system by arranging a $100 million loan to the Reichsbank, a credit joined in by the Bank of England, the Bank of France, the New York Fed, and several other central banks. But the run on the German banks, both by the German people and their foreign creditors, proved devastating. By mid-July the German banking system collapsed from internal runs, and Germany went off the gold standard. Since the German public feared runaway inflation above all else and identified the cause of the inflation as exchange rate devaluation, the German government felt it had to maintain the par value of the mark, now highly overvalued relative to gold. To do so, while at the same time resuming inflationary credit expansion, the German government had to "protect" the mark by severe and thorough exchange controls.

With the bank runs in Austria and Germany, it was clear that England would be the next to suffer a worldwide lack of confidence in its currency, including runs on its gold reserves. Sure enough, in mid-July sterling redemptions in gold accelerated, and the Bank of England lost $125 million in gold in nine days.

The remedy for this situation under the classical gold standard was clear: a sharp rise in the bank rate to tighten English money supply and to attract gold and foreign capital to flow back into England. In classical gold standard crises, the Bank of England had raised its bank rate to 9 or 10 percent until the crisis passed. And yet, so wedded was England to cheap money, that it entered the crisis in mid-July at the low bank rate of 2 1/2 percent. It grudgingly raised the rate only to 4 1/2 percent by the end of July, keeping the rate at this low level until finally, on Black Sunday, 20 September, it went off the very gold-exchange standard that it had recently foisted upon the rest of the world. Indeed, instead of tightening money, the Bank of England made the pound still shakier by inflating credit further. Thus, in the last two weeks of July, the Bank of England purchased nearly $115 million in government securities.

England went off gold even as foreign central banks tried to prop up the Bank of England and save the gold-exchange standard. Answering Norman's pleas, the Bank of France and the New York Fed each loaned the Bank of England $125 million on 1 August, and then later in August another $400 million was provided by a consortium of French and American bankers. All this aid was ineffectively used to pursue the policies of inflationism and a 4 1/2 percent bank rate. As Benjamin Anderson concluded, "England went off the gold standard with the bank rate at 4 1/2 percent. To a British banker in 1913, this would have been an incredible thing—the collapse of the gold standard in England was absolutely unnecessary. It was the product of prolonged violation of gold standard rules, and, even at the end, it could have been averted by the return to orthodox gold standard methods" (Anderson 1949, 245–50; Benham 1932, 9–10).

England not only betrayed the countries that aided the pound but also the countries it had cajoled into adopting the gold-exchange standard in the 1920s. It also specifically betrayed those banks it had persuaded to keep huge sterling balances in London: specifically, the Netherlands Bank and the Bank of France. Indeed, on Friday, 18 September, G. Vissering, head of the Netherlands Bank, phoned Montagu Norman and asked him about the crisis of sterling. Vissering, who was poised to withdraw massive sterling balances from London, was assured without qualification by his old friend that England would, at all costs, remain on the gold standard. Two days later, Britain betrayed Norman's word and the Netherlands Bank suffered severe losses (Anderson 1949, 246–47, 253).

The Netherlands Bank was strongly criticized by the Dutch government for keeping its balances in sterling until it was too late. In its defense, the bank quoted repeated assurances from the Bank of England about the safety of foreign funds in London. The bank made it clear that it was betrayed and deceived by the Bank of England (Palyi 1972, 276–78).

The Bank of France also suffered severely from the British betrayal, losing about $95 million. Despite its misgivings, the Bank of France had loyally supported the English gold standard system by allowing sterling balances to pile up. The Bank of France sold no sterling until after England went off gold; by September 1931, it had amassed a sterling portfolio of $300 million, one-fifth of France's monetary reserves. In fact, during 1928–31, the sterling portfolio of the Bank of France was at times equal to two-thirds of the entire gold reserve of the Bank of England.

Despite Montagu Norman, who began to blame the French government for his own egregious failure, it was not the French authorities
who put pressure on sterling in 1931. On the contrary, it was shrewd
private French investors and commercial banks, correctly sensing the
weakness of sterling and the British refusal to employ orthodox measures in its support, that decided to make a run on the pound in exchange for gold (Palyi 1972, 187–90; Kooker 1976, 105–06, 113–17).
The run was aggravated by the fact that Britain had a chronic import
deficit. It was scarcely in a position to save the gold standard through
tight money when the British government, at the end of July, projected
a massive fiscal 1932–33 deficit of 120 million pounds, the largest
since 1920. Attempts in September to cut the budget were overridden
by union strikes—and even by a short-lived, sit-down strike by British
naval personnel—which convinced foreigners that Britain would not
take sufficient measures to defend the pound.

In his memoirs, the economist Moritz J. Bonn summed up the significance of England's action in September 1931:

> September 20, 1931, was the end of an age. It was the last day of the age of eco-
> nomic liberalism in which Great Britain had been the leader of the world.... Now
> the whole edifice had crashed. The slogan "safe as the Bank of England" no longer
> had any meaning. The Bank of England had gone into default. For the first time in
> history a great creditor country had devalued its currency, and by so doing had
> inflicted heavy losses on all those who had trusted it." (Bonn 1948, 278)

As soon as England went off the gold standard, the pound fell by 30
percent. It is ironic that, after all the travail Britain had put the world
through, the pound fell to a level—$3.40—that might have been vi-
able if she had originally returned to gold at that rate. Twenty-five
countries followed Britain off gold and onto floating, and devaluating,
exchange rates. The era of the gold-exchange standard was over.

Epilogue

Due to the events discussed above, the world was plunged into a
monetary chaos of fiat money, competing devaluations, exchange controls, and warring monetary and trade blocs, accompanied by a network of protectionist restrictions. These warring blocs played an
important though neglected part in paving the way for World War II.
The trend toward monetary and economic nationalism was accentu-
ated when the United States, the last bastion of the gold coin standard,
devalued the dollar and went off that standard in 1933.

Moreover, this inflationary system under the cloak of the prestige of gold was destined to last a great deal longer than the British venture, finally collapsing at the end of the 1960s.[66] The retreat from the classical gold standard had been years in coming, but the effects continue today. The politicians, financial manipulators, and demagogues who spent their careers attempting to free themselves and their home nations from the constraints imposed by an international gold standard system finally got their wish. The consequences of that wish, in my view, have been both dire and unnecessary. Discipline is difficult precisely because of human weaknesses, and the story of gold is no different from many other, similar human proclivities to thwart natural or artificial constraints. Although it is unlikely in the near future that the world will return to gold, its history and the history of its decline remains instructive for all of us.

Notes

1. Germany, which multiplied its money supply eightfold during the war, would soon spiral into runaway inflation, propelled by accelerated monetization of government deficits and of private credit; France and Austria also went into hyperinflation after the war to a lesser extent than Germany (Palyi 1972, 33; Moggridge 1972).
2. Precisely, British currency had traditionally been defined so that one ounce of gold was equal to 77s. 10 1/2 d. Comparing the prewar ratios of the dollar and the pound to gold, the pound sterling was therefore set at $4.86656. The gold ounce was also set equal to $20.67.
3. The word "inflation" has changed in meaning when used in economic theorizing over the past two centuries. From the earliest writings of the Classical School, whose founder was Adam Smith, up to around the middle of this century, the term meant an increase in the supply of money. Many dictionaries still define the term that way. For example, *The Oxford Dictionary of the English Language* (1989) provides the following definition: "An undue increase in the quantity of money in relation to the goods available for purchase: (in lay use) an inordinate rise in prices." Today, most economists accept the "lay" definition and have abandoned the older view expressed above. But, unfortunately, there is no really good substitute for the term when discussing expansions of money and/or credit. In this article, the term used to denote an increase in the quantity of money is "expansion." *Inflation* is used solely to indicate an increase in the level of some price index, as in the modern (non-lay) usage. The terminology change to *inflation* as a measurable phenomenon has occurred gradually in this century and is now common. That being the case, I will adhere to this terminological convention throughout this chapter, although I personally prefer the older approach. Others also prefer the older approach on grounds both of simplicity and demonstrated causation. If the central bank is increasing the supply of money, then they are engaging in a process of inflation relative to production, regardless of what is happening overall to output. Further, if prices rise because of the policy, the cause of that rise is clear. Under the new definition, potential causes are limited

solely by one's ability to imagine them, the direct definitional causal link having been cut. Perhaps this is progress; perhaps not.

4. A recent flurry of scholarly interest in the gold standard, the 1920s, and the Great Depression has unfortunately continued the dominant view of the past half-century: that the gold standard chained governments with restrictive fetters that prevented them from instituting the expansionist monetary and fiscal policies necessary to economic recovery. Thus, see Eichengreen 1992a and 1992b. On the problem of the valuation of the French franc, see Mouret 1991; Sicsic 1992.

5. See Palyi 1972, 1–21, 118–19; and Calleo 1976. Calleo shows that the pre-1914 gold standard was a genuine, multicentered gold standard and not a British sterling standard.

6. Far from showing that moneys of account can be "imaginary" in relation to media of exchange, the historical research of Luigi Einaudi on "imaginary money" in the Middle Ages reveals various countries' experiences with various relationships between gold and silver, both commodity moneys (Einaudi 1953; Timberlake 1991).

7. Prices during the boom did not necessarily increase in historical terms. If a secular price fall was occurring due to increased production, as happened in much of the nineteenth century, the inflationary boom took the form of prices being higher than they would have been in the absence of the expansion of money and credit.

8. While the United States, alone of major powers before 1914, lacked a central bank, the quasi-centralized national banking system performed a similar function in the years between the Civil War and 1914. Instead of the government conferring a monopoly note-issuing privilege upon the central bank, the federal government conferred that privilege upon federally chartered "national banks," which pyramided their credit upon a handful of central reserve city national banks located in New York and a few other Eastern financial centers.

9. For an early English critique of not going back at a realistic par, see Robbins 1934, especially 77–87.

10. The pound sterling was depreciated by 45 percent before the end of the Napoleonic War. When the war ended, the pound returned nearly to its prewar gold par. This appreciation was caused by (a) a general expectation that Britain would resume the gold standard and (b) a monetary contraction of 17 percent in one year, from 1815 to 1816, accompanied by a price deflation of 63 percent (Fetter 1965).

11. See the classic article by D. Benjamin and L. Kolchin, "Searching for an Explanation for Unemployment in Interwar Britain" (Benjamin and Kolchin 1979). It is unfortunate that Melchoir Palyi, in his valuable, perceptive, and solidly anti-inflationary work on the interwar period, is blind to the problems generated by the insistence on going back to gold at the prewar par. Palyi dismisses all such considerations as "Keynesian" (Palyi 1972 passim).

12. Address to the Annual General Meeting of the F.B.I. in November 1921. See Hume 1970, 141.

13. *Round Table* XIV (1923, 28), quoted in Hume 1970, 136.

14. *The Times* (London), 29 April 1925, cited in Hume 1970, 144.

15. Bradbury to Farrer, July 24, 1924 (Moggridge 1972, 47).

16. Undoubtedly the most trenchant testimony before the committee was by the free-market, hard-money economist from the London School of Economics, Edwin Cannan. In contrast to the other partisans of $4.86, Cannan fully recognized that the return to gold would require considerable deflation and that the needed reduction in wage rates would cause extensive difficulty and unemployment in

view of the new system of widespread unemployment insurance which made the unemployed far "more comfortable than they used to be." The only thing to be done, counselled Cannan, was to return to gold immediately at $4.86 and get it over with. As Cannan wrote at the time, the necessary adjustments "must be regarded in the same light as those which a spendthrift or a drunkard is rightly exhorted by his friends to face like a man" (Moggridge 1972, 45–46; Cannan, 1925, 105: cited in Milgate 1987, I:316). Cannan's sentiment and passion for justice are admirable, but, in view of the antagonistic political climate of the day, it might have been the better part of valor to return to gold at a realistic, depreciated pound.

17. Actually, the old Gold Embargo Act remained in force until allowed to expire on 31 December 1925. Since gold exports were prohibited until then, the gold standard was really not fully restored until the end of the year (Palyi 1972, 71).

18. In a memorandum to Churchill, Sir Otto Niemeyer delivered an eloquent critique of the Keynesian view that inflation would serve as a cure for the existing unemployment. Niemeyer declared: "You can by inflation (a most vicious form of subsidy) enable temporary spending power to cope with large quantities of products. But unless you increase the dose continually there comes a time when having destroyed the credit of the country you can inflate no more, money having ceased to be acceptable as a value. Even before this, as your inflated spending creates demand, you have had claims for increased wages, strikes, lockouts, etc. I assume it will be admitted that with Germany and Russia before (i.e., runaway inflation) we do not think plenty can be found on this path." Niemeyer concluded that employment can only be provided by thrift and accumulation of capital, facilitated by a stable currency, and not by doles and palliatives (Moggridge 1972, 77). Unfortunately, Niemeyer neglected to consider the crucial role of excessively high wage rates in causing unemployment.

19. France also appointed the House of Morgan its fiscal agent, having long had close connections through the Paris branch, Morgan Harjes (Chernow 1990, 104–05, 186, 195; and Clay 1957, 87).

20. On the interconnections among the Morgans, the Allies, foreign loans, and the Federal Reserve, and on the role of the Morgans in bringing the United States into the war, see Tansill 1938, 32–134. Also see Chernow 1990, 186–204. It is instructive that the British exempted the House of Morgan from its otherwise extensive mail censorship in and out of Britain, granting J. P. Morgan, Jr., and his key partners special code names (Chernow 1990, 189–90).

21. Rothbard 1984, 107–08, 111–12; Willis 1936, 90–91; and Chandler 1958, 105. The massive U.S. deficits to pay for the war were financed by Liberty Bond drives headed by a Wall Street lawyer, Russell C. Leffingwell, who would become a leading Morgan partner after the war (Chernow 1990, 203).

22. Rothbard 1984, 114; and Chandler 1958, 93–98. While some members of the Federal Reserve Board (FRB) had heavy Morgan connections, its complexion was scarcely as Morgan-dominated as Benjamin Strong. Of the five FRB members, *Paul M. Warburg* was a leading partner of Kuhn-Loeb, an investment bank rival of Morgan, and during the war suspected of being pro-German; *Governor William P. G. Harding* was an Alabama banker whose father-in-law's iron manufacturing company had prominent Morgan as well as rival Rockefeller men on its board; *Frederic A. Delano,* uncle of Franklin D. Roosevelt, was president of the Rockefeller-controlled Wabash Railway; *Charles S. Hamlin,* an assistant secretary to McAdoo, was a Boston attorney married into a family long connected with the Morgan-dominated New York Central Railroad; economist *Adolph C. Miller,* professor at Berkeley, had married into the wealthy, Morgan-connected

Sprague family of Chicago. At that time, Secretary of Treasury McAdoo and his longtime associate, John Skelton Williams, comptroller of the currency, were automatically FRB members, but only *ex officio*. Thus, setting aside the two *ex officio* members, the FRB began its existence with one Kuhn-Loeb member, one Morgan man, one Rockefeller person, a prominent Alabama banker with both Morgan and Rockefeller connections, and an economist with family ties to Morgan interests. When we realize that the Rockefeller and Kuhn-Loeb interests were allied during this era, we can see that the FRB scarcely could be considered under firm Morgan control (Rothbard 1984, 108).

23. Too much has been made of the fact that this discovery of the inflationary power of open market purchases by the Fed was the accidental result of a desire to increase Fed earnings. The result was not *wholly* unexpected. Thus, Strong, on April 18, 1922, wrote to Undersecretary of the Treasury S. Parker Gilbert that one of his major reasons for these open-market purchases was "to establish a level of interest rates...which would facilitate foreign borrowing in this country...and facilitate business improvement." Gilbert went on to become a leading partner of the House of Morgan.

24. Money supply equalling currency + total adjusted bank deposits. If savings and loan shares are added, the money supply rose by 9.0 percent during 1924 (Rothbard 1972, 88, 102–05).

25. Strong to Pierre Jay, 23 April and 28 April 1924; and Strong to Andrew Mellon, 27 May 1924 (Moggridge 1972, 51–53; Rothbard 1972, 133–34; and Chandler 1958, 283–84, 293ff.).

26. Grenfell to J. P. Morgan, Jr., 23 March 1925 (Chernow 1990, 274–75).

27. Hughes was both attorney and chief foreign policy adviser to Rockefellers' Standard Oil of New Jersey. On Hughes' close ties to the Rockefeller complex and their being overlooked even by Hughes' biographers, see the important but neglected article by Thomas Ferguson, "From Normalcy to New Deal: Industrial Structure, Party Competition, and American Public Policy in the Great Depression" (Ferguson 1984, 67).

28. "Morrow and Thomas Cochran, although moving spirits in the whole drive, remained in the background. The foreground was filled by the large, devoted, the imperturbable figure of Frank Stearns" (Nicolson 1935, 232). Cochran, a leading Morgan partner and board member of Bankers Trust Corporation, Chase Securities Corp., and Texas Gulf Sulphur Company, was a Midwesterner and not an Amherst graduate. He therefore had no reason of friendship to work strongly for Coolidge. Stearns, incidentally, had not met Coolidge before being introduced to him by Morrow (Burch 1981, 274–75, 302–03).

29. In addition to being a director of the Merchants National Bank of St. Paul, Kellogg had been general counsel for the Morgan-dominated U.S. Steel Corporation for the Minnesota region and, most important, the top lawyer for railroad magnate James J. Hill, long allied with the Morgan interests.

30. Morgan partner Dwight Morrow became ambassador to Mexico that year, and Nicaraguan affairs came under the direction of Wall Street lawyer Henry L. Stimson, longtime leading disciple of Elihu Root and a partner in Root's law firm (Burch 1981, 277, 305).

31. The latter phrase is in a letter from Sir Otto Niemeyer to Winston Churchill, 25 February 1925 (Moggridge 1972, 83).

32. Contrast Norman's view to that of pro–gold-coin-standard economist Walter Spahr: "A gold-coin standard provides the people with direct control over the government's use and abuse of the public purse...a manner that raises doubts as to their value as compared with gold, those people entertaining such doubts will

demand gold in lieu of...paper money, or bank deposits...The gold-coin standard thus places in the hands of every individual who uses money some power to
express his approval or disapproval of the government's management of the
people's monetary and fiscal affairs" (Spahr 1947, 5, cited in Palyi 1972, 122).

33. The theory, of course, was that the world required a more elastic currency system
that could grow as trade grew. In fact, to the extent productivity and growth do
improve, the supply of money can be expanded without driving up the average
level of existing relative prices. Unfortunately, monetary discipline tends to break
down under such arrangements, and the predicted breakdown occurred in this
case. It would be but a few short years before the European problem was repeated in the United States. Wherever these arrangements have been tried, long-
term inflation has been the inevitable result.

34. When the gold-exchange standard broke down in 1931, the economist H. Parker
Willis noted that "the ease with which the gold-exchange standard can be instituted, especially with borrowed money, has led a good many nations during the
past decade to 'stabilize' at too high a rate" (Willis 1931, 626ff.).

35. Skidelsky 1986, 275, 272–74; Palyi 1972, 155–57. While Keynes's book was
largely an apologia for the existing system in India, he also gently chided the
British government for not going far enough in managed inflation by failing to
establish a central bank (Skidelsky 1986, 276–277).

36. Since the Industrial Revolution, prices have tended to fall secularly in response
to an increased supply of goods, except for prices rising during wartime in response to inflationary war finance. This secular trend was reversed after the international abandonment of the gold standard in the 1930s.

37. Davis 1981, 219. Hawtrey's speech was published as "The Gold Standard"
(Hawtrey 1919). Fisher's proposal is in Fisher 1911, 332–46.

38. See Hawtrey 1919, 131–47. The text of the Genoa Resolutions themselves can
be found in the *Federal Reserve Bulletin* (June 1922), 678–79, reprinted in
Lawrence 1928, 162–65.

39. Peter Temin has shown that the 1839–43 monetary contraction in the United
States, in contrast to the 1929–33 contraction, had few ill effects because prices
and wage rates were free to fall (Temin 1969, 155ff.).

40. See the illuminating 1969 work by S. B. Saul, *The Myth of the Great Depression,
1873–1896.*

41. For contemporaneous critiques of Hawtrey's stabilizationism as a mask for inflationism, see Lawrence 1928, 326, 432–33; Deutscher 1990, 211–15.

42. Hogan 1977. On Strong's misgivings on the gold-exchange system, see Stephen
V. O. Clarke 1967, 36–40.

43. Finland acted on the advice of the great classical liberal Swedish economic historian, Eli Heckscher of the University of Stockholm. See Lester 1937, 433–67;
and Palyi 1972, 73, 107.

44. Entry of 6 February 1928 (Rothbard 139; Chandler 1958, 379–80). Also see the
entry in October 1926, in which Moreau comments on a report of Pierre Quesnay,
general manager of the Bank of France, on the "doctrinaire, and without doubt
somewhat Utopian or even Machiavellian" schemes of Montagu Norman and
his financier associates such as Sir Otto Niemeyer, Sir Arthur Salter, and Sir
Henry Strakosch, aided and abetted by Benjamin Strong, to establish and dominate the "economic and financial organization of the world by Norman and his
fellow–central bankers" (Palyi 1972, 134–35).

45. Draft memorandum to Chancellor of Exchequer Churchill, April 1929 (P. Clarke
1990, 186). Also see P. Clarke 1990, 179–80, 184–87.

46. Benham 1932, 27f. A manifestation of this obstructive and restrictive trade union
spirit circulated to the members of the union of Building Trade Workers in 1926:

"You should keep a keen control of overtime. Adopt a militant policy against all forms of piece work; be watchful and limit apprentices, remember the power you now occupy is conditioned by the scarcity of your labor" (Palyi 1972, 79).

47. Anderson estimates that it would have been safer for France to have gone back at 3.5 cents (which it could have done at the market rate in November) (Anderson 1949, 58). On the saga of France and the French franc in this period, see Anderson 1949, 54–61, 168–73; Palyi 1972, 185–90. For the influence of Moreau and Rist, see Kooker 1976, 91–93.

48. See the lucid exposition in Anderson 1949, 168–70.

49. The open-market discount rate in Paris fell from 7.0 percent in August 1926 to 2.0 percent in August of the following year (Anderson 1949, 172).

50. Thus, in 1925, the last full year of the hyperinflation, French exports were 103.8 percent of imports. The surplus was concentrated in manufactured goods, which had an export surplus of 23.8 billion francs, partially offset by a net import deficit of 5.4 billion in food and 16.8 billion in industrial raw materials (Palyi 1972, 185).

51. Palyi 1972, 187. The recycling of pounds and francs was pointed out by a leading French banker, Raymont Philippe (Philippe 1931, 134, cited in Palyi 1972, 194).

52. Moreau did resist Norman's pressure to inflate the franc further, and he repeatedly urged Norman to meet Britain's gold losses by tightening money and raising interest rates in England, thereby checking British purchase of francs and attracting capital at home. All this urging was to no avail, Norman being committed to a cheap money policy (Rothbard 1972, 141).

53. Anderson 1949, 181. Schacht had stabilized the German mark in a new Rentenmark after the old mark had been destroyed by a horrendous runaway inflation ending in 1923. The following year, he put the mark on the gold-exchange standard.

54. Unfortunately, Hoover shortsightedly attacked only credit expansion *in the stock market* rather than credit expansion *per se* (Rothbard 1972, 142–43; Anderson 1949, 182; Robey 1928; and Reed, 1930, 32).

55. O. Ernest Moore to Sir Arthur Salter, 25 May 1928, in Chandler 1958, 280–81.

56. Willis was a leading and highly perceptive critic of America's inflationary policies in the interwar period (Willis 1929, 553). Clark's study was written as a doctoral thesis under Willis (Clark 1935, 344).

57. Page was the Anglophile ambassador to Great Britain under Wilson who played a large role in getting the United States into the war (Clark 1935, 315).

58. On the real estate boom of the 1920s, see Hoyt 1947, 57.

59. On the unfortunate Fed acceptance policy of the 1920s, see Rothbard 1972, 117–23.

60. *Business Week* (October 22, 1930); *Commercial and Financial Chronicle* 113 (August 2, 1930) 690–91. The leading "bull" speculator of the era was former General Motors magnate William Crapo Durant, who was wiped out in the crash. He hailed Coolidge and Mellon as the leaders of the boom (*Commercial and Financial Chronicle* [April 20, 1929] 2557ff.).

61. Some of Strong's apologists claim that if he had been at the helm, he would have imposed tight money in 1928. See Snyder 1940, 227–28. Snyder worked under Strong as head of the statistical department of the New York Fed. In a letter from Strong to Walter W. Stewart on 3 August 1928, Strong protested against even the feeble restrictive measures during 1928 as being too severe. Dr. Stewart, formerly head of the division of research at the Fed, had a few years earlier become economic advisor of the Bank of England and had written to Strong warning of unduly tight restriction on American bank credit (Chandler 1958, 459–65).

62. Undersecretary of Treasury Ogden Mills, Jr., who was to replace Mellon in 1931 and who was close to Hoover, was a New York corporate lawyer from a family long associated with the Morgan interests.
63. Burch 1981, 280. For the important but private influence on President Hoover of Morgan partner Thomas W. Lamont, including Lamont's inducing Hoover to conceal his influence by faking entries in a diary Hoover left to historians, see Ferguson 1984, 79. The Morgans, in the 1928 Republican presidential race, were torn three ways: between inducing, unsuccessfully, President Coolidge to run for a third term; Vice President Charles G. Dawes, who had been a Morgan railroad lawyer and who dropped out of the 1928 race; and Herbert Hoover. On Hoover's worries before the nomination about the position of the Morgans, and on Lamont's assurances to him, see the illuminating letter from Thomas W. Lamont to Dwight Morrow, 16 December 1927, in Ferguson 1984, 77.
64. For a recent revival of similar views, see White 1990, 143–87.
65. *Business Week* (22 October 1930); *Commercial and Financial Chronicle* 131 (2 August 1930) 690–91. In addition, Albert Wiggin, head of the Chase National Bank, then clearly reflecting the views of the bank's chief economist, Benjamin M. Anderson, denounced the new Hoover policy of propping up wage rates and prices in depressions and of pursuing cheap money. "When wages are kept higher than the market situation justifies," wrote Wiggin in the Chase annual report for January 1931, "employment and the buying-power of labor fall off…. Our depression has been prolonged and not alleviated by delay in making necessary readjustments" (*Commercial and Financial Chronicle* 132 [17 January 1931], 428–29; Rothbard 1972, 191–93, 212–13, 217, 220–21).
66. For an overview of the monetary struggles and policies of the New Deal, see Rothbard 1980, 79–129. Some of the details in this account of the economic and financial interests involved have been superseded by Ferguson, 1984, "From Normalcy to New Deal," 41–93; and Ferguson 1989, 3–31.

References

Anderson, Benjamin M. 1949. *Economics and the Public Welfare: Financial and Economic History of the United States, 1914–1946*. Princeton, NJ: D. Van Nostrand.
Beckhart, Benjamin H. 1931. "Federal Reserve Policy and the Money Market, 1923–1931." In *The New Money Market,* Beckhart et al. New York: Columbia University Press.
Benham, Frederic C. 1932. *British Monetary Policy*. London: P. S. King.
Benjamin, D., and L. Kolchin. 1979. "Searching for an Explanation for Unemployment in Interwar Britain." *Journal of Political Economy* 87: 441–78.
Bonn, Moritz J. 1948. *Wandering Scholar.* New York: John Day.
Boyle, Andrew. 1967. *Montagu Norman.* London: Cassell.
Brown, William Adams, Jr. 1940. *The International Gold Standard Reinterpreted, 1914–1934.* New York: National Bureau of Economic Research.
Burch, Philip H., Jr. 1981. *Elites in American History.* New York: Holmes & Meier.
Calleo, David P. 1976. "The Historiography of the Interwar Period: Reconsideration." In *Balance of Power or Hegemony: The Interwar Monetary System,* edited by Benjamin M. Rowland. New York: Lehrman Institute and New York University Press, 227–60.
Cannan, Edwin. 1925. *The Paper Pound: 1797–1821.* 2d ed. London: P. S. King.
Chandler, Lester V. 1958. *Benjamin Strong, Central Banker.* Washington, DC: Brookings Institute.

Chernow, Ron. 1990. *The House of Morgan: An American Banking Dynasty and the Rise of Modern Finance*. New York: Atlantic Monthly Press.

Clark, Lawrence E. 1935. *Central Banking Under the Federal Reserve System*. New York: Macmillan.

Clarke, Peter. 1990. "The Treasury's Analytical Model of the British Economy Between the Wars." In *The State and Economic Knowledge: The American and British Experiences*, edited by M. Furner and B. Supple. Cambridge: Cambridge University Press.

Clarke, Stephen V. O. 1967. *Central Bank Cooperation, 1924–31*. New York: Federal Reserve Bank.

Clay, Sir Henry. 1957. *Lord Norman*. London: Macmillan.

Davis, Eric G. 1981. "R. G. Hawtrey, 1879–1975." In *Pioneers of Modern Economics in Britain*, edited by D. P. O'Brien and J. R. Presley. Totowa, NJ: Barnes & Noble.

Deutscher, Patrick. 1990. *R. G. Hawtrey and the Development of Macroeconomics*. Ann Arbor: University of Michigan Press.

Eichengreen, Barry. 1922a. *Golden Fetters: The Gold Standard and the Great Depression, 1919–1939*. New York: Oxford University Press.

———. 1992b. "The Origins and Nature of the Great Slump Revisited." *Economic History Review* 45 (May): 213–39.

Einaudi, Luigi. 1953. "The Theory of Imaginary Money from Charlemagne to the French Revolution." In *Enterprise and Secular Change*, edited by F. C. Lane and J. C. Riemersma. Homewood, IL: Richard D. Irwin, 229–60.

Einzig, Paul. 1932. *Montagu Norman*. London: Kegan Paul.

Ferguson, Thomas. 1984. "From Normalcy to New Deal: Industrial Structure, Party Competition, and American Public Policy in the Great Depression." *International Organization* 38 (Winter): 41–94.

———. 1989. "Industrial Conflict and the Coming of the New Deal: The Triumph of Multinational Liberalism in America." In *The Rise and Fall of the New Deal Order, 1920–1980*, edited by S. Fraser and G. Gerstle. Princeton, NJ: Princeton University Press.

Fetter, Frank W. 1965. *Development of British Monetary Orthodoxy, 1797–1875*. Cambridge, MA: Harvard University Press.

Fink, Carole. 1984. *The Genoa Conference: European Diplomacy, 1921–1922*. Chapel Hill: University of North Carolina Press.

Fisher, Irving. 1911. *The Purchasing Power of Money*. New York: Macmillan.

Hardy, Charles O. 1932. *Credit Policies of the Federal Reserve System*. Washington, DC: Brookings Institution.

Hawtrey, R. G. 1919. "The Gold Standard." *Economic Journal* 29: 429–42.

Hogan, Michael J. 1977. *Informal Entente: The Private Structure of Cooperation in Anglo-American Economic Diplomacy, 1918–1928*. Columbia: University of Missouri Press.

Hoyt, Homer. 1947. "The Effect of Cyclical Fluctuation upon Real Estate Finance." *Journal of Finance* (April).

Hume, L. J. 1970. *The Gold Standard*, edited by S. Pollard. London: Methuen & Company.

Kooker, Judith L. 1976. "French Financial Diplomacy: The Interwar Years." In *Balance of Power or Hegemony: The Interwar Monetary System*, edited by Benjamin M. Rowland. New York: Lehrman Institute and New York University Press.

Lawrence, Joseph Stagg. 1928. *Stabilization of Prices*. New York: Macmillan.

Lester, Richard A. 1937. "The Gold Parity Depression in Norway and Denmark, 1924–1928." *Journal of Political Economy* (August): 433–67.

May, A. Wilfred. 1935. "Inflation in Securities." In *The Economics of Inflation*, edited by H. Parker Willis and John M. Chapman. New York: Columbia University Press.

Milgate, Murray. 1987. "Cannan, Edwin." In *The New Palgrave: A Dictionary of Economics*. Vol. 1. New York: Stockton Press.

Miller, Adolph C. 1935. "Responsibilities for Federal Reserve Policies, 1927–1929." *American Economic Review* (September): 442–58.

Mogenstern, Oskar. 1930. Developments in the Federal Reserve System. *Harvard Business Review* (October).

Moggridge, D. E. 1972. *British Monetary Policy, 1924–1931: The Norman Conquest of $4.86.* Cambridge: Cambridge University Press.

Mouret, Kenneth. 1991. *Managing the Franc Poincaré.* New York: Cambridge University Press.

Nicolson, Harold. 1935. *Dwight Morrow.* New York: Harcourt, Brace.

Orde, Anne. 1990. *British Policy and European Reconstruction After the First World War.* Cambridge: Cambridge University Press.

Palyi, Melchior. 1972. *The Twilight of Gold, 1914–1936.* Chicago: Henry Regnery.

Philippe, Raymont. 1931. *Le Drame Financier de 1924–1930.* 4th ed. Paris: Gallimard.

Reed, Harold L. 1930. *Federal Reserve Policy, 1921–1930.* New York: McGraw-Hill.

Rist, Charles. 1955. "Notice Biographique." *Revué d'Economie Politique* (November–December).

Robbins, Lionel. 1934. *The Great Depression.* New York: Macmillan.

Robey, Ralph W. 1928. "The Capedores of Wall Street." *Atlantic Monthly* (September): 388–97.

Rothbard, Murray M. 1972. *America's Great Depression.* Kansas City, MO: Sheed and Ward.

———. 1980. "The New Deal and the International Monetary System." In *The Great Depression and New Deal Monetary Policy.* San Francisco: Cato Institute.

———. 1984. "The Federal Reserve as a Cartelization Device: The Early Years." In *Money in Crisis,* edited by Barry Siegel. San Francisco: Pacific Research Institute for Public Policy.

Saul, S. B. 1969. *The Myth of the Great Depression, 1873–1896.* London: Macmillan.

Sayers, R. S. 1970. "The Return to Gold, 1925." In *The Gold Standard and Employment Policies Between the Wars,* edited by S. Pollard. London: Methuen & Company.

Sicsic, Pierre. 1992. "Was the Franc Poincaré Deliberately Undervalued?" *Explorations in Economic History* 29: 69–92.

Silverman, Dan P. 1982. *Reconstructing Europe After the Great War.* Cambridge, MA: Harvard University Press.

Skidelsky, Robert. 1986. *John Maynard Keynes, Vol. 1, 1883–1920.* New York: Viking Press.

Snyder, Carl. 1940. *Capitalism, the Creator.* New York: Macmillan.

Spahr, Walter E. 1947. *Monetary Notes* (December 1).

Tansill, Charles Callan. 1938. *America Goes to War.* Boston: Little Brown.

Temin, Peter. 1969. *The Jacksonian Economy.* New York: W. W. Norton.

Timberlake, Richard. 1991. *Gold, Greenbacks, and the Constitution.* Berryville, VA: Durell Foundation.

Vedder, Richard, and Lowell Gallaway. 1993. *Out of Work: Unemployment and Government in Twentieth-Century America.* New York: Holmes and Meier for The Independent Institute.

White, Eugene N. 1990. "When the Ticker Ran Late: The Stock Market Boom and Crash of 1929." In *Crashes and Panics: The Lessons from History,* edited by Eugene N. White. Homewood, IL: Dow Jones-Irwin.

Willis, Henry Parker. 1929. "The Failure of the Federal Reserve." *North American Review.*

———. 1931. "The Breakdown of the Gold Exchange and Its Financial Imperialism." *The Annalist* (October 16).

———. 1936. *The Theory and Practice of Central Banking.* New York: Harper and Brothers.

5

Gold Standard Policy And Limited Government

Richard H. Timberlake

*An "automatic" gold currency is part and parcel of a
laissez-faire and free-trade economy.... It is extremely
sensitive to government expenditure and even to
attitudes or policies that do not involve expenditure
directly, for example, to foreign policy, to certain
policies of taxation, and, in general, to precisely all
those policies that violate the principles of economic
liberalism.... It is both the badge and the guarantee of
bourgeois freedom.... From this standpoint a man may
quite rationally fight for it, even if fully convinced of
the validity of all that has ever been urged against it on
economic grounds. From the standpoint of etatisme and
planning, a man may not less rationally condemn it,
even if fully convinced of the validity of all that has
ever been urged for it on economic grounds.*

—Joseph A. Schumpeter
History of Economic Analysis, 1954, 405–406

The State's Involvement with Money

The world has known precious-metals money for millennia. Through
the ages from ancient times, monetary devices have evolved spontane-

I have an extensive list of people to thank for reading and commenting on parts or all
of this monograph. The list includes William Beranek, the late Alfred Bornemann,
Kevin Dowd, Milton Friedman, Thomas Humphrey, Huston McCulloch, John Robbins,
Anna Schwartz, George Selgin, David Theroux, Richard Wagner, Larry White, Walter
Witt, Leland Yeager, and my wife, Hildegard Timberlake.

ously for much the same reason that wheels, levers, calculators, and other such innovations have also appeared: they significantly reduce the real costs of living and thereby add to the total product that people can enjoy. Money, however, has had an evolutionary history somewhat different from that of other commonly used technical devices. It has often been a mystical symbol that has lent itself to charlatanism and priestcraft; and because of its unique properties, it has become everywhere an object of state intervention and control.

Commodity money reached its evolutionary zenith with the multinational adoption of the gold standard in the late nineteenth and early twentieth centuries. During this same period, ironically enough, many governments initiated legal tender paper money systems and central banks that took control over monetary systems away from the self-regulating gold standard. The rule of law in monetary affairs very definitely gave way to the rule of men.

While the operations of the gold standard system are no puzzle, the pervasive intrusion of the state into monetary systems has had only limited treatment. This paper explores the evolution of the state's relationship to the precious metals, paper money, and central banks with the following questions in mind:

1. Did the constitutional gold standard lead to a noninterventionist constitutionally constrained state, or was it the other way around, or were both of these institutions the result of a more fundamental influence?
2. Has a gold standard proven to be a means for insulating the monetary system from the state, or has it been a device that the state could manipulate to its own advantage?
3. How did paper money and central banks come to replace gold and silver-based currencies?
4. Has the state's influence been benign or malignant, or both, and under what circumstances?
5. How might a gold standard be reinstituted in the contemporary world?

Coined Money Becomes Legal Tender

Money evolved from commodities that were not money. As ancient economies began to specialize, they first bartered goods and services directly. In time, they learned to barter indirectly, obtaining some intermediate items only for a subsequent final exchange. These indirect bartering devices were rudimentary media of exchange that had nascent monetary properties (Menger [1871] 1981, 262; Glasner 1989, 3–10).

Metallic currencies exhibited superior monetary properties at least as early as the seventh century B.C. Thereafter, the state assumed the prerogative of coinage. The seal on coins became a trademark. Wealthy and powerful merchants whose coins were current, and who themselves could assume political office, used their power to establish coining monopolies.[1] Mintage became almost exclusively a state function (Glasner 1989, chapter 2).

State authorities realized many benefits from their coinage powers. First, coinage provided a means for exploiting the booty from military conquests and mining enterprises. It also facilitated the state's collection of tribute and taxes, which, noted Arthur R. Burns, "the Romans for the first time made efficient." Religious authorities also coined ornaments and temple treasures in order to obtain usable moneys (Burns [1927] 1965, 458). All these features of coined money emphasize the great utility that monetization bestowed on commodity metals.

The state did not at first exploit its coinage monopoly by debasement. The city-state of Athens, for example, had a respectable and widely accepted coinage. However, charged Burns, the Romans, both the republicans and emperors, "attended more to the exploitation than the perfection of coining....They gave the world the inestimable curse of practical knowledge of all the possible methods of inflation apart from the use of paper money" (Burns [1927] 1965, 465).

In order to make coinage profitable, the state extended the routine practice of stamping coins with a seal of weight and fineness to a stamp of coercive authority that forced acceptance of the state's debased money. Burns observed that Greek coins did not reflect any direct evidence of legal tender. Nonetheless, he concluded:

> It is beyond doubt that legal tender regulations existed in some form or other from the earliest times. No unit of account could come into general use until it was legally defined, and this [legal specification] would involve a statement of the means by which a debt expressed in the unit could be settled....The Roman state fixed the rate at which coins were to pass, and presumably at this rate they were legal tender and had to be accepted. They were at no period merely punch-marked ingots to be placed in the balance at the option of the payee. (Burns [1927] 1965, 378–80)[2]

Burn's and Glasner's careful studies of the evolution of coined money suggests a Jekyll-Hyde sequence. While acting in a Dr. Jekyll capacity, the state saw to the certification of the weight and fineness of coined metal and stamped the coins to verify their material content. When the state assumed the monopoly of coinage, however, it became a Mr. Hyde.

Roman heads of state learned how to obtain real returns from seigniorage and debased the coinage for centuries. The experiences of these
systems demonstrated that adoption and ubiquitous use of metallic
moneys by itself did not provide an effective barrier to the state's exploitation of the payments system once the state assumed for itself
monopoly over the coinage.

Precious Metals Become Standards

Gold, although coined frequently, did not become a standard for at
least the first thousand years of coinage. Rather, the currencies of medieval Europe were based almost entirely on silver. The practical commercial reason for the monetization of gold in the thirteenth century
was the growth of European trade with Byzantium after the Crusades,
and with other Eastern areas that used gold. Florence and Venice became
the commercial centers for this trade. Silver was still the common currency in Europe, so the introduction of monetary gold stimulated a
movement toward bimetallism. Official bimetallism meant that the state
had to specify the unit of account in both gold and silver. In practice,
however, the "endless change in the [market] ratio of gold to silver,
necessitat[ed] continual revision of the [official] rate of exchange"
(Shaw [1896] 1967, 13).

The extensive use of gold and silver moneys in Europe and the
gradual adoption of de facto bimetallic standards gave rise to a mercantilist mind-set. "The wish of the 14th and 15th century ruler," observed Shaw, "was not only to defend his own stock of precious
metals,...but to attract to himself the stock of his neighbors by whatever craft" (Shaw [1896] 1967, 17). Minting operations continued to
be the prerogative of the king, and the "development of the law of
tender," Shaw wrote, "is to be traced to royal proclamations of the
King in Council long before it became the subject of parliamentary
legislation." These royal edicts prohibited the export of precious metals, banished foreign coins, or, if permitting them, prescribed "the rough
tariff or rate according to which coin for (native) coin should be
current....The two metals had grown to be the exchange medium; they
were actually there, and all that had to be done was to keep them there"
(Shaw [1896] 1967, viii–ix).

The regent's power to fix exchange rates by edict, and otherwise to
control the coinage, led to the perpetually recurring phenomenon of
devaluation. The nature of coined money, Shaw observed, "permitted

literally anything in the way of arbitrary manipulation" (Shaw [1896] 1967, xii). While gold and silver standards were very much a part of the mercantilist picture, this association did not result in a liberal economy and a free society. Rulers in the mercantilist era manipulated their precious metal standards primarily to generate revenues for their military expeditions and other state projects.

The mercantilistic dogma with its ideology of accumulated gold and silver gradually gave way to a new philosophy. By the end of the seventeenth century, as Shaw noted, devaluation and debasement "began to be impugned on theoretic grounds and in the course of the 18th century fell into disuse. Since that time [until the late nineteenth century] no Mint or legislative change...was made on the expressed value or [precious metal] content of any European coinage." The practice of state manipulation of the coinage ceased. Arbitrary mint ratios gave way to naturally determined commercial ratios, "and the regulation of the international flow of the precious metals was left to the oscillation of trade balances." This change was a revolution in theory, Shaw concluded. For before state monitoring of the "supply of precious metals at any cost and consideration could go by the board, the whole Mercantile theory must have lost its force in men's minds" (Shaw [1896] 1967, 160–61; Glasner 1989, 41–42).

Problems of Bimetallic Standards

A recurring technical problem with metallic standards that led to a great deal of governmental manipulation and downright bungling was the fact that both gold and silver vied for the stamp of standard. This condition arose naturally. Throughout history the relative scarcity of the two metals constantly altered their relative values, which varied from 13:1 in medieval times, to 40:1 by 1900, and to 80:1 by 1931 (Jastram 1981, 8). The superior monetary characteristics of both metals often resulted in both being minted as full-bodied coins with precise legal monetary values for each. The logical idea was to provide natural denominational differences for coinage systems.

Governments that instituted full-bodied bimetallic standards always had a housekeeping problem to contend with. The coins that were actually in use—silver as hand-to-hand currency and gold as a clearing medium for banks and international transactions—would in time wear down. Their denominations would become illegible and their reduced weights would belie their full-bodied values. The prince or other regent administering the coinage, if acting responsibly and in good faith, had then two options for managing the depreciated coin. First, he could offer publicly to recoin the pieces that were worn below some specified weight by supplementing the lost gold and silver from his own stocks. Since the prince had the fiscal power of taxing his dominion, the taxes used to furnish the precious metal necessary to bring the coins to full weight could have been viewed as a generalized "users' fee." A second option was for the ruling authority to call in all the coins worn below a certain amount, to recoin them into their old forms and denominations, and then to reissue them with slightly less precious metal in them.

If the ruling government used the first option, prices in the currency area served would tend to be less buoyant than otherwise; the lesser amount of precious metal would generate a smaller quantity of currency. Whether prices would fall or rise secularly would depend on the technical state of the art in the precious metals industry. If gold and silver production was generally booming, prices would rise in spite of the lost metal. Under the second option, prices would be more buoyant or less depressed because a given quantity of precious metal would produce a greater quantity of money. With the proper amount of devaluation, the internal price level could be maintained roughly constant.

Indeed, according to Luigi Einaudi, this general scheme of precious metal coinage was the one actually practiced in Europe during the medieval era (Einaudi [1937] 1970). Domestic households and businesses recognized and stated prices in what Einaudi described as "imaginary" money, or in what is now known as an abstract unit of account. They used "effective" money—precious metal coins of different weights—for settling international accounts. When prices fell, the local prince would issue a proclamation that reduced the metallic content of coins of given denominations—ideally, a reduction of the same proportion as the decline in prices. By this means, the effective quantity of money was increased, and prices tended to return to their former level. True, princes often mismanaged the coinage systems by extracting various amounts of seigniorage in addition to the nominal fees of recoinage (called brassage). To prevent such abuses of currency stewardship, men threw up constitutional obstacles. However, the abuses to the system, Einaudi concluded, did not gainsay the productive utility of a properly managed coinage (Einaudi [1937] 1970, 265–68).

A related problem within a bimetallic coinage system was a change in the relative market values of the two metals due to changes in their supply and demand factors. Over the long run the practical problem turned out to be the secular decline in the real value of silver, with respect especially to gold, but also relative to all other goods and services. If a responsible government wanted to maintain both coins in circulation when their relative market value changed, it had to decide whether to increase the silver content of the silver coins or to reduce the gold content of the gold coins. The latter policy was the one usually followed, for example, the 6 percent devaluation of the U.S. gold dollar in 1834 (McCulloch, 1995).

Any devaluation of this sort had two notable characteristics. First, it was a small-percentage marginal change undertaken in an attempt to maintain both metals in circulation. Second, it was for housekeeping purposes only. The change in the defined metallic medium was not supposed to provide any significant amount of seigniorage for the government. Otherwise, the metal that became cheaper in the market would go to the mint, while the now dearer coin would be converted into bullion and exported or used for nonmonetary purposes. This phenomenon, known as Gresham's Law, has been observed for centuries. It can only occur, however, when the state defines quantities of both metals and invests both of them with legal tender properties (Einaudi [1937] 1970, 260; Rothbard 1962).

The tendency for the cheaper metal to go to the mint did not ordinarily mean that the dearer metal would disappear entirely from circulation. Market values change gently and incrementally. So even as the cheaper metal began to dominate the coinage, much of the dearer metal would remain in circulation. The costs of removing it from the coinage system exceeded the profits arbitrageurs could realize from their well-publicized swaps (Friedman 1992, chapter 6).

Neil Carothers noted in his classic work, *Fractional Money*, that the disparity between the mint and market ratios of silver and gold in the United States in the period 1834 to 1859 was only about 1 percent. Since many silver coins, especially Spanish pieces, were worn down by more than 1 percent of their original size, and since the costs of arbitrage transactions of silver for gold averaged around 1 percent, most of the fractional silver coins remained in circulation. Only when the U.S. Treasury in 1844 started recoining the worn and defaced silver pieces into new quarters and dimes were they driven out by the adverse ratio (Carothers [1930] 1967, 98–101).

A change in the market ratio that triggered Gresham's Law was a part of the bimetallist strategy. As one metal became cheaper, either

from natural causes or from legislated changes in the official mint ratio, the "burden" of monetization would shift to the cheaper metal.
Since the actual event of monetization added significantly to the market demand for either metal, monetization of the cheaper metal arrested
the real decline in its value (Friedman 1992). That is, the price level
would stop rising and stabilize until one or the other metal again became cheaper. Finally, whenever a much cheaper currency, such as fiat
paper, drove up all market prices, full-bodied coins disappeared entirely because their commodity values far exceeded their fixed mint
values. Private businesses, banks, and municipalities then produced
token and paper currencies to serve as exchange media (Timberlake
1981, 856–66).

In England gold was monetarily undervalued relative to silver until
the early eighteenth century. On the recommendation of Sir Isaac New-
ton, who was Master of the Mint at the time, Parliament raised the mint
value of gold and the ratio of gold-to-silver in 1717 from 14.485:1 to
15.21:1, which was the highest relative mint value in Europe. England,
consequently, was on a de facto gold standard until 1797. In 1798 the
government discontinued the unused service of free silver coinage altogether (Hawtrey 1939, 82).

Enter the French Revolution and the Napoleonic era. The monetary
end product of these upheavals left the French system on a bimetallic
standard with a ratio of 15.5:1. Silver was the standard in all other
European countries, while gold, already the de facto standard in England, became the exclusive standard de jure after the passage of the
Coinage Act of 1816.

In the United States the ratio was 15:1 until 1834; but by the Currency Act in that year, the ratio became almost 16:1. Consequently,
England and the United States, who were major international trading
partners, were effectively on gold standards, while France and the rest
of Europe remained on de facto silver standards (Hawtrey 1939, 82–
86; Fetter [1965] 1978, 64–67).

Neil Carothers noted that the favorable-to-gold ratio of 16:1 adopted
in 1834 in the United States had at least three roots. First, commercial
interests wanted gold in circulation for general business purposes and
to enhance trade with England. Second, provincial interests in Georgia
and North Carolina wanted to subsidize home industry. Third, antibank ideologues wanted a gold currency to replace the notes of the
Second Bank of the United States in order to "hasten the destruction of
that ill-fated institution" (Carothers [1930] 1967, 92). Carothers noted

nothing about minimizing the role and scope of the government in monetary affairs. Ratification of the Constitution and the Bill of Rights had presumably settled that issue.

The Nineteenth-Century Gold Standard as an Obstacle to State Intervention

Specie standards or not, governments flooded many of the world's monetary systems with legal tender, or quasi-legal tender, paper money at various times during the nineteenth century. The injections of paper money had similar effects in virtually all cases. As governments spent the money in the private sector, business firms and households, who received it for goods and services, would deposit it in banks. Because the paper money was receivable for government dues, it would become bank reserves and initiate bank credit expansions. Banks would issue their own notes and create new derivative deposits. Prices would rise. At some point banks, private households, business firms, and government treasuries would realize that too much common money was present for the maintenance of specie payments. Everyone would then begin to redeem bank money and hoard gold and silver in the anticipation that mint prices would be unsustainable. Sure enough, suspension of note and deposit redemptions would follow. This pattern of events occurred, not just during the American Civil War, but also in England during the Napoleonic Wars. After hostilities and the issues of paper money ended, questions always arose of how, when, where, and—sometimes—whether to return to specie convertibility.

When the question of the return to a metallic standard was prominent in England before the Act of 1819, the adherents of the gold standard relied on "dogmatic assertions of the injustice of any other system" and the impossibility of devising any system of currency that would have more stability of value than a precious metal standard (Viner 1937, 214). David Ricardo was one who furthered such arguments. "The only use of a standard," he wrote, "is to regulate the quantity, and by the quantity the value of the currency....Without a standard [the value of the monetary unit] would be exposed to all the fluctuations to which the ignorance or the [special] interests of the issuers might subject it" (Ricardo [1816] 1923, 162).

Circumstances as much as ideology, however, were responsible for the ponderous trend toward a universal gold standard in the latter half of the nineteenth century. The primary circumstance was the discovery of new low-cost gold supplies in the western United States and Australia near mid-century. This development tended to lower the market value of gold and put a monetary premium on silver. Since much of the now cheaper gold was monetized and thereby displaced silver, "pragmatists" argued that gold should be the only standard. In addition, the loss of silver currency due to its undervaluation at the mint seemed to necessitate something beyond improvisation by private business firms as a means for satisfying the need for smaller denominational currency. Fiduciary silver currency was a logical answer. To fill the important role of a fractional money, the conventional wisdom held, silver could not remain one of the standards. It had to become a knave instead of a king, and gold had to become the exclusive standard (Carothers [1930] 1967, 137).

The conventional wisdom in this case, as in many others, turned out to be wrong. Just as gold became cheaper in the 1850s, so silver became cheaper after 1875. It could just as easily have shared the monetary function with gold, except that one country after another between 1870 and 1900 demonetized it as a standard money metal. Silver went begging and declined significantly in value relative to gold—all of which proved, not any great volatility in the value of silver, but only the significant impact that standardization had on the value of the money metal chosen as the standard (Friedman 1992, chapter 3; Timberlake 1993, chapter 12).

Other political and social circumstances moved the world's monetary systems toward monometallic gold standards between 1840 and 1900. Germany took its first step toward gold as a result of the payment of the French indemnity during 1871–73. The new German unit of account, the mark, was a gold unit, and the mints were closed to the free coinage of silver. By the Gold Currency Act of 1900, gold also became the exclusive standard in the United States (Hepburn 1924, 376–78). In Russia the gold standard became law in 1897 (Conant [1896] 1969, 263–65). In Austria-Hungary the gold standard was restored in 1892 after a prolonged period of fiat paper money, similar to what occurred in the United States between 1862 and 1879. Leland Yeager notes, "Its Austrian supporters saw the gold standard less as a transmitter of foreign disturbances than as a means of cushioning domestic disturbances by linkages with the presumably more stable world economy" (Yeager 1984, 653). There, as well as in Russia, arguments for monetary reform with a dominant gold standard also reflected state hegemony rather than a move toward a monetary rule of law. In case a future war should encourage another bout of inflationary paper currency, a government could extract more resources by issues of paper money if it started its inflation from an uninflated base! (Yeager 1984, 654; Rist [1938] 1966, 321; Glasner 1989, chapter 2).

The second round of gold discoveries in the Yukon and South Africa in the 1890s provided enough gold even for populist consumption. The pleasing buoyancy of world trade up to 1914 complemented the formal adoption of gold standards throughout the trading world.

Specie Standards Compromised by Central Banks

Unannounced, however, a new institution had appeared keeping company with the gold standard: the central bank. Although not originally labeled as such, institutions that came to be known as "central banks" were not at first true central banks in the modern sense. They were, like the Bank of England and the banks of the United States, *public* banks doing banking business for the governments that sponsored or chartered them, and they were also *commercial* banks dealing with private households and business firms. They became *central* banks, having a contrived and deliberate effect on national monetary systems, only as a derivative of their prior governmental connection (Timberlake 1993, chapter 16; Smith [1936] 1990, 8–24, 167–69; Dowd 1989, chapter 5).

Metallic standards, central banks, and legal tender laws all had an interrelated historical development in the nineteenth century. As gold and silver standards became widespread and prominent, embryonic central banks appeared as though the adoption of the former prescribed the emergence of the latter. These institutions were sometimes state chartered and partially controlled by the state's representatives on their boards of directors, or they were strictly regulated by the state, or they were completely owned by the state. Their commercial and public connections made them a sort of liaison between the private financial world and their governments, which generously endowed them with deposits of tax revenues, monopoly control of note issue, and other privileges. Central bank notes were widely accepted because of the ubiquitous presence of the banks and their branches, because the notes originally were redeemable on demand in precious metals, and because governments received the notes as tender for taxes and duties. When financial crises threatened, all eyes both in the private sector and in the government turned to the financial professionals who managed the banks of

178 The History of the Modern International Monetary System

issue. If the now central bank was on its toes, it followed the Bagehot principle of lending freely on any "subjunctive" security—a security that would be good in normal times—at high interest rates. Only in central banks were there reserves of a magnitude that could alleviate a liquidity crisis (Bagehot 1906, 199–201; Timberlake 1993, chapter 16; Goodhart 1988, 85–102; Smith [1936] 1990, 14–16, 167–70).

Central bank currency was not only redeemable in specie but was frequently made a forced tender for debts due to and payable by the sponsoring governments. Gold and silver, while still the official standards, became more and more concentrated in central banks and of concern only to central bankers (Conant [1896] 1969). In the United States, which had no central bank, the Treasury Department performed a virtually identical central banking role as an issuer of paper currency and as the specie reserve-holding agency that administered the government's issues of legal tender notes (Timberlake 1993, chapter 16; Taus 1943).

The world's currencies in the latter half of the nineteenth century thus tended to become fiduciary—not gold or silver themselves, but redeemable in the precious metals if anyone wanted to go to the trouble. Most people were satisfied with central bank notes, which were, with their gold backing and legal tender properties, unquestionably acceptable. Hence, the precious metals went into central bank sequestration just as the governments of the world almost universally adopted gold standards (Dowd 1989, chapter 6).

World War I broke the link between central bank note issues and the gold reserved for their redemption. Even though the postwar period witnessed the gradual and partial return to ongoing gold standards, those systems were now gold bullion standards or gold-exchange standards. Gold was so remote from ordinary transactions of households and business firms that the general public saw only token amounts— five-dollar gold pieces for birthdays and such. Nevertheless, the reserves of gold in the central banks and government treasuries still operated as a constraint on the issue of governmental currencies. Even if private citizens no longer had occasion to redeem paper currency for gold, international traders did. So central banks had a vital interest in guarding and claiming the gold that gave their note issues respectability (Rist [1938] 1966, 423–25).

The extension of central bank prerogatives in the 1930s and 1940s saw yet another phase in the developing schism between gold and common moneys. During the worldwide depression of the time, central banks and the governments they served engaged in a competitive scramble for the gold that was still by law the basis of official currencies (Glasner 1989). But by now the central banks had assumed the initiative for money creation. From an exogenous element that ebbed and flowed because of international market forces, gold became a manipulable variable to be fit into the monetary system in a way that would not threaten official policy goals, such as "full" employment, balances of trade, interest rates, and all the rest. "The central banks of issue," Charles Rist wrote critically, "had departed further and further from the position of distributors of gold among the world's money markets, and had become purely national instruments for the creation of money" (Rist [1938] 1966, 425).

Ludwig von Mises, one of the most persuasive of contemporary gold standard advocates, noted in 1912: "[The gold standard] introduces an incalculable factor into economic activity." Nonetheless, he emphasized, the gold standard also acts as "an instrument for the protection of civil liberties against despotic inroads on the part of governments. Ideologically it belongs in the same class with political constitutions and bills of rights" (von Mises [1912] 1980, 27, 454).

Mise's elegant statement reflected a large body of classical liberal thought on the hoped-for-role of the gold standard as a major element in the rule of law. Aside from the question of whether the gold standard was devised for this purpose, the important question is whether this particular "emperor" had any clothes. Were the strictures that the gold standard would impose on arbitrary and discretionary actions by the state rigorous enough to thwart determined efforts by political pragmatists to manipulate monetary systems to their own benefit?

An opinion to the contrary—a very jaundiced opinion—on this question was given by Gustav Cassel in his book, *The Downfall of the Gold Standard* (1936). Cassel extended and elaborated on Rist's criticisms, which were written at about the same time. In the first place, Cassel noted, the gold standard as an international system was short-lived. It lasted only from the mid-1870s to 1914, or for about forty years. Even this brief period was enough to expose the "inherent weakness of the system," which was a high degree of instability in the values of the national money units tied to gold. Cassel argued, in agreement with Rist, that central banks would seldom allow the adjustment mechanism of the international gold standard to work if doing so violated "national" interests. Rather, they established gold reserve positions so that they could counteract what they considered undesirable movements of gold. Even without central banks, capital flows in financial markets could have accomplished the same neutralizing effects (Cassel 1936, 1–6).

Central bank gold policy, Cassel continued, became a competition among central banks to accumulate gold. The demand for gold was no longer a spontaneous market reaction based on economic behavior but a central bank demand based on political motivations. This kind of contrived "gold standard" had several undesirable features, including an increase in protectionism to prevent outflows of gold due to balance of trade deficits, and a reluctance of wealthier economic units to invest their resources abroad because of monetary uncertainties prompted by central bank infighting. The system had, in fact, regressed to mercantilist policies with central banks taking over the role formerly played by royal treasuries (Cassel 1936, 12–15). Cassel claimed that only the British were on a true gold standard prior to 1914, in that only in the London gold market was gold always freely available and the redeemability of sterling unlimited. Therefore, he concluded, the "international" gold standard was in practice a "pound sterling" gold standard (Cassel 1936, 16; Bordo 1984, 67–77).

Cassel's review was not so much a criticism of the gold standard as it was an indictment of central bank interference with what would have been the purely economic operations of the gold standard. He noted that of all the forces arrayed against an operational gold standard in the 1930s, U.S. government policies were the most formidable. Huge quantities of gold came into the United States in the 1920s and 1930s. By January 1933, Cassel reported, the U.S. Treasury's gold reserves exceeded $4 billion and were more than one-third of the world's total. At about the same time, all of this gold was declared "off limits" to any private demands for conversion because the President and Congress had determined that private gold transactions were "contrary to the public interest." Policies of the U.S. government discouraged both the ownership and use of monetary gold at the same time that politicians were lauding its function of "backing" legal tender paper money. Devaluation of the gold dollar in 1934 increased the dollar value of the government's gold stock 69 percent (Cassel 1936, 112–34). Subsequently, a continuing tide of gold flowed into the U.S. Treasury. By 1940 this stockpile amounted to over twenty thousand tons! More and more gold accumulated in the U.S. and other world treasuries, but became less and less available for satisfying demands for the redemption of common money.[3]

The Metallic Standard as a Force Promoting
Constitutional Money

The evolution of metallic commodity moneys to metallic standard moneys coincided at times with the evolution of individual rights to life, liberty, and property, and constitutional government. The argument that links the concept of a limited role for the government in monetary affairs to enhanced economic freedom and general social well-being is appealing. If the correlation is also causation, the case for a return to a true gold standard is very strong.

The summary evidence on metallic moneys over three millennia suggests the following conclusions:

1. Commodity money evolved as naturally and as spontaneously as the wheel, the screw, the hydraulic press, the inclined plane, a national language, and common law. Its emergence was economic and natural, not political and contrived. Nonetheless, as Friedman and Schwartz observe, "History suggests both that any privately generated unit of account will be linked to a commodity and that government will not long keep aloof" (Friedman and Schwartz 1986, 8, 11). If free private competitive enterprise can produce a viable money without government, they note, it has yet to do so.[4]

2. Government's initial intervention in commodity-money systems was often excusable—simply the certification of weight and fineness by stamp and seal. If the governmental function had stopped at simple specifications for coin denominations, monetary systems would have suffered no more abuse than systems of weights and measures. But as frequently and as universally as governments adopted the power of standardizing the units of currency, just as inevitably they assumed the monopoly right to coin the metal themselves. Monopoly coinage became a device for raising state revenue. The nominal fee that the state charged for the minting function was easy to exploit. If the charge was, say, one-fourth of 1 percent of the coined metal, what was to prevent it from becoming 10 percent or 20 percent?

3. Metallic money failed not only in protecting against usurpation of private wealth by the state, it even lent itself to the fleecing process, as the research of Shaw indicated. Strong-armed state mercantilism in European economies occurred in the presence of metallic standards, which were at that time simply vehicles of state policy. Not until constitutional republics appeared in the eighteenth and nineteenth centuries was the principle of a metallic standard linked to the principle of

limited government. Otherwise, the standard was not the lever that constrained governments.

4. The gold standard that became an international system in the nineteenth century was not only, nor even primarily, a reaction to state excesses. It was more a result of favorable circumstances—particularly, of two fortuitous expansions of world gold production in the 1850s and 1890s. With gold supplies of this magnitude, the popular norms of buoyant prices and low interest rates were realized without recourse to the free coinage of ever more abundant silver or the excessive circulation of ever prevalent fiat money.

5. The emergence of central banking was a most pernicious influence on the viability of the gold standard. In order to function as a self-regulatory, undirected monetary institution, the gold standard did not need state accommodation or support in any sense. Governments did not need to create central banks to keep gold reserve balances or to print paper money with gold backing. They did not need to establish mints in order to coin precious metals, nor to specify gold reserve requirements for commercial banks, nor to prohibit private bank notes and branching. If any of these "protective" actions had been beneficial, free private competitive enterprises would have initiated them without central bank intervention because the costs and benefits of each such action would have been (or were) clearly recognized by the economic agents in those markets. For example, private coin smiths in the United States produced gold coins a few grains above the standard set by federal law until their enterprises were stopped in the 1860s by proscriptive laws that gave the federal government a monopoly on all coinage (Carothers [1930] 1967, 128; White 1984b).

6. Central banks became surrogates for the gold standard. To begin with, they held government balances that arose from tax or tariff collections. Since even a limited government's balances were substantial, and since governments wanted their deposits secure, the central bank depositories had to maintain sizable specie reserves. Their recognized relationships to their sponsoring governments also argued for endowing their notes with partial legal tender properties. Consequently, their notes, rather than specie, came to serve as reserves for commercial banks, and only they had substantial gold reserves. When a liquidity crisis appeared in the commercial banking sector, the central banks were the only institutions that had the means to save anyone and everyone (Humphrey and Keleher 1984; Timberlake 1993, chapter 16).

Ancient, medieval, renaissance, and classical thinkers could envisage only one kind of money—one based on a precious metal—that would maintain its real value for any length of time. This property was desirable for both economic and political reasons. A specie standard was, therefore, necessary for its time but proved not to be sufficient for insulating monetary systems from state indiscretion.

Decline of Gold Standards and Rationalizations for Paper Money

The gold standard status quo prior to 1914 may have lulled constitutionalists into the false notion that the greenbacks and other government-issued paper moneys were no longer a threat to monetary security. As an adjunct to the gold standard, the early Federal Reserve System promised to make the monetary system work more smoothly, and to do so on the solid basis of a monetary standard reaffirmed in gold (Timberlake 1993, chapter 15).

Over the following decades, however, especially in the 1930s, another momentous sea change in monetary practices took place. After 1934, federal law prohibited gold altogether for domestic monetary use. Federal Reserve notes—latter day greenbacks—became the legal tender medium. While some economists, such as Walter Spahr and other gold standard "extremists," objected to this kind of unconstitutional manipulation, the large majority of economists accepted the change as both necessary and desirable (Rothbard 1962, 113–28). Managed money, they held, was necessary to mitigate boom and bust. Under a gold standard, the "guidance of human wisdom" could not function because the monetary system was on an automatic pilot that was insensitive to signals for adjustment. The few economists and historians who treated the legal tender issue looked at the Supreme Court's monetary decisions and found them both valid and good because the decisions enlarged Congress' hands-on control of the monetary system (Kemp 1956).

The banking historian Bray Hammond was one who applauded the evolution of monetary control from a self-regulating specie standard to a politically controlled central bank. Hammond interpreted the money clauses in the Constitution as implying that the framers wanted the federal government, and not the state governments, to control the money supply. The federal government, Hammond argued without any supporting citation, had "responsibilities imposed upon it by the Constitution" to regulate the supply of money, whatever that money happened to be. Wrapping all of Congress' express powers into one package—to lay and collect taxes, regulate commerce, coin money, fix standards of weights and measures—plus everything else that was "necessary and proper," Hammond claimed, substantiated Congress' powers over the monetary system. The judicial arguments that support this interpretation, Hammond admitted, lead to the "anomaly of the monetary function being considered...with little attention to what the Constitution says about [money], but with attention chiefly to what the Constitution says about interstate commerce[!]" (Hammond 1957, 109–13).

Hammond's arguments, including the reference to the interstate commerce clause, simply parroted earlier Supreme Court decisions on the greenbacks.[5] Neither Hammond nor others who used this line of thought ever addressed the question of why a document as profoundly reasoned as the Constitution would provide principles for monetary policy by implication from the clauses on interstate commerce. What is to say that the clauses on interstate commerce were not based on the norms in the clauses on money, or for that matter on the clauses dealing with foreign affairs?

Gerald Dunne, a legal historian of monetary court cases, agreed with Hammond's principle contention—that the Constitution's primary monetary purpose, rather than limiting severely the monetary powers of the state and federal governments, was to provide sovereign federal controls over the supply of money (Dunne 1960, "Preface," 24 n). Dunne observed that "judicial appraisal of legal tender began by considering it as a provisional [Civil War] expedient and closed by investing it with a legitimacy that was both permanent and beyond judicial control" (Dunne 1960, 83).

An even later treatise, *A Legal History of Money in the United States* by James Willard Hurst, cited and supported Hammond's and Dunne's arguments on Congress' alleged powers over the money supply. The legal tender power, Hurst claimed, "served the general interest in ready conduct of market transactions and in ready government allocation of economic resources." One "contribution" that legal tender status gave to money tokens, Hurst claimed, was the "help" it provided in determining the quantity of money; a second "contribution" was its "help" in promoting "the practical acceptance of given money tokens" (Hurst 1973, 40–43).

Hurst found no constitutional problem with any of the federal government's assumptions of monetary powers. He also seemed ignorant of the monetary operations of a gold standard. He concluded that Congress and the Court "did not go beyond the limit, in light of the indicated constitutional intent [?] that the national government *fully control the system of money* and that it enjoy broad authority to promote a truly national economy" (Hurst 1973, 195–96, emphasis added). And Hammond fatuously observed that "changes in [federal] statutes and [Supreme Court] jurisprudence have strengthened the Constitution's ban on issues of money by individual states *but have nullified completely the original intent* that the federal government should have no power to make anything but the precious metals legal tender" (Hammond 1957, 109, emphasis added). If a constitution can be so frivolously interpreted, it is no longer a constitution.

The Government's Monetary Role
Under a "Perfect" Constitution

Up until the time of the Civil War, almost no one had seriously considered interpreting the money clauses in the Constitution in any light except that of prohibiting state and federal issues of paper currency on the basis of discretionary authority. "To coin money" meant to provide the technical facilities for minting coins. "Regulate the value thereof" meant only to specify a weight of fine gold or silver as equal to a number of the units of account, which were dollars. "Regulate," while it may have been a questionable choice for the proper verb, did not mean "determine the supply of money," either of precious metal or of paper. Indeed, the very act of adopting a specie standard precluded the idea or possibility that "regulate the value" meant anything more complex than simply "specify the weight." The specie standard by its very nature is self-regulating, as all the framers knew or sensed. Clearly, a self-regulating system is incompatible with any kind of policy-inspired manipulation. The only regulation implied by "regulate" was the small-scale kind of housekeeping change in the specifications of the units of account that would keep both precious metals current as money. This problem was inherent and chronic in the management of bimetallic standards.

The First and Second Banks of the United States were not examples of governmental *monetary* agencies, as Bray Hammond and later observers alleged. Congress created both these institutions to assist the Treasury with its fiscal operations. Not only were the banks not vested with either express or implied powers to control the quantity of money, but the debates on their creation explicitly denied them such license. In the circumstances of their existence, the banks' directors were able to assume some unauthorized monetary controls; but no grant of such powers appears anywhere in their charters nor by any implied understanding between their directors and the government (Timberlake 1993, chapter 16).

The framers knew what they were doing. They founded a simple monetary system—a gold and silver standard—that would regulate itself. Their system would work no matter how many unchartered commercial banks issued currency and deposits. As long as banking enterprises obeyed the rules prohibiting force and fraud, redeemed their demand obligations in specie, and were subject to the pressures of free and open competition, they needed no more regulation than blacksmiths or cart-wrights (White 1984a; Selgin 1988).

One may wonder, in reviewing monetary history from the time of the Founding Fathers to the present, just where was the Achilles' heel in policy that allowed Congress, presidents, and Supreme Courts the opportunity to breach the rule of law and substitute fiat paper money for the gold and silver of the Constitution.

Robert Greenfield and Leland Yeager have recently proposed a norm for monetary policy that suggests an answer to this question. The Greenfield-Yeager proposal distinguishes the monetary unit of account from the medium of exchange, the distinction that Luigi Einaudi recounted as unofficial medieval policy. The unit of account in the United States is the dollar, while the medium of exchange is the Federal Reserve note. Greenfield and Yeager contend that only an accident of polity makes the two things synonymous in people's minds. For the practical purpose of getting the government (in the guise of the Federal Reserve System) out of any policy-making role, Greenfield and Yeager prescribe that Congress specify the unit-of-account dollar to be of a value equal to a market price index made up of a limited array of staple, conventional, basic commodities—items that would ideally mirror an all-markets average of prices. The government would not involve itself in keeping this price index constant by manipulating the quantity of money, nor by other means. It would leave this function to dealers and arbitrageurs in financial and commodity markets (Greenfield and Yeager 1983; Einaudi [1937] 1970; White 1984b).

Greenfield and Yeager's analysis and prescription serve to illustrate what the constitutional framers, if they had been omniscient, should have done, and what the fatal weakness in Congress' monetary powers turned out to be. "Regulate the value" of gold and silver coins is analogous, with obvious qualifications, to the specification of the unit of account as the value of a bundle of commodities in the Greenfield and Yeager model. The framers put this provision in the same clause that had Congress providing a system of weights and measures. Unfortunately, they also allowed Congress the power to coin the money that it was supposed to regulate. Coining money is analogous to producing the medium of exchange in the Greenfield-Yeager system—a function they deny the government. However, a viable and stable monetary system no more requires government coinage than a usable weights and measures system requires government production of weights and yardsticks (McCulloch 1995). Apparently, the prevailing sentiment for governmental coinage at the time of the Constitutional Convention was an uneasiness that private coin smiths might not do an effective job, or that the prevalence of Spanish-produced coins in use at the time sullied the prestige of the fledgling U.S. government.

Without the coinage power, Congress would have had no reason to debase the coinage and to monopolize currency production in their ongoing quest for seignorage. Likewise, the Supreme Court would have had no opportunity nor incentive to validate Congress's transgressions of its constitutional limits. William Brough stated the case: "Clearly there is no need of making coin a legal tender at any specified weight. If governments would confine their legislation to fixing by enactment the fineness of the precious metal and the number of grains that shall constitute each piece of a given name, they may safely leave the maintenance of coinage...and the value of the pieces to be regulated [to] individual interest and action" (Brough [1896] 1969, 34–35).

The valid part of Schumpeter's quotation used as an epigraph above is the idea of an "automatic" institution free of governmental manipulation. The gold standard might have qualified as Schumpeter's "badge," but experience has denied that it is the "guarantee" of bourgeois freedom. What is needed to maximize individual freedoms and economic productivity is a market-directed monetary system completely free from any possible governmental intervention.

To insist on a gold-standard monetary system in today's world would very possibly shut out technically more efficient payment systems that would also more effectively constrain the state (Friedman and Schwartz 1986, 9–10). Also, a return to a gold standard at the present time would likely be accompanied by mercantilist trade policies and extensive central bank manipulation to prevent the economic adjustments that are constantly necessary under a truly automatic gold standard.

If a gold (or gold and silver) standard is to be a viable system, and not just a facade for a central bank's discretionary control, it must be an exclusive institution that develops endogenously from inside the monetary community. To reinstitute a metallic standard in the United States today, all the federal government connections to and controls over money and monetary institutions would have to be severed so that the system would revert to the status quo of the Constitution. The steps for undoing that which ought not to have been done would include the following: First, all Federal Reserve Banks and branches would have to be privatized. They would very likely become a modern day counterpart of the nineteenth century's clearinghouse associations. Second, the Federal Reserve Board of Governors and its institutional trappings in Washington would have to be abolished. Third, the Federal Reserve's already created money stock—Federal Reserve notes and depository institution deposit accounts—would have to be frozen at existing levels. Fourth, the U.S. Treasury's gold stock—8,200 tons— would have to be popularly distributed.[6] I would suggest a per capita distribution of one ounce to every legal citizen of the United States in some early year as an income tax "rebate." This gold, which would now be owned by private citizens, could become (and likely would become) the basis for a true, operational gold monetary system. Individuals would deposit their gold in banks as gold checking accounts redeemable only in gold. The gold units would have a market price in the frozen stock of Federal Reserve greenbacks. But since gold would now be used extensively as money, the gold money unit would also have a price in terms of ordinary goods and services. Henceforth, the stock of common money would grow only as the gold stock grew.

The advantages of a restored gold money as an entrée to a government-free monetary system are that it could be made intuitively plausible and acceptable to the general public, and that it is technically feasible without any significant monetary or financial upheaval. But while gold is the most attractive vehicle for uncoupling money from governmental manipulation, acceptance of a gold system should not preclude, by law or otherwise, alternative monetary arrangements from developing in the presence of a competitive private market for money. Gold has been the money of the ages, but innovations such as money market deposit accounts would perhaps in time supplant gold. We should always provide for the possibility that better things than what we can imagine today may emerge.

The fundamental lesson given by the history of monetary insitutions is that some set of principles, rules, or covenants—such as a constitution—must constrain the state generally if the state's discretion with respect to money is also to be limited. A metallic monetary standard is a complementary constraining principle in a constitution, but it cannot by itself keep the state in check.

Notes

1. See especially Glasner's discussion of the complementary functions of coinage and sovereignty as an explanation of the state's eternal monopolization of the coinage and base money.
2. Burns here makes the common mistake of regarding state certification as a necessary condition for the existence of money. The state could (and did) assume for itself legal tender powers, but money came into existence before the state had anything to do with it. Indeed, the state and its legal tender powers turned good private money into bad "official" money.
3. For a contemporary account of how and why central banks manipulated gold stocks and moneys in pursuit of various objectives, see Goodfriend 1991, section 4, and Glasner 1989, chapter 2.
4. For possible microeconomic exceptions, see Timberlake 1987; White 1984b.
5. For an account of the Supreme Court's astounding "constitutional" justification of the greenbacks, see Timberlake 1991, 11–42.
6. Murray Rothbard discusses some of these institutional prerequisites in his article, "The Case for a 100 Percent Gold Dollar" (Rothbard 1962). However, Rothbard's revision would (1) eliminate all existing Federal Reserve money, (2) commission the government to try and find an appropriate gold price, and (3) prescribe that gold at the previously fixed price back other money 100 percent. For many diverse reasons, I do not concur on these points. The principal desideratum for stability in the monetary system is to abolish all government controls and powers over the production of money. Rothbard's system would retain much of the government's presence.

References

Bagehot, Walter. 1906. *Lombard Street*. 12th ed. London: Kegan Paul, Trench, Trubner and Co.

Bordo, Michael. 1984. "The Gold Standard: The Traditional Approach." In *A Retrospective on the Classical Gold Standard*, edited by Michael Bordo and Anna J. Schwartz, 23–117. Chicago: University of Chicago Press.

Brough, William. [1896] 1969. *The Natural Law of Money*. New York: Greenwood Press. Original edition, New York: G.P. Putnam's Sons.

Burns, Arthur Robert. [1927] 1965. *Money and Monetary Policy in Early Times*. New York: Augustus M. Kelly. Original edition, New York: Alfred A. Knopf.

Carothers, Neil. [1930] 1967. *Fractional Money*. New York: Augustus M. Kelly. Original edition, New York: John Wiley and Sons.

Cassel, Gustav. 1936. *The Downfall of the Gold Standard*. Oxford: Clarendon Press.

Conant, Charles A. [1896] 1969. *A History of Modern Banks of Issue*. New York: Augustus M. Kelly.

Dowd, Kevin. 1989. *The State and the Monetary System*. New York: St. Martin's Press.

Dunne, Gerald T. 1960. *Monetary Decisions of the Supreme Court*. New Brunswick, NJ: Rutgers University Press.

Einaudi, Luigi. [1937] 1970. "The Medieval Practice of Managed Currency." In *The Lessons of Monetary Experience, Essays in Honor of Irving Fisher*, edited by

Arthur D. Gayer, 259–68. New York: Augustus M. Kelly. Original edition, New York: Rhinehart and Co.

Fetter, Frank Whitson. [1965] 1978. *Development of British Monetary Orthodoxy.* Fairfield, NJ: Augustus M. Kelly. Original edition, Cambridge, MA: Harvard University Press.

Friedman, Milton. 1992. *Money Mischief.* New York: Harcourt Brace Jovanovich.

Friedman, Milton, and Anna J. Schwartz. 1986. "Has Government Any Role in Money?" *Journal of Monetary Economics* 11 (January): 37–62.

Glasner, David. 1989. *Free Banking and Monetary Reform.* Cambridge, MA: Cambridge University Press.

Goodfriend, Marvin. 1991. "Central Banking under the Gold Standard." *Carnegie-Rochester Series on Public Policy.* Rochester, NY: University of Rochester.

Goodhart, Charles. 1988. *The Evolution of Central Banks.* Cambridge, MA: MIT Press.

Greenfield, Robert L., and Leland B. Yeager. 1983. "A Laissez-Faire Approach to Monetary Stability." *Journal of Money, Credit and Banking* 15, 3 (August): 302–15.

Hammond, Bray. 1957. *Banks and Politics in America.* Princeton, NJ: Princeton University Press.

Hawtrey, R. G. 1939. *The Gold Standard in Theory and Practice.* 4th ed. London: Longmans, Green and Co.

Hepburn, A. Barton. 1924. *A History of Currency in the United States.* Rev. ed., New York: MacMillan.

Humphrey, Thomas, and Robert E. Keleher. 1984. "The Lender of Last Resort: A Historical Perspective." *The Cato Journal* 4 (Spring/Summer): 275–318.

Hurst, James Willard. 1973. *A Legal History of Money in the United States, 1774–1970.* Lincoln: University of Nebraska Press.

Jastram, Roy W. 1981. *Silver the Restless Metal.* New York: John Wiley and Sons.

Kemp, Arthur. 1956. *The Legal Qualities of Money.* New York: Pageant Press.

McCulloch, Huston. 1995. "The Crime of 1834: Comment." In *Money and Banking: The American Experience,* edited by John W. Robbins. Fairfax, VA: George Mason University Press.

Menger, Carl. [1871] 1981. *Principles of Economics.* New York: New York University Press. Translated by James Dingwall and Bert Hoselitz. Original German edition, Vienna.

Ricardo, David. [1816] 1923. *Economic Essays,* edited by E. C. D. Gonner. London: G. Bell and Sons.

Rist, Charles. [1938] 1966. *History of Monetary and Credit Theory.* New York: Augustus M. Kelly. Original edition, Paris.

Rothbard, Murray. 1962. "The Case for a 100 Percent Gold Dollar." In *In Search of a Monetary Constitution,* edited by Leland Yeager. Cambridge, MA: Harvard University Press.

Schumpeter, Joseph A. 1954. *History of Economic Analysis.* New York: Oxford University Press.

Selgin, George. 1988. *The Theory of Free Banking.* Totowa, NJ: Rowan and Littlefield.

Shaw, W. A. [1896] 1967. *The History of Currency.* 2d ed. New York: Augustus M. Kelly. Original edition, London: Wilsons and Milne.

Smith, Vera. [1936] 1990. *The Rationale of Central Banking and the Free Banking Alternative.* Indianapolis, IN: Liberty Press. Original edition, Westminster, England: P.S. King and Son, Ltd.

Taus, Esther R. 1943. *Central Banking Functions of the U.S. Treasury, 1789–1941.* New York: Columbia University Press.

Timberlake, Richard H. 1981. "The Significance of Unaccounted Currencies." *Journal of Economic History* 41 (December): 853–66.

———. 1987. "Private Production of Scrip-Money in the Isolated Community." *Journal of Money, Credit and Banking* 19 (November): 437–47.

———. 1991. *Gold, Greenbacks and the Constitution*. Berryville, VA: Durrell Foundation.

———. 1993. *Monetary Policy in the United States*. Chicago: University of Chicago Press.

Viner, Jacob. 1937. *Studies in the Theory of International Trade*. New York: Harper and Brothers.

von Mises, Ludwig. [1912] 1980. *The Theory of Money and Credit*. Translated by H. E. Batson. Indianapolis, IN: Liberty Classics. Original edition, Germany.

White, Lawrence H. 1984a. *Free Banking in Britain*. Cambridge, MA: Cambridge University Press.

———. 1984b. "Competitive Payments Systems and the Unit of Account." *American Economic Review* 74, 1 (September): 699–712.

———. 1989. *Competition and Currency*. New York: New York University Press.

Yeager, Leland, ed. 1962. *In Search of a Monetary Constitution*. Cambridge, MA: Harvard University Press.

———. 1984. "The Image of the Gold Standard." In *A Retrospective on the Classical Gold Standard*, edited by Michael Bordo and Anna J. Schwartz, 651–69. Chicago: University of Chicago Press.

II

Modern Money and
Central Banking

6

U.S. Financial Policy in the
Post–Bretton Woods Period

Thomas F. Cargill

The end of the Bretton Woods system in 1973 was significant for U.S. financial policy in two respects. First, the failure to maintain a system of exchange rates inconsistent with market forces demonstrated the ineffectiveness of binding regulations on financial markets. The collapse of the managed exchange rate system was a precursor to the collapse of policies designed to limit competitive forces in domestic financial markets. Second, the same economic and technological forces ending the Bretton Woods system brought pressure on U.S. policy makers to remove or relax a number of binding constraints on domestic financial markets. Inflation and high interest rates, market innovations, and regulatory-market conflicts of the type described by Kane (1981) forced U.S. financial policy to shift focus. The new focus was a radical departure from the past.

U.S. policy during the Bretton Woods period had been predicated on the view that competitive financial markets were inherently unstable. As a result, financial policy was designed to limit market forces by administering a rigid exchange rate system at the international level and imposing a wide variety of constraints on portfolio flexibility and interest rate movements at the domestic level. The collapse of Bretton Woods in 1973 coincided with a growing inability to enforce regulatory constraints in domestic financial markets that were inconsistent with market forces. The failure to insulate domestic financial markets from competitive forces eventually required U.S. policy to shift focus from one that limited market forces to one that permitted market forces to play a more significant role in the allocation of credit.

The shift in focus is referred to as deregulation[1] and while a few reforms were enacted in the 1970s, the official start of the deregulation process is frequently associated with passage of the 1980 Deregulation and Monetary Control Act. Sufficient time has passed to provide some historical perspective on the shift in financial policy. Three aspects of the shift during the post–Bretton Woods period are particularly interesting.

First, U.S. financial policy has been reactive rather than active. Deregulation became an accepted principle only after market innovations rendered most of the efforts to manage the financial system a failure. In many ways the 1980 Deregulation and Monetary Control Act merely ratified innovations introduced by market participants during the 1970s. The same can be said for the decision to end the Bretton Woods system in 1973. Having won flexible exchange rates by default and likewise, the shift of U.S. policy to permit greater competition in domestic financial markets was by default.

Second, the commitment to enhance the role of competitive forces in the financial system is less than complete. Critics of the market view complain exchange rates fluctuate "too much" in the short run and persistent large trade imbalances, such as between the United States and Japan, are offered as evidence that flexible exchange rates have failed. The 1980s witnessed increased efforts of the United States and other "G" countries to intervene in the foreign exchange market. At the domestic level some argue that the insolvency of the thrift[2] industry is the result of "too much" deregulation.

Third, the transition toward more open and competitive financial markets has yet to be completed and the record, especially at the domestic level, is mixed at best. The insolvency of the thrift industry, the high cost of the thrift bailout, and weakened financial condition of the banking system suggest regulatory reform has failed to establish an efficient and stable financial environment.

Thus, the period starting with the end of the Bretton Woods system has witnessed a major shift in U.S. financial policy toward establishing more competitive financial markets and institutions. The shift, however, was a response to the failure of past efforts, both domestically and internationally, to regulate important aspects of the financial system. The revised focus, however, has experienced many problems and the commitment to enhance market forces is not firmly in place.

This paper focuses on the domestic financial transition and argues that much of what has gone wrong with financial reform is traceable to a series of poorly designed past and current policies. In sum, U.S. policy makers have hindered the transition process toward more open and competitive financial structures and generated a financial structure that is weak and imposes a serious deadweight loss on the economy.

The Domestic Transition in the Context
of Flexible Exchange Rates

The post–Bretton Woods system is based on something less than market-determined exchange rates since it incorporates the principle of government intervention to "smooth" short-run exchange rate movements. Central bank intervention throughout the trading world has become an accepted policy instrument, especially since 1985 when the United States along with Germany, Japan, and sometimes other major industrialized countries aggressively conducted foreign exchange intervention to influence the value of the dollar (Belongia 1990). At the same time the post–Bretton Woods system—even with central bank intervention—permits market forces greater latitude in determining exchange rates than prior to 1973.

The start of financial reform in domestic markets coincided with the end of the Bretton Woods system. Beginning in the early 1970s, the structure of financial markets and institutions came into conflict with an economic environment of high and uncertain interest rates and a technological environment that increased the return on financial innovation. By the end of the decade, government policy was forced to relax or remove a number of key constraints on market forces. Changes in domestic finance were not the direct result of the end of the Bretton Woods system; however, the two events share a common basis for at least three reasons.

First, the Bretton Woods system ended because governments were unsuccessful in their efforts to insulate exchange rates from market forces; likewise, domestic financial policies changed because they failed to limit market forces. Second, the end of the Bretton Woods system represented a shift from regulated to market-determined exchange rates; likewise, the domestic changes eventually removed most of the binding interest rate constraints. Third, international and domestic market forces have become interrelated and mutually reinforcing since 1973. Once price constraints are relaxed in one financial market (international or domestic), it becomes more difficult to maintain price constraints in the other financial market (domestic or international). This reinforcing interaction has been especially important in countries such as Japan.[3]

The specific catalysts for the domestic transition vary from country to country; however, in almost all cases the shift toward market-determined financial transactions resulted from conflicts generated by a system of regulation that limited portfolio flexibility and a new economic and technological environment that demanded greater flexibility.[4] Like the end of the Bretton Woods system, changes in government policy were reacting to a set of market forces that made it impossible to continue the previous regime of regulated and controlled financial transactions.

The transition of financial structures at this point in history is unique in at least three ways. First, the transition of domestic financial systems is widespread. Despite differences in cultural, economic, and social structure, and differences in historical experiences, a large number of developed and developing economies have—and continue—to make their financial structures more sensitive to market forces than previously. Second, the transition of domestic financial systems is taking place in the context of a potentially more integrated world trading and financial system than has ever been previously possible. The emergence of market-oriented economies in Eastern Europe and Russia suggests the reality of a world trading and financial system is closer than at any earlier time. Third, the transition is taking place in the context of a revolution in computer and telecommunications technology. Advances in the technology of financial transactions make it easier to circumvent binding regulations and, as a result, make it difficult for government to rationalize existing constraints on market forces or to impose new constraints. The interaction between the market and the regulatory authorities has been best described as a regulatory-market dialectical process where binding regulation induces innovation which in turn induces reregulation which in turn induces re-innovation and so on (Kane 1981).

The Domestic Transition in Detail

The U.S. financial structure in the Bretton Woods period was significantly influenced by the events of the Great Depression and their interpretation. In the wake of the financial collapse the Roosevelt administration and Congress enacted a series of reforms designed to restore public confidence in the financial system (Cargill and Garcia

1985). These reforms constrained portfolio activities and limited competition. New regulatory entities such as the Federal Home Loan Bank Board (FHLBB), Federal Deposit Insurance Corporation (FDIC), Federal Savings and Loan Insurance Corporation (FSLIC), Federal Bureau of Credit Unions, and the Securities and Exchange Commission were established. Existing agencies were provided with expanded powers to regulate and supervise the financial system.

The resulting financial structure was unable to function under normal conditions until the 1950s. The remainder of the 1930s was depressed, and the 1940s were dominated by war financing and postwar adjustment. During the 1950s and early 1960s, the financial structure nonetheless appeared to adequately fulfill its responsibilities for three reasons.

First, price stability generated a narrow gap between unregulated and regulated interest rates and, as a result, Regulation Q was not binding. Second, the lack of incentives to disintermediate between direct and indirect finance permitted the rapid and profitable growth of the thrift industry even though they loaned long and borrowed short. Third, the technology of financial transactions was still relatively stable and had not yet been influenced by the later advances in computer and telecommunications technology.

Thus, the incentives to circumvent portfolio restrictions were undeveloped into the early 1960s. The situation changed by the end of that decade, however. The Johnson administration took a more aggressive activist role in managing the economy and at the same time expanded the war against North Vietnam. The Federal Reserve was pressured to accommodate increased government spending. Additionally, the Federal Reserve adopted an operating procedure focused on the federal funds rate that insured inflationary monetary growth. Interest rates in the money and capital markets rose as nominal rates incorporated anticipated inflation; for the first time a visible thrift problem emerged. Regulation Q introduced in 1933 originally applied only to banks. As a result, thrifts raised interest rates to maintain deposit growth; but the concentration of loan portfolios in long-term, fixed-rate mortgages exposed them to interest-rate risk. The thrift industry sought the protection of government and in September 1966, the Interest Rate Adjustment Act extended deposit rate ceilings to federally insured thrift institutions.

This decision was a major policy error. According to Mayer (1982), policy makers at the time were aware of the potential for disintermediation, but did not regard this as a serious issue since they were

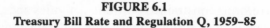

FIGURE 6.1
Treasury Bill Rate and Regulation Q, 1959–85

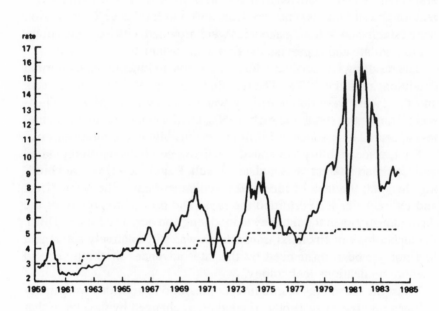

Source: Cargill and Garcia (1985, p. 83)

confident the Federal Reserve would stabilize the economy. Unfortunately, the Federal Reserve for the next fifteen years conducted an inflationary monetary policy which in turn generated a series of disruptions in the U.S. financial system.

Regulatory response was slow to evolve. The market response in the form of innovation, however, was immediate and made easier because of rapid advances in computer and telecommunications technology. The innovation process became the major event in the U.S. financial system during the 1970s and forced policy makers to initiate regulatory reforms that continue to the present. The process of innovation is most easily illustrated by the effects of Regulation Q.

Figure 6.1 illustrates the gap between the three-month Treasury Bill rate (unregulated rate) and Regulation Q. As the gap increased in the

1970s, depositors withdrew funds and transferred them to the open money markets to earn market-determined rates. At several points the disintermediation process became intense enough to generate a "credit crunch" in which depository institutions, as major suppliers of consumer and mortgage credit, had insufficient funds to loan at even high interest rates. All depository institutions (banks, savings and loan associations [S&Ls], savings banks, and credit unions) experienced disintermediation to varying degrees; however, S&Ls and savings banks (collectively referred to as thrifts) were the most severely impacted because they had limited fund-raising powers compared to commercial banks.

S&Ls and savings banks innovated by offering negotiable orders of withdrawal (NOW) in the early 1970s to broaden their fund-raising base to compete more directly with bank demand deposits. Credit unions introduced a similar deposit called a credit union share draft. Banks were in a better position to innovate because of their size; and they increasingly relied on funds obtained from Eurodollar deposits, bank-holding company issues of commercial paper, and large CDs.

The most dramatic innovation used to circumvent Regulation Q, however, was the money market mutual fund (MMMF) first introduced in 1971. By 1982 MMMF assets totaled $220 billion. MMMFs offered shares in a managed portfolio of money market instruments paying market rates of return less a management fee. Share accounts could be purchased in minimum amounts of $100 and offered limited transaction features. While not federally insured, they possessed low credit and interest rate risk, and the public regarded them as substitutes for many of the deposits offered by depository institutions.

At the end of the 1970s a crisis situation existed in the U.S. financial system. Innovation had at least circumvented the most binding regulations, and incentives to innovate increased dramatically as inflation and high interest rates reached historical highs by 1979–80. The innovation process, however, was not available to all participants and exposed the financial system to new risks. The deteriorating external trade balance, decline in the value of the dollar, the Hunt Brothers scandal in the silver market, the need for a large federal bailout of Chrysler Corporation, and the increased failure rate in the banking system all raised concern about the stability of the U.S. financial system. The fiftieth anniversary of the Great Depression also contributed to a sense of crisis as it rekindled fears of serious financial collapse.

It was this crisis environment that provided the incentive for significant regulatory reform. Several incomplete efforts at regulatory reform were taken in the early 1970s and 1978; however, passage of the 1980 Deregulation and Monetary Control Act initiated the official deregulation process from a regulatory perspective. A brief review of these reforms follows:

1. 1970–73: Removal of large CDs from Regulation Q deposit ceilings.

2. 1978: Establishment of money market certificates (MMCs) with minimum denomination of $10,000 and six-month maturity. The MMC rate was market determined and set at the discount yield on six-month Treasury bills.

3. 1978: Permit thrift institutions in New England states to issue negotiable orders of withdrawal (NOW) accounts.

4. 1980: Passage of the Depository Institutions Deregulation and Monetary Control Act. The 1980 act established deregulation as official policy. Most importantly, the act (a) expanded the sources of funds for banks and thrifts by permitting nationwide authorization to issue NOW accounts; (b) expanded the uses of funds for thrift institutions by permitting them to offer a limited amount of consumer credit and relaxed restrictions on mortgage loans; (c) expanded powers of thrifts to issue credit cards and provide fiduciary services; (d) initiated a six-year phase-out of Regulation Q deposit ceilings; (e) provided a federal override to a number of state-imposed usury restrictions on lending rates; (f) established a new reserve requirement system for all federally insured depository institutions in that all federally insured institutions were required to meet Federal Reserve–imposed requirements on transaction deposits—i.e., demand deposits, NOW accounts, automatic service transfer or ATS accounts, and credit union share draft accounts—and certain types of managed liabilities (primarily Eurodollar deposits and large CDs); and (g) established a new relationship between depository institutions and the Federal Reserve. Institutions that were required to satisfy Federal Reserve–imposed reserve requirements could obtain services from the Federal Reserve on a nondiscriminatory fee basis irrespective of membership status including the right to request a loan from the Federal Reserve. In effect, the 1980 act made all federally insured depository institutions de facto members of the Federal Reserve. Official membership status is moot at this point in time.

5. 1982: Garn–St Germain Depository Institutions Act enhanced some of the features of the 1980 act. The most important features of the 1982 act were: (a) authorized a money market deposit account

(MMDA) with no maturity, minimum denomination of $2,500, limited transactions features, and a market-determined rate of interest; (b) thrifts were permitted to offer demand deposits under limited conditions; and (c) expanded the uses of funds powers for thrift institutions. While not directly authorized by the 1982 act, the Depository Institutions Deregulation Committee established by the 1980 act authorized the super-NOW account which had the same features as the MMDAs, except that unlimited transfers were permitted.

6. 1986: All interest rate ceilings were eliminated per the 1980 act with the exception of demand deposit accounts which remain subject to a zero deposit ceiling.

7. 1987: The Competitive Equality Banking Act was the first official response to the thrift problem. The act recapitalized the FSLIC, called for relaxed regulatory treatment of Texas thrift institutions until the regional economy improved, and made it easier for banks to acquire failed or failing thrifts.

8. 1989: The Financial Institutions Reform, Recovery, and Enforcement Act was offered as a solution to the thrift crisis. The 1989 act: (a) abolished the FHLBB and transferred its functions to a newly formed Office of Thrift Supervision (OTS) within the U.S. Treasury; (b) abolished FSLIC and transferred its functions to the FDIC; (c) thrift asset powers were reduced and thrifts were further restricted to allocate up to 70 percent of their funds to real estate–related loans; (d) deposit insurance premiums for both banks and thrifts were raised; (e) a thrift bailout agency called the Resolution Trust Corporation (RTC) was established to liquidate assets of failed thrifts; (f) capital requirements for thrifts were raised, but still left at levels below those of banks; and (g) bank holding companies were given permission to purchase both insolvent and solvent thrifts.

9. 1991: The Federal Deposit Insurance Improvement Act started out as a major restructuring of the banking system; however, it finally emerged as an act focused only on the FDIC (Cargill and Mayer 1992). The act's objectives were to require a least-cost resolution of insolvent depository institutions, to improve supervision and examination procedures, to establish a "trip wire" system for regulatory intervention based on a bank's capital-asset ratio, to establish a system of risk-based deposit insurance premiums, to initiate development of a market valuation approach to asset valuation, and to provide additional resources to the Bank Insurance Fund (BIF) of the FDIC.

10. 1994: The Riegle-Neal Interstate Banking and Branching Effi-

ciency Act authorized interstate branching and reversed a long-standing policy of geographic constraints on bank operations.

These regulatory reforms brought about the most extensive restructuring of the U.S. financial system since the reforms of the Great Depression period.[5] They increased the degree of competition in the intermediation sector of the financial system by expanding the sources of funds for all depository institutions, expanding the uses of funds for thrift institutions, and removing or relaxing constraints on deposit and lending rates.

Financial Transition in the United States: Evaluation

The financial transition during the past two decades has been successful in many respects. The consumers of financial services now have a wider choice than previously, competition between different depository institutions has increased, competition between intermediation and direct financial markets has increased, deposit rates (with the exception of demand deposits) along with the majority of lending rates are now free to fully reflect market forces, depository institutions possess greater ability to manage liquidity and interest-rate risk, and the disruptive periods of disintermediation and credit crunch have ended.

Unfortunately, these positive elements pale in comparison to the failures of omission and commission of the regulatory reforms. To fully understand what happened three questions need to be addressed:

1. Would the financial transition have occurred if price stability had been maintained?
2. What were the specific policy failures?
3. What is the proper role for government regulation in a more market-sensitive financial environment?

Government and the Initiation of Financial Transition

There is little doubt conflict between market forces and the financial structure of the Bretton Woods period would have emerged sometime in the 1970s even in the absence of high inflation and interest rates. The advances in computer and telecommunications technology combined with increased linkages between developed and developing economies would have provided incentives to innovate around restrictions that limited competition. The innovation process, however, would have been considerably less intense and less disruptive than it was.

Four factors transformed what would have been an orderly process of financial evolution into a series of financial disruptions. First, Federal Reserve inflationary policy in the 1960s and 1970s generated large gaps between unregulated and regulated interest rates (figure 6.1); second, regulatory authorities were slow to remove or relax constraints on portfolio behavior for fear that this would lead to the demise of the thrift industry; third, when regulatory authorities finally recognized the need to enhance the portfolio flexibility of thrifts, it was done in such a manner that thrifts were exposed to new risks and were provided with enhanced incentives to assume imprudent levels of risk; and fourth, during the 1980s regulatory authorities increasingly resorted to forbearance—allowing weak and insolvent thrifts to remain open—as a policy of dealing with troubled thrift institutions.

Policy Failures

Seven policy failures can be identified from the U.S. experience.

First, the Federal Reserve failed to maintain price stability, especially in the second half of the 1970s. This policy failure alone is responsible for the wide gap between regulated and unregulated interest rates which in turn led to disintermediation and credit crunches, and weakened the depository institutions, especially thrift institutions.[6]

Second, reflecting the widespread support of Congress and the administration, regulatory authorities sought to maintain thrifts as primary mortgage lenders to support the nation's housing objectives. The 1982 act expanded thrift asset diversification powers; yet, on close examination, these new powers were essentially real estate oriented and ultimately more risky than tradition thrift lending.

Third, regulatory policy towards thrifts in particular was unbalanced in that deregulation of the sources of funds occurred more rapidly than deregulation of the uses of funds. Thrifts were permitted to offer more market sensitive deposits while, at the same time, asset diversification powers grew more slowly. Combined with a large backlog of low-yielding fixed-rate mortgages, thrifts found their condition deteriorating in the early 1980s as their cost of funds rose. The 1978 decision to introduce money market certificates (MMCs) clearly illustrates this point. Thrifts and other depository institutions were permitted to offer MMCs without any corresponding change in their asset diversification powers. MMCs raised the cost of funds and, combined with a loan portfolio dominated by fixed-rate long-term mortgages, exposed thrifts to interest rate risk. Thus, MMCs merely changed the type of risk exposure for thrifts from disintermediation to interest rate risk.

Fourth, tax policy contributed to the thrift problem in two ways: (1) thrifts continued to receive significant tax advantages through 1986, if they allocated the majority of their loan assets to residential mortgages. Thus, thrifts received conflicting messages about asset diversification until the tax advantage was removed in 1986; and (2) the Tax Reform Act of 1981 raised the rate of return on real estate investment by accelerating depreciation schedules. With new powers granted by the 1982 act thrifts aggressively pursued real estate investments without adequate experience to assess risk. The Tax Reform Act of 1986 removed the favorable depreciation, thereby turning many commercial real estate loans into problem loans and increasing credit risk to thrifts.

Fifth, regulatory authorities, Congress, and the administration failed to recognize the declining profitability of thrifts in the early 1980s as a reflection of a more fundamental problem. They attributed the growing thrift problem to adverse economic conditions—high interest rates and recession—that would shortly end and return the thrift industry to profitability. There was an unwillingness to see the thrift problem as a reflection of a fundamental flaw in the deregulation process. During the first half of the 1980s, policy makers relaxed accounting standards to measure thrift net worth, adopted a policy of capital forbearance, lowered required thrift capital, and failed to expand the supervision staff of the FHLBB. The outcome was a growing number of insolvent but operating thrift institutions elegantly referred to as "zombies" by Kane (1989).

By 1985 the thrift industry and the FSLIC were insolvent. A Government Accounting Office (GAO) report (1986) indicated that FSLIC had insufficient reserves to close the some 500 insolvent thrift institutions for which it insured deposits. Failure to close insolvent thrifts had a major adverse impact and ultimately resulted in one of the most serious financial policy failures ever experienced by the United State.[7] Insolvent but operating thrifts had every incentive to assume high levels of risk in their loan and investment decisions and to raise deposit rates to attract funds needed to expand loans. There was no effective check on this process since regulatory authorities were unable to close insolvent institutions because of insufficient reserves and depositors had little reason to impose discipline on the insolvent institution since deposits were federally insured up to $100,000.

The failure to deal with insolvent thrift institutions in a timely manner permitted the insolvency problem to reach levels that would require a major taxpayer input of funds. By the late 1980s it was becoming difficult for regulatory authorities to mislead the public about the magnitude of the thrift problem as they had done earlier in the decade. Regulatory authorities knowingly covered up the magnitude of the problem hoping economic conditions would improve and thrifts could "work their way out" of the problem.

The Competitive Equality Banking Act of 1987, designed to recapitalize the FSLIC insurance fund, reflected the official denial of the seriousness of the problem. The act was cosmetic and purposely misled the public about the magnitude of the problem. The act sought to recapitalize the fund with an infusion of $10.8 billion, when at the same time, official estimates of the thrift problem being published by the GAO in 1986 were in the range of $16 to $25 billion (GAO 1986). Outside estimates exceeded the GAO estimates. Not only did the 1987 act accept a low estimate of the cost of closing thrift institutions, but increased the forbearance problem by requiring special regional considerations to be taken into account when handling a troubled thrift.

Sixth, the Financial Institutions Reform, Recovery, and Enforcement Act was enacted in August 1989 as the next major official response to the thrift problem (Brewer 1989), but it failed to address the fundamental earlier policy failures. The act understated the cost of the bailout and, most importantly, it failed to address a fundamental failure of U.S. financial policy: the act relied on regulatory discipline rather than market discipline to limit depository institution risk and to protect the deposit insurance fund.

Seventh, policy makers paid little attention to the conflict between incentives to assume risk embedded in the system of deposit guarantees and the enhanced ability of depository institutions to manage risk made possible by market and regulatory innovations. Federal deposit insurance was based on fixed-rate premiums with no allowance for individual risk. Once a troubled institution is identified, policy makers resort to procedures to protect all depositors without regard to ultimate cost or to the effect this has on the willingness of institutions to assume risk. In fact, incentives embedded in government deposit guarantees to assume risk increased significantly in the 1980s, because the 1980 act raised deposit insurance from $40,000 to $100,000—far beyond any inflation adjustment. This fundamental problem has yet to be adequately addressed; however, the 1991 FDIC

Improvement Act does take steps toward dealing with troubled institutions in a timely manner (Cargill and Mayer 1992; Bentson and
Kaufman 1997).

The above policy failures fall into three general categories: first,
and probably most important, is the failure to maintain price stability;
second, misguided regulatory actions designed to maintain thrifts as
primary real estate lenders; and third, failure to deal with the conflict
between enhanced opportunities to assume and manage risk and the
risk incentives embedded in government deposit guarantees.

The thrift problem has received the most attention during the past
decade as the chief failure of U.S. financial policy. By the end of the
1980s, however, there was also increasing concern over the condition
of the banking system. While not exhibiting the same degree of financial duress as the thrift industry, banks found themselves with significant backlogs of problem loans—especially in commercial real estate.
There are several dimensions here.

First, the number of bank failures increased significantly. In the 1970s
less than ten banks per year failed, while as many as 200 banks failed
at the end of the 1980s. While still a small percentage of the total number of banks, the increased failure rate caused concern. In the past it
had been mainly small banks that failed, but increasingly larger banks
were failing as well.

Second, the number of "problem banks" significantly increased. A
"problem bank" is one determined to need close regulatory attention
based on an on-site examination by regulatory authorities. In the 1960s
and 1970s the number of problem banks ranged from 100 to 200 banks
per year. But that number increased in the 1980s, and after 1984 it did
not fall below 1,000 banks each year. Like the failure rate statistics, the
banks on the problem list were getting larger.

Third, the FDIC reserve fund steadily declined in the 1980s. In 1988
the FDIC lost income for the first time since establishing operations in
1934; by 1990 it was insolvent in that reserves were insufficient to
close the projected number of bank failures. Like the defunct FHLBB
and FSLIC, FDIC officials at first denied any problem with the reserve
level, then admitted that some taxpayer funds might be required to
sustain operations, every few months revising upward the estimate of
needed funding. While few believe the potential problems with the
banking system and the FDIC would equal those of the thrift industry
and the now defunct FSLIC, there was a growing sense of unease about
U.S. banking.

Fourth and finally, a comprehensive report to Congress in December 1990 by Barth, Brumbaugh, and Litan (1990) presented a bleak picture of the condition of U.S. banking. They concluded the U.S. banking industry was financially weak despite reported measures of accounting profits and industry-wide equity capital-to-asset ratios. The report drew a disturbing parallel to the thrift crisis: "There is very good evidence that the BIF is in the same position as FSLIC was in the mid-1980s—without sufficient resources to pay for its expected caseload of failed depositories" (Barth, Brumbaugh, and Litan 1990, 6).

One year later the banking system remained weak, but there was some reason for optimism (Keehn 1991). Asset quality problems were identified, banks raised credit standards, and banks built up loan loss reserves significantly. In addition, the real estate decline appeared to have bottomed out and there were signs the economy was emerging from a recession that started in July 1990.

Most important, the 1991 Federal Deposit Insurance Improvement Act brought about important changes in the way regulatory authorities deal with troubled institutions (Bentson and Kaufman 1997, Keehn 1991). The 1991 act, actions by the banks to write off bad loans and increase bad loan reserves, easy monetary policy, and improvement in several regional sectors of the national economy (Texas and California in particular) combined to significantly improve the condition of the banking system by 1996.

Despite signs of a turnabout in banking and an improved thrift industry, there remains much to be concerned about the future of the U.S. financial system. The past two decades have shown that whatever failures the deregulation process has manifested are mainly the result of policy failures on the part of government.

Responsibilities of Government
in the Financial Transition

The experiences of U.S. financial policy in the post–Bretton Woods period suggest four responsibilities for government in the future. First, government should permit the central bank to pursue price stability to limit large and unpredictable movements in interest rates. It appears U.S. policy has recognized the importance of price stability. Price stability by the mid-1980s was one of the more important policy achievements of the Federal Reserve in recent times. Whether this commitment to price stability will persist remains unknown, however.

Second, government should recognize financial innovation and market forces are the driving force of the transition and, as a result, resist interfering with them. Unfortunately, regulatory policy continues to resist utilizing those forces to assist government regulation and supervision. To illustrate, the FDIC Improvement Act of 1991 ignored a large number of well-developed proposals to impose greater market discipline on banks as a way to relieve the burden on deposit insurance. The act explicitly accepts the premise regulatory discipline is a substitute for market discipline as a way of monitoring the risk of depository institutions.

Third, government should cease credit allocation policies designed to maintain a class of depository institutions as primary mortgage lenders. Such a policy is inconsistent with market forces and distorts the allocation of credit. The declining competitiveness of the U.S. economy is partly due to a low savings rate and a national policy which directs much of the limited savings into real estate rather than industrial development and research.

Lastly, government needs to recognize the fundamental conflict between incentives to assume risk and opportunities to assume risk in a more open and competitive financial environment. The financial reform process in the United States will not achieve the objectives of an efficient, adaptable, and sound financial system unless the entire system of government deposit guarantees is reformed and made compatible with a more open and competitive financial environment. According to Kane (1991, 1–3), the prospect for meaningful deposit insurance reform is not optimistic:

> [T]he U.S. deposit-insurance mess provides considerable evidence that the world's greatest regulatory difficulties do not reside in instrumental defects. They are rooted in incentive defects that systematically encourage government officials to misoperate their machines when they find themselves under stress. The fundamental weakness is the lack of a timely accountability for losses that accrue to taxpayers from governmental acts of financial misregulation...For over two decades, top regulatory officials, federal politicians and thrift-institution trade associations cooperated in denying and covering up the size of their industry's growing capital shortage. They did this by using and creating accounting gimmicks to delay the formal realization of developing losses and by fighting politically the efforts of outside critics to size the need to recapitalize the deposit-insurance funds realistically.

Kane (1995) has been one of the most severe critics of deposit insurance, and his views are now widely held. Regulatory authorities failed in their public trust and will likely continue to perform in unsatisfactory ways to deal with troubled financial institutions as long as discretion remains the major characteristic of regulation.

Future Developments and Implications for Other Countries

There is widespread agreement among observers that the financial reform process erred in significant ways. What is more frustrating is the slowness with which regulatory authorities took to even recognize the conflict, let alone deal with it. It was the insolvency of FSLIC, the insolvency of the thrift industry, the weakened condition of U.S. banks, and most recently the insolvency of the FDIC that finally alerted policy makers to the fundamental conflict facing the U.S. financial system.

The failures of U.S. financial policy have important implications for other countries. At least two can be identified. First, price stability is of tremendous importance to the stability of the financial system. It permits a more orderly financial transition driven by market innovations and provides time for regulatory authorities to react to changes in the structure of finance. It goes a long way towards limiting crisis reactions, which have been so frequent in the U.S. case. Second, all governments rightly guarantee deposits up to some limit; however, these guarantees introduce a moral hazard problem in that they provide incentives to assume risk. As domestic and international financial markets continue to evolve toward more open and competitive structures, risk incentives embedded in government deposit guarantees will become more of a problem to the stability of the financial system. The lesson to be learned from the U.S. experience is that government should not only avoid hindering market forces, but just as importantly, government needs to reform its deposit guarantee system to reduce incentives to assume risk by issuers of the nation's money supply (Barth 1990). Ultimately, market forces via depositor and equity-holder discipline provide the best means toward this end.

Notes

1. The term "deregulation" was not meant to imply the removal of government regulation over the financial system, but rather it was used to describe a process of removal or relaxation of key binding constraints on the financial system, especially indirect finance. Other countries prefer to characterize the process as "financial liberalization."
2. S&Ls and savings banks are collectively referred to as thrifts since they possessed similar loan and deposit portfolios. Most important, they both allocated a major part of their assets to real estate loans. S&Ls, however, are the most im-

210 Modern Money and Central Banking

portant component of the thrift industry in terms of number of institutions and level of assets.

3. Suzuki (1986) has argued that the shift to flexible exchange rates played a major role in Japan's domestic reforms.

4. Cargill and Royama (1988) present a taxonomy of the financial reform process applicable to any country.

5. The majority of the reforms focused on deregulation of intermediation finance; however, the 1980 act devoted considerable attention to monetary control issues. Monetary control was not the most important issue even in this piece of legislation (Timberlake 1985), however.

6. In contrast to the United States, the financial reform process in Japan through the mid-1980s had been more gradual and less disruptive because of the successful price stabilization policies of the Bank of Japan (Cargill and Royama 1988). This description of a smooth transition, however, is no longer applicable. Japan's "bubble" and "burst of the bubble" economy of the second half of the 1980s and the first half of the 1990s, respectively, have revealed serious problems both in the structure of finance and regulation (Cargill, Hutchinson, and Ito 1997, chapters 5 and 6).

7. The most serious was the failure of the Federal Reserve to provide lender of last resort services during the Great Contraction period (1929–33).

References

Barth, James R. 1990. "Post-FIRREA: The Need to Reform the Federal Deposit Insurance System." *1990 Conference on Bank Structure and Competition.* (May) Chicago: Federal Reserve Bank.

Barth, James R., R. Dan Brumbaugh, Jr., and Robert E. Litan. 1990. *The Banking Industry in Turmoil: A Report on the Condition of the U.S. Banking Industry and the Bank Insurance Fund.* Report prepared for the House Committee on Banking, Finance and Urban Affairs. 101st Cong., 2d sess. Washington, DC: U.S. Government Printing Office.

Belongia, Michael T. 1990. "Foreign Exchange Intervention by the United States: A Review and Assessment of 1985–89." *Review* (May–June): 32–51. St. Louis: Federal Reserve Bank.

Benston, George J. and George G. Kaufman. 1997. "FDICA after Five Years: A Review and Evaluation." *Journal of Economic Perspectives.* Forthcoming in 1997.

Brewer, Elijah III. 1989. "Full-blown crisis, half-measure cure." *Economic Perspectives* (November–December): 2–17. Chicago: Federal Reserve Bank.

Cargill, Thomas F., and Gillian G. Garcia. 1985. *Financial Reform in the 1980s.* Stanford, CA: Hoover Institution Press.

Cargill, Thomas F., and Thomas Mayer. 1992. "U.S. Deposit Insurance Reform." *Contemporary Policy Issues* 10 (July): 95–103.

Cargill, Thomas F., and Shoichi Royama. 1988. *The Transition of Finance in Japan and the United States: A Comparative Perspective.* Stanford, CA: Hoover Institution Press.

Cargill, Thomas F., Michael M. Hutchinson, and Takatoshi Ito. 1997. *The Political Economy of Japanese Monetary Policy.* Cambridge, MA: The MIT Press.

Kane, Edward J. 1981. "Accelerating Inflation, Technological Innovation, and the Decreasing Effectiveness of Banking Regulation." *Journal of Finance* 36 (May): 355–67.

———. 1985. *The Gathering Crisis in Federal Deposit Insurance.* Cambridge, MA: MIT Press.

————. 1989. *The S&L Insurance Mess: How Did it Happen?* Washington, DC: Urban Institute.

————. 1991. "The Festering U.S. Deposit-Insurance Mess." Working Paper. (February).

Keehn, Silas. 1991. "First and ten: A fresh start for banks in the 1990s." *Chicago Fed Letter*. (October).

Mayer, Thomas. 1982. "A Case Study of Federal Reserve Policymaking: Regulation Q in 1966." *Journal of Monetary Economics* 10 (September): 259–71.

Suzuki, Yoshio. 1986. *Money, Finance, and Macroeconomic Performance in Japan.* New Haven, CT: Yale University Press.

Timberlake, Richard H., Jr. 1985. "Legislative Construction of the Monetary Control Act of 1980." *American Economic Review* 75 (May): 97–102.

U.S. General Accounting Office. 1986. *Thrift Industry: Cost to FSLIC of Delaying Action on Insolvent Savings Institutions.* Washington, DC: GAO.

7

Bank Deposit Guarantees: Why Not Trust the Market?

Genie D. Short and Kenneth J. Robinson

Despite a long history of sporadic periods of severe banking difficulties, the United States continues to search for solutions to financial-sector problems that have been perpetuated by legal restrictions that foster a fragmented banking system. There is now general agreement about the sources of U.S. banking problems. Geographic and product restrictions under which banks operate have hampered their ability to compete in the financial marketplace and limited their ability to diversify their portfolios. And problems with the financial safety net, including the system of federal deposit insurance and the Federal Reserve's operation of the discount window, have made depositors indifferent to the financial conditions of insured depository institutions, with the result that incentives to control risk-taking have been blunted.

While the sources of U.S. banking difficulties are generally accepted, agreement has not been reached on how to untangle the current financial structure and institutional arrangements that have been in place for nearly sixty years. Since 1980 five major congressional banking reform bills have been passed: the Monetary Control Act of 1980; the Garn–St. Germain Depository Institutions Act of 1982; the Competitive Equality Banking Act (CEBA) of 1987; the Financial Institutions Reform, Recovery, and Enforcement Act (FIRREA) of

The authors would like to thank Kelly Klemme and Lydia L. Smith for their participation in preparing this paper.

1989; and, most recently, the Federal Deposit Insurance Corporation Improvement Act of 1991. But thus far, the United States has been unable to introduce a comprehensive reform bill that establishes an institutional framework that enables U.S. banks to compete effectively in the global marketplace.

As in the early 1980s, the debate about financial reform in the United States centers on how to eliminate the legal restrictions that prevent U.S. banks from competing in today's marketplace while at the same time controlling the moral-hazard problem that is present with mispriced federal deposit guarantees. Yet, unlike the early 1980s, the focus of attention today has shifted from whether we need to change the system of deposit guarantees to how we can change this system of federal guarantees without fostering a financial crisis.

In our view, effective financial reform in the United States will require a fundamental reexamination of the long-standing disagreement about the extent to which deposit market forces can and should be trusted to discipline banks. Federal deposit insurance was introduced to offset what was viewed to be the inherent instability of bank deposit markets. Over time, however, reliance on these guarantees increased to virtually 100 percent coverage. Along with extended coverage came greater problems from mispriced risk incentives, higher bank resolution costs, and further reliance on government-mandated restrictions and regulatory oversight as a means to offset the moral-hazard problem generated at the outset by the program of deposit guarantees.

In this chapter, we explore how the history of deposit guarantees has evolved in the United States. We then offer a comparative analysis of the deposit insurance programs that have been introduced elsewhere in the world and review the reasons why 100 percent deposit guarantees have become an accepted policy norm for maintaining deposit market stability throughout the world. We argue that, rather than minimizing deposit market instability, the expanded role given to the financial safety net has contributed to and exacerbated financial-sector problems throughout the world. We conclude by arguing that changes are needed that allow bank deposit markets to function more freely to improve the price-signaling mechanism for monitoring risk-taking in banking. Absent a fundamental rethinking of the benefits derived from market pricing of bank deposits, the prospects for successful banking reform in the United States remain dim.

Deposit Insurance in the United States from the 1930s to the Present

Deposit Insurance and the Great Depression

Much of the U.S. financial structure that is currently in place originated in the aftermath of the Great Depression. The banking legislation of the 1930s reflected the outgrowth of concerns about a banking system that was uniquely prone to deposit runs. The thrust of the legislation, however, was aimed at combating what was alleged to be the impact of excessive competition that fostered imprudent risk-taking on the part of banks. It was argued that deposit insurance, together with tighter regulations and supervision over the commercial banking system, could restore public confidence in the banking industry while restraining incentives for banks to undertake excessive risk that could lead to bank failures (Schwartz 1988, 34–62).

The Banking Act of 1933, also known as the Glass-Steagall Act, separated commercial and investment banking, prohibited the payment of interest on demand deposits, and subjected interest rates paid on time and savings deposits to regulation. Banks were limited primarily to accepting deposits and making loans, mostly in their home states or counties, and paying interest on deposits no higher than allowed by federally authorized ceilings. The Glass-Steagall Act also established the system of federal deposit insurance to help restore confidence in the banking system in the United States. The Federal Deposit Insurance Corporation (FDIC) was thus created as part of an overall legislative effort to ensure the safety and soundness of the financial system by imposing regulations to constrain bank risk-taking.

Deposit insurance was introduced in the United States ostensibly to accomplish two objectives. The first (and most publicized) objective was the protection of small depositors. The second goal was a monetary policy objective—the protection of the circulating medium of exchange. However, a third, much less publicized role for federal deposit insurance was to support branching restrictions by offering protection to small, independent banks. The problem of depositor confidence that erupted during the banking crises in the early 1930s was not unique to that period, and the solution of providing federal deposit guarantees was not a novel idea at the time. Both federal and state branching restrictions originated and perpetuated a banking system that consisted of a large number of banks, many of them quite small in size. These and other restrictions gave rise to a unique banking structure in the United States with a unique set of problems—i.e., U.S. banks were unusually prone to runs and suspensions.[1]

Between 1886 and 1933, 150 separate proposals for deposit insurance or guaranty were introduced in Congress. Sponsors of these proposals came from over thirty different states in all parts of the country and represented a cross section of the political spectrum (Golembe 1961, 188). In fact, as Carter Golembe has pointed out, one of the key reasons behind the establishment of deposit insurance in the United States was to protect the existing structure of thousands of independent banks.

> Yet it is not reading too much into history to say that bank-obligation insurance systems and proposals between 1892 and 1933 reflected and influenced...attempts to maintain a banking system composed of thousands of independent banks by alleviating one serious shortcoming of such a system: its proneness to bank suspension, in good times and bad.... In the United States in 1933...public disillusionment with the independent banking system had reached a point at which fundamental change in the banking structure could easily have been obtained.... Whether this would have taken the form of nation-wide branch systems, nationalization, or something different will never be known. (Golembe 1961, 199)

This same fragmented banking structure survives in the United States today. Although during the interim from 1933 through the early 1980s financial institutions were quite adept at developing financial innovations to circumvent regulatory constraints in banking, the period since the 1980s has been characterized by mounting problems for insured depositories.[2]

Deposit Insurance in the Postdepression Environment

Excessive competition in the deregulated environment of the 1980s has been cited by industry experts as an important causal factor behind many of the banking difficulties that emerged in the 1980s. But research on the issue characterizes the financial difficulties of the 1980s as a melding of a number of interrelated factors—economic, regulatory, and managerial.[3] Moreover, it is now widely acknowledged that the unprecedented bank and thrift difficulties that developed in the United States were directly linked to two factors: the expanded scope of federal deposit guarantees that had evolved to virtual 100 percent coverage, and the ineffectiveness of bank regulatory oversight as a

FIGURE 7.1
Share of Financial Assets Held by Major Intermediaries

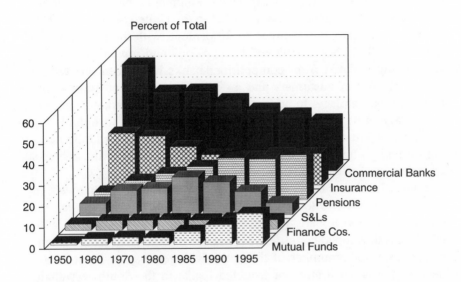

Percent of Total

Commercial Banks
Insurance
Pensions
S&Ls
Finance Cos.
Mutual Funds

1950 1960 1970 1980 1985 1990 1995

Source: Board of Governors of the Federal Reserve System, *Annual Statistical Digest.*

means to offset the mispriced risk incentives at insured financial institutions (SFRC 1989; Brumbraugh 1988; Feldstein 1991).

Throughout most of the period following the Great Depression, the institutional setting established by the Banking Act of 1933 performed fairly well in minimizing the number of U.S. bank failures. From 1934, when the FDIC was officially established, through the decade of the 1960s, the failure rate for U.S. banks was low. During this entire period only 621 U.S. banks failed (an average of seventeen per year), all of which were very small in size. Except for episodes of severe economic downturn, misuse of banking resources by inept or corrupt managers caused most of the bank failures that occurred after the 1930s (Benston et al. 1986).

By the mid-1970s, however, the banking industry was in the early stages of a major restructuring. Banks began to face increasing competition from new providers of financial services.

Figure 7.1 shows the considerable inroads made by nonbank competitors into banking markets. In 1950, commercial banks held about 50 percent of the financial-asset market in the United States. By 1991, their market share had declined to 30 percent, with the most notable gains over that period achieved by pensions and mutual funds. Far from being isolated from competition, banks have been left with a shrinking pool of customers and a declining relative position in the financial marketplace. In addition to this decline in market share, the percentage of banks that the FDIC labeled as problems rose markedly in the early part of the 1980s. More ominously, not only did the number of bank failures rise during the 1980s, but the size of those banks experiencing financial difficulties also increased.

Figure 7.2 shows the percentage of U.S. banking assets that were in failed banks from 1980 to 1995. The chart identifies the marked increase in large U.S. bank failures. In the early 1980s, problems with LDC (less developed countries) debt raised questions about the financial viability of a number of the nation's largest banks. Later in the decade, the concentration of troubled banks in the Southwest again underscored the vulnerability of large banks to failure. Nowhere was this more evident than in Texas during the latter part of the 1980s, when nine of the state's ten largest bank holding companies, representing two-thirds of the state's banking assets, were either acquired by out-of-state institutions or provided new management with federal assistance. Extensive financial problems also developed in New England, throughout the Southeast, and in California, with a number of the major financial institutions in those regions experiencing severe asset quality problems and failure. Moreover, the 1980s also witnessed the meltdown of the nation's thrift industry.

The high concentration of troubled assets at large banks represented an important change from the banking difficulties during the 1920s and 1930s. During the 1980s, the asset quality problems of the largest U.S. banks became the primary source of instability, and the focus of policy attention shifted from concerns about deposit runs at the nation's smaller institutions to concerns about runs at the largest institutions. In part because of the criticisms over the inadequate policy response taken during the 1933 banking panics to offset deposit market instability, a more proactive policy stance was taken in the 1970s and 1980s. This

FIGURE 7.2
Proportion of U.S. Commercial Bank Assets in Failed Banks

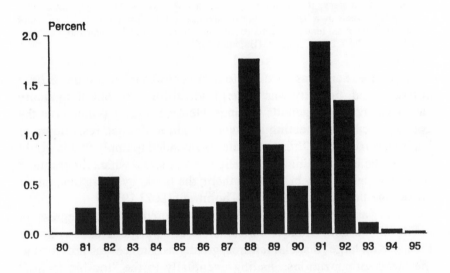

Sources: Federal Deposit Insurance Corporation; Reports of Condition and Income.

new policy focused on avoiding unwanted deposit market instability by providing direct assistance to troubled institutions rather than concentrating on the macroeconomic liquidity needs of the banking system as a whole.[4] Unfortunately, U.S. policy makers failed to heed the warnings expressed in the early discussions of the appropriate use of the financial safety net for avoiding financial panics.[5]

In the nineteenth century, Walter Bagehot emphasized the classical view of the role of lender of last resort as primarily macroeconomic. To Bagehot, the central bank's responsibility was to guarantee the liquidity of the whole economy but not that of particular institutions. The difficulty, of course, which Bagehot recognized, was how to establish and maintain an institutional framework that enabled the central banking authorities to respond to a shock before it "got out of hand" *without* protecting individual insolvent institutions. The emphasis was on responding to liquidity pressures at healthy financial institutions.

> A panic, in a word, is a species of neuralgia, and according to the rules of science you must not starve it. The holders of the cash reserve must be ready not only to keep it for their own liabilities, but to advance it most freely for the liabilities of others. They must lend to merchants, to minor bankers, to "this man and that man" whenever the security is good. (Bagehot 1962, 25)

Under these circumstances, as long as central bank lending was fully collateralized, liquidity was to be provided liberally, but at a penalty rate. Even before Bagehot's writings, Henry Thornton pointed out the consequences of protecting insolvent institutions when responding to banking difficulties: "It is by no means intended to imply that it would become the Bank of England to relieve every stress which the rashness of country banks may bring upon them; the Bank, by doing this, might encourage their improvidence" (Thornton [1802] 1939).

These warnings, however, were largely ignored in the postdepression environment. And because concerns about contagious bank runs are greater with large financial failures, greater assistance was provided to the larger organizations, leading eventually to the "too-big-to-fail" policy that is a major aspect of bank regulatory policy.[6]

With the settlement of Continental Illinois National Bank in 1984, then the nation's seventh largest bank, the too-big-to-fail doctrine became an acknowledged policy option for settling large bank failures in the United States. During congressional testimony concerning the resolution of Continental, C. Todd Conover, the U.S. comptroller of the currency, stated that the federal government would not allow the nation's eleven largest banks to fail (Carrington 1984). That statement provided a verbal guarantee of 100 percent coverage to all depositors and general creditors of the nation's largest banks. But this verbal guarantee merely made explicit a perception that previous policy actions had already led U.S. depositors to believe.[7] This practice now fuels the political stalemate on bank reform.[8]

Throughout most of the postdepression environment, the resolution technique that was most widely used for settling both large and small bank failures was the purchase and assumption transaction, in which all nonsubordinated liabilities, including uninsured deposits, are transferred to an assuming bank. But in some instances, alternative forms of deposit payoffs were used that did not provide full coverage to uninsured depositors. Virtually all of these cases involved small banks (Short 1985). This practice of providing full coverage to large banks, but less than full coverage to small banks, established a serious competitive equity issue on the basis of bank size. The greater protection given to large banks also fostered distortions toward more excessive risk-taking at the larger banks and made them more vulnerable to failure. And as difficulties at large institutions mounted, concerns about systemic-risk implications increased. In contrast to the warnings expressed by Thornton, actions were taken to forestall failures at these large institutions to avoid systemic risk, rather than to respond to any liquidity crises that emerged.[9]

In responding to banking difficulties, policy makers argue that they need too-big-to-fail exemptions for emergency measures to avoid a financial crisis. With too-big-to-fail, large banks receive broader protections than small banks; and with this greater implicit protection, small banks continue to demand explicit 100 percent deposit guarantees to compete on an equal footing with their more protected large bank competitors. The current gridlock on financial reform is directly linked to this policy issue. The result of this gridlock is the 1991 FDIC Improvement Act (FDICIA), which once again relies on regulatory oversight and mandatory capital requirements as a means of disciplining banks, rather than addressing the moral-hazard problem present with federal deposit guarantees.

The original intent of the 1991 banking reform legislation was to establish a comprehensive plan to reform and modernize the U.S. financial system. The proposal that the U.S. Department of the Treasury developed to provide the framework for the legislation identified four interrelated problems that needed to be addressed: (1) the decline in the competitive position and financial strength of U.S. banks in both domestic and international markets; (2) the fragmented regulatory structure; (3) the overextension of the federal safety net for deposits; and (4) the undercapitalized deposit insurance fund. The solutions to these issues recommended by the Treasury were: (1) to expand the geographic and product markets in which U.S. banks compete; (2) to streamline the bank regulatory framework to avoid overlapping responsibilities across regulatory agencies; and (3) to reduce the scope of deposit insurance coverage to minimize taxpayer exposure to losses from the deposit insurance fund and to reintroduce greater market discipline against excessive risk-taking (U.S. Department of Treasury 1991).

The actual legislation, however, achieved none of these objectives. Rather than establishing a comprehensive bill to modernize the U.S. financial system, the FDIC Improvement Act of 1991 concentrated on establishing tighter regulatory standards and enforcement actions without adequately addressing the need to roll back deposit guarantees and remove geographic and product market restrictions. The final bill included measures to recapitalize the deposit insurance fund. The FDIC's line of credit to the U.S. Treasury was increased from $5 billion to $30 billion but without reaching agreement on how to pay for this extended credit. The regulatory structure remained essentially unchanged, and no progress was made on removing geographic barriers or expanding bank powers.

Most of the language in the bill concentrated on establishing a set of requirements for bank regulators to follow in order to avoid another replay of the banking and thrift debacle of the 1980s. Regarding efforts to roll back deposit insurance guarantees, the statute includes a legal requirement that after 1994 the FDIC cannot take any action to protect uninsured depositors if such actions would increase losses to the insurance fund. (But the statute also includes a systemic-risk exception that leaves open the policy option to provide broader coverage if there is evidence of systemic risk.)[10] With this exception, the too-big-to-fail doctrine remains in place in the United States, and the impasse on financial reform remains unchanged.[11]

In addition to the alleged destabilizing effects that might result from a reduction in deposit guarantees in U.S. domestic markets, it is also argued that such changes will place U.S. banks at a competitive disadvantage in the global marketplace. This issue of 100 percent guarantees is now imposing constraints on financial integration worldwide ("Deposit Insurance" 1992). An examination of deposit guarantee systems in other industrialized countries indicates that the use of 100 percent deposit guarantees for large bank depositors has become an accepted policy norm for resolving large bank failures throughout the world.

Deposit Guarantees: A Comparative Analysis

Global Evolution of Government Deposit Insurance Coverage

The U.S. system is the oldest national system of deposit insurance currently in operation, and other industrialized countries used the U.S. system as a model for developing their own deposit guarantee programs. There are now over thirty other countries that offer some type of depositor protection. Most of these other deposit guarantee systems were established fairly recently—seven were established in the 1960s, seven were established in the 1970s, and seventeen were created during the 1980s. In addition, while a number of countries do not have a formal national system of deposit guarantees, implicit guarantees are often provided. These implicit guarantees take the form of either central bank funding or cash infusions from healthy institutions to troubled institutions that prevent failures or losses to depositors.

With Italy's establishment of the Interbank Deposit Protection Fund in 1987, all of the G-7 countries—Canada, France, Germany, Italy, Japan, the United Kingdom, and the United States—now have some type of national deposit insurance system. (Table 7.1 summarizes the main characteristics of the different deposit insurance programs that are now operating in these countries.) In addition, the twelve countries (the G-7 countries plus Belgium, the Netherlands, Luxembourg, Sweden, and Switzerland) that signed the Basle Accord on Capital Measurement and Capital Standards all have formal systems of national deposit insurance. Most of the systems currently in operation have been established since the accord and were created in an effort to formalize existing implicit deposit guarantees to troubled banks (Bartholomew and Vanderhoff 1991, 243–48).

Deposit Insurance System: Structure and Organization

The formal structure of the different insurance schemes can be characterized under four broad issues: (1) whether membership is voluntary or compulsory; (2) whether administration of the fund is through public, private, or joint efforts; (3) the method of maintaining the fund; and (4) the type and amount of coverage provided by the fund. Of the national deposit insurance schemes shown in Table 7.1, membership in the systems in three of the countries is voluntary. Deposit insurance schemes in Canada, the United Kingdom, and the United States are officially administered, while the other G-7 countries' deposit insurance systems consist only of industry arrangements.

The two primary means by which governments fund deposit insurance schemes are regular premium assessments and post-failure levies. France and Italy use strictly post-failure funding, as does the United Kingdom's System for Building Societies. If necessary, the Association of French Banks can require contributions to cover settlement prac-

TABLE 7.1

Selected Characteristics of Deposit Insurance Systems in the G-7 Countries

Country	Membership	Administration	Method of Maintaining the Fund	Type and Amount of Coverage Provided (Domestic Currency)
Canada	Compulsory	Officially Sponsored & Administered	0.1% of insured deposits	C $60,000
France	Voluntary	Industry Arrangement	Collected as needed; assessments based on deposits	FF 400,000
Germany				
Deposit Security Fund (DSF)	Voluntary	Industry Arrangement	0.03% of total deposits	30% of the bank's liable capital per depositor
Savings Bank Security Fund (SBSF)	Compulsory	Industry Arrangement	0.03% of claims on customers	100% of deposits & credits
Credit Coorperatives Security Scheme (CCSS)	Compulsory	Industry Arrangement	Complex premiums and mutual guarantees	100% of deposits & credits
Italy	Voluntary	Industry Arrangement	Unfunded Arrangement	100% of first L 200 million 75% of next L 800 million
Japan	Compulsory	Industry Arrangement	0.012% of covered deposits	¥10,000,000
United Kingdom				
Deposit Protection Fund (DPF)	Compulsory	Officially Sponsored & Administered	Progressive levy with effective rate not to exceed 0.3% of domestic sterling deposits	75% of deposit balance up to £20,000
Building Societies Investor Protection Board (BSIPB)	Compulsory	Officially Sponsored & Administered	Unfunded Arrangement	90% of deposit balance up to £20,000
United States	Compulsory for national banks & members of the Federal Reserve	Officially Sponsored & Administered	0.23% of domestic deposits as of July 1, 1991	$100,000

Source: Philip F. Bartholomew and Vicki A. Vanderhoff. 1991. "Foreign Deposit Insurance Systems: A Comparison," *Consumer Finance Law Quarterly Report* 45, 3 (Summer).

tices over the preceding two years, as well as advances on the next two years. The remaining G-7 countries' funds are financed through a regular assessment of premiums. The rates and bases vary widely. The various bases on which the premiums are levied include total deposits, domestic deposits, and insured deposits. To date, only the FDIC plans to implement any form of risk-based premiums. In its original structure, U.S. banks were assessed a flat-rate deposit premium, independent of risk profile. The 1991 FDICIA legislation mandated that the FDIC change this flat-rate premium structure to a system of risk-based deposit insurance premiums. This new system has a rising-scale premium structure that increases from 23¢ per $100 of domestic deposits for banks included in the lowest risk classification to 31¢ per $100 of domestic deposits for banks identified in the highest risk classification.

All of the deposit insurance systems have an explicit coverage ceiling. In practice, though, the actual coverage provided may be either limited by the resources of the fund or expanded to unlimited de facto coverage. Germany's Deposit Security Fund for commercial banks is considered a unique coverage scheme because coverage is limited to 30 percent of a bank's stated equity capital, based on the last quarterly report. Since coverage declines as the level of capital diminishes, depositors have an incentive to move their deposits out of an insured financial institution as its reported financial condition deteriorates. But despite attempts to establish insurance schemes with incentives for some deposit market discipline, virtually all governments have indicated that they would, under some circumstances, step in and rescue an insolvent institution. In such cases deposit protection would be complete. So while the deposit insurance systems of the G-7 countries carry formal explicit limits to coverage, there is now the practice of providing de facto 100 percent coverage of deposits in many cases, especially large bank failures.[12]

In settling bank failures, policy makers worldwide have become less and less willing to expose banks, especially large banks, to depositor losses. And while it is generally accepted that the steady erosion of deposit market discipline that results from these guarantees has contributed to the unprecedented increase in the cost of resolving bank failures worldwide, thus far no progress has been achieved toward reaching agreement on how to roll back these guarantees. A reexamination of some of the views that contributed to the belief that bank deposit markets are inherently unstable may lead to a better understanding of how to proceed with meaningful reform.

Philosophical Underpinnings of Views on Banking Instability

Are Banks Special?

Questions about the inherent instability of the banking system stem from the view that banks are different from other financial and nonfinancial firms because of the unique nature of banks' liabilities, which are payable on demand at par value. Many economists also accept the view that banks play a special role in the economy through their role in the monetary policy process and their role in the payments mechanism. Because banks have been viewed as special, they have been subjected to much greater supervision and regulation than similar lines of commerce. The policy issues stemming from the view that banks are special predate the writings of Adam Smith, but Smith, too, pointed out over 200 years ago those features of the banking enterprise that make it a unique entity:

> Over and above the expenses which are common to every branch of trade; such as the expense of house-rent, the wages of servants, clerks, accountants, &c; the expense peculiar to a bank consists chiefly in two articles: First, in the expense of keeping at all times in its coffers, for answering the occasional demands of the holders of its notes, a large sum of money, of which it looses the interest; And, secondly, in the expense of replenishing those coffers as fast as they are emptied by answering such occasional demands.

To Smith, the unique nature of banks' liabilities conferred on them their specialty. Adam Smith also made a case for why regulatory oversight in banking is needed, despite the potential infringements on liberty inherent in such regulations:

> To restrain private people, it may be said, from receiving in payment the promissory notes of a banker, for any sum whether great or small, when they themselves are willing to receive them; or to restrain a banker from issuing such notes, when all his neighbors are willing to accept them, is a manifest violation of that natural liberty which it is the proper business of law, not to infringe, but to support. Such regulations, may, no doubt, be considered in some respects a violation of natural liberty. But those exertions of the natural liberty of a few individuals, which might endanger the security of the whole society, are, and ought to be, restrained by the laws of all governments; of the most free, as well as of the most despotic. The obligation of building party walls, in order to prevent the communication of fire, is a violation of natural liberty, exactly of the same kind with the regulations of the banking trade which are here proposed. (Smith 1965, 285)

This public-good aspect to the business of banking implies some amount of regulation and oversight to promote social welfare. But few would doubt that the array of federal supervision and regulation under which U.S. banks operate far exceeds what Smith would view as necessary to promote the general welfare. And what he envisioned as necessary was even then a result of the Bank of England's monopoly privileges and the restrictions and prohibitions on the activities of private banks.

The system of federal guarantees and regulatory oversight, in place in the United States since the Great Depression, has now broken down. The bankruptcy of the FSLIC, the insolvency of the FDIC, and a taxpayer bailout of the thrift industry of at least $200 billion contributed to a widespread consensus that reform was urgently needed. On an international scale, the global implications of the activities of the Bank of Credit and Commerce International offer stark evidence of a breakdown in the established framework in the banking industry. There remains, however, an entrenched belief against a role for deposit market discipline in banking. The currently accepted regulatory paradigm in banking views banks as inherently unstable, and because of this, supervision and regulation are seen as necessary in order to avert widespread financial crises. Fundamental reform of the financial system, both in the United States and worldwide, requires a reevaluation of this widely accepted view of how the regulatory framework affects banks and a reconsideration of what constitutes a financial crisis.

Banking and Regulatory Oversight

In Search of a New Paradigm

The current debate on financial reform in the United States centers on two fundamentally different viewpoints, or paradigms, concerning the role of regulation and market forces. On one side of the debate is the view that greater regulatory efforts are needed to cope with an increasingly complex international financial marketplace. Alternatively, there is the view that regulation is the source of many of our current difficulties, and that what is needed is less, rather than more, reliance on regulatory oversight. This dichotomy reflects fundamentally different views regarding the roles of regulation and market forces as means of disciplining the banking industry. And these views are influencing the debate on financial reform worldwide.

The perspective that greater regulation is required to monitor financial performance stems from the view that financial markets are themselves a source of the problem, and thus cannot be relied upon to provide the proper signaling mechanisms in banking that markets do in other sorts of businesses. According to this view, unprecedented technological change has fostered an increasingly interdependent international financial marketplace in which major transactions are completed in a very short period of time. As a result, financial markets are more volatile today than ever before, with the inevitable outcome that the private actions of individual participants may not lead to the public-sector goal of maintaining financial-sector stability. In short, Adam Smith's invisible hand may not be applicable to banking, or to financial markets in general, so the argument goes (Corrigan 1991, 44–53).

A radically different viewpoint on the role of regulation in the financial marketplace stresses that regulation itself is a major factor contributing to the current difficulties faced by the U.S. banking system. Extensive reliance on an ever-expanding scope of federal safety nets has undermined both the signaling mechanism and the allocative role of the financial marketplace. As a result, distortions exist in the financial markets that inhibit the self-correcting forces that would normally operate in competitive markets. In this view, the United States is currently faced with a highly inefficient system of regulatory taxes and subsidies, which has created a more fragile banking system and contributed to the insolvency of the thrift industry. Supervision and regulation have been relied upon to provide some defense against the moral-hazard problem associated with the fixed-rate deposit insurance system; however, this process has failed to accomplish its goal. The massive concentration of troubled bank and thrift assets contributed to the insolvency of the FSLIC and the need to recapitalize the FDIC fund in the United States. And this experience was not unique to the United States, as evidenced by the unprecedented public-sector costs of resolving the financial-sector difficulties that emerged worldwide during the past decade (Hoskins 1989).

Barriers to Reform: Can We Trust Deposit Markets?

Given this poor record, why have policy makers persisted in relying on regulatory oversight and government guarantees as a means of avoiding unwanted financial-sector crises that may result from bank failures? Unraveling the system of deposit guarantees that has evolved over the past fifty years presents a formidable task and a radical departure from the status quo. In testimony on deposit insurance reform before the U.S. Congress in October 1990, Alan Greenspan, chairman of the Federal Reserve Board, described the current dilemma when he stated: "The ideal is an institutional framework that, to the extent possible, induces banks both to hold more capital and to be managed *as if there were no safety net,* while at the same time shielding unsophisticated depositors and minimizing disruptions to credit and payment flows" (emphasis added).

The benefits of the market process cannot be replicated without letting the process work. Banks, as a group, cannot be managed as if there were no safety net when a safety net is in place that protects and shields depositors from losses and minimizes disruptions to credit flows and the payments system. But policy makers are reluctant to allow the deposit market to operate freely, because of the allegedly destabilizing consequences that will result from deposit market discipline. Thus, while there is now at least widespread agreement about the problems inherent in a system of 100 percent deposit guarantees, the debate persists about the role that deposit market discipline should play in banking. The fundamental question—"Can we trust the market to discipline banks?"—remains at the forefront. Answers to this question involve the long-standing debate about the advantages and disadvantages of the market system.

Market Discipline Versus Government Deposit Guarantees

Market Benefits: What Do We Give Up?

Without deposit guarantees, depositors have greater incentives to monitor the asset quality of banks, *because* they face the potential of financial losses. This monitoring process assists bank managers in controlling their exposure to risk. Financial losses, just like profits, provide a signaling mechanism that helps produce an efficient allocation of resources. In the bank deposit market, this signaling mechanism has not been allowed to operate freely, because of concerns about systemic deposit runs, or banking panics. These concerns about banking panics are deeply rooted in U.S. government restrictions and regulatory practices.

As financial-sector difficulties continue to evolve, more attention has been paid to various alternatives to restrain excessive bank risk-taking. These alternatives do not attempt to eliminate risk-taking but aim at allowing financial markets to price accurately the risk-reward trade-off inherent in investment projects.[13] Suggested changes to deposit insurance coverage, though, have been criticized as ineffective methods of controlling bank risk-taking (Randall 1989, 3–24). Much of this evidence, however, is derived from markets as they currently operate, under a system of virtual 100 percent deposit coverage.[14] This evidence does not and cannot reflect conditions that would exist under different institutional settings.[15]

The failure to discern a consistent pattern regarding the potential role of market discipline on bank risk-taking is not surprising given the current institutional environment of de facto 100 percent deposit guarantees. Markets make use of all available information to process and evaluate a bank's risk profile. As expectations of implicit coverage of all deposits have evolved, depositors would not be expected to monitor and penalize the risk-taking activities of insured depositories. Under other institutional arrangements—principally where 100 percent guarantees are absent—depositors would have stronger incentives to monitor the risk profiles of insured financial intermediaries and to price risk appropriately.

These alternative institutional arrangements have not been allowed to operate in bank deposit markets, because of widely held views about the inherent instability of banks. This instability, it is alleged, would inevitably give rise to recurring financial crises if banks were allowed to operate based on market pricing signals. What constitutes a real financial crisis, therefore, remains at the forefront of the deadlock on how to reform the financial system.

Real Versus Pseudo-Crises

As asset quality problems continue to escalate, interest among academics and policy makers in what constitutes a financial crisis has heightened.[16] In a recent work on financial-market crises, Anna Schwartz offers a definition of "financial crisis" that distinguishes between "real" and "pseudo" crises:

> A financial crisis is fueled by fears that the means of payment will be unobtainable at any price and, in a fractional-reserve banking system, leads to a scramble for high-powered money. It is precipitated by actions of the public that suddenly squeeze the reserves of the banking system. In a futile attempt to restore reserves, the banks may call loans, refuse to roll over existing loans, or resort to selling assets.... The essence of a financial crisis is that it is short-lived, ending with a slackening of the public's demand for additional currency.... No financial crisis has occurred in the United States since 1933.... All the phenomena of recent years that have been characterized as financial crises—a decline in asset prices of equity

stocks, real estate commodities; depreciation of the exchange value of a national currency; financial distress of a large non-financial firm, a large municipality, a financial industry, or sovereign debtors—are pseudo-financial crises. (Schwartz 1986, 11–31)

To Schwartz, a real financial crisis occurs when depositors indiscriminately withdraw funds from the financial system by converting financial instruments into currency. Her definition thus distinguishes between a flight to currency and a movement of funds among financial intermediaries. A widespread conversion of deposits into currency would constitute a financial crisis. If actions are not taken to offset a shift out of deposits and into currency, a generalized contraction in the banking industry and in the money supply would occur, as happened in the Great Depression. And this shift would likely generate damaging effects on economic activity.

On the other hand, a transfer of deposits among different banks or other financial intermediaries based on the changing risk/reward assessments of depositors would not constitute a financial crisis, because a contraction in the banking industry as a whole would not follow. This criterion would not apply only to the banking industry. In fact, given the declining relative position of banks in financial markets, it is important to note that other types of financial institutions could also be involved in a financial crisis.[17] But here, too, a transfer of financial assets among financial institutions changes the composition of deposits that are held at banks and other intermediaries. Rather than necessarily causing severe adverse effects on economic activity, though, this movement of funds can actually strengthen the financial system by encouraging insured institutions to price their deposit liabilities to reflect more accurately the risk/reward preferences of depositors (Kaufman 1988, 9–40). Relative prices of financial assets would change, which would likely impact the allocation of financial capital, but the extent to which this reallocation would affect economic activity is unclear.[18] But even if direct real-sector effects emerge, the financial crises of the 1980s—and their impact on taxpayers—have generated serious problems that will likely impact economic activity in the future. The resource misallocation that resulted from the financial difficulties of the 1980s should not be understated when evaluating the costs of policy actions, however well-intentioned, aimed at avoiding financial-sector instability.

A misinterpretation of what constitutes a true financial crisis remains a stumbling block to financial reform. Among economists a financial crisis results when financial-sector difficulties become so acute as to cause severe adverse consequences to real economic activity. But among policy makers, the distinction between a financial crisis that has severe economic consequences and movements of deposits among banks has become blurred. Policy makers have treated large deposit flows from one bank to another—especially those involving large banks—as if they have systemic implications. Policy actions are thus taken *to avoid* the possibility of a systemic panic rather than to formulate a response to an actual panic.

This view that a shift of deposits, especially at large banks, has systemic implications and thus constitutes a crisis has produced a regulatory framework in banking that prevents banks from receiving deposit market pricing signals on risk-taking activities. Ironically, this framework has enhanced the very instability that it was supposed to minimize.

Conclusions

Throughout U.S. banking history, from the First Bank of the United States chartered in 1791, through the Second Bank of the United States established in 1816, the National Banking Act of 1863, the Federal Reserve Act of 1913, and the host of regulatory legislation enacted in the aftermath of the Great Depression, a basic distrust of deposit market forces to discipline bank risk-taking activities has been a pivotal factor in the formulation of bank regulatory policy.

The basic framework underlying financial reform is a set of beliefs about how financial markets work—what we referred to as the current paradigm for banking reform. We are skeptical that an institutional framework that relies on regulation and supervision can replace the marketplace as an effective means of allocating financial capital. This is particularly evident given the increasingly integrated nature of the global marketplace. A move to a safer, more efficient financial system will require a reconsideration of several myths about banking, the most prominent being its inherent instability and the concomitant need for 100 percent deposit guarantees. The U.S. banking industry is now one of the most heavily regulated industries worldwide. The conflicts between federal deposit guarantees, regulatory oversight, and the social responsibilities that have been imposed on insured depository institutions place these more regulated institutions at a severe competitive disadvantage in today's global marketplace.

The regulatory framework that grew out of the view that bank deposit markets are unstable has exacerbated the problems inherent in the fragmented U.S. banking industry. The regulatory framework put in place during the Great Depression has now unraveled, and the structure imposed by the 1991 banking legislation will not solve the underlying problems facing U.S. banks. To be effective, financial reform efforts must rely less on government decision making and guarantees and look more to the role of individual decision makers in reaping the rewards and accepting the responsibilities of the risk-reward trade-offs in a market economy. Banks do not need 100 percent deposit guarantees to operate, and governments do not need a too-big-to-fail doctrine to maintain a safe and sound banking system.

Appendix A
Handling Distressed Banks—The U.S. Record

U.S. Settlement Practices in the 1970s

In the postdepression environment in the United States, large bank failures were virtually nonexistent until the 1970s.[19] The first billion-dollar bank failure in the United States occurred in October 1973 and involved the United States National Bank of San Diego. This was quickly followed in 1974 by the failure of Franklin National Bank of New York, the nation's twentieth-largest bank. In both cases, the FDIC arranged a purchase and assumption transaction in which all general creditors were made whole.[20]

U.S. Settlement Practices in the 1980s

Banking difficulties escalated in the 1980s, both in the United States and worldwide. The FDIC's handling of bank failures continued to evolve during the decade, as the number of failures increased and as some of the nation's largest banks failed or requested financial assistance. The unprecedented number and size of banking difficulties in the 1980s in the United States placed great strains on the deposit insurance fund. Moreover, as banking difficulties increased over the course of the decade, the settlement practices utilized by the FDIC evolved to include virtual 100 percent coverage of bank deposits.

During the July 4 weekend in 1982, the Comptroller of the Currency closed Penn Square Bank in Oklahoma City. The FDIC set up a Deposit Insurance National Bank (DINB) to pay off insured depositors. The FDIC pursued a payoff because it was not possible to assess the cost of arranging a purchase and assumption transaction. Due to the heavy volume of loan participations and questions about the accuracy of information given to loan purchasers, a large number of lawsuits were anticipated. By paying off insured depositors, the FDIC's maximum loss was the $250 million in insured deposits, which would ultimately be reduced by the FDIC's share of receivership collections (FDIC 1984, 97–98).

The FDIC's payout to Penn Square took financial markets somewhat by surprise. Analysts have argued that the use of the payout may have been an attempt to alter depositors' perceptions of the too-big-to-fail doctrine and thus refocus attention toward risk-taking at insured institutions. While Penn Square was the largest bank to receive a payout, it was much smaller than any money-center bank. Therefore, the Penn Square failure may have only altered perceptions as to what are large and small banks, rather than contributed to any significant debate about whether large banks would be permitted to fail (Benston et al. 1986, 181; Short 1985).

Of the $2 billion in oil and gas participations in which Penn Square Bank had been involved, one-half, or $1 billion, was held by Continental Illinois National Bank (Sprague 1986). Following the failure of Penn Square Bank, Continental's stock price dropped from $25 a share in June to $16 in mid-August. Its credit ratings were downgraded, and it was eventually forced to seek deposits in the more expensive Eurodollar market.

In May of 1984, persistent rumors of financial difficulties at Continental Illinois triggered outflows of billions of dollars of uninsured deposits. The perception that a too-big-to-fail doctrine would be used to settle the nation's largest bank failures was strengthened by the actions taken to settle Continental Illinois. When faced with a liquidity run, the FDIC announced that it would guarantee *all* of Continental's deposits, including those over $100,000. The deterioration in Continental's loan portfolio resulted in a lack of interest by potential bidders for Continental. As a result, the bank was taken over by the FDIC, which owned 80 percent of the bank's stock. Equity holders lost most of the value of their stock in the company, as well as managerial control. As a consequence of the bailout, nondeposit creditors of the corporation and uninsured depositors were reimbursed in full (Woodward 1989, 11).

The Continental Illinois rescue triggered more debate over the too-big-to-fail doctrine. Prior to the Penn Square rescue, all large banks were settled with a purchase and assumption. This explicit guarantee to the nation's largest banks was in stark contrast to the treatment of several smaller banks that were settled with modified payoffs. Uninsured depositors at these smaller banks did incur financial losses under these payoffs, with initial payouts ranging from 35 to 75 percent of the dollar volume of their holdings (Short 1985, 12–20). These modified payouts represented attempts by regulators to introduce greater deposit market discipline on bank risk-taking activities. However, the use of modified payouts was derailed by the obvious competitive inequities that result from following a policy of too-big-to-fail.

In the latter part of the 1980s, banking difficulties in the United States were concentrated in Texas. In fact, from 1985 to 1989, bank failures in Texas accounted for over 50 percent of U.S. failures. Of note were failures of three of Texas's largest banking organizations. In these three cases, the resolutions undertaken by the FDIC protected all deposits in full, with an estimated cost of over $4 billion (Robinson 1990, 13–24; O'Keefe 1990).

U.S. Settlement Practices in the 1990s

Banking problems in the United States moved from the Southwest to the Northeast during the early 1990s. Real estate–related credit problems, once concentrated in the energy-dependent states of the Southwest, began to emerge in New England. In January 1991, the comptroller of the currency closed the three subsidiary banks of the Bank of New England Corporation and appointed the FDIC as receiver. The FDIC assumed all deposits and most other liabilities and assets of Bank of New England, N.A., Boston, Massachusetts (total assets of $13.9 billion); Connecticut Bank and Trust Company, N.A., Hartford, Connecticut (total assets of $7.1 billion); and Maine National Bank, Portland, Maine (total assets of $1 billion). All deposits, including uninsured deposits, were fully protected. Nonsubordinated creditors will share pro rata with the FDIC in the receivership estates of the banks. The new banks did not assume any liabilities of the parent holding company, Bank of New England Corporation, or its creditors. As part of the transaction, the FDIC infused $750 million of capital into the banks. In April 1991, Fleet/Norstar Financial Group together with Kohlberg Kravis Roberts and Company agreed to purchase the bridge banks from the FDIC (FDIC 1991). The failure of the Bank of New England unit was, at the time, the third-largest failure, following that of Continental Illinois Bank and Trust Company in 1984 and First Republic Bancorp in Texas in 1988 (Suskind and Bacon 1991).

Appendix B
Handling Distressed Banks—
The International Record

Banking difficulties were not exclusively confined to the United States. Beginning in the 1970s, banking-sector stress was emerging in other industrialized countries as well. Moreover, policy actions to resolve these difficulties also followed the U.S. policy of evolving to 100 percent coverage to all depositors, especially those at large banks.

International Settlement Practices in the 1970s

The 1974 collapse of Bankhaus I. D. Herstatt was the culmination of years of concern in international banking circles over the vulnerability of interbank lending (FDIC 1989). At the time of its failure, Herstatt was one of Germany's largest privately owned banks, with assets of approximately $900 million. By June 1974, Herstatt had incurred such large losses from foreign exchange trading that it was forced to ask the Bundesbank (Germany's central bank) for help. Efforts to reorganize the bank failed, and the German central bank closed Herstatt on 26 June 1974 at 4:00 P.M. local time, while New York banks were still trading, leaving many foreign banks exposed to losses (U.S. Department of Treasury 1991, xxi–8). Germany's commercial banks set up a fund to reimburse Herstatt depositors of less than $8,000. All depositors with accounts exceeding this amount lost some portion of their funds. Of the remaining creditors, German banks received 45 percent of their claims, foreign banks received 55 percent, and other small creditors received 65 percent (Woodward 1989, 8).

International banking supervision was strengthened as a result of the Herstatt failure. In September 1974 the Group of Ten central-bank governors met in Basle, Switzerland, to establish a framework that would ensure the long-term health of international banking. In December 1975 the committee issued the Basle Concordat, which attempted to establish guidelines for supervision of banks that operate in more than one country. The concordat assigned primary responsibility for supervising liquidity and solvency to the host authority, but acknowledged that the parent authorities have a moral commitment to supervise the solvency of their foreign branches.

International Settlement Practices in the 1980s

The United States was not the only country experiencing banking difficulties and an expansion of implicit coverage of all bank deposits into the 1980s. As in the United States, a pattern of resolution policies emerged in other industrialized countries in which regulators appeared increasingly unwilling to allow depositors to suffer losses.

The financial regulatory system in Canada was overhauled in June 1987 in response to earlier failures there. Although no Canadian banks failed between 1923 and 1985, twelve trust companies have required assistance from the Canada Deposit Insurance Corporation (CDIC) since its inception in 1967. In March 1985, the Canadian government announced a C$255 million ($187 million) plan for resolving Canadian Commercial Bank (CCB) of Edmonton, Alberta, the country's tenth-largest commercial bank with C$3 billion ($2.2 billion) in assets. The support package consisted of a capital infusion from the CDIC, taxpayer contributions from the Alberta and federal governments, and funding from the "Big Six" commercial banks.[21]

Six months after announcing the rescue of CCB, the Canadian government was forced to liquidate it. At this time the government also took control of Northland Bank of Calgary, a C$1.4 billion ($1.0 billion) bank. The change in the government's position toward CCB was prompted by an examination in which many of the bank's loans were classified as unsatisfactory. Instead of restoring confidence in CCB, the bailout focused on its problems and those of other regional banks, causing deposit withdrawals. By 1 September, when the Bank of Canada withdrew its support from CCB and Northland, the central bank had pumped C$1.8 billion ($1.3 billion) in secured short-term loans into the two banks, both of which were eventually liquidated. No depositors, though, either insured or uninsured, lost money. The final cost to the Canadian government was almost C$900 million ($660 million) of which C$430 million ($315 million) represented uninsured deposits. None of the initial C$225 million ($187 million) was ever recovered.

Following these two failures, three other Canadian banks experienced difficulty. These banks were either taken over or assisted through their problems, and again no depositors suffered losses. As a result of the Canadian banking crisis, the Office of Superintendent of Financial Institutions was created as an integrated regulatory body with greater supervisory powers than those of the former agencies, and the CDIC's role in providing deposit insurance to the general public was strengthened (U.S. Department of Treasury 1991, xxi–8).

In 1983 the Basle Concordat was tested in Germany when Schroeder, Munchmeyer, Hengst & Co. (SMH) neared insolvency due primarily to loans extended to a single company by its Luxembourg subsidiary. The company, IBH Holdings, defaulted on its DM 900 million ($405 million) loan, which was roughly one-third of all SMH assets. It was also revealed that SMH held a 9 percent equity stake in IBH. In making the loans, SMH violated at least the spirit of a law that limited a bank's loans to a single borrower to 75 percent of capital. For SMH this would have totaled only DM 83 million ($37 million). SMH circumvented the law by lending through its Luxembourg subsidiary.

At the request of the Bundesbank, a group of German banks came to the aid of SMH, and the deposit guarantee fund also contributed some cash. Existing management was ousted, and the banks assumed control. Three months later, Lloyd's Bank International acquired parts of SMH's commercial banking business and all of its investment banking business. As was the case in other countries, no depositors lost money, although some of the creditor banks' contribution was never recovered. As a result of the failure, lending restrictions were altered to cover partially owned domestic or foreign subsidiaries (U.S. Department of Treasury 1991, xxi–10).

International Settlement Practices in the 1990s

The 1990s have seen some abatement of banking difficulties, especially in the United States. However, the recent collapse of Barings Bank and the fraudulent activities uncovered at Daiwa Bank's New York office highlight the challenges that regulators face in today's increasingly complex and integrated financial marketplace. Regulators ultimately allowed Barings to fail with no discernible long-term effects on the international financial markets. The ability of regulators to keep pace with the increasingly complex financial marketplace was called into question in the Daiwa case, however, where unauthorized bond trading had taken place for more than a decade at a cost to the bank of over $1 billion.

New lending rules in the United Kingdom that were adopted as a result of banking difficulties of the 1970s were tested with the June 1990 failure of British Commonwealth and Merchant Bank (BCMB), with assets of about £430 million ($780 million). BCMB was considered a sound, well-capitalized bank, but it faced a liquidity crisis when its owner was forced to write off £550 million ($990 million) in loans to one of its subsidiaries. Fears of a run on the bank led to the creation of a £100 million ($180 million) "lifeboat" operation in which the primary clearing banks recycled funds to healthy secondary banks to meet maturing deposit obligations.[22] Much debate centered around the handling of depositor and creditor funds, which were frozen in June. While some depositors began receiving money on 1 October, it was not clear to what extent they were repaid. It was believed that the delay would be over once the bank's holding company was sold. Thus far, however, the only bid has come from a Turkish conglomerate, and the Bank of England is reluctant to give its approval to the sale.

BCCI and International Regulatory Efforts

In the international arena, the closure of the Bank of Credit and Commerce International (BCCI) in July 1991 captured attention around the world. BCCI was a worldwide institution based in Luxembourg. Its seizure by banking authorities in several different countries influenced the debate over both expanded powers in the banking industry and the ability of regulatory oversight to monitor the risk-taking activities of international institutions.

BCCI was founded in 1972 in Luxembourg, its registered home, by a Pakistani financier with backing from Bank of America and Arab investors. BCCI's assets totaled approximately $20 billion and were scattered in a branch network that encompassed sixty-nine countries. Some analysts estimated that losses from the bank's closure could total anywhere from $5 to $15 billion. Most of these losses will be incurred by thousands of depositors in Europe, the Mideast, and Asia. The biggest single loser probably will be Zayed bi Sultan al-Nahayan, Abu Dhabi's ruler, who invested $1 billion in BCCI stock in 1990. The royal family and government of Abu Dhabi owned 77 percent of BCCI.

Although several major U.S. banks denied any exposure to BCCI, a *Wall Street Journal* article stated that U.S. financial institutions, including big banks and brokerage houses, may have to absorb losses of up to $500 million from credit lines granted to BCCI. BCCI has been linked to at least four U.S. banks. It had secretly acquired a stake in both First American Bankshares, Inc., a holding company based in Washington, D.C., with $11 billion in assets, and Independence Bank, an organization based in Encino, California, with $640 million in assets. There was one incident in which BCCI apparently drew funds from First American by having the bank purchase another institution, National Bank of Georgia, which also was secretly controlled by BCCI. In addition, BCCI has been linked to CenTrust Savings Bank, a Miami-based institution that failed. The Federal Reserve has ordered BCCI to divest itself of the unspecified stakes in both First American and Independence Bank and barred it from conducting any business with them.

BCCI's closure raised questions from depositors, banking experts, and politicians around the world regarding charges that regulators were much too slow (or too fast) in closing the bank. These charges spurred investigations in several countries of whether financial markets were made aware of BCCI's possible illegal activities, and whether despite this, many banks and government institutions continued to do business with the bank. In the end, financial institutions and governments around the world had billions in deposits and trading accounts with BCCI when it was shut down.

As a result of this exposure, regulators in many countries tried to begin liquidation proceedings against the bank's local offices. However, several court decisions, including some in the United States and Britain, stalled these proceedings in an effort to protect the bank's assets for the benefit of all creditors. Touche Ross, BCCI's liquidator, was successful in negotiating a $2.3 billion settlement with the bank's main shareholders, the government of Abu Dhabi and a Saudi Arabian bank. Payouts from this settlement were due to start in the summer of 1995, but were delayed by an appeal to a Luxembourg court by former BCCI employees. One of the frustrations in the BCCI case has been the lack of an international forum for coordinating the liquidation of a company facing difficulties in several countries at once.

Notes

1. Other restrictions on banks included reserve requirements, prohibitions on note issues, and laws against option clauses and due bills, all of which served to reduce considerably banks' flexibility to respond to changing market conditions.
2. For more on how financial innovations develop to circumvent banking regulations, see Kane 1981, 355–67.

3. For more on this issue, see Robinson 1990, 13–24.
4. See Friedman and Schwartz (1963) for a description of the shortcomings of the monetary policy response to the Great Depression. Also, Goodfriend and King (1988) present an overview of the appropriate monetary policy response to banking difficulties.
5. For an overview of U.S. resolution practices, see Appendix A.
6. It is important to note that too-big-to-fail practices often do not provide protection to the stock- and bondholders of the failed institution. Depositors are covered in full, but bond- and stockholders frequently lose all the value of their investments in the failed institution. A policy distinction has thus been made between the merits of market discipline from bond- and stockholders versus market discipline from bank depositors. For more on this issue, see Evanoff 1992.
7. For more on the role of FDIC settlement practices, and the different treatment given to large and small bank depositors, see Short 1985, 12–20.
8. In early 1990 the New York Clearinghouse Association voted to oppose the too-big-to-fail doctrine. Members of the association include some of the largest money-center banks, such as Chase Manhattan, Citicorp, and J. P. Morgan. See Horowitz 1990.
9. Recent policies for handling large bank failures are in marked contrast to the policy response to the 1987 stock market crash, when liquidity was provided liberally to the financial markets, but with no protections given to individual institutions.
10. See Title I—Safety and Soundness, Subtitle E—Least Cost Resolution, of FDICIA for the systemic-risk exception for too-big-to-fail.
11. For more on these issues, see Short and Robinson 1992.
12. For settlement practices in other industrialized countries, see Appendix B.
13. Ely (1994) has proposed a system of cross-guarantees on banks. Other proposals include implementing a coinsurance feature to deposit insurance, limits on the amount of coverage, and a role for the private provision of deposit insurance. See White (1989) for a summary of various reform proposals.
14. There exists some evidence that deposit markets could and did discipline banks before the advent of implicit 100 percent guarantees. Several large banks encountered serious difficulties in the 1970s, including U.S. National Bank of San Diego and Franklin National Bank. In addition, real estate investment trusts began to sour at this time, placing pressures on bank earnings. During this time, deposit markets did exert discipline on institutions by penalizing those intermediaries engaged in more risky activities. An interest rate "tiering" was observed in the market for large certificates of deposit in that those banks with a higher risk profile were forced to pay higher rates on their large CDs. Deposit holders required risk premiums in light of the less than 100 percent coverage by the FDIC. See Crane 1976, 213–24.
15. More recent evidence on the potential role of market discipline is mixed. A recent study found that the market for large, uninsured certificates of deposit still extracts a price for bank risk-taking—measures of perceived bank risk were found to be positively correlated with yields on these deposits. See Hannan and Hanweck 1988, 203–11; Baer and Brewer 1986, 23–37. However, an examination of the potential for subordinated notes and debentures to exert market discipline on banks revealed that the return on these instruments was unrelated to what regulators considered to be important determinants of bank riskiness, including both the index proposed by the FDIC for assessing risk-related insurance premiums and various balance sheet measures. See Avery et al. 1989; Gordon and Santomero 1990.

16. For different perspectives on what constitutes a financial crisis, see Feldstein 1991. For an analysis of financial crises spanning over 200 years, see Kindleberger 1978. See also Minsky 1977.
17. For more on the declining relative importance of banks see Kaufman 1991.
18. For an overview of these issues, see Gertler 1988, 559–88.
19. "Failure" in the presence of federal deposit insurance occurs when the primary regulator declares the bank insolvent and either closes the institution or temporarily assumes its operations.
20. In a purchase and assumption, the FDIC arranges for a healthy bank to purchase the assets of the failed bank and assume its deposit liabilities. See Federal Deposit Insurance Corporation 1984, 91.
21. Canada's Big Six Commercial Banks are the Bank of Montreal, the Bank of Nova Scotia, Canadian Imperial Bank of Commerce, the National Bank of Canada, the Royal Bank of Canada, and Toronto Dominion Bank.
22. For more on the "lifeboat," see Fforde 1986, 186–87.

References

Avery, Robert B., Terrence M. Belton, and Michael Goldberg. 1989. "Market Discipline in Regulating Bank Risk: New Evidence from the Capital Markets." *Journal of Money, Credit, and Banking* 20 (November).

Baer, Herbert, and Elijah Brewer. 1986. "Uninsured Deposits as a Source of Market Discipline: Some New Evidence." *Economic Perspectives* (September/October). Chicago: Federal Reserve Bank.

Bagehot, Walter. *Lombard Street.* 1962. As quoted in Thomas M. Humphrey, "Lender of Last Resort: The Concept in History." *Economic Review* (March–April 1989: 8–16). Richmond: Federal Reserve Bank.

Bartholomew, Philip F., and Vicki A. Vanderhoff. 1991. "Foreign Deposit Insurance Systems: A Comparison." *Consumer Finance Law Quarterly Report* 45, 3 (Summer).

Benston, George J., Robert A. Eisenbeis, Paul M. Horvitz, Edward J. Kane, and George G. Kaufman. 1986. *Perspectives on Safe and Sound Banking: Past, Present, and Future.* Cambridge, MA: MIT Press.

Brumbaugh, R. Dan, Jr. 1988. *Thrifts Under Siege: Restoring Order to American Banking.* Cambridge: Ballinger Publishing Company.

Carrington, Tim. 1984. "U.S. Won't Let 11 Biggest Banks in Nation Fail." *Wall Street Journal* (20 September).

Corrigan, E. Gerald. 1991. "The Risk of a Financial Crisis." In *The Risk of Economic Crisis,* edited by Martin Feldstein. Chicago: University of Chicago Press.

Crane, Dwight B. 1976. "A Study of Interest Rate Spreads in the 1974 CD Market." *Journal of Bank Research.* (Autumn).

"Deposit Insurance: Euro-muddle." 1992. *Economist* (19 December): 74.

Ely, Bert. 1994. "Financial Innovation and Deposit Insurance: The 100 Percent Cross-Guarantee Concept." *Cato Journal* 13 (Winter).

Evanoff, Douglas D. 1992. "Issues in Financial Regulation." *Working Paper Series.* (30 November). Chicago: Federal Reserve Bank.

Federal Deposit Insurance Corporation (FDIC). 1984. *The First Fifty Years: A History of the FDIC 1933–1983.* Washington, DC: FDIC.

———. 1989. *Deposit Insurance for the Nineties: Meeting the Challenge.* Washington, DC: FDIC.

———. 1991. *News Releases,* PR–3–91 and PR–61–91. (6 January and 22 April).

Feldstein, Martin, ed. 1991. *The Risk of Economic Crisis*. Chicago: University of Chicago Press.

Fforde, J. S. 1986. "Walter Bagehot and the Theory of Central Banking: A Comment." In *Financial Crisis and the World Banking System*, edited by Forrest Capie and Geoffrey Wood. New York: St. Martin's Press.

FIDCIA. *Title I—Safety and Soundness, Subtitle E—Least Cost Resolution.*

Friedman, Milton, and Anna J. Schwartz. 1963. *A Monetary History of the United States, 1867–1960*. Princeton, NJ: Princeton University Press.

Gertler, Mark. 1988. "Financial Structure and Aggregate Economic Activity: An Overview." *Journal of Money, Credit, and Banking* 20, 3, part 2 (August).

Golembe, Carter H. 1961. "The Deposit Insurance Legislation of 1933: An Examination of Its Antecedents and Its Purposes." *Political Science Quarterly* 76.

Goodfriend, Marvin, and Robert G. King. 1988. "Financial Deregulation, Monetary Policy, and Central Banking." *Economic Review* (May–June). Richmond: Federal Reserve Bank.

Gordon, Gary, and Anthony M. Santomero. 1990. "Market Discipline and Bank Subordinated Debt." *Journal of Money, Credit, and Banking* 22 (February).

Hannan, Timothy H., and Gerald A. Hanweck. 1988. "Bank Insolvency Risk and the Market for Large Certificates of Deposit." *Journal of Money, Credit, and Banking* (May).

Horowitz, Jed. 1990. "Banks in NY Clearinghouse Vote to Oppose 'Too Big to Fail' Credo." *American Banker* (January).

Hoskins, W. Lee. 1989. "Reforming the Banking and Thrift Industries: Assessing Regulation and Risk." American College/Bryn Mawr Frank M. Engle lecture (22 May).

Kane, Edward J. 1981. "Accelerating Inflation, Technological Innovation, and the Decreasing Effectiveness of Banking Regulation." *Journal of Finance* (May).

Kaufman, George G. 1988. "The Truth About Bank Runs." In *The Financial Services Revolution: Policy Directions for the Future*, edited by Catherine England and Thomas Huertas. Boston: Kluwer Academic Publishers.

———. 1991. "The Diminishing Role of Commercial Banking in the U.S. Economy." *Financial Regulation Working Paper Series*. (May). Chicago: Federal Reserve Bank.

Kindleberger, C. P. 1978. *Manias, Panics, and Crashes: A History of Financial Crises*. New York: Basic Books.

Minsky, H. P. 1977. "A Theory of Systematic Fragility." In *Financial Crises: Institutions and Markets in a Fragile Financial Environment*, edited by E. I. Altman and A. W. Sametz. New York: Wiley.

O'Keefe, John. 1990. "The Texas Banking Crisis: Causes and Consequences 1980–1989." Federal Deposit Insurance Corporation *Banking Review* 3, 2 (Winter).

Randall, Richard E. 1989. "Can the Market Evaluate Asset Quality Exposure in Banks?" *New England Economic Review* (July–August). Boston: Federal Reserve Bank.

Robinson, Kenneth J. 1990. "The Performance of Eleventh District Financial Institutions in the 1980s: A Broader Pespective." *Financial Industry Studies* (May). Dallas: Federal Reserve Bank.

Schwartz, Anna J. 1986. "Real and Pseudo-Financial Crises." In *Financial Crises and the World Banking System*, edited by Forest Capie and Geoffrey E. Wood. New York: St. Martin's Press.

———. 1988. "Financial Stability and the Federal Safety Net." In *Restructuring Banking and Financial Services in America*, edited by W. S. Haraf and R. M. Kushmeider. Washington, DC: American Enterprise Institute.

Shadow Financial Regulatory Committee Statement (SFRC). 1989. "An Outline of a Program for Deposit Insurance and Regulatory Reform." 41 (February 13).

Short, Genie D. 1985. "FDIC Settlement Practices and the Size of Failed Banks." *Economic Review* (March). Dallas: Federal Reserve Bank.

Short, Genie D., and Kenneth J. Robinson. 1992. "Banking Conditions and Legislation: What Is the Appropriate Role of Government in the Economy?" *Financial Industry Issues* (Third Quarter). Dallas: Federal Reserve Bank.

Smith, Adam. 1965. *An Inquiry into the Nature and Causes of the Wealth of Nations.* New York: The Modern Library.

Sprague, Irvine H. 1986. *Bailout.* New York: Basic Books.

Suskind, Ron, and Kenneth H. Bacon. 1991. "U.S. Recession Claims Bank of New England as First Big Victim." *Wall Street Journal* (7 January): A1.

Thornton, Henry. [1802] 1939. *An Enquiry into the Nature and Effects of the Paper Credit of Great Britain*, edited with an introduction by F. A. von Hayek. New York: Rinehart and Company.

U.S. Department of the Treasury. 1991. *Modernizing the Financial System: Recommendations for Safer, More Competitive Banks* (February). Washington, DC: GPO.

White, Lawrence J. 1989. "The Reform of Deposit Insurance." *Journal of Economic Perspectives* 3 (Fall).

Woodward, G. Thomas. 1989. "Deposit Guarantees in Other Countries." *Congressional Research Report for Congress,* Congressional Research Service report no. 89–637E (27 November): 11.

8

The IMF's Destructive Recipe:
Rising Tax Rates and Falling Currencies

Alan Reynolds

The International Monetary Fund (IMF) is one of the three major institutions created at Bretton Woods, New Hampshire, in 1944 to facilitate international economic expansion. The General Agreement on Tariffs and Trade (GATT) was designed to help negotiate and arbitrate reduced barriers to world commerce, the World Bank was intended to provide longer-term development assistance in poorer countries, and the primary role of the International Monetary Fund was to foster global stability of exchange rates and prices by providing short-term financing to countries in which temporary balance of payments problems threatened to result in currency devaluations.

After 1971, when the United States ended the global system of fixed exchange rates by refusing to redeem foreign dollars for gold, the IMF was left with no clear mandate or reason for existence. In the early 1980s the debt crisis of less developed countries (LDCs), mainly in Latin America and Eastern Europe, provided an opportunity for the IMF to expand into a new field—namely, providing loans to troubled countries on the condition that these countries adopt policies and goals dictated, or at least approved, by an IMF team. This process is called "conditionality."

Although other lending agencies, such as the World Bank and regional development banks, are often involved, it is the IMF that usually decides whether a borrowing country's economic policies warrant financial support. Other lenders, including private banks, usually follow the IMF lead.

There must, of course, be conditions attached to any loan. The critical question about IMF conditions, though, is whether they typically improve or worsen the economic performance of the debtor countries. If the strings attached to IMF loans are not helpful, or are even harmful to economic growth, the private sectors of borrowing countries may simply end up burdened by more foreign debt that their governments have wasted. Government debts to the IMF are no less burdensome than debts to foreign banks. As Peter Kenen points out, "repayments of Fund credits will figure prominently in total debt service payments due from many countries, because many of their other debts [to foreign banks] have been rescheduled" (Kenen 1986, 46).

Taxpayers in the major industrial countries are once again providing many billions of dollars of additional funding to the IMF, as they did in the 1980s, but this time the main purpose is to expand the Fund's leverage over policies in the former Soviet Union and the rest of Eastern Europe. Nearly all countries in that region have suffered several years of hyperinflationary depression, weakening the entire world economy and provoking fears that public unrest in these deeply troubled economies may lead to political extremism that could threaten international security. The stakes are high. There is not much room for error. Given the gravity of the task, it is not unreasonable for the donor countries to ask for convincing evidence of IMF effectiveness. What, for example, has been the IMF's record of "graduating" countries from an IMF loan program into economic stabilization, growth, and independence from successive IMF programs?

There is, in fact, no commonly recognized group of IMF "success stories" at all. Indeed, we have been unable to find a single example of IMF intervention unambiguously improving an economy's performance over a sustained period, though we show many examples of countries that have made dramatic improvements on their own. Many regular patients of the IMF—such as Yugoslavia, Haiti, Peru, Nicaragua, Zaire, Papua, New Guinea, Somalia, Uganda, and the Ivory Coast—have been on the critical list for many years. The long list of obvious failures, and the absence of any clear successes, raises the central question: What is the nature and effect of the package of economic policy "reforms," or "conditionality," that accompanies most IMF loans?

The IMF never makes public the "letter of intent" the borrower signs, which outlines the conditionality to which it agrees. But several recent IMF agreements have been reprinted by the de Tocqueville Institute in Washington, and others have been leaked to the press, so the usual elements of IMF conditionality and surveillance programs are well known. Governments seeking loans are well aware of what policies they have to adopt in order to placate the IMF.

A typical package of policies required to keep IMF money flowing in contains at least three elements: (1) devaluation of the currency, ostensibly to reduce trade deficits; (2) restrictions on the growth of certain measures of money or credit; and (3) numerical targets for reducing the budget deficit. In practice, as we show throughout this paper, the IMF's short-term goals for smaller budget and trade deficits are often translated into increased tax rates, and sometimes higher tariffs. We will argue that this IMF-subsidized blend of higher tax rates and a weaker currency invariably fosters slower economic growth and faster inflation.

This paper begins with a brief history of recent IMF programs and an analysis of the economic theology behind the strings attached to IMF loans. Subsequent sections describe how severely damaged economies have turned into "economic miracles" in the past, and what policies they had in common. Toward the end, we observe that some IMF publications have recently questioned the Fund's policy advice of the 1980s, along the same lines as proposed in this paper, particularly with respect to exchange rates, tariffs, and tax rates. Unfortunately, we find no evidence, from IMF programs adopted in Yugoslavia, Haiti, Russia, and Latin America in 1988–93, that the IMF had yet incorporated these well-tested, successful policies into its recommendations to countries that remain troubled with high inflation and stagnant or declining living standards.

The Genesis of International Central Planning

When the Mexican government suspended payments on its foreign loans in 1982, the unprecedented bailout package devised by U.S. Federal Reserve Chairman Paul Volcker and IMF Managing Director Jacques de Larosiere thrust the IMF and its resources to the center of an extensive U.S.-led strategy. That strategy was designed to mobilize new loans to developing nations to keep them from defaulting on old loans. It was at that time that the IMF's obsession with currency devaluation became the centerpiece of so-called "adjustment" policies, and the main "conditionality" attached to getting and keeping IMF loans. Sebastian Edwards investigated the thirty-four conditionality-oriented programs that the IMF approved in 1983 and found that almost every one required devaluation (Edwards 1989, 32–34).

The required devaluations are sometimes camouflaged as a switch to "floating" exchange rates. There were forty-nine countries with such floating exchange rates by the third quarter of 1993, compared with only seventeen in 1988 (*International Financial Statistics* 1993, 6). Yet it is clear from experience that the IMF's view of "floating" is a euphemism for sinking. The IMF has gone public with loud complaints whenever one of its debtors dared to let its currency float up, rather than down (e.g., Russia in early 1992).

There is an element of irony or hypocrisy in the fact that industrial countries have condoned the IMF's habit of promoting currency devaluations among the less developed countries, since (1) the IMF was created to prevent such devaluations, and (2) the industrial countries have been trying to stabilize their own exchange rates through G-7 meetings and the European Monetary System.

Within the IMF's institutional ideology, currency devaluations are supposed to improve the balance of payments (which is incorrectly treated as almost synonymous with the balance of trade, thus neglecting capital flows). This is what "adjustment" usually means—trying to turn trade deficits into surpluses in order to devote export revenues to the servicing of foreign debt, including IMF debt. Limits on budget deficits and money growth are likewise aimed at cutting imports by restraining "domestic demand." These primary policy recommendations have often been supplemented by government wage controls in IMF-supported "adjustment programs" (e.g., Brazil in 1983, Israel in 1984, Yugoslavia in 1988). Combining wage controls with devaluation is designed to lower real wage rates (through inflation), and thus to make a country's exports more "competitive."

As we will demonstrate, the IMF's standard policy package involves some contradictions. The quest for a balanced budget has often fostered destructive taxes and tariffs, which weaken the economy and therefore the country's ability to service foreign debts. The obsession with manipulating an economy into a trade surplus through currency devaluation invariably results in high inflation, which makes it quite impossible to comply with IMF limits on the growth of money or credit. Defining "adjustment" as a current account surplus (which requires a matching capital outflow) often encouraged protectionist measures, as did the pursuit of smaller deficits through tariff receipts. And the stagflation that results from destructive tax and exchange rate policies eroded real tax receipts and inflated the governments' interest expense, thus making budget deficits larger, not smaller. This will all be explained later, with examples.

Devaluation and Austerity Theories

When hyperinflationary depressions began to break out in Latin America in the early 1980s, and later in the former Soviet Union, IMF missionaries to the afflicted countries rarely seemed to have any sense of which policies had worked in the past and which had always failed. Instead, IMF prescriptions seem based on theory rather than experience. They frequently included a mix of repeated devaluations, import restrictions, wage controls, and a tax policy that punishes investment and success. A 1983 *Fortune* magazine account of the Fund's advice to Brazil is typical of media reports of IMF programs throughout the 1980s:

> The Brazilian government is pinning its hope on the IMF staff.... To meet this year's [IMF] target, Brazil has cut imports drastically.... Brazil carried out a 23 percent devaluation last February and several smaller ones later...however, inflation has been accelerating.... Wage law 2045 [was] designed to damp inflation by limiting semi-annual wage adjustments.... The IMF staked approval of its new package on the measure.... At the same time, the law raised taxes on interest, profits and dividends. (Boyer 1983)

Brazilian hopes were soon dashed by runaway inflation, which has continued into the 1990s. In hundreds of years of world history, neither wage controls nor higher tax rates have ever stopped inflation. *As we will demonstrate, no serious inflation in world history has ever been stopped without a nation's monetary authorities guaranteeing to redeem the currency for either a more credible foreign currency or a precious metal.* Yet the IMF's "devaluation theory" has systematically undermined the essential process of defining and guaranteeing the value of a country's currency in order to end inflation.

IMF programs typically lend money to governments only on condition that they devalue the currency. The devaluations hurt the private sector, but the loans benefit politicians. Indeed, a mere promise to devalue is not usually sufficient. The loans usually arrive only after a "preparatory" devaluation. A survey of conditionality by the de Tocqueville Institute notes that "the general pattern was for most of...a given depreciation to take place during the negotiations leading up to a formal conditionality agreement.... In 1985, fund officials quietly promoted a continuing, gradual depreciation of Costa Rica's currency against the U.S. dollar.... From 1986 to 1988, Fund officials grew concerned...with growing prospects of an unsustainable deficit in China's balance of payments. A Fund surveillance mission recommended that the Chinese...allow a declining exchange rate against the dollar and other major currencies" (*IMF Conditionality* 1992, 21, 25, 45). Such stories have been repeated, over and over, throughout the world. The IMF insists the way to make an economy strong is to make its money weak.

The principal tenets of the IMF's devaluation theory are: (1) that a current account deficit is always a sign of economic weakness, something that policy should attempt to fix; and (2) that devaluation of the currency is an effective and appropriate method by which to eliminate such undesirable current-account deficits. A typical 1980s press report on an IMF program (this one in Argentina) thus noted that "the IMF is keen for the Government to devalue the currency, the austral, to boost export prospects" (Coone 1988). Taken to the extreme, it seems as though the IMF believes that all countries ought to run trade surpluses with each other, and they can do that by devaluing their currencies against all the others. But this, of course, does not add up. In a world of increasingly free mobility of capital, some countries will have a surplus on the capital account (i.e., a net inflow of foreign investment), and therefore a deficit on the current account.

The devaluation theory's main objective is quite clear, in light of the IMF's post-1982 mission of making sure that developing countries paid their bills to foreign lenders. Devaluation was supposed to shrink imports and free-up more export revenues to be devoted to servicing debts to foreign banks, including the IMF. Yet a country may have balanced trade and still have a current account deficit, because interest paid to foreigners exceeds interest received on foreign investments. And *because interest on foreign debt is a large part of the current account in third world countries, the IMF objective of balance on current account requires running a huge surplus on trade*. In practice, this has meant cutting back on investment, so that domestic savings exceed investment and the capital account is therefore in deficit. There is an unflattering phrase for this IMF goal of a capital account deficit—it is called "capital flight."

Martin Feldstein once estimated that a typical Latin American interest bill, then amounting to about 5 percent of GNP, "can be financed without new funds from abroad only if the country's exports exceed imports by five percent of GNP. That is possible only if it saves five percent more of its GNP than it invests" (Feldstein 1989). That is, devaluation could "work"—in the sense of promoting a current account surplus—only by increasing domestic savings or reducing investment. This is so because the gap between investment and savings equals the current-account deficit. And the only way to finance a current-account deficit is for foreigners to invest more in the country than its own citizens invest abroad. *In order to "work," devaluation must either make it more attractive to save or less attractive to invest.* But nobody wants to save a shrinking currency, so the "adjustment" that supposedly follows devaluation must come through lower investment. Weak investment (and savings export) is indeed a likely effect of devaluation; but weak investment certainly is not helpful to economic growth, without which future repayment of debts becomes quite difficult (Reynolds 1989, 113–22).

The Rationale for Punitive Taxation

Devaluation theory is closely related to "austerity theory," which advocates deliberate contraction of "demand" (investment and living standards) in order to (1) curb imports, (2) divert production from domestic uses toward exports, and (3) earmark export revenues for servicing debts to the IMF and foreign banks. According to the IMF's model, budget deficits "stimulate domestic demand" directly by causing monetary expansion. And this, in turn, supposedly causes imports to exceed exports. "Curing" current-account deficits, then, also requires cutting the budget deficit—the dubious "twin deficits" theory that was once so popular in the United States. This is where IMF prescriptions for new and/or higher taxes come into play.

IMF officials have long maintained that they merely set a target for a nation's budget deficit and offer only "technical" advice about the specific tax and spending measures involved. For example, Vito Tanzi, head of fiscal policy research at the IMF, writes:

> [If] the country wanted advice on its tax structure, on the structure of its public spending, or on their respective administration, it could request technical assistance from the Fund. No conditionality was attached to the provision or the use of this advice, although *Fund missions have occasionally used technical assistance reports to provide advice to the countries, especially on how to raise revenue.* (Tanzi 1989, 18; emphasis added)

Nations on IMF programs have commonly slashed public infrastructure investment to comply with IMF deficit targets, but capital outlays (including education) are the easiest forms of government spending to defer. And IMF programs have usually imposed new taxes and/or higher tax rates in order to appear to comply with the IMF deficit-reduction targets. Indeed, Edwards' previously noted review of the thirty-four

IMF programs initiated in 1983 found that 74 percent of the programs required higher tax rates. "Moreover," he continues, "in a number of cases, the *Fund programs have called for a hike in trade taxes* as a way to strengthen the fiscal side and reduce the fiscal imbalance" (Edwards 1989, 32; emphasis added). Wards of the IMF commonly retain or increase import tariffs—not only in pursuit of added revenues but also to comply with the IMF objective of generating a trade surplus (even though import restrictions do not, in fact, reduce trade deficits).[1] In January 1991, for instance, the Philippines bowed to IMF pressure and instituted a 9 percent supplemental levy on imports in order to obtain a new IMF loan (Hutchinson 1991, 4). Thus, whether the IMF calls it "conditionality" or not, indications point to an IMF pattern of guiding nations to higher tax rates and tariffs as the surest way to close budget and trade deficits.

By taking more savings out of the private sector (through higher taxes) and making producers' imported capital and intermediate goods more expensive (through higher tariffs), austerity theory forces a cutback in private investment (which is also jeopardized by devaluation). "In Brazil 1983 real growth was running at minus 2–3 percent," wrote John Makin, *"with the economy strangled by austerity aimed at squeezing down consumption to free up funds to pay the loans.* And investment-hampering, chaotic inflation was approaching 200 percent a year" (Makin 1984, 249; emphasis added). We later show that this has been the typical pattern of IMF adjustment programs. As Peter Kenen had warned in 1986, "the Fund...is in danger of attaching too much weight to bankers' standards of creditworthiness and too little weight to...the need for the long-term [structural] policy reforms" (Kenen 1986, 53).

Depressing investment and economic growth through devaluation and tax-induced austerity is not even in the narrow self-interest of foreign creditors who want their LDC debts repaid. No borrower has ever been made more creditworthy by deliberately shrinking current and future income.

Another rationale for austerity theory is the "Phillips Curve," which holds that inflation is caused by excessive wage demands due to tight labor markets—in short, the idea that high unemployment and weak growth cure inflation.[2] If this theory had any merit, however, inflation would be highest in the rapidly expanding Asian NICs and lowest in such shrinking economies as Russia. That is clearly not the case.

Devaluations Bring Inflation, Not Trade Gains

The idea that devaluations can reduce trade deficits—that cheaper money means cheaper exports—remains a theory in search of some facts. Richard Blackhurst, chief economist for GATT, surveyed the major studies on devaluation a decade ago and found an "absence of credible support for the popular view that an exchange-rate change has an independent and predictable effect on the current account balance" (Blackhurst 1983, 88). In 1986 John Spraos of the University of London surveyed several of the IMF's studies of its own programs and found a pattern of "ineffectiveness of Fund programs on the external [balance of payments] front" (Spraos 1986, 5, 27). Rose and Yellen (1989), examining the U.S. experience, likewise found that "there is little evidence of…any reliable link between the balance of trade and the exchange rate." Similarly, John Chipman of the University of Minnesota found "very slender empirical support for the hypothesis that a decline in the value of the dollar will improve the U.S. current account balance" (Bradley 1989). And when *The Economist* reviewed exchange-rate theories, it concluded: "A change in the nominal exchange rate has no lasting effect on an economy's competitiveness; a currency devaluation will eventually produce higher domestic wages and prices, canceling out any benefit" ("Why Exchange Rates Change" 1984, 66–67). Indeed, Edwards' review of IMF programs found that, "on average…inflation increased quite significantly," and a "steep reduction" in real economic activity followed (Edwards 1989, 34).

Guillermo Ortiz, who served as Mexico's Undersecretary of Finance and Public Credit, has correctly argued that in his country "the rise in the fiscal deficit has been caused by the rise in inflation and not vice versa [and] inflation was caused by the policy actions (i.e., massive devaluations) taken to protect the balance of payments" (Ortiz 1988). This is a critical point. *Repeated devaluations of the currency reduce the public's willingness to hold local money (i.e., they reduce the demand for money) and thus cause inflation. Chronic inflation, in turn, increases the budget deficit. Inflation raises government spending immediately, partly by raising the interest rate on past government debts. Tax collections, moreover, lag behind because they are based on incomes or sales during a previous period when prices were lower.*

The IMF's penchant for devaluation cannot be reconciled with its equally passionate anxiety about budget deficits. That is because repeated, large devaluations are always inflationary, and rapid inflation always shrinks tax receipts. In Bolivia, for example, tax revenues fell from 9.4 percent of GDP in 1980 to 1.9 percent during the hyperinflation of 1984. In Argentina, tax revenues fell from 15.1 percent of GDP in 1986 to 4.7 percent in 1988. In Peru, tax revenues fell from 14 percent of GDP in 1985 to 6.4 percent in 1989 (Inter-American Development Bank 1990, 275, Table C-1). Since real GNP also fell during these hyperinflations, a declining tax share of declining output meant that real government revenues from progressive income taxes became virtually impossible to collect, just as they were in Germany in 1923.

It is often supposed that big budget deficits and/or rapid growth of the monetary base (bank reserves and currency) precede and cause major devaluations. That may be the case in some circumstances, though even in these instances a decision to devalue represents a capitulation to inflation as an alternative to ending inflationary policies. In the extreme cases that were common in Latin America in the 1980s, and in the former Soviet Union more recently, the dominant direction of causality is often just the opposite. Deep devaluations, undertaken with the hope of improving the trade balance, often precede and cause larger budget deficits and subsequent rapid money growth. The budgetary effect occurs, in part, through the process illustrated by the hyperinflations just mentioned—namely, a collapse of real tax receipts. But devaluations also inflate government spending, most obviously by raising interest rates on the government debt.

Countries that repeatedly devalue always have to pay high interest rates, which raises the nominal budget deficit. Even though inflation may be eroding the real national debt, it is the nominal deficit that must be financed by printing money. In Mexico, for example, the devaluation of September 1976 was followed—not preceded—by an acceleration of growth in the monetary base from 12 percent in 1976 to 109 percent in 1978 (when the budget deficit was only 2.7 percent of GDP). Another Mexican devaluation in early 1981 was likewise followed by a doubling of the growth of monetary base in 1982. Mexico's budget deficit, which had been below 3 percent of GDP before the 1981 devaluation, soared to nearly 15 percent in the following year. After Mexico adopted a quasi-fixed exchange rate in 1989, inflation and interest rates came way down, reducing the budget deficit by an amount equal to nearly 17 percent of GDP.

Since hyperinflationary countries with inflated expenditures and plunging revenues cannot possibly finance their inflated deficits by selling fixed-rate bonds, they are left with no alternative but the printing press.

Moreover, any devaluation of, say, the Russian ruble against the U.S. dollar must raise prices of important commodities priced in dollars (such as oil, metals, and grains). If the devaluation is to stick, as the IMF requires, there is no option but to accommodate those increases in ruble prices with an increase in the supply of rubles. The supply of money thus soars even as the public's willingness to hold that money collapses (that is, as velocity soars), creating pressures for additional devaluations, larger budget deficits, more money creation, and so on.

Frequent devaluations not only cause inflation, they also generally fail to make exports cheaper (because export prices are also inflated) or imports less desirable. The fact that import prices are widely expected to rise shortly after a devaluation naturally creates a surge of demand for such imports on any rumor of devaluation. Louka Katseli of Yale thus suggests, "a devaluation can give rise to inflationary expectations that lead to an increase in consumption and imports" (Katseli 1983).

Devaluations impoverish workers—particularly those subject to IMF-mandated wage controls—because their real wages shrink in relation to the rising prices of imports and import-competing goods. Devaluations also injure important industries which depend on imported equipment and materials. A study of Mexico's past experience by Edward Buffie and Allen Krause emphasizes this type of damage caused by devaluation:

> In Mexico...intermediate inputs and capital goods account for over 90 percent of total imports.... A reduction in imports, whether imposed directly by import controls or induced by a real devaluation, *exerts a powerful contractionary effect upon economic activity*. Cutbacks in imported intermediates lower labor demand at a given real wage and discourage investment by reducing the productivity of capital. (Buffie and Krause 1989, 163; emphasis added)

The resulting economic contraction, in turn, further expands a nation's budget deficit through depressed tax receipts and accelerated welfare outlays.

Devaluations also work to increase the government's budget deficit in more subtle ways. Once domestic and world investors recognize that any government has adopted devaluation as a policy tool, that country's interest rates must remain very high. The expectation of devaluation adds a risk premium to holding the country's bonds or bills, causing nominal interest rates to rise to a level that may even exceed the domestic inflation rate. A government's expenditures for servicing internal debt can then balloon substantially. (Inflation would erode the real burden of any debts in which the nominal interest rate was fixed, but such longer-term, fixed income securities soon cease to exist in countries with a habit of devaluation). Conversely, a credible institutional commitment that requires a central bank or currency board to slow the growth of domestic credit whenever the exchange rate threatens to fall always results in lower interest rates. It is a hoary myth that high interest rates are necessary to "defend a currency." Countries with sound currencies always have reasonably low interest rates. When the bond yields of Country A are higher than those of Country B, the market expects that Country A's currency will fall against the currency of Country B.

Devaluation, in short, raises interest rates; and the added interest expense raises budget deficits. Rapid inflation also shrinks real tax receipts because of lags in collections (paying tax bills after the money is worth less) and because of increased use of barter and foreign currencies (which escape tax collectors). Inflation also reduces the incentive to work and invest in the formal economy—and thus pay higher taxes on rising real incomes—because it pushes people into higher tax brackets and results in confiscatory taxation of paper profits and illusory, inflated capital gains. Inflation pushes even low-income workers into the highest tax brackets, resulting in capital flight, a "brain drain," and "underground" or "informal" enterprises that must remain inefficiently small to escape detection. All of these unfortunate consequences of devaluation result in growing budget deficits that cannot possibly be financed by selling fixed-rate bonds, which leaves no alternative to abusing the central bank to print more money—even as devaluation reduces the public's willingness to hold that money. What might be called the "devaluation-deficit syndrome" results in inflationary pressures that create conditions for yet another devaluation and even more chaos.

Repeated use of devaluation to make exports competitive is very bad policy. And devaluations often lead to other bad policies. Many third world governments then resort to wage and price controls in a naive attempt to outlaw inflation; but price controls only add uncertainty to business plans (which depresses investment) and produce shortages of consumer goods (which governments often feel compelled to remedy through budget-busting subsidies).

Monetary Manipulation Is No Substitute for Structural Reform

The current account depends on relative incentives and capacities to save and invest. It is a real phenomenon, not merely a monetary one.

Any real effects of devaluation—including effects on investment, savings, and trade—are simply by-products of the resulting inflation (such as a decline of investment due in part to a nonindexed tax system, a decline of consumption due to shrinking real wages, or a reduction of savings due to capital flight).

In a series of papers published between 1968 and 1971, Columbia University professor Robert Mundell (1971) proposed that different policy tools be assigned to different objectives. In particular, he argued that monetary policy is most effective in stabilizing nominal values such as exchange rates and prices. Current-account deficits, on the other hand, mirror real activity, particularly real investment and real savings. A current-account deficit simply means that real investment in a given nation's economy exceeds real savings within that nation by its own citizens (which is to be expected in any poor country that, through economic reform, becomes an attractive place to invest). Mundell correctly argued that to influence real activity, including growth and employment, governments should use structural tools such as tax reform and increased competition through privatization, freer trade, and deregulation. To attempt to influence real activity by manipulating the quantity and value of money is ultimately futile and dangerous; it causes only high interest rates and large debts. If the tax and regulatory situation is not conducive to expansion of real activity, a monetary stimulus (including devaluation) will simply result in higher inflation.

The overall balance of payments (which includes capital flows as well as trade) is a reasonable concern of monetary policy and one that monetary policy can easily handle. A drain on foreign-exchange reserves (which signifies that capital inflows are inadequate to handle the current-account deficit) should simply be met by firmer restraint on domestic credit expansion—that is, a government should not finance budget deficits by creating new bank reserves and currency. When people are too eager to exchange a developing country's currency for foreign goods and assets, fixing that problem requires a tighter monetary policy, not higher tax rates, and not capitulation to escalating rates of inflation through repeated devaluations.

When a country repeatedly succumbs to the temptation to devalue, it soon becomes difficult or impossible to finance government borrowing in a responsible, noninflationary manner. Governments then lose the option of financing even capital projects with longer-term fixed-rate bonds, and so do aspiring homeowners and private enterprises. To restore that option requires two things. First, a tax system with low rates on a broad base must be implemented so that economic growth can be revived; fair and reasonable taxes can be collected; and expected real tax receipts can be expanded by the real growth of taxable sales, profits, and salaries. The expectation of a growing stream of real receipts in future decades raises the discounted present value of government securities and is quickly capitalized in the ability to roll over past debts at lower interest rates and longer maturities.

Second, the government and central bank (or currency board) must announce and maintain a "clean" fixed exchange rate—one without capital controls—eventually bringing interest rates down toward international levels. In this situation, there will be far less temptation to resort to the printing press to pay government expenses. With the prospect of improved economic growth (due to tax, trade, regulatory, and monetary reform) the demand for the local currency and for financial assets denominated in that currency will rise, thus facilitating stabilization of the currency at moderate interest rates. One obvious example is the worldwide rush to buy Mexican stocks and Treasury bills that followed exchange rate stabilization, lower tariffs, and lower tax rates in 1989–93.

A Kind Word for Current-Account Deficits

The basic idea that trade and/or current accounts should never be in deficit is mainly a hangover from seventeenth-century mercantilism. Even today, because of ancient mercantilist habits of speech, people still describe a trade surplus as a "favorable" balance, even though such a surplus requires a *deficit* on capital accounts—otherwise known as "capital flight." A country that keeps taking in more foreign money than it spends on foreign goods has no other option but to accumulate foreign assets. World capital flows toward superior investment opportunities. As Jurg Niehans put it, "countries are debtors if their investment opportunities exceed their wealth and are creditors when their wealth exceeds their investment opportunities" (Niehans 1984, 107). A deficit on current account—with one major exception—simply means that investment opportunities are superior to those elsewhere, which causes domestic capital to remain in the country and attracts foreign capital as well. The important exception occurs when governments borrow from institutions such as the IMF. Such borrowing is motivated by considerations other than profitable production and efficiency, and thus does not represent a flow of capital to superior investment opportunities.

Developing countries can clearly benefit by exploiting investment opportunities beyond those that can be financed by their own past accumulations of wealth. Therefore, it is not inherently sinful for growing economies to remain debtor nations—that is, run current-account deficits—for many years or even decades. If current-account deficits are financed by voluntary, private capital inflows, they reflect improved opportunities for profitable investment and production and make such improved production possible (e.g., by financing imports of high-tech equipment). In turn, it is growth-oriented policies that make the financing of current-account deficits possible, because the prospect of enlarged output in the future can be discounted in higher prices of equity and bonds today. At an economic growth rate of 7 percent a year—which is by no means unprecedented among developing countries with growth-oriented policies—an economy will double in size in less than a decade. Even if such a country's foreign debt remains unchanged over that period, it will be cut in half as a percentage of the doubled GDP.

Much of the "debt crisis" debate assumed that there was no alternative to continued borrowing by LDC *governments* from banks, the IMF, and the World Bank. Mexico's 1989 debt agreement with commercial banks, for example, was criticized by some commentators for not including enough new lending. But it is quite possible to finance new capital projects and any related current-account deficits with *private* equity and *private* debt from both domestic and foreign sources. This involves bringing flight capital back home and attracting foreign portfolio investment (e.g., selling stock in new ventures and formerly state-owned enterprises to foreigners) as well as direct investment. To do that requires combining an attractive tax, regulatory, and monetary environment with greater development of capital markets. One extremely promising mechanism for capital-market development is the type of country fund listed on major international stock exchanges, such as the Mexico, Argentina, Turkey, Indonesia, and India funds on the New York Stock Exchange.

Table 8.1 shows that a decade of large current-account deficits preceded most of the success stories that are discussed later in this survey.

These nations, with large and prolonged current-account deficits, are some of the most successful turnaround economies ever seen. Yet IMF adjustment programs nonetheless continue to emphasize the alleged need to avoid current-account deficits. By the IMF's standard, these countries could not have been impressive success stories by the mid-1980s but must instead have been dismal failures. They did not

TABLE 8.1
Average Current-Account Deficits, 1976–85 (as a percentage of GDP)

Mauritius	8.0 percent
Chile	7.0
Singapore	6.6
Thailand	5.3
S. Korea	3.3
Colombia	2.5

Source: IMF, *International Financial Statistics Yearbook*, 1990.

"adjust" their current-account deficits. To IMF bureaucrats, eliminating any and all current-account deficits is the single most important "macroeconomic ceiling" that defines "adjustment." Yet *nearly all reforms that have been truly successful, in the sense of launching a major surge in economic activity and wealth, have been accompanied by at least a decade of current-account deficits.*

This worldwide experience suggests that the current-account deficits of many troubled debtor economies have been too small, not too large, in relation to their potential growth. Weaker economies have failed to attract the private financial capital needed to import private equipment and skills into industry, agriculture, commerce, and services. This problem can be solved, and the countries in Table 8.1, among others, have shown the way—through reduced tax rates, reduced trade barriers, and relatively strong, stable currencies.

Export-Led Growth Follows Import-Led Investment

In examining the factual record of countries with prolonged current-account deficits (such as the United States in the first century of its existence), the expression "export-led growth" is extremely misleading. Most of the "Asian Tigers" actually began with import-led growth. South Korea ran enormous current-account deficits nearly every year for three decades up until 1986—amounting to 9 percent of GNP in 1961, more than 12 percent in 1974, and 9.5 percent in 1980. South Korea's foreign debt exceeded 50 percent of GNP by the early 1980s, and Western experts thought the country needed an austerity plan (briefly imposed by the IMF in 1980) to slow the economy and thereby cut imports (Reynolds 1987). Starting in 1986, South Korea's prolonged current-account deficits turned to surpluses in some years—because domestic savings rose enough, with rising incomes, to exceed investment—and much of the foreign debt accumulated over three decades was rapidly and easily repaid out of the much larger economy.

Another example of import-led growth is Japan—a country which ran large trade deficits with the United States from 1945 through 1965. A 1958 Rockefeller Foundation study, *Japan's Postwar Economy*, typifies the antigrowth austerity advice given to Japan by the West's orthodox economists of the day:

> The growth of prosperity in Japan seems inevitably to set in motion forces which tend to widen the trade gap.... If, however, the import component of Japan's gross national product can be reduced to less than the present 13 percent, then a smaller volume of both imports and exports will be sufficient.... It is also possible to put aside the goal of full employment and to economize in some sectors of imports. (Cohen 1958, 134, 217)

But as Western economists were wondering what Japan was going to do with all that machinery it was importing—no doubt some were thinking that surely little Japan could never produce autos—the damage their advice could do was limited. Western economists could not advise Japan to devalue the yen because the Japanese currency had been fixed at 360 yen to the dollar. That meant that Japan was blessed with a currency considered virtually "as sound as a dollar" because yen could be redeemed for dollars at a known rate.

The U.S. Occupation imposed confiscatory tax rates (85 percent) at relatively modest incomes until Japan was allowed to make her own policies after September 1951.[3] Even long after the occupation, however, American experts continued to lecture the Japanese about the irresponsibility of cutting tax rates or raising exemptions—see, for example, the 1958 Rockefeller Foundation study cited earlier. Tax cuts were nonetheless made repeatedly in Japan—in nearly every year from 1951 to 1978, and again in 1985 and 1987. If Japan in the early postwar years had followed the sort of advice now routinely given to countries with similar current-account deficits—namely, to keep tax rates and tariffs high and the currency low—Japan would never have been the economic power that it was through 1989 (before adding new taxes on savings, sales, and securities transactions).

Developing countries can prudently experience current-account deficits for many years, as Japan and South Korea did, by making their countries attractive places for private investment, both domestic and foreign, and by expanding and deepening capital markets to facilitate such investments. Regardless of whether such countries experience current-account deficits, however, monetary and exchange-rate policy must *never* be used as tools for targeting trade objectives—as the IMF's devaluation theory requires—because that leaves inflation adrift without an anchor, inviting monetary chaos.

Lessons from Successful Stabilizations of the 1920s

In the 1920s the creditor nations, usually working through the League of Nations, insisted that devaluation be stopped. They recognized that any system in which government monopolizes the issue of currency, currency is part of the national debt. Devaluation thus constitutes a partial repudiation of government obligations. They also recognized that devaluation means austerity for private citizens—who get stuck holding the government's debased money—but not for the politicians who acquired control over labor and products by issuing such deceptive promises to pay. Benjamin Anderson, chief economist at Citibank in the 1920s, explained U.S. policy toward the German hyperinflation:

> The [U.S.] Department of State informally made it clear that American participation in the proposed Dawes Plan loan to Germany would not be regarded favorably by the American government unless Germany went immediately to the gold standard.... The Dawes Committee...had no doubt that industry and finance would revive if sound currency were established, if men once more had money in which they believed and in which they could safely make contracts. (Anderson 1979, 119, 121)

On 12 November 1923 Hjalmar Schacht was appointed Reich Currency Commissioner, virtually the czar of monetary policy. Three days later, the paper mark, which had depreciated to 4.2 trillion per dollar, was declared equivalent to one trillion new Rentenmarks. This policy effectively fixed the exchange rate of the new mark at the prewar parity of 4.2 per dollar (23 cents). Exchange controls were also abolished by 20 November. The exchange rate of the new mark was held within a narrow range of 21.8 to 23.4 cents in the first half of 1924, then formally pegged at 23.8 cents (Sargent 1984, 76, Table G2). Overnight interest rates, which averaged 10,950 percent in 1923, quickly fell as low as 13 percent in late 1924 (Homer 1977, 476).

Some observers have attached undue significance to the psychological impact of introducing a new currency, an illusion that may have inspired several purely cosmetic reforms that failed in recent years, such as the ill-fated Austral Plan in Argentina. In reality, Germany's substantive changes of 15 November 1923 were that (1) the exchange rate against the dollar was deliberately fixed, and (2) the newly independent central bank stopped discounting Treasury bills and instead discounted only sound commercial paper ("real bills"). Credibility was also greatly enhanced by the fact that it was well known that "Schacht had always considered the introduction of the Rentenmark as an intermediary step toward the introduction of the gold standard," which did in fact occur nine months later (Simpson 1969, 17).

Quantity theorists (monetarists), who have had much influence at the IMF, sometimes emphasize the fact that the issue of new Rentenmarks was limited to only 3.2 billion (the amount of capital secured by compulsory mortgage bonds on farm land and businesses), with nearly half of that available to the government. Those high ceilings, however, were not binding. The old depreciated mark continued to circulate after the reform, partly because Rentenmarks were not issued in denominations below one mark; and Rentenmarks were not legal tender except for payments to the government (which also accepted old marks). In fact, the volume of currency in circulation quintupled in the six weeks following the reform, and the stock of Rentenmarks alone tripled between January and March of 1924 (Sargent 1984, 81, Table G4). Deposits in commercial banks rose 155 percent in 1924 and another 40 percent in 1925 (Mitchell 1978, 364). As Thomas Sargent documented for all four hyperinflations of the 1920s that he studied, "in each case the note circulation continued to grow rapidly after the exchange rate and price level had been stabilized" (Sargent 1984, 90). What happened was that the *demand* for money increased sharply (i.e., velocity fell) once the market found it could expect its value to be guaranteed in gold—not that the nominal supply of currency or deposits was rigidly fixed. Indeed, as Edwin Kemmerer noted in 1937, the "reduction of velocities was so great at the start that it resulted in an actual scarcity of money and the authorities were compelled to increase the volume of paper money somewhat at the beginning in order to maintain the approximate price level prevailing at the time of the Rentenmark stabilization" (Kemmerer 1937, 316).

Fiscal theorists such as Sargent, on the other hand, stress reductions in the budget deficit, usually with suspiciously inexplicit references to "increased taxes." There were substantial reductions of government jobs in Germany, particularly in overstaffed government railroads and postal services, which undoubtedly helped. Moreover, the hyperinflation slashed the national debt to only 2.9 percent of GNP, which meant the budgetary cost of debt service nearly vanished by de facto default (Webber and Wildavsky 1986, 446). And the Dawes Committee suspended payments of external (war) debts while also providing a large loan to stabilize the mark. Still, more than 99 percent of government spending was financed by new money at the peak of the inflation, so economizing on government spending could not possibly have been the key to filling such a huge gap.

Instead, the most significant fiscal change was on the revenue side, but not in the way that Sargent supposed. It is extremely important to understand that *the increase in tax receipts was the result of monetary stability, not higher tax rates or new taxes*. That is, monetary reform fixed the fiscal crisis, not the other way around. Taxes were indeed part of the problem during the hyperinflation, but because tax rates were too high, not too low. In early 1920 Germany attempted to impose a progressive income tax with rates as high as 40 percent. This tax damaged the economy and yielded little revenue. But any income tax is uniquely unsuited to keeping up with inflation (unlike sales taxes expressed as a percentage of the price). "It took time to make a tax levy and…it took further time to collect the tax after it had been levied. But, during the inflation…the longer the delay, the less in real value was the tax" (Kemmerer 1937, 310).

Measured in gold marks, total tax receipts collapsed from 5.2 billion in fiscal 1921–22 to an annual rate of only 758 million by November 1923. After the exchange rate was fixed, however, tax revenues immediately rebounded to an annual rate of over 6 billion by January 1924 (Sargent 1984, 83, Table G5). Obviously, a nearly tenfold increase in real revenues in a little over two months could not have been the result of a tenfold increase in tax rates. In reality, there was no increase in tax rates. Two years after the currency reform, fiscal revenues were 40 percent higher, measured in gold, than the Dawes Committee had expected (Anderson 1979, 160). This unexpected windfall allowed tax rates to be *reduced*, not increased, and lower tax rates in 1926 helped bring about a doubling of the German stock market and a brisk recovery. "By the middle of 1926 the economy began to show signs of marvelous recuperative powers," notes a biographer of Hjalmar Schacht: "The internal tax burden had been *decreased* and was in the process of being more completely reformed."[4]

Under the guidance of the League of Nations, Austria, Hungary, and Poland were likewise compelled to commit to converting their currencies into hard (gold) currencies on demand at a fixed exchange rate. As in the German case, they were usually offered a line of credit to back them up in that effort (i.e., the "conditionality" was the opposite of what the IMF imposed in the 1980s). Thus from 1923 to 1926, the hyperinflations in Germany, Austria, Hungary, and Poland were all ended by fixing those nations' exchange rates to a hard currency. The Russian hyperinflation at the same time was ended in 1922–24 by defining and backing the new chervonets in terms of gold. In all of these cases, devaluation was made illegal. There was often discussion among experts from the League of Nations or U.S. State Department about the need for balancing national budgets, as a later stage of reform. But *the return of stable money always resulted in enormous, immediate increases in real tax receipts which automatically reduced the budget deficits. Exchange-rate stabilization came first, and budget balance was an unexpected result.*

Moreover, the resulting increases in revenue receipts were real, not inflated, because the currencies had been fixed to those of gold-standard countries with negligible inflation. In Austria, for example, the currency stock rose by 520 percent from August 1922 to December 1924, yet the exchange rate was stabilized at the same time and the 9,200 percent inflation of 1922 was stopped almost immediately (Sargent 1984, 50, Table AZ). As a consequence of the newly fixed exchange rate—together with some tax cuts—Austria's real GNP rose 10 percent in 1924 alone and tax receipts soared far above what the experts had predicted. Table 8.2 shows actual revenues in Austria, compared with the earlier estimates of the League of Nations.

The experience was the same in every country that stopped a runaway inflation in the 1920s, as noted earlier in the case of Germany. Two years after Hungary stabilized its currency, for example, real government revenues were 54 percent higher than Western experts had projected (Pasvolsky 1928, 321, 324).

TABLE 8.2
Government Revenue in Austria
(millions of gold shillings)

	Estimated	Actual
1923	524.1	697.4
1924	659.7	900.6

Source: L. Pasvolsky, *Economic Nationalism of the Danubian States*, Brookings Institution, Macmillan, 1928, p. 127.

The situation in France in 1926 is perhaps more comparable to that of countries troubled with inflation rates around 50–150 percent (such as Mexico a few years ago), rather than the more extreme hyperinflations that have recently plagued Brazil, Peru, Nicaragua, and Russia. The French inflation rate in 1926 peaked at about 100 percent. France had adopted a "monetarist" rule, which put a limit on the amount of currency issued. This rule, however, was secretly breached, resulting in scandal and a change of government. France also had a serious problem with capital flight, as French investors sought the better investment opportunities available in the United States—with its 1921–25 reductions in income tax rates from 77 percent to 25 percent, as well as the superior insurance of the U.S. gold standard.

In 1926 the new French government, under Poincaré, first instituted a rule that prohibited the central bank from issuing any new currency without new reserves of gold or gold-convertible foreign currencies. This turned out to be too effective, with deflationary results and a brief recession. The franc was then pegged to the gold dollar and pound, and later made directly convertible into gold until 1936. (The French economy performed relatively well until 1936, long after the United States and the United Kingdom had largely abandoned gold.)

Real tax receipts in Poincaré's France increased after the end of inflation and restoration of real growth, repeating the earlier experience of Austria, Hungary, Poland, and Germany. Although some excise taxes and public utility rates were adjusted to compensate for past inflation, of far more significance was the fact that Poincaré slashed the highest income-tax rates in half—from 60 percent to 30 percent—with the explicit aim of encouraging entrepreneurship and instigating the repatriation of flight capital. "Poincaré reversed the [Committee of Experts'] recommendation on taxes," wrote Charles Kindleberger. "The purpose was to appeal to the capitalist class in France, to persuade it to repatriate its money" (Kindleberger 1984, 357).

Since the "Poincaré Miracle" of 1926, the postwar paradigm has been Ludwig Erhard's very similar tax and monetary reforms executed in West Germany after 1948. The top tax rate imposed by the Allied Control Council was blatantly punitive—95 percent on any income above $15,000.[5] Since the occupation tax brackets were set in old marks, however, the 1948 monetary reform (which converted ten old marks into one new Deutschemark) automatically increased tenfold the income thresholds at which the highest tax rates applied. Moreover, Germany repeatedly reduced marginal tax rates as well, to the point where the highest rate of 53 percent only applied at income above $250,000, which was an extremely high income at the time. Tariffs and other trade restrictions were also slashed, price controls were abolished, and the exchange rate was fixed to the gold dollar (Reynolds 1993b, 245). The result was that inflation immediately stopped, trade flourished, and the West German economy grew much faster than that of the United States for more than a decade.

Successful Stabilizations of the 1980s

In addition to such past stabilization success stories as Poincaré's France in 1926 and Erhard's Germany in 1948, there have also been quite a few promising economic turnarounds in recent years. Because the policies that led to these dramatic improvements are difficult to identify through conventional, demand-side macroeconomics, the results are often vaguely characterized as "economic miracles" by observers such as *The Economist*. These so-called miracles, however, should be no mystery. They invariably result from a combination of currency stabilization, low tax rates, and low tariffs—a policy mix that flies in the face of the IMF paradigm.

Bolivia

In 1985, Bolivia had an inflation rate of 23,000 percent. Real GDP fell by 16 percent annually from 1978 through 1986. Yet inflation suddenly dropped below 15 percent by 1987 and to 12 percent by 1992. How did a runaway hyperinflation stop so quickly? One reason, explains Juan-Antonio Morales of the Catholic University of Bolivia, is that "stabilization has focused explicitly on the exchange rate."[6] According to Morales, Bolivia ignored the IMF's advice to devalue, and instead moved to halt the currency's decline by reducing the budget deficit (through tax reform and reduced subsidies), by not "monetizing" government debt, and by intervening in foreign-exchange auctions to stabilize the currency.[7] Jeffrey Sachs likewise observed:

> The exchange rate stabilized almost immediately, and with a stable exchange rate, the price level stopped rising.... The remarkable break in the hyperinflation began no more than one week after the inception of the program! Inflation fell from a rate of more than 50 percent per month to price stability almost immediately.... *The stabilization program eschewed all wage and price controls...and indeed freed many controls at the inception of the program.* (Sachs 1986, 75. emphasis added)

The new Boliviano of January 1987 (equal to one million old pesos) was not literally fixed after that, but depreciation was confined to 15 percent per year from 1986 to 1989—a so-called "crawling peg." Inflation has hovered between 12 percent and 20 percent from 1987 through 1992, which is modest by Latin American standards. The Bolivian economy soon began to grow, with real GNP increasing by 3.1 percent annually from 1987 to 1992.[8] This economic expansion occurred despite the failure of Argentina to pay for Bolivia's biggest export (natural gas), weakness in the price of Bolivia's second biggest export (tin), and a continuation of the sustained decline in production of crude oil that began in 1973.

This modern miracle, like that of France in 1926 and Germany in 1948, began with a rather extreme reduction of tax rates. Tax reform came first, and exchange-rate stabilization second. The highest income tax rate in Bolivia, which had already been reduced from 45 percent to 35 percent, was slashed to a flat rate of only 10 percent. A 30 percent corporate tax was replaced with a three percent tax on net worth, except for oil and mining. Some 400 sales taxes were also combined into a 10 percent value-added tax (both the income tax and VAT were raised to 13 percent in 1992). What was unique, however, was that *the new 10 percent VAT was entirely deductible from the 10 percent income tax!* With a 10 percent income tax, there was little incentive to cheat. And by simply keeping receipts for VAT paid, the income tax could be largely avoided anyway. As a result, Bolivians began demanding sales receipts in order to claim the tax break for VAT. Much of the informal, underground economy's advantage in being outside the tax system was thereby eliminated. Tax receipts soared. In addition, the Bolivian government ended gasoline subsidies, with important budgetary effects. Government spending did not fall, but in fact rose from 8.1 percent of GDP in 1986 to 11.6 percent in 1988. Tax receipts rose from 1.9 percent of GDP in 1984 to seven percent in 1987–88, reducing the budget deficit from 19.6 percent of GDP in 1984 to 4.2 percent in 1988 (Inter-American Development Bank 1990, 275–76). With the added receipts from tax reform, it became feasible to slash tariffs from 80 percent to 20 percent. And just as with the European countries in the 1920s, stabilizing the exchange rate also improved the real value of tax collections. Although the increased tax receipts resulting from lower tax rates were critical in minimizing the need to print money to cover budget deficits, the commitment to eschew regular, massive devaluations as a policy tool was also essential to creating credibility for the new currency.

Jamaica

In Jamaica, real output and income began falling in 1974 and continued to drop almost every year through 1986, by a total of 23 percent. The currency was repeatedly devalued following an IMF program in 1978. In 1985 it took five times as many Jamaican dollars to buy a U.S. dollar as it did in 1977. Tax brackets were not adjusted for inflation, so the top tax rate of 57.5 percent eventually fell on incomes as low as $700 a year. At least one-third of the professionals and managers left the country. In 1986, after six years in power, Prime Minister Edward Seaga finally cut the highest tax rate nearly in half, to 33.3 percent; he also reduced tariffs and refused to comply with another IMF demand to devalue the currency. Measured in constant 1985 Jamaican dollars, real tax receipts rose by almost 17 percent in the first year tax rates were reduced. Without price controls, inflation dropped from 27 percent in 1984–85 to less than 10 percent in 1987–89, and the Jamaican economy expanded far more rapidly from 1988 to 1991 (by 3.7 percent per year) than it had in more than fifteen years, despite falling prices for a major export, bauxite.

In 1990–91 the IMF was back, peddling mischief. "IMF technical advisers urged Jamaica to speed up the delayed introduction of a General Consumption Tax" (*IMF Conditionality* 1992, 22). That 10 percent VAT became fully effective in 1992 (albeit largely as a replacement for other indirect taxes). The currency was devalued by 69 percent in 1991; GDP slowed to less than one percent in 1992, and inflation rose to 77 percent.

Colombia

Mainstream economists do not simply ignore the role of lower marginal tax rates in successful stabilizations, as in Jamaica, Mexico or Bolivia, they sometimes get it exactly backwards. The usual error is in observing an increase in tax receipts and assuming that it occurred because of higher, not lower, tax rates. Michael Urrutia of the Inter-American Development Bank, for example, writes that "Colombia was the only country in Latin America that adjusted successfully after 1982. It did it by almost wiping out the fiscal deficit in 1984–85, not only by decreasing expenditures, *but also by increasing taxation*" (Sachs 1989, 216. emphasis added).

This is much worse than misleading. What actually happened in Colombia (which, by the way, was not under an IMF program) was that the highest tax rates were repeatedly and deeply *slashed*—from 56 percent in 1979 to 49 percent in 1984, to only 30 percent in recent years. Moreover, the income thresholds at which those lower rates applied were also substantially increased in real terms. Economic growth in Colombia averaged well over 4 percent per year from 1984 to 1993—with no recession in a decade—after languishing at 1.6 percent in the previous three years. Progress has been broadly based throughout industry and agriculture. Colombia has reduced the ratio of foreign debt to GDP by the unorthodox approach of raising GDP; that is, by allowing private producers to keep 70 percent of the increases in output and income.

For all the IMF's concern about "investment-savings gaps" (another subtle IMF target) and the matching capital inflow, it is worth noting that Colombia's "gap" between investment and domestic savings averaged 3.9 percent of GNP from 1980 to 1987—three times the rate (1.3 percent) of Mexico at that time ("Special Survey on Colombia" 1989, II). Yet Mexico was then in far worse financial shape. Investment exceeded savings by a wide margin in Colombia in the 1980s (as it did in Mexico after 1987) because constructive tax, trade, and exchange rate policies made Colombia an attractive place to invest.

Chile

Colombia, Bolivia, and Jamaica are not the only countries in Latin America that have eschewed the IMF approach in favor of lower marginal tax rates, freer trade, and a more-or-less stable currency. Chile also adjusted successfully, but only long after "floating" the Chilean peso along traditional IMF lines. The currency was allowed to go into a free fall in June 1982—an experiment that resulted in a 15 percent drop in real GDP, a doubling of unemployment to 20 percent, and a soaring budget deficit which was met through the disastrous expedient of increasing tariffs from 10 percent to 35 percent. This "floating" (sinking) exchange rate was accompanied by an increase in marginal tax rates at low and middle incomes in 1983—a set of suicidal policies rewarded with a two-year IMF loan in January 1983 (*IMF Conditionality* 1992, 132). *The Economist*—which still cannot imagine how the IMF's Cambridge Keynesianism could possibly cause the problems it aims to cure—proudly announced that "Chile's bureaucrats need no arm-twisting to run their economy according to the IMF handbook" ("Chile's Economy" 1985). Yet Chile's remarkable recovery after 1984 actually consisted of abandoning the brief 1982–83 flirtation with IMF exchange rate, tax, and tariff policies, choosing instead to reduce tariffs and tax rates and slow the depreciation of the currency.

The first and most important tax cut in Chile was the reduction in taxes on trade—that is, tariffs. Average tariffs were reduced from 94 percent in 1973 (with a maximum rate of 220 percent) to 10 to 15 percent after 1983 (Frankel, Froot, and Salces 1987, 13). After 1985, income tax rates were also reduced at most income levels, and to 50 percent from 65 percent at the top (35 percent for one year, 1985). The corporate rate was more deeply cut in 1985, to 32.5 percent from 47.5 percent; and the VAT was later trimmed to 18 percent from 20 percent. Individual income tax rates are not quite as high as they look because social security taxes are deductible, and only "real" interest income (after adjustment for inflation) is taxed. There have been virtually no limits on privatization of state enterprises, which has mostly occurred through shares sold to Chilean pension funds, workers, and investors rather than debt-equity swaps (Graham 1988). Chile also privatized the social security system, replacing it with a private, competitive system in which workers must pay a tax-free minimum of their salaries in a pension fund. Deregulation has opened entry into the taxi, bus, and airline industries, with competitive pricing. Private schools are reimbursed for the cost of educating a child in public schools (Rosett 1982).

The Chilean economy grew at an impressive annual rate of 5.3 percent from 1986 through 1992—up from 1.8 percent in 1975–84. Inflation—which hit 350 percent in the mid-1970s and averaged 64 percent from 1975 to 1984—has recently been held at 15–25 percent through a crawling peg regime. The value of Chilean foreign debt on secondary markets has long been among the highest of third world debtors. Early in 1991, Chile was even able to market $320 million in bonds to a group of twenty international banks (Crawford 1991). It is now difficult to recall that at the time of the disastrous 1983 IMF-sponsored experiment with devaluation, higher tax rates, and 35 percent tariffs, Chile had the highest per capita foreign debt in Latin America.

Philippines

The Philippines, an Asian country burdened with historic Spanish mercantilist institutions and ideas, provides yet another example of how changes in the policy mix can turn things around quickly. In 1983 Ferdinand Marcos complied with an IMF demand to let the peso "float"—which of course meant sink. The peso's value was quickly cut in half, and inflation jumped from 10 percent to 50 percent. Because the tax system was not indexed, taxpayers with even low and middle incomes suddenly found that higher tax brackets now applied at half as much real income as previously. The late Warren Brookes explained the tax policy that accompanied the devaluation: "At the IMF's urging, Marcos raised business tax rates in 1984 by more than 30 percent, with a 45 percent rate now starting on only $6,800 in net business profits, and a new top rate of 60 percent on anything above $23,000" (Brookes 1986).

Real GNP fell by 12 percent in 1984–85, followed by revolution. Still, the IMF took no notice. "The IMF is pushing for a free float of the peso," reported the *Journal of Commerce* in the fall of 1985. "Of particular concern to the IMF inspection team is the continuing strength of the peso, which it believes is...being secretly propped up by the government" (Bangsberg 1985a, 1985b). Shortly thereafter, the new Aquino government ignored the IMF, virtually fixing the peso (inflation fell from 23.1 percent in 1985 to 3.8 percent in 1987), reducing tariffs, and cutting the top tax rate from 60 percent to 35 percent. "In June 1986, a bold new program of tax reform was adopted...including a sharply reduced tax rate at the highest income ranges [and] reform of import tariffs" (Gurgen 1986). Economic growth quickly rebounded to 4.8 percent in 1987, 6.3 percent in 1988, and 6.1 percent in 1989. Real tax receipts (deflated by the CPI) rose from 78 billion pesos in 1986 to 97 billion in 1987 and over 118 billion in 1989—an increase of more than 50 percent in four years.

Unfortunately, the Philippine government again resorted to a sizable devaluation of the peso in 1990—to comply, of course, with conditions on a new IMF loan. Inflation rose to nearly 19 percent in 1991 (*International Financial Statistics* 1993, 59). The 1986 relief from high tax rates and tariffs was also undermined by this new "stabilization" program. The World Bank reports that "the government imposed a nine percent import levy" under "a new stabilization program supported by an IMF standby arrangement" (World Bank 1992, 448). The program also included another increasingly common IMF panacea—a new 10 percent VAT. From that point on, tax and tariff receipts stopped growing much in real terms. Interest rates in 1990 were double what they had been in 1987, which is another reason the budget deficit doubled between 1989 and 1990. The Philippine stock market, which had risen 57 percent in dollar terms in 1989, fell by 55 percent in 1990 (Moore

1991). Real GDP growth suddenly slowed from 6.2 percent in 1988–89 to 2.4 percent in 1990, and fell by 1 percent in 1991.

Asian Tigers

Only one of the expanding group of "Asian Tigers" has suffered the sort of IMF supervision that has inflicted such damage to the Philippine economy in the past decade. Taiwan's lack of universal recognition as a country separate from China has been a distinct advantage in this respect, because the island was not allowed to belong to the IMF.

South Korea was under tight IMF supervision for a single year, 1980, because the current account deficit had reached 6.4 percent of GDP in the previous year (and to 8.4 percent in 1980), which alarmed creditors. The IMF's adjustment policy for 1980 included a huge increase in the highest income tax rates, to 89 percent, plus a 17 percent currency devaluation. Inflation soared to 35 percent and real GDP fell by five percent. The IMF standby loan ended in February 1981, and Korean authorities were then free to repair the damage. "During 1981–82," notes a retrospective IMF study, "structural policies were aimed at increasing the productivity and efficiency of the economy. These policies encompassed...a comprehensive tax reform, and trade liberalization" (Aghevli and Marquez-Ruarte 1987, 101). Top tax rates were slashed from 89 percent to 70 percent at once and to 50 percent later. Tariffs fell. Lower tax rates and tariffs greatly invigorated the real economy, as always, by reducing costs and raising incentives. Since the IMF was no longer around, promoting the chimera of "real devaluation," inflation dropped to 12 percent in 1981 and 5 percent in 1982. That this drop of inflation coincided with (and indeed helped create) a 6 percent growth of real GDP is yet another repudiation of the Phillips Curve theory. It is extremely doubtful that the tax, tariff, and exchange rate policies that pulled Korea out of the 1980 stagflation would ever have been permitted if the IMF program had not expired in February 1981. Just as the adoption or resumption of IMF programs has so often been followed by stagflation or worse, the rapid dismantling of IMF programs, as in South Korea in 1981 and Mexico in 1989, has likewise brought economic progress and low inflation.

The "newly industrialized" Asian countries either always had low tax rates and tariffs (Hong Kong), or emulated such policies during the 1980s. China began its remarkable renaissance by granting farmers secure property rights (long-term transferable leases), and by allowing them to sell all produce above a fixed quota on the open market. This was essentially a zero marginal tax rate—anything produced above quota was tax free. China, like Hong Kong, had no VAT and no Social Security taxes (though there were some turnover taxes, usually about 3 percent). The maximum income tax rate on foreigners working in China was less than 23 percent in 1993, which facilitated importing knowledge. Large free trade zones were also established, attracting capital from Hong Kong and elsewhere.

Singapore found itself in recession in 1985 and responded by reducing income tax rates (the top rate fell from 45 percent to 30 percent) and sharply reducing the percentage of payrolls devoted to mandatory savings plans. Malaysia followed by cutting its top tax to 34 percent. Economic growth from 1987 to 1992 averaged 8.2 percent in both countries. Indonesia likewise reduced tariffs and cut maximum tax rates in the mid-1980s to 35 percent from 50 percent, and real GDP grew by an average of 6.2 percent a year from 1987 to 1992. Another thing the Asian NICs have in common, aside from falling tax rates, is that the IMF was not involved (aside from the 1980 fiasco in South Korea).

Mauritius and Botswana

The IMF has been pushing its economic recipe throughout Africa for a long time. As the *Financial Times* observed in 1985, "only a handful of African countries have managed to avoid the unwelcome embraces of the IMF in the past few years."[9] A United Nations report found that "of the 12 least developed countries which have applied [IMF] programs for most of the 1980s, the growth rates of only three— Bangladesh, Gambia and Mali—were above the average for all the [42] least developing countries" (Bollag 1989).

Indeed, the prolonged absence of meaningful development on the continent with the highest tax rates in the world—a region which has long labored under continual IMF tutelage—is evidence of the importance of tax policy. Gerardo Sicat and Arvind Virmani of the World Bank calculated that marginal tax rates in 1984–85, at the equivalent of only two times the average family income (which is still well below the U.S. poverty level), were 51 percent in Sierra Leone, 56 percent in Somalia, 60 percent in Ghana, and 63 percent in Tunisia (Sicat and Virmani 1988, Table 1. See also Bartlett 1989, 307). For comparison, tax rates on those earning twice the average family income were 13 percent in Chile at that time (after tax reform) and 17 percent in Hong Kong (which has been the maximum tax rate in Hong Kong for many years).

Among the lucky handful of African countries who have avoided "the IMF embrace" is the most successful African democracy, Botswana. The government of Botswana has repeatedly reduced its highest tax rates to a maximum of 40 percent (from 60 percent in 1979), with the higher tax rates applying only at an increasingly high real income. Economic growth in Botswana has long been the fastest in the world, averaging 14 percent per year, despite droughts, from 1972 through 1989. That awesome performance was broadly based in agriculture and manufacturing; it is often too easily dismissed as entirely due to diamonds, or to interaction with South Africa (which, in fact, has not grown nearly as fast as Botswana).

Perhaps the most instructive case of economic renaissance in Africa has been the island country of Mauritius, which has become known as the "Hong Kong of Africa." In 1982 Mauritius had an unemployment rate of 22 percent, and one fifth of the people were attempting to emigrate. Since then, by contrast, real economic growth has averaged well above 5 percent per year, and unemployment has been negligible since 1988. Inflation, which was 30 percent in 1979–80 when price controls were in force, averaged 4.4 percent from 1983 to 1987—that is, after price controls were removed. The budget deficit was cut from 14 percent of GDP in 1982 to 1 percent in 1988.

What caused this amazing switch from despair to prosperity? There should be no mystery. At a 1992 World Bank conference, Paul Romer emphasized that *"income and corporate tax rates were halved in 1983 (from about 70 to about 35 percent)."* He also observed that free trade zones were set up, which allowed "unrestricted, tariff-free imports of machinery and materials, no restriction on ownership or repatriation of profits, [and] a ten-year income tax holiday for foreign investors" (Romer 1992, 77).

Romer, a major architect of the "new growth" economics, is unusually perceptive. More conventional explanations of how Mauritius was turned around in 1983 completely ignore tax rates and tariffs. For example, a March 1989 *Financial Times* survey on Mauritius stated that "under successive IMF programs...the Government devalued the rupee" (Survey on Mauritius 1989). This is a classic example of the triumph of IMF theory over reality. The only big devaluation was back in 1980; it was accompanied, as usual, by a 10 percent drop in real GDP, 22 percent unemployment, and 30 percent inflation. From 1982 through

1987, when inflation slowed and growth began, the rupee was on a de facto crawling peg, slipping by less than 4 percent per year. Real GDP growth was 9.3 percent per year from 1986 to 1988. Unfortunately, the IMF did succeed in demanding a 12 percent devaluation between the fourth quarters of 1988 and 1989, ostensibly to reduce a current-account deficit (which instead grew by 14 percent in 1990). As a result, inflation bounced back to 13.2 percent in 1989–91 and interest rates rose, turning a budget surplus into deficit. Growth nonetheless remained above 5 percent, thanks in part to an additional cut in income tax rates from 35 percent to 30 percent.

Israel

Israel's stabilization program of July 1985 is instructive, because it shows that even a mild version of the policy reforms that we have been discussing have the same beneficial effects in a relatively advanced economy. Before the mid-July policy change, Israel was suffering another unsuccessful experiment with IMF-style "Nixonomics"—that is, trying to combine currency devaluations with wage and price controls. Indeed, Israel had been under considerable pressure in 1984 from two former advisers to President Nixon—George Shultz and Herbert Stein—whose heavy-handed recommendations could have been ignored only at the risk of losing U.S. and IMF funding.[10]

Stanley Fischer, former chief economist with the World Bank, has written that in 1981 Israel's new finance minister, Yoram Aridor, "came to office with his own brand of supply-side economics" (Fischer 1985, 78). It is true that Aridor cut tariff rates (not tax rates) and that revenues from the tariff subsequently increased. But Aridor never quite grasped the global monetary message of Robert Mundell and other supply-siders. Instead, he claimed that inflation was simply a matter of "inertia" or "expectations," to be dealt with through wage-price controls and subsidies. This led him to press—again and again—for a currency devaluation for "balance of payments" reasons.

Aridor left office at the end of 1983, amid a controversy surrounding his sound proposal to "dollarize" the Israeli currency, the shekel. Another devaluation of 23 percent followed, and by early 1985 the inflation rate was approaching 1000 percent. It is important to note that comprehensive wage and price controls had already been adopted in November 1984. Yet inflation exploded under those controls, and both inflation and controls rapidly worsened the fiscal situation (wage controls result in substitution of benefits for taxable cash and greater misreporting of income). As Alvin Rabushka pointed out, "Tax receipts fell sharply in 1984 [from 50.3 percent of GNP to 39.3 percent] as inflation eroded the value of tax payments...but recovered with the 1985 stabilization plan" (Rabushka and Hanke 1988).

What really made the July 1985 Israeli stabilization successful was not price controls—which had already been eased in April of 1985 and were largely dismantled in 1986—but rather the formal and explicit repudiation of the IMF's devaluation theory, the idea of sinking the exchange rate to make exports "competitive." Yakir Plessner, former Deputy Governor of the Bank of Israel, writes, "The complete absence of anything resembling a monetary policy persisted for over six years, until July 1985." Before the 1985 reform, as Plessner rightly empha- sizes, "the exchange rate was...used for balance of payments correc- tions, with complete disregard of the monetary effects" (Rabushka and Hanke 1988, 75). After the reform, Stanley Fischer confirms, "the Bank of Israel would conduct monetary policy with the exchange rate as its main nominal target" (Fischer 1987, 277). A recent statistical com- parison of Israel with Argentina and Brazil, by Peter Montiel of the IMF, likewise came to the following momentous conclusion:

> The case of Israel also does not provide support for the fiscal view [that inflation is caused by budget deficits].... The recent inflationary episodes that gave rise to the attempts at heterodox stabilization seem to have been much more closely asso- ciated with nominal exchange rate movements than with base money growth.... *The pursuit of external adjustment through nominal exchange rate devaluation may be associated with a substantial, sustained, and...extremely stubborn increase in the rate of inflation.* (Montiel 1989, 547–48. emphasis added)

As in the European stabilizations of the 1920s, stabilizing the ex- change rate in Israel raised the real value of tax receipts and reduced interest expenses and subsidies. But the budget deficit was also fur- ther reduced by the positive effects on economic growth arising from lower tariffs and tax rates. A retrospective IMF report on Israel in 1987 expressed apparent astonishment that *"the rising revenues stemmed mainly from the positive effect of declining inflation and buoyant wages, consumption and imports"* ("Israel Curbs Inflation" 1987. emphasis added). Had Israel instead followed the IMF recipe of attempting to curb wages, consumption, and imports—through wage controls, devaluation, and higher tax rates and tariffs—one re- sult would have been much smaller tax revenues, though that would have been the least of many troubles.

Like nearly all other *successful* stabilizations—that is, stabilizations in which the real economy expands as inflation declines—Israel's reform also included a reduction in tax rates. In 1986–87 marginal tax rates on individuals were reduced from 60 percent to 48 percent. The VAT was cut from 17 percent to 15 percent, an import deposit fee was reduced by 15 percent, and an employment tax in commerce and services was also cut from 7 percent to 4 percent. Effective tax rates on business income (including double-taxation of dividends) were reduced from 61 percent to 55 percent. Although "tax revenue was not projected to show much change," what actually happened was that "*tax revenue was higher than expected in all categories, and particularly in the case of the income tax*" (Kreis 1989, 378–79. emphasis added). Economic growth averaged 6.2 percent from 1990 to 1992, and inflation was down to about 12 percent by 1992, belying the IMF's Phillips Curve notion that rapid real growth raises inflation.

Mexico and Argentina

Two more recent economic "miracles" were the result of policies designed by elected political leaders responsible to their citizens, not by some paternalistic foreign team of aspiring central planners.[ll] These reforms were the precise opposite of those typically proposed by the IMF, as an explicit or de facto condition for loans. Instead of devaluing, currencies were fixed or semi-fixed. Instead of imposing new and higher taxes, existing tax rates were sharply reduced. And instead of maintaining protectionist policies, ostensibly to close the trade deficit, tariffs were sharply reduced and current account deficits expanded along with enormous inflows of foreign investment.

The IMF had a long history of intervention in Mexico. A World Bank report summarizes the record with remarkable objectivity:

> In 1983, an IMF-supported stabilization program was launched. In a single year...inflation was running at 100 percent. The results were a severe recession with GDP falling by more than 4 percent.... A new [IMF] adjustment program was adopted in July 1986.... Economic stagnation and triple-digit inflation continued into 1987, while...frequent exchange rate adjustments to maintain export competitiveness created inflationary pressures. (World Bank 1992a, 355)

The new Salinas government had seen enough of this sort of "stabilization," and opted for something quite different. The peso was put on a crawling peg, initially allowed to depreciate by only one peso per day, later a half-peso, and so on. The maximum income tax rate was reduced, in stages, from 55 percent to 35 percent, and the real income threshold at which the 35 percent rate applied was raised above those at which the 55 percent rate used to apply (particularly in 1994). The value-added tax was reduced from 15 to 20 percent to 10 percent. Tariffs that had commonly been 50 to 100 percent were reduced to no more than 20 percent (and an average of 10 percent), and later were scheduled to be phased out entirely under the North American Free Trade Agreement.

The results of the Salinas reforms were rapid and dramatic. Inflation fell from 159 percent in 1987, to 20 percent in 1989, and to 10 percent by early 1993 (regardless of money supply growth above 80 percent in the previous two years). Growth of real GDP rebounded to 3.5 percent a year from 1989 to 1992. And there was a massive infusion of net foreign investment (and equally massive current account deficit), mostly due to repatriation of Mexican capital and to foreign portfolio investment in Mexican stocks and Treasury bills. The budget also swung into surplus, even aside from privatization revenues, largely for reasons that are not widely appreciated.

As mentioned before, particularly in the section on success stories of the 1920s, a beneficial side effect of slowing or stopping inflation is lower government interest expense on the domestic national debt. As inflation fell from 159 percent in 1987 to 12 percent in 1992, short-term interest rates also fell from 103 percent to 16 percent (note that "real" interest rates rose with the improved productivity of capital). *The Mexican government's cost of debt service thus fell from 19.8 percent of GDP to 3.9 percent—reducing the nominal budget deficit by an amount equal to nearly 17 percent of GDP!* This is an extremely clear example of just one way in which good monetary policy can produce good budgetary results, rather than the other way around. The easiest way for countries with high inflation to meet the IMF's targets for lower budget deficits is usually to ignore the IMF's targets for currency depreciation. And Mexico also shows that another way to improve the budget is to use lower marginal tax rates to improve incentives to work and invest in the formal economy, thus generating growing real tax revenue through the growth of payrolls, profits, and sales.

No country has endured more IMF programs over the years than Argentina, with endless failures. A "letter of intent" with the IMF on 13 October 1989, negotiated shortly after President Carlos Menem took office in July, stated, once again, that Argentina's government "recognizes the importance of continuing with a competitive type of exchange that stimulates exports" (*IMF Conditionality* 1992, Appendix B). Inflation was 2,315 percent in 1990 and real GDP fell once again (it had already fallen by 1.9 percent in 1988 and 6.2 percent in 1989).

President Menem soon surprised everyone, probably including the IMF, by adopting policies quite similar to those of Mexico, only more so. The maximum income tax rate was slashed to only 30 percent. Tax enforcement was toughened, as in Mexico, but it is always much easier to collect reasonable taxes than to collect unreasonable taxes. Export taxes were eliminated in 1990–91. Tariffs were completely eliminated on capital goods and reduced to no more than 20 percent on almost everything else. The telephone company and many other enterprises were wholly or partly privatized, including (as in Mexico) private toll roads. There are plans to privatize Social Security, as in Chile, which could reduce the still onerous payroll tax. But the most astonishing change involved totally repudiating the October 1989 pledge to the IMF to keep devaluing the currency in the vain hope of making exports "competitive."

Instead of merely slowing the rate of devaluation on a predictable schedule, as Mexico and others have done, Argentina pegged the new peso at one to the dollar in April 1991 and required that any new issue of currency be 100 percent backed by foreign exchange or gold. The results were immediate. Inflation, which had been 3,082 percent in 1989 and 2,315 percent in 1990, promptly dropped to about 13 percent by early 1993 (even lower for wholesale prices). And Argentina proved, once again, that low inflation is scarcely synonymous with "austerity." Real GDP growth was nearly 9 percent in both 1991 and 1992.

An economy that is growing by 9 percent a year needs to use some of the industrial goods at home that it might otherwise export, and it is likewise sure to need imported materials and machinery to keep expanding production. Argentina soon began repatriating some of the huge Argentine investments that had flowed abroad to avoid taxes and inflation (about $60 billion), and the country attracted considerable foreign direct and equity investment. The result was a large capital-account surplus and matching $8.4 billion current-account deficit. Imports (many from the U.S.) rose from $4 billion in 1990, to $8.1 billion in 1991, and to $14.9 billion in 1992. Naturally, those of the IMF school of thought (as well as some local special interests) quickly pointed to the rise in imports and trade deficits as a reason for higher tariffs and another dose of devaluation. This would be a huge mistake. Inflows of private capital to businesses were a sign that Argentina was doing things right, not a sign of "crisis" requiring an IMF "adjustment."

Reasonable Tax Rates = Faster Growth of Real Tax Revenue

We have shown that *all successful economic turnarounds in the twentieth century, without exception, have had at least two of the following three features in common:* (1) tariffs and other trade barriers were reduced; (2) exchange rates were tied to a stronger currency, through a pegged or crawling exchange rate regime; and (3) high marginal tax rates on human and physical capital were sharply reduced. The IMF certainly does not object to lower trade barriers in principle, though the institutional emphasis on trade balances sometimes has the effect of aborting liberalization. At least some IMF economists have recently questioned the wisdom of perpetual currency devaluations, though to our knowledge no IMF program (unlike the League of Nations in the 1920s) has ever made currency stability a condition for loans to less developed countries. It is at least conceivable that a country seeking IMF credit today might be able to propose a plan to stabilize exchange rates or reduce tariffs without encountering overt opposition, though it seems unlikely that the IMF itself has ever proposed currency stabilization except in the aftermath of a truly massive devaluation (Poland).

Table 8.3 shows a small sample of sizable reductions in the highest marginal tax rates in the 1980s and early 1990s.

TABLE 8.3
Maximum Marginal Tax Rates on Individual Income

	1979	1989	1993
Argentina	45	35	30 %
Bolivia	48	10	10
Botswana	75	50	40
Brazil	58	25	25
Colombia	56	30	30
Indonesia	50	35	35
Jamaica	58	33	33
Malaysia	60	45	35
Mauritius	60	35	30
Mexico	55	40	35
Pakistan	55	45	39
Portugal	84	68	40

Source: Price Waterhouse; International Bureau of Fiscal Documentation.

This third policy tool—alleviating high marginal tax rates on human capital—remains the one topic on which IMF appears most reluctant to bend (though the IMF has been more tolerant of lower corporate tax rates). Even the slightest reduction in any tax rate on individuals still appears to be viewed with great suspicion, due to the dogma that revenues will necessarily decline and budget deficits will rise. However, tax reform did not have that effect in countries such as Britain and the United States, where real revenues soared following sharp reductions of marginal tax rates.

Were the widespread reductions of income or sales tax rates among less developed countries fiscally irresponsible? Was government revenue actually reduced, either in real terms or as a share of (rising) GDP? The record for Latin America, using revenue figures from the Inter-American Development Bank, is quite clear:[12]

- Mexico cut the top income tax rate from over 60 percent to 35 percent in 1990. Revenues (about 90 percent from taxes) rose from 15.9 percent of GDP in 1986 to 18.6 percent in 1990. It is particularly noteworthy that income taxes rose from 23.2 percent of all current revenue in 1987 to 31.1 percent in 1990 (before the VAT was cut from 15–20 percent to 10 percent).
- Jamaica cut the top tax from 58 percent to 33 percent in 1986. Revenues rose from 25.2 percent of GDP in 1985 to 33.4 percent in 1990.
- Colombia cut the top tax from 60 percent to 30 percent in 1984–86. Revenues rose from 7.8 percent of GDP in 1983 to about 10 percent from 1986 through 1990.
- Chile cut both corporate and individual tax rates in 1984–85. Tax revenues promptly rose from 7.8 percent of GDP to 10.6 percent.
- Bolivia cut the top tax from 45 percent to 10 percent in 1985–86, slashed tariffs, substituted a 10 percent VAT for several hundred sales taxes, and let taxpayers deduct that value-added tax from income taxes. Revenues jumped from 1.7 percent of GDP in 1984 to 6.3 percent by 1987.
- Puerto Rico cut the top tax from 68 percent in 1985 to 41 percent in 1988, and tax revenues increased by 28 percent (de Soto 1993).

By contrast, in those Latin American countries that had not yet adopted competitive tax policies by 1990, punitive tax rates began yielding less and less real revenue, obliging governments to print money to pay their bills. Peru, while under an IMF adjustment program, routinely overtaxed all productive activity; and revenues dropped from 14.1 percent of GDP in 1985 to 6.4 percent in 1989—both a cause and effect of Peru's hyperinflation. Argentina's revenues likewise fell from 15.1 percent of GDP in 1986 to only 4.7 percent in 1988. In 1991–92, though, Argentina sharply reduced income tax rates, to a top rate of 30 percent, as part of a successful end to hyperinflation, involving, as usual, much lower tariffs and a fixed exchange rate.

The Latin American experiences of strong revenue gains from lowering high marginal tax rates were confirmed by a survey article on taxation and development by Robin Burgess and Nicholas Stern of the London School of Economics. In case studies of those tax reforms which involved a significant reduction of marginal income tax rates, Burgess and Stern had the following comments:[13]

- S. Korea: "Tax revenue/GDP rose considerably"
- Mexico: "Reforms...now revenue-positive."
- Jamaica: "There was an increase in overall revenues."
- Indonesia: "Revenue effect broadly neutral"—but oil tax fell from 60 percent to 30 percent of total.
- Sri-Lanka: "There was a positive effect on overall revenues" (which rose by 3 percent of GDP).

Even relatively timid tax relief has brought revenue gains. Turkey's highest marginal rate was 68 percent in 1984, applied at an income of only about $34,000 a year. The big reduction was in 1986, when the top rate fell to 50 percent at about $63,000 or more. Revenues from the personal income tax alone rose from 5.4 percent of GDP in 1985, to 6.1 percent in 1986, and to 7.4 percent in 1990. More important, real GDP grew briskly as tax rates came down, so that a rising share of GDP meant rapid growth of real tax receipts from a wide variety of taxes (Reynolds 1993c, chapter 2).

A recent World Bank study of thirty-two countries (Easterly and Rebelo 1992) notes that all growth theories predict that "increases in [marginal] income taxes lead to permanent declines in the rate of economic expansion," and that "high statutory schedules [may] significantly distort behavior while generating little revenue." Easterly and Rebelo found that *"about two thirds of the countries in our sample generated less revenue than would be collected by implementing a linear [flat rate] tax with a rate that coincides with lowest statutory rate"* (Easterly and Rebelo 1992, 5). That is, all tax rates above the lowest bracket not only failed to yield any revenue at all in two-thirds of the countries studied, but actually generated less revenue than simply applying the lowest tax rate to everyone. This is confirmed by the cross-country analysis of Gerald Scully, which suggest that income tax rates much above about 23 percent reduce long-term tax receipts by slowing economic growth and therefore shrinking the tax base (Scully 1991, 9).

A National Bureau of Economic Research paper by Eric Engen and Jonathon Skinner reviewed nearly a dozen recent studies which found that increases in tax rates do lasting damage to economic growth (Engen and Skinner 1992). Their research, based on 107 countries over fifteen years, estimates that "a 10 percentage point tax increase is predicted to reduce output growth by 3.2 percentage points per annum." Philip Trostel found that even small increases in marginal tax rates have very large effects on young peoples' willingness to invest time and money in their education. A 1 percent increase in tax rates was found to permanently shrink the stock of human capital by nearly 1 percent, with progressive tax rates having even stronger effects (Trostel 1993, 347). Another study by William Easterly and Sergio Rebelo for the World Bank looked at evidence going back to 1870, as well as recent comparisons between twenty-eight countries. They, too, found "a negative association between growth and...the marginal income tax rate" (Easterly and Rebelo 1993).

Another multicountry study of individual income tax rates by Reinhard Koester and Roger Kormendi of the University of Michigan came up with the following dramatic result: "Holding average tax rates constant, a 10 percentage point reduction in marginal tax rates would yield a 15.2 percent increase in per capital income for LDCs" (Koester and Kormendi 1989, 367–86).

Since 1986 the IMF has at times seemed willing to condone lower income tax rates, but only on two conditions: The first condition is that lower income tax rates be accompanied by new or higher value-added taxes. The de Tocqueville Institute survey of fifty-two IMF-supported programs between 1986 and 1991 found that 64 percent included raising or broadening value-added or other sales taxes, though 43 percent also reduced income tax rates at the equivalent of the U.S. poverty level. "The Fund has been particularly impressed with Chile's experience with the value-added tax.... Fund technical missions to other countries...have regularly recommended emulation of the Chilean model" (*IMF Conditionality* 1992, 126–27). We noted earlier that a new 10 percent VAT accompanied IMF programs in Jamaica and the Philippines in the early 1990s, and (unlike the earlier experiences of Chile and New Zealand) these recent VATs were not matched by reductions in income tax rates.

A VAT may have less adverse effects on savings than an equivalent income tax, but it is the combined income, Social Security, and VAT rate that matters for incentives. As Burgess and Stern put it, "VAT is a tax on wages and profits" (Burgess and Stern 1993, 815). Very few rapidly expanding economies have any value-added tax, and some (such as Hong Kong and China) have no payroll tax for Social Security (though Chile and Singapore have mandatory private savings plans). Even some of the countries that do have a value-added tax have found high rates counterproductive. Mexico recently reduced its VAT from 15–20 percent to 10 percent, Ireland from 25 percent to 16–21 percent, and Chile from 30 percent to 18 percent. In any case, the actual revenue growth from lower income tax rates, demonstrated above, makes it quite unnecessary to offset the assumed static revenue losses with some other tax, as the IMF appears to require.

The second IMF precondition is that countries that refuse to devalue their currencies are not permitted to reduce any tax rates. The 1992 de Tocqueville study notes, "the Fund's fiscal advisors have not encouraged African countries to emulate Latin American tax reforms." The authors of that study suggest that this is because the IMF views devaluation as one way to "adjust" (i.e., to run a trade surplus), so that countries that do not devalue must supposedly keep tax rates high in order to restrain domestic demand. Since fourteen African currencies are tied to the French franc, those countries (and most others) are discouraged from reducing punitive marginal tax rates if they hope to continue getting IMF loans. This may well explain why taxpayers with modest incomes still faced punitive 1993 tax rates of 50 percent in Congo and Senegal, 55 percent in Zimbabwe, 60 percent in Gabon and Zaire, plus Social Security taxes (19.4 percent in Congo, 24.6 percent in Gabon) (*Individual Taxes* 1993). The results of trying to impose Swedish tax rates on poor countries (or on Sweden, for that matter) can only be described as tragic.

Whenever combined marginal income, payroll, and sales tax rates have been reduced to internationally competitive levels, this has resulted in (1) substantially increased net capital inflows and therefore a stronger currency and lower interest rates; (2) reduced "brain drain" and increased personal investment in education; and (3) reduced tax evasion, more rapid economic growth, and therefore increased real tax collections from all sources.

If one looks at such crisis-prone wards of the IMF as Russia, Yugoslavia, and Haiti, and compares their tax rates with those of bold tax reformers such as Singapore, Indonesia, Mexico, Argentina, or Mauritius, it is hard to see why any country would prefer being in the former group—even as a condition for getting deeper in debt to the IMF.

In Search of an IMF "Success Story"

A survey of IMF programs by Jeffrey Sachs demonstrated that "there are almost no success stories of countries that have pursued IMF austerity measures and World Bank structural adjustments to reestablish creditworthiness and restore economic growth" (Sachs 1986, 402–03; see also Farnsworth 1985; Wolman 1983; IMF's Austerity Prescriptions 1983). Indeed, the list of countries "helped" by recent IMF programs reads like a casualty list. The IMF formula was applied to Peru and Jamaica in 1978, and real per capita GDP subsequently fell by 13 to 14 percent in those countries. The next IMF adjustment programs were in Nicaragua and Bolivia after 1980, and real output in those countries fell by 13 percent and 28 percent respectively, accompanied by the two worst hyperinflations since the 1920s. The IMF record was not much better in the Philippines, which immediately quintupled inflation and sank into depression and riots in 1985–86, just after the U.S. State Department actively supported an "IMF arrangement involving...a floating peso and broad new taxes."[14]

We have previously cited the decidedly unpleasant results of IMF-endorsed programs of the early 1980s in the Philippines, Mexico, and elsewhere. The experience was essentially the same following other IMF programs—inflation rose, real GDP slowed, or both. Economic growth had averaged better than 4 percent a year for a decade before Cote d'Ivorie embraced an IMF program in 1986, but then real GDP fell every year from 1987 through 1992. Economic growth averaged 7.4 percent a year in Niger from 1975 to 1984, but Niger adopted an IMF program in 1985 and growth averaged only 1.3 percent from 1985 through 1992. Guyana received an IMF loan in 1990, the currency was massively devalued, as usual, and interest rates on Treasury bills, at 30 percent, was nearly triple what it had been in 1988 (a 30 percent short-term interest rate makes this country's seemingly low inflation statistics quite implausible, which implies that Guyana's real GDP figures are even weaker than they appear). There was an IMF deal in Guatemala in late 1988, and inflation rose from 11 percent in that year to 41 percent by 1990.

Those who feel obliged to defend the IMF's track record assert that the economies entrusted to IMF medical attention would have fared even worse without their adjustment programs. That sort of speculation about what might have happened is not terribly persuasive. Others, such as the de Tocqueville Institute, have argued that the bad policy advice was just so much ancient history, and that the IMF has become much more sensible since 1986 after making so many mistakes in the early 1980s. But we have some examples of IMF adjustment programs that began in 1988–90, such as Yugoslavia and Haiti, and they look no different from past programs nor any less disastrous.

In 1988, in what used to be Yugoslavia, the IMF once again bankrolled its favorite combination of "real devaluation" and "incomes policy" (wage controls). In the following year the World Bank reported,

"The dinar was devalued in real terms [i.e., by more than the previous inflation rate] by 19.3 percent [and] strict limits were imposed on the growth of nominal wages, public spending and monetary aggregates up to the end of 1988. The program was supported by the IMF.... On the external front, results have been favorable, with the current account of the balance of payments...recording an overall surplus of around $2 billion in 1988, well above anticipated levels. In contrast development in the domestic economy has been unsatisfactory. Output declined by about two percent, and inflation accelerated to 251 percent at the end of the year. The unemployment rate has been rising, and the real income of the population declined by at least two percent. (World Bank 1989, 504)

This could only be counted a success by IMF standards—that is, the current-account surplus became "favorable" for a while, as the people of Yugoslavia became too impoverished to import. There were subsequent attempts to engineer a "real devaluation," by devaluing at an ever-increasing rate, but the internal results were also "unsatisfactory." Inflation quickly jumped to 1,258 percent in 1989 and was well over 6,000 percent by 1992. Real GDP fell by 7.5 percent in 1990, 17 percent in 1991, and 34 percent in 1992. The inflationary collapse of Yugoslavia, due to policies endorsed and financially underwritten by the IMF, was an ominous precursor to IMF conditional lending in the former Soviet Union.

And there have been even more recent IMF programs, also followed by social chaos and political revolution. In Haiti, notes the World Bank, "the government adopted an economic program for fiscal 1990, supported by an IMF standby.... The government adopted a number of measures to increase fiscal revenues.... While government spending remained within acceptable levels [due to 'cutbacks in capital outlays'], revenue collections...deteriorated sharply.... In its last months in office the Aristide government was moving deliberately to implement further reforms and stabilization programs with the assistance from the IMF." The Haitian economy, which had grown by 2.4 percent a year from 1975 to 1984, shrank by 3 percent in 1990, 4 percent in 1991, and about 11 percent in 1992. While it would be unfair to blame

Haiti's collapse on the IMF, but it has not been unusual to see total economic and political chaos in the wake of IMF programs.

Taxing Russia to Death

That the IMF has been deeply involved with Russia, and other remnants of the former Soviet Union, is well known. What advice they have given is anyone's guess. But there were some early clues from the IMF program in Yugoslavia, as well as IMF publications.

In early 1991 the IMF, World Bank, OECD, and the European Bank for Reconstruction and Development issued a three-volume tome with the ill-fated title, *A Study of the Soviet Economy*. A key chapter describes the tax policies being implemented by the USSR in its final death throes:

- A tax on enterprises of 45 to 90 percent.
- A tax on personal income of up to 60 percent at a modest level of income.
- A 1991 Social Security tax of 26 percent (up from 9 percent in 1989).
- An additional payroll tax of up to 200 percent on "excess" wages.
- A turnover (sales) tax that averaged 28 percent.
- A tax of up to 50 percent on energy and raw material exports.
- A tariff of up to 630 percent on imports.

In short, the former Soviet Union, in its final hours, was attempting to impose marginal tax rates on the rewards for productive labor of up to 286 percent, on business success of 90 percent, on the most desirable exports and imports of 50 to 630 percent. This appeared to be the result of an infection of Western ideas (Soviet "reformers" spoke with affection about Sweden), since there were little or no Social Security taxes in the heyday of communism, and the top income tax was 13 percent. Instead, the "communist" tax system mainly consisted (and to some extent still does) of exploiting workers with wage controls and farmers with price controls, then using the state's monopoly power to sell many goods to consumers with a fat profit margin, despite notoriously high costs.

What did the four leading international institutions have to say about the oppressive and suicidal tax regime on the eve of the Soviet empire's implosion? They thought the Soviet tax system looked just fine, by and large. There was some quibbling about needing to adjust the profits tax for inflation. And the IMF et al., opined that "Social Security reform [meaning more benefits] is in many ways at the center of the economic and social policy agenda." There was not the slightest suggestion that any tax rate or tariff might be too high, least of all the newly tripled Social Security tax. On the contrary, the main complaint was that the tax on consumption was *too low!* The Western experts proposed that "a [new] general sales tax should be accompanied by the introduction of excise duties—at relatively high rates—on selected 'nonmerit' or luxury goods" (IMF et al., 254).

Since then, the tax system in Russia itself has improved in some respects, but worsened in others. The top income tax was reduced to 40 percent, then 30 percent by 1993; but the system was not indexed for inflation, meaning virtually all productive private workers were theoretically subject to a 30 percent tax on most of the earnings. Making matters much worse, the Social Security tax in 1993 was up to 39 percent! (*Individual Taxes* 1993 and *Corporate Taxes* 1993). That raised the total income and payroll tax to a prohibitive level on formal employment, driving employment into small commercial enterprises that can more easily evade these and other taxes. The turnover tax was originally replaced with a more efficient value-added tax, but at a brutally high rate of 28 percent. The VAT was mercifully lowered to 20 percent in 1993, and to 10 percent on food, though there were many additional excise taxes. Exporters of natural resources continued to face a 40 percent tax on their hard currency earnings. And all exporters were required to surrender their hard currency earnings to the state, which acted as form of taxation, too: it meant export industries could not use such earnings to expand by importing needed materials and machines. The Russian tax on business income was first cut to 45 percent, then to 32 percent, but there were also significant local property taxes that applied to inventories and real estate. However, the greater problem was not taxation of business per se, but punitive, demoralizing taxation of individual effort, employment, and entrepreneurship, through income, Social Security, and sales taxes.

To become part of the integrated world economy, tax rates on human capital, as well as physical capital, must become more competitive with those of successful economies. Instead, Russia and its neighbors continued to tax economic success out of existence, at least in the formal economy, in order to shore up inefficient state enterprises, the military-industrial complex, and an unaffordable welfare state. The predictable result was that entrepreneurial spirits were confined to tiny commercial ventures—small-scale marketing of foreign products rather than medium-scale production at home—because such activities could more easily evade taxes.

No economy in world history has ever prospered, or even survived for long, with a tax system as onerous as the one now crippling Russia. Will the IMF ever even hint that the rapacious Russian tax authorities ought to consider reducing, for example, the 39 percent payroll tax before it will be remotely feasible for private businessmen to employ people "on the books"? The record does not suggest much room for optimism.

Turkey: An IMF Success?

Is it too much to ask for a single example of an IMF program that worked? Jeffrey Sachs could find only one "notable success"—Turkey. Yet Turkey followed a different drummer: the late President Turgut Ozal. In 1985–86 Turkey's income tax rates were sharply reduced from 40–75 percent to 25–50 percent. Tariffs were also reduced in 1984, from an average of 49 percent to 20 percent (Levinsohn 1991). Subsequently, economic growth averaged nearly 6 percent a year. Indeed, a 1987 retrospective IMF report on Turkey noted: "most taxpayers were placed into income brackets subject to very high marginal rates. This contributed to a steady erosion of work and savings incentives" (Kopits 1987, 15).

There is no evidence that the IMF supported, much less initiated, President Ozal's reduction of marginal tax rates and tariffs in the mid-1980s.[15] But there is ample evidence of what happened earlier, when the IMF really dictated Turkish policy.

In 1958, 1970, and 1978-79, Turkey adopted "IMF-supported programs involving stabilization with devaluation. Domestic political difficulties and unrest were heightened at each instance, paving the way for military interventions in 1960, 1971 and 1980.... The IMF was called on to administer a series of stabilization programs...one in early 1978 and the other in 1979. But both programs...proved unsuccessful" (Celasun and Radrik 1989, 194, 197–98). After the 1979 IMF plan, for example, Turkey's real growth turned negative in 1979–80, under the paradoxical "stabilization with devaluation," and inflation climbed to 110 percent. The result was social chaos and another military coup.

Has the IMF Really Changed?

Surprisingly, some of the strongest objections to the IMF's traditional approach have been voiced by some of the top economists within the IMF itself. Consider, for example, the following comments by Vito Tanzi, Director of the Fund's Fiscal Affairs Department:

> The design of adjustment programs should integrate stabilization with growth, or demand-management policies with structural, supply-side policies...such as changes in various taxes and tax rates.... The more far reaching the structural reform agreed to by the country, the greater will be that supply response (in terms of output, exports, capital repatriation, and the like). Such a supply response may imply that a less stringent demand-management policy is necessary.
>
> Excessive reliance on macroeconomic ceilings may divert attention away from the *quality*, as well as the *durability*, of the specific measures used.... Work effort, exports, productive investment, savings, capital flight, foreign investment, and so on can be affected by the choice of specific fiscal instruments.... Sometimes countries have raised payroll taxes or taxes on interest income with undesirable repercussions on employment, saving, and capital flight. (Tanzi 1989, 15–23. emphasis in original)

Tanzi implies that the IMF's macroeconomic bias against structural, supply-side reforms has been reduced in recent years, although he offers no specific examples (Tanzi once cited Peru as an IMF victory in a *Wall Street Journal* article, but that was surely an unfortunate choice). In fact, he notes that "according to the present guidelines on conditionality, under which the Fund staff operates, the change advocated in this paper *might not be possible*" (ibid., emphasis added).

A 1991 report by the U.S. National Advisory Council on International Monetary and Financial Policies "affirms the IMF's role 'at the forefront' of promoting 'market oriented reforms' throughout the world, including...safety nets to help offset the hardships to the most vulnerable groups (Romania), increased social services (Ghana), crop price incentives (Mozambique), increased public investment (Niger) and worker retraining programs (Senegal)" (*IMF Conditionality* 1992, 18). Yet, such programs all involve *subsidizing increased government spending*, not increased private production. This is not helpful. A study of twenty-seven countries by Charles Wolf of the Rand Corporation found that "a 10 percent increase in the ratio of government spending to GDP results in...an expected decrease of four percent in the average annual rate of [GDP] growth" among low-income countries (Wolf 1988, 146).

When asked to consider microeconomic, structural reforms, the IMF has responded by simply redefining supply-side economics to mean currency devaluation: "The success of an adjustment program will depend on eliciting an adequate response from the supply side of the economy. Macroeconomic variables such as the interest rate and the exchange rate are of singular importance in this respect" ("Conditionality" 1983, 3).

When asked to consider the contradiction between the practice of rich countries, all of which reduced marginal tax rates in the 1980s, and the advice offered to poorer countries by the IMF, the IMF has responded that high tax rates cannot do much damage in poor countries because they collect so little money:

> Revenues from personal income taxes in industrial countries are generally much higher than in developing countries.... Presumably this explains why the great bulk of literature on the incentive effects of tax regimes and of changes in marginal tax rates on labor, savings and investment decisions pertain to the developed world.... Regressions show that the ratio of income taxes to total revenue (as well as to GDP) and the growth rate of output are negatively related and that the regressions coefficients are significant, but this result does not hold in all specifications. (Gandhi 1987)

Yet, the damage of suffocating taxation cannot be measured by the revenues it yields, any more than a prohibitive tariff (a tariff that stops trade) could be judged as harmless because it yields nothing. Revenues from income taxes in developing countries with the highest marginal tax rates are typically trivial, often less than 1 percent of GDP. But that certainly does not mean that such economies are not damaged by the methods by which such onerous taxes are evaded—such as working in inefficiently small and secretive "informal" enterprises, hiding capital in other countries or in gold hoards, and emigration of skilled people.

Some economists at the World Bank—such as Keith Marsden, Deepak Lal, and Chad Leechor—have been more candidly critical of the IMF's almost total lack of attention to structural, supply-side reforms. Leechor made the following particularly courageous comments:

> The importance of tax policy is well recognized in the more advanced market economies. In the context of developing countries, however, tax policy has received relatively little attention.... Policy advice has often consisted of recommendations to increase taxes...without adequately evaluating the effect on the supply side of the economy.... Even if revenue increases temporarily, the change may take place at the expense of potential growth, in which case future revenue will be diminished. (Leechor 1986, 2, 6; Marsden 1983; Lal 1983)

There has also been some welcome, though muted reconsideration of the merits of perpetual currency debasement. An internal October 1990 paper prepared by IMF staff for the Fund's Executive Board— the policy-making body composed of officials from member nations' finance ministries—suggests that recently there has been a significant (though quiet) debate within the board over the merits of the IMF's devaluation theory. The paper begins:

[I]n recent Board discussions, Executive Directors have questioned the perceived readiness of the staff to recommend a flexible exchange rate policy as a way of correcting external imbalances because of the possible adverse effects of such a policy on inflation and overall macroeconomic stability.... The concerns raised by the Executive Directors carry the implication that Fund advice has tended to favor excessive flexibility in exchange rate management, and that, in certain cases, this flexibility may have had a deleterious effect on financial discipline.... Increased stability of the exchange rate is believed, by some Directors, to enhance financial discipline, and thus improve the conditions for sustained improvement in the external accounts, a lower rate of inflation, and a better growth performance. (IMF Research Department 1990, 1)

The IMF economists' response to their directors' concerns is full of typically bureaucratic defenses such as "the need to strike an appropriate balance." Nonetheless, the study acknowledges that "the average rate of inflation has been lower in countries with pegged exchange rates." Furthermore, the study properly censures the IMF's advocacy of devaluing by (at least) the amount of inflation: "Real exchange rate rules designed to protect external competitiveness by rigidly linking exchange rate adjustment to domestic inflation could be quite destabilizing and even lead to hyperinflation." Moreover, the report also recommends that "[i]n cases in which the authorities are genuinely determined to establish financial discipline and price stability, but lack credibility...a commitment to precommit to fix the nominal exchange rate for an extended period would help provide a strong anchor for price stability." Lest that suggest an impending major shift in IMF exchange-rate conditionality, however, an adjoining recommendation lets many IMF economists (and officials of developing nations) off the hook: "In countries in which the authorities are not in a position to refrain completely from resorting to inflationary finance...flexibility in the exchange rate will be needed to prevent a deterioration in external competitiveness."[16]

It is only mildly encouraging to see IMF publications at least paying lip service to common sense. A recent *IMF Outlook* briefly mentions that recent inflation in the former Soviet Union is similar to other cases, "*with inflation being fueled by devaluations intended to improve competitiveness*.... Typically, ending hyperinflation has involved... establishing currency convertibility, *often at a fixed exchange rate* (IMF 1993, 93–95. emphasis added). But there is no corresponding suggestion that countries threatened with hyperinflation should fix their exchange rates, and certainly no such conditionality has been applied to IMF loans to places like Russia.

IMF publications have begun to at least hint that their past advice about devaluing currencies has been wildly inflationary, and sometimes even that it is possible to push tax rates too high. But it is what the IMF does that matters, not what it writes. There is no sign that such overdue rethinking of the traditional IMF program has yet filtered down to the IMF negotiating teams, which continue to muscle countries in the direction of new and higher taxes, as well as more "devaluations intended to improve competitiveness." In mid-1992, after the Russian ruble had staged a brief recovery, "a visiting IMF team" was "attempting to persuade the authorities to stick to their original idea of floating the ruble" (Boulton 1992). This attempt was evidently quite successful. The ruble did indeed resume its downward "float" toward hyperinflationary collapse.

A Myopic Focus on Macroeconomic Targets Still Dominates

Even though a few IMF and World Bank economists are critical of the devaluation theory, or sympathetic with the importance of tax incentives, the teams who actually negotiate deals with third world countries are nonetheless likely to revert to an excessive reliance on macroeconomic ceilings—such as attempted limits on budget and current-account deficits, or on some increasingly arbitrary measures of money or credit. The whole ritualistic process of setting macroeconomic targets leads to a bias against structural, microeconomic reforms. "Financial variables," notes Graham Bird, "say practically nothing about what is happening on the supply side, or real sector of the economy. Output, productivity, investment and trade performance are neglected [by the IMF]" (Bird 1982, 435).

Since actual outcomes depend on actual economic performance, the IMF's narrow emphasis on macroeconomic financial targets will often fail, even on its own terms. An economy thrown into recession will usually meet the IMF target for a lower trade deficit, because impoverished economies cannot afford to import. For the same reason, though, an economy suffering from serious inflation and depression will not be able to meet the IMF target of a smaller budget deficit. The impossibility of reducing the budget deficit after repeated devaluations allows the IMF to proclaim "noncompliance" as the excuse for repeated failures of its favorite policy mix of devaluation and tax increases. A reasonable definition of insanity is continuing to do the same thing, over and over, while expecting quite different results.

Because of the IMF's obsession with short-term budget deficits, it might well favor trade liberalization—in the abstract—and yet condone or even require high tariffs. In 1989, for example, *The Economist* observed that "one country began to negotiate a [World] Bank policy loan just after finalizing an IMF one. The Bank called for a reduction in import duties that was at odds with the IMF's budgetary targets" ("Twins That Won't Tango" 1989, 17–18). That sort of excessive emphasis on short-term revenues may prevent reductions of tariffs that would otherwise reduce the cost of production and cost of living, while moving resources out of inefficient, protected industries. Even reductions in nontariff import barriers may be resisted because of the Fund's self-imposed mission of pushing developing countries prematurely into trade surpluses in order to extract more export revenue for foreign debt service (import restrictions actually hurt exports and therefore do not really reduce trade deficits, but "trade officials" typically believe otherwise).

Similarly, the IMF's timidity about short-term revenue losses apparently prevents it from recommending reductions in punitive marginal tax rates, even when those tax rates obviously yield nothing but growth-inhibiting distortions and disincentives, tax evasion, and capital flight. Despite IMF assurances to the contrary, the news continues to show the Fund's yearning for ever-increasing tax rates. *Business in Latin America* thus reported on 24 June 1991 that in Argentina, "The IMF seeks to boost the country's fiscal surplus by raising the value-added tax, reintroducing export taxes and increasing fuel taxes." The same journal had also reported on 10 June 1991 that in Honduras "tax hikes necessitated by the [IMF] program are generating serious labor and social unrest." And on 15 July 1991 *Business in Latin America* likewise reported that taxes in Peru "will be hiked sharply in an effort to narrow the deficit to the IMF-mandated target of two percent of GDP."

The words coming out of the IMF have improved in the 1990s, but there is no sign that the words have yet been translated into action.

Conclusion

Countries plagued by hyperinflation and economic contraction need not continue in that sad condition. We have at least seven decades of global experience to draw upon, and it shows quite clearly that economic crises are curable and that the cure always involves quite similar policies. Economists should know by now what works and what fails. The policies that Hong Kong has followed for decades (free trade, low taxes, and a fixed exchange rate) obviously work; the policies that

Russia has followed (protectionism, punitive taxes, and a sinking exchange rate) obviously do not. The conditions attached to IMF loans all over the world have long resembled the policies being pursued in Russia, not those of Hong Kong. Yet there were still no signs in 1988–93, in Russia or elsewhere, that the discredited terms of IMF "conditionality" had been substantially changed. The IMF still sanctions and underwrites the policies of perpetual failure.

The most successful "economic miracles" of the 1920s, 1950s, and 1980s invariably shunned wage and price controls, guaranteed to convert the currency to a more credible currency or commodity, and reduced marginal tax rates and tariffs. By emulating such successful tax, trade, and exchange-rate policies, third world and former communist countries could likewise put an end to runaway inflation, reduce interest rates and related budget deficits, and unleash incentives for productive effort, entrepreneurship, and investment.[17] Unfortunately, there appears to be little hope of getting this sort of policy advice from the "economic development" establishment, including the IMF. The IMF's recipe has been one of destructive devaluation and suffocating taxation, often accompanied by wage controls and high tariffs. This formula has yet to play a constructive role in helping any country out of its economic difficulties.

Notes

1. Abba Lerner's symmetry theorem shows that restrictions on imports are equivalent to restrictions on exports. (Laffer and Miles 1982, 101).
2. For a critical history of the analytical errors behind the Phillips Curve, see Burstein 1993.
3. See, for example, Lockwood 1965, 470: "Still another heritage left by the war and the Occupation was high taxes.... Tax cuts were made repeatedly after [occupation ended in] 1951."
4. Simpson 1969, 24. With the 1926 tax relief in Germany and France, the German stock market doubled from January to November 1926, and the French market rose by 28 percent, even as the U.S. and British stock markets stagnated (Kindleberger 1973, 122).
5. "The Allied Control Council imposed extremely heavy taxes on West Germany [in order to promote] further weakening of the German economy" (Webber and Wildavsky 1986, 536).
6. Morales 1988, 321. Curiously, some observers (including the IMF) have wrongly labeled Bolivia's quasi-fixed exchange rate as "floating." See, for example, the otherwise perceptive description of the Bolivian tax reform in Raiford 1987.
7. That is, the central bank tightens the supply of money (for example, by selling Treasury bills to "mop up" surplus cash) whenever it is running short of foreign-exchange reserves. The Bolivian government thus committed itself to restrain what they call "inorganic emission"—that is, new currency or bank reserves not backed by new foreign reserves.

8. All GDP growth figures from the late 1980s to early 1990s, for this country and others, are from International Monetary Fund (IMF), *World Economic Outlook* 1993, Table A-6.

9. Kaletsky 1985. The black homelands of Ciskei kept maximum tax rates at 15–20 percent, due to the influence of the late C. Northkote Parkinson (of "Parkinson's Law" fame), and enjoyed a reportedly rapid boom (Robinson 1986).

10. Gowa 1983, 150n. Others who advised President Nixon in 1971 to devalue the dollar for alleged trade advantages included two leaders of the "Concord Coalition," Peter G. Peterson and Paul Volcker.

11. "The Fund must treat its members as adults. Government must have the right to make their own mistakes as they alone are responsible to their citizens" (Kenen 1986, 49).

12. Inter-American Development Bank 1990, 284; Table C-1. We are using the "top" tax rates as a rough proxy for the tax schedule. This is not always accurate, since some countries follow the Japanese practice of appearing to have high tax rates at high incomes, but offering numerous "loopholes" that reduce taxable income. The income thresholds at which high tax rates apply are obviously important, as are sales and Social Security taxes. For countries that have reduced the top tax rate to 10–35 percent, though, it is clear enough that marginal tax rates at lower incomes are modest, too.

13. Burgess and Stern 1993, Table 7. The authors claim the deep marginal rate reductions in Colombia were "roughly revenue neutral," but our data suggest otherwise—revenues rose sharply, both in real terms and as a percent of GDP, as tax rates fell.

14. Wolfowitz 1985. Mr. Wolfowitz was U.S. Assistant Secretary of State for East Asia. It was unusual for a U.S. official to be so candid about actively promoting devaluation or meddling with other domestic policies in a foreign country.

15. Celasun and Rodrik 1989, 203. The authors also note that "it is rather surprising that exchange rate policy has played such a moderate role [in explaining export growth] in view of the vast depreciations achieved since 1980" (ibid, 207).

16. IMF Research Department 1990, 33, 19, 35, and 35, respectively. Several other IMF and World Bank economists who have recently criticized the heavy reliance on devaluation are cited in Miles 1991.

17. Empirical research in the "new growth" or "exogenous growth" theories of scholars such as Paul Romer and Robert Barro has been, as one recent survey puts it, "based on the idea that long-run growth is determined by economic incentives" (Gould and Ruffin 1993). Taxation is only one part of incentives, but it is the one over which government policies have the most control (see Reynolds 1993a, 329–32).

References

Aghelvi, Bijan, and Jorge Marquez-Ruarte. 1987. "A Case of Successful Adjustment in a Developing Country: Korea's Experience During 1980–84." In *Economic Adjustment: Policies and Problems*, edited by Sir Frank Holmes. Washington, DC: International Monetary Fund.

Anderson, Benjamin M. 1979. *Economics and the Public Welfare*. Indianapolis, IN: Liberty Press.

Bangsberg, P. T. 1985a. "IMF Team Inspects Philippine Compliance." *Journal of Commerce* (12 August).

———. 1985b. "Philippines, IMF Near Credit Deal." *Journal of Commerce* (18 September).

Bartlett, Bruce. 1989. "The State and Market in Sub-Saharan Africa." *The World Economy* (September).

Bird, Graham. 1982. "A Role for the International Monetary Fund in Economic Development." *Banca Nazionale del Lavoro Review* (December).

Blackhurst, Richard. 1983. "The Relation Between the Current Account and the Exchange Rate: A Survey of the Recent Literature." In *Exchange Rates in Multicountry Econometric Models,* edited by P. de Grauwe and T. Peters. London: Macmillan.

Bollag, Burton. 1989. "U.N. Critical of IMF Austerity Plan." *The New York Times* (6 September).

Boulton, Leila. 1992. "Roubles Are Free, But Some Freer Than Others." *Financial Times* (1 July).

Boyer, Edward. 1983. "Why Lenders Should Still Be Scared." *Fortune* (12 December).

Bradley, Pamela J. 1989. "Conference Participants Discuss Ability of Exchange Rates to Affect Trade Balances." *IMF Survey* (12 July).

Brookes, Warren T. 1986. "IMF Helped Bring Marcos Down." *The Boston Herald* (22 March).

Buffie, Edward F., and Allen S. Krause. 1989. "Mexico 1958–86: From Stabilizing Development to the Debt Crisis." In *Developing Country Debt and the World Economy,* edited by Jeffrey D. Sachs. Chicago: NBER/University of Chicago Press.

Burgess, Robin, and Nicholas Stern. 1993. "Taxation and Development." *Journal of Economic Literature* (June).

Burstein, M. L. 1993. "Keynes and Wicksell on Bank Rate." Chapter 1 in *Three Economic Studies.* Ontario: York University.

Business in Latin America. 1991. [incomplete reference] (10 June).

Business in Latin America. 1991. [incomplete reference] (24 June).

Business in Latin America. 1991. [incomplete reference] (15 July).

Celasun, Merih, and Dani Rodrik. 1989. "Turkish Experience with Debt." In *Developing Country Debt and the World Economy,* edited by Jeffrey D. Sachs. Chicago: NBER/University of Chicago Press.

"Chile's Economy." 1985. *The Economist* (19 August).

Cohen, Jerome B. 1958. *Japan's Postwar Economy.* Bloomington: Indiana University Press.

Coone, Tim. 1988. "Argentina's Balance of Trade Slides to Low Point for Decade." *Financial Times* (6 January).

"Conditionality." 1983. *IMF Survey* (September).

Corporate Taxes: 1993. 1993. New York: Price Waterhouse.

Crawford, Leslie. 1991. "Chile Makes Successful Return to World Finance." *Financial Times* (15 January).

de Soto, Irene Philippe. 1993. "Is There Life After 936 in Puerto Rico?" *The Wall Street Journal* (2 April).

Easterly, William, and Sergio Rebelo. 1992. "Marginal Income Tax Rates and Economic Growth in Developing Countries." Working Paper WPS 1050. Washington, DC: World Bank.

———. 1993. "Fiscal Policy and Economic Growth: An Empirical Investigation." Paper presented at the World Bank Conference, 8–9 February, Washington, DC.

Edwards, Sebastian. 1989. "The International Monetary Fund and the Developing Countries: A Critical Evaluation." *Carnegie-Rochester Conference Series on Public Policy.* New York: Elsevier North-Holland.

Engen, Eric M., and Jonathon Skinner. 1992. "Fiscal Policy and Economic Growth." Working Paper 4223. (December). Cambridge, MA: National Bureau of Economic Research.

Farnsworth, Clyde. 1985. "The IMF's Help Can Sometimes Hurt." *The New York Times* (14 April).

Feldstein, Martin. 1989. "A Wrong Turn in LDC Debt Management." *The Wall Street Journal* (15 March).

Fischer, Stanley. 1985. "Inflation and Indexation: Israel." In *Inflation and Indexation,* edited by John Williamson. Washington, DC: Institute for International Economics.

————. 1987. "The Israeli Stabilization Program." *The American Economic Review.* (May).

Frankel, Jeffrey A., Kenneth A. Froot, and Alejandra Mizala Salces. 1987. "Credibilty, the Optimal Speed of Trade Liberalization, Real Interest Rates, and the Latin American Debt." Working Paper 94720 (19 August). Berkeley: University of California.

Gandhi, Ved, ed. 1987. *Supply Side Economics: Its Relevance to Developing Countries.* Washington, DC: International Monetary Fund.

Gould, David M., and Roy J. Ruffin. 1993. "What Determines Economic Growth?" *Economic Review.* (2nd Quarter). Dallas: Federal Reserve Bank.

Gowa, Joanne. 1983. *Closing the Gold Window.* Ithaca, NY: Cornell University Press.

Graham, Robert. 1988. "Few Limits Have Been Set by the Country Over Privatization. Special Survey on Chile." *Financial Times* (28 September).

Gurgen, Emine. 1986. "Philippine Program of Economic Reform Entails Policy Shifts to Revive Growth." *IMF Survey* (17 November).

Homer, Sidney. 1977. *A History of Interest Rates.* New Brunswick, NJ: Rutgers University Press.

Hutchinson, Greg. 1991. "Philippines Austerity Awaits IMF Seal of Approval." *Financial Times* (20 February).

IMF Research Department. 1990. "Analytical Issues Relating to Fund Advice on Exchange Rate Policy." Washington, DC: International Monetary Fund. (16 October).

IMF, World Bank, OECD, European Bank for Reconstruction and Development (EBRD). 1991. *A Study of the Soviet Economy* 1 (February). 3 vols.

"IMF's Austerity Prescriptions Could Be Hazardous." 1983. *Business Week* (21 February).

IMF Conditionality. 1992. Washington, DC: Alexis de Tocqueville Institute.

Individual Taxes: 1993. 1993. New York: Price Waterhouse.

Inter-American Development Bank. 1990. *Economic and Social Progress in Latin America: 1990 Report.* Baltimore: Johns Hopkins University Press.

International Financial Statistics. 1993. Washington, DC: International Monetary Fund. (November).

International Monetary Fund (IMF). 1993. *World Economic Outlook.* (October).

"Israel Curbs Inflation, Improves Budget Balance." 1987. *IMF Survey* (14 September).

Kaletsky, Anatole. 1985. "Wanted: A Revolution in Economic Thought." *Financial Times* (15 April).

Katseli, Louka T. 1983. "Devaluation: A Critical Appraisal of the IMF's Policy Prescriptions." *American Economic Review* (May).

Kemmerer, Edwin W. 1937. *Money.* New York: Macmillan.

Kenen, Peter. 1986. *Financing, Adjustment and the International Monetary Fund.* Washington, DC: Brookings Institution.

Kindleberger, Charles P. 1973. *The World in Depression.* Berkeley: University of California Press.

————. 1984. *A Financial History of Western Europe.* London: George Allen and Unwin.

Koester, Reinhard B., and Roger C. Kormendi. 1989. "Taxation, Aggregate Activity and Economic Growth: Cross-Country Evidence on Some Supply-Side Hypotheses." *Economic Inquiry* (July).

Kopits, George. 1987. "Structural Reform, Stabilization and Growth in Turkey." *IMF Occasional Paper* 52 (May).

Kreis, Eliahu. 1989. "The Inflationary Process in Israel." In *Fiscal Policy, Stabilization, and Growth in Developing Countries,* edited by Mario I. Blejer and Ke-young Chu. Washington, DC: International Monetary Fund.

Laffer, Arthur B., and Marc A. Miles. 1982. *International Economics.* Glenview, IL.: Scott Foresman.

Lal, Deepak. 1983. *The Poverty of Development Economics.* London: Institute of Economic Affairs.

Leechor, Chad. 1986. "Tax Policy and Tax Reform in Semi-Industrial Countries." Industry and Finance Series 13 (January). Washington, DC: World Bank.

Levinsohn, James. 1991. "Testing the Imports-as-Market-Discipline Hypothesis." Working Paper 3657. Washington, DC: National Bureau of Economic Research.

Lockwood, William W. 1965. *The State and Economic Enterprise in Japan.* Princeton, NJ: Princeton University Press.

Makin, John. 1984. *The Global Debt Crisis.* New York: Basic Books.

Marsden, Keith. 1983. "Links Between Taxes and Economic Growth: Some Empirical Evidence." Working Paper 605. Washington, DC: World Bank.

Miles, Marc A. 1991. "The IMF's Destructive Focus on Devaluation." Paper presented at Cato Institute Conference on Multilateral Aid (8 May).

Mitchell, B. R. 1978. *European Historical Statistics: 1750–1970.* New York: Columbia University Press.

Montiel, Peter J. 1989. "Empirical Analysis of High-Inflation Episodes in Argentina, Brazil, and Israel." *IMF Staff Papers* (September). Washington, DC: International Monetary Fund.

Moore, Jacqueline. 1991. "Latin Americans Produce the Year's Best and Worst." *Financial Times* (11 January).

Morales, Juan-Antonio. 1988. "Inflation Stabilization in Bolivia." In *Inflation Stabilization,* edited by Michael Bruno et al. Cambridge, MA: MIT Press.

Mundell, Robert A. 1971. "The Dollar and the Policy Mix." Essays in International Finance 85 (May). Princeton, NJ: Princeton University Press.

Niehans, Jurg. 1984. *International Monetary Economics.* Baltimore: Johns Hopkins University.

Ortiz, Guillermo. 1988. "Public Finance, Trade, and Economic Growth: The Mexican Case." Istanbul: International Institute of Public Finance. (22–25 August).

Pasvolsky, Leo. 1928. *Economic Nationalism of the Danubian States.* New York: Macmillan.

Rabushka, Alvin, and Steven Hanke. 1988. *Toward Growth: A Blueprint for Economic Rebirth in Israel.* Jerusalem: Jerusalem Institute for Advanced Political and Economic Studies.

Raiford, William N. 1987. "Bolivia's Monetary Reform Leads to Supply-Side Revolution." *The Wall Street Journal* (24 July).

Reynolds, Alan. 1987. "Japan, Korea Had Trade Deficits, Too." *The Asian Wall Street Journal Weekly* (9 March).

———. 1989. "Commentary." In *U.S. Trade Deficit: Causes, Consequences, and Cures,* edited by Albert E. Burger. Federal Reserve Bank of St. Louis. Norwell, MA: Kluwer Academic Publishers.

———. 1993a. "Marginal Tax Rates." In *The Fortune Encyclopedia of Economics,* edited by David R. Henderson. New York: Warner Books.

———. 1993b. "Reconsidering Economic Masochism in Germany." In *Germany in a New Era,* edited by Gary L. Geipel. Indianapolis, IN: Hudson Institute.

———. 1993c. *Turkey Beyond 2000.* Indianapolis, IN: Hudson Institute.

Robinson, Anthony. 1986. "The Supply-Siders of Ciskei." *Financial Times* (19 November).

Romer, Paul D. 1992. "Two Strategies for Economic Development: Using Ideas and Producing Economic." *Proceedings of the World Bank Annual Conference on Development Economic: 1992.* Washington, DC: World Bank.

Rose, A., and J. Yellen. 1989. "Is There a J-Curve?" *Journal of Monetary Economics.*

Rosett, Claudia. 1982. "Chile's Economic Revolution." *Reason* (April).

Sachs, Jeffrey D. 1986. "Managing the LDC Debt Crisis." *Brookings Papers on Economic Activity.* 2. Washington, DC: Brookings Institution.

Sargent, Thomas J. 1984. "The Ends of Four Big Inflations." In *Inflation: Causes and Effects,* edited by Robert E. Hall. Chicago: University of Chicago Press.

Scully, Gerald W. 1991. *Tax Rates, Tax Revenues, and Economic Growth.* Dallas: National Center for Policy Analysis. (March).

Sicat, Gerardo, and Arvind Virmani. 1988. "Personal Income Taxes in Developing Countries." *The World Bank Economic Review* (January).

Simpson, Amos E. 1969. *Hjalmar Schacht in Perspective.* The Hague: Mouton.

"Special Survey on Colombia." 1989. *Financial Times* (28 July).

Spraos, John. 1986. *IMF Conditionality: Ineffectual, Inefficient, Mistargeted.* Essays in International Finance 166. Princeton, NJ: Princeton University Press.

"Survey on Mauritius." 1989. *Financial Times* (20 March).

Tanzi, Vito. 1989. "Fiscal Policy, Growth, and the Design of Stabilization Programs." In *Fiscal Policy, Stabilization, and Growth in Developing Countries,* edited by Mario I. Blejer and Ke-young Chu. Washington, DC: International Monetary Fund.

Taylor, Lance. 1987. "IMF Conditionality: Incomplete Theory, Policy Malpractice." In *The Political Morality of the International Monetary Fund,* edited by Robert J. Myers. New Brunswick, NJ: Transaction Books.

Trostel, Philip A. 1993. "The Effect of Taxation on Human Capital." *Journal of Political Economy* (April).

"Twins That Won't Tango." 1989. *The Economist* (11 March).

Webber, Carolyn, and Aaron Wildavsky. 1986. *A History of Taxation and Expenditure in the Western World.* New York: Simon and Schuster.

"Why Exchange Rates Change." 1984. *The Economist* (24 November).

Wolf, Charles, Jr. 1988. *Markets or Governments.* Cambridge, MA: MIT Press.

Wolfowitz, Paul D. 1985. "U.S. Encourages Constructive Change in the Philippines." *The Wall Street Journal* (15 April).

Wolman, William. 1983. "The IMF's Perilous Plan for Growth." *The New York Times* (2 October).

World Bank. 1992a. *Trends in Developing Countries: 1992.* Washington, DC: World Bank.

———. 1992b. *Trends in Developing Economies: 1992.* Washington, DC: World Bank.

9

Global Economic Integration: Trends and Alternative Policy Responses

Robert E. Keleher

Deregulation of financial markets, revolutions in telecommunications and information processing, and global integration of financial markets have dramatically transformed the environment in which both private financial entities and public policy makers operate. These enormous changes have spawned recommendations for alternative approaches to public policy making. Many economists, for example, have concluded that since this heightened international interdependence limits the degree of control and scope for independent policy action, more coordination of economic policy making among countries is needed.

"Policy coordination" means different things to different economists. Two competing approaches to coordinating economic policy have recently emerged. These approaches differ in terms of (1) macro-stabilization versus micro-structural policies; (2) assumptions about the centralization of information and knowledge; and (3) discretionary versus rules-based policy making. Proponents of one approach—which is premised on Mundell-Fleming macroeconomic models and game theoretic approaches to macro-policymaking and which relies more heavily on centralized, public sector decision making—argue that since increased international interdependence constrains traditional forms of domestic macroeconomic policy, international coordination of monetary and fiscal policy is essential to stabilize the business cycle. Relevant information and knowledge are assumed to be readily available for centralized policy makers to execute this strategy; acquiring appropriate information does not pose much of a problem for macro-policymaking.

A second approach is premised on the Hayekian notion that information and knowledge are decentralized and dispersed; increased economic integration and interdependence simply broaden the realm of this decentralized information and knowledge. Accordingly, proponents of this alternative view argue that economic activity can be best coordinated by relying on the price system and decentralized decision making through market processes. The role of government policy making should be to establish those institutions and structures that enable the price system to work most efficiently and to promote certain policy rules, standards, and legal conventions. Once such rules are in place, market price signals can work both to coordinate economic activity and ensure the most effective use of decentralized information and knowledge. The functioning of markets as well as tax and regulatory competition from decentralized government bodies work to discipline and constrain the public sector.

Recent Trends

Recent trends provide necessary, important background for discussing these approaches. The effects of (1) deregulation and innovation in financial markets; (2) revolutions in telecommunications and information processing; and (3) global economic and financial integration on the environment in which both financial institutions and public policy makers operate have been analyzed carefully and at length.[1] Deregulation of financial markets impacts the financial and economic environment by reducing *artificial* barriers among segregated or segmented financial markets and by promoting the development of more universal financial institutions. Deregulation has taken many forms and has occurred in many markets in most countries.[2]

U.S. depository institutions, for example, have experienced price, product, and geographic deregulation; the deregulation of interest rate (price) controls; the elimination of some product restrictions; and the dismantling or erosion of some geographic restrictions on financial institutions. This deregulation often happened in response to innovative circumventions of existing regulations.[3] Regulatory change has also affected the securities industry; for example, the deregulation of brokerage commission charges, the emergence of shelf registration, as well as the development of new products (check writing) and new institutions (nonbank banks) (Khoury 1990, 91).

Moreover, international banking and securities market deregulation has been accompanied by the scrapping of various forms of capital controls in the United States and elsewhere, as well as liberalization of entry restrictions on foreign financial instruments and foreign financial institutions.[4] The proliferation of globally diversified multinational firms and banks has accelerated these developments.

While deregulation reduces important artificial barriers to market integration, technological advances reduce key *natural* barriers to such integration. Revolutions in telecommunications and information processing, for example, have dramatically lowered the costs of acquiring and processing information. Estimates suggest that since 1964 the real cost of processing information has fallen more than 95 percent (Smith 1990, 7). Diminishing information costs—like lowered transportation costs—reduce "natural barriers" to market integration, as Scitovsky pointed out years ago (Scitovsky 1950). Not only are information costs lower, but the quantity of information has greatly increased and is available more quickly and continuously, twenty-four hours a day. Consequently, the knowledge and sophistication of market participants have increased dramatically.

Risk assessment is cheaper. Lower costs of information processing have spawned new developments and innovations, including the securitization of corporate and mortgage lending. Securitization, by (in effect) transforming loans into securities, is synonymous with the integration of the loan and securities markets. More specifically, computer record keeping enables financial institutions to bundle a portfolio of small-denomination loans economically and sell them to a third party, while earning fees for doing so. Computer technology enables financial institutions to tailor such loan packages so that their payment streams are attractive in the market (Mishkin 1990, 9). Securitization has occurred not only for mortgage and corporate lending, but also for automobile lending, credit card receivables, and commercial and computer leasings.

Lower information costs, however, have much broader implications than integrating loan and security markets. Computer technology, for example, has fostered the development of program trading, which involves computer-driven trading between stock index futures and the stocks' spot price index. Such trading is synonymous with sophisticated arbitrage operations between future and spot equity markets. Thus, lower information costs work to integrate heretofore segregated or segmented financial markets.

Information cost reduction has impacted both domestic and foreign markets. Information and knowledge now quickly transcend political boundaries and circumvent regulatory barriers, thereby integrating markets previously separated by sector, time, and geography. In short, economists recognize that lowering artificial (regulatory) and natural (information cost) barriers to factor and product mobility fosters a third trend: namely, the global integration of key economic and financial markets.

Integration, "the bringing together of parts into a whole," unites segmented markets into one market. The more markets are integrated, the more they are interconnected and behave as a unified whole. Thus, economic integration can alternatively be defined as (1) the extent to which markets are connected; (2) the degree of responsiveness and sensitivity to foreign disturbances; or (3) the degree of openness. Integration of two markets is sometimes gauged by the law of one price, the extent to which the prices of identical but geographically separated goods behave as one price. "Global integration," therefore, implies that domestic and international prices move together.

Evidence that economies are more open and that financial markets are increasingly integrated is provided in a number of ways.[5] For example, evidence demonstrates that: (1) ratios of both imports and exports to GNP in the U.S. have substantially increased (Cooper 1986); (2) the foreign presence in major domestic markets is rising (Frenkel and Goldstein 1991, 11); (3) inflation rates among industrialized countries have converged; (4) interest differentials between the costs of domestic and offshore interbank funds (denominated in the same currency) have fallen dramatically;[6] and (5) covered interest parity holds in many short-term financial markets.[7] The evidence pertaining to uncovered interest parity and real interest rate parity is more difficult to interpret (Goldstein, Mathieson, and Lane 1991, 8–9). Nonetheless, the evidence suggests that short-term financial markets are highly integrated; and returns on longer-term debt and equity instruments in various countries have also shown increasing tendencies to move together (ibid., 9–10).

Implications for Policy

These three trends have important implications not only for the performance of markets but also for the behavior of policy makers, who recognize that policies now have different effects than they used to. Policies, for example, impact alternative variables in differing magnitudes so that policy transmission mechanisms are now different than previously.[8]

These developments are also associated with some important empirical regularities. For example, financial market prices—specifically, (real) exchange rates, interest rates, and commodity prices—are now more volatile than in the 1950s and 1960s. Additionally, foreign exchange rates often dramatically and persistently overshoot reasonable estimates of their "equilibrium" values. Both large capital flows and sizable, persistent trade imbalances have impacted several countries in recent years.

Policy makers recognize that in a globally integrated economy, public policy making may contribute importantly to these empirical regularities; unexpected policy innovations diverging from international norms can affect exchange rates and other financial market prices. Such policies can contribute to exchange rate volatility and "overshooting," as well as sizable capital flows and trade imbalances. Some policy makers argue that with global integration, economies are more vulnerable to foreign policy disturbances as well as policy "spillovers" or externalities.[9] In short, policy makers recognize that policy making is now more complex.

In response, many policy makers and economists advocate coordinating public policy making to improve economic performance. But "coordinating public policy making" means different things to different economists. Policy coordination proposals can be classified into two broad categories, each premised on different views of how economies operate. Generally, these two categories can be differentiated on the basis of (1) macro-stabilization versus micro-structural policies; (2) assumptions about the centralization of information and knowledge; and (3) discretionary versus rules-based policy making.

Macroeconomic (Keynesian) Policy Coordination and Centralized Decision Making

A Keynesian view, which has long occupied center-stage among most conventional macro-economists and governmental policy makers, holds that policy decision making necessarily is both highly centralized and largely discretionary. The intellectual heritage of the approach emanates from international income-expenditure (Mundell-Fleming or IS-LM) models,[10] game theoretic frameworks, or assignment problem approaches to policy making,[11] whereby decision makers are central authorities who manipulate policy instruments to manage (stabilize) the macro-economy or redistribute income. Decisions relating to policy coordination are always made by centralized government decisionmakers and centralized international policy making is the centerpiece of the policy approach endorsed by this view.[12]

These proponents endorse international policy coordination, believing that macroeconomic policies deviating from international norms create sizable spillovers or externalities that produce market volatility and overshooting. Payment imbalances result. Independent pursuit of national objectives results in suboptimal global outcomes; thus, the price system malfunctions in that externalities mandate the international coordination of macro-policy making. In short, these spillovers can be embodied into the decision-making calculus via international policy coordination.

These international Keynesians prescribe using various macroeconomic quantity variables (e.g., national income account statistics, budget deficits, monetary aggregates, current-account imbalances) as guides to coordinate policy so as to internalize these externalities and find the optimal policy mix. Policy makers control and coordinate aggregate demand by manipulating *both* monetary and fiscal policy to stabilize economic activity; management of income-expenditure flows receives primary emphasis. In this way, proponents argue that public policy makers can exploit policy trade-offs, thereby improving economic performance.

Notably, fiscal policy plays a very prominent role in determining aggregate demand in these Keynesian (Mundell-Fleming type) models; and fiscal policy is a key tool in managing policy coordination efforts. Budget deficit measures are used to reliably gauge the stance of fiscal policy; changes in the budget deficit are viewed as reliably impacting aggregate demand and its important components.[13] Indeed, sometimes fiscal policy is assigned to "manage" external balance (Swoboda 1990). In sum, fiscal policy coordination boils down to budget deficit coordination.[14]

Discretionary management of monetary policy also plays a key role in determining the preferred macroeconomic policy mix for policy coordination. Monetary policy, along with fiscal policy, is a complementary rather than a principal determinant of aggregate demand. Seen as a tool to manage aggregate demand, monetary policy is normally *not* assigned exclusive responsibility for price or exchange rate stability. In accordance with their economic "fine tuning" perspective, many proponents of this approach currently view the exchange rate as a tool useful in managing the trade balance. And regulatory policies such as the imposition of capital controls are sometimes also prescribed as aids helpful in managing external imbalances.

In this view, coordination is carried out *entirely* by centralized public authorities using aggregated macroeconomic accounting data produced by government statistical offices rather than by the private sector using the price system. The data and method are akin to centralized government planning agencies using accounting data (and presumed superior centralized knowledge) to substitute for the price system.

Microeconomic Policy Coordination/Harmonization and Decentralized Decision Making

An alternative approach to economic policy coordination has recently materialized.[15] This approach maintains that information and knowledge necessarily are dispersed and decentralized and that the costs of acquiring information are significant. Accordingly, as demonstrated by the calculation debate of the 1930s, centralized decision makers are not the all-knowing entities portrayed by proponents of centralized decision making.

Therefore, the Hayekian approach argues that the market price system is the most efficient mechanism utilizing decentralized information and knowledge. Market prices are information-aggregating devices; decentralized decision makers can readily take advantage of dispersed knowledge and information by using the price system, which can best direct business enterprise, allocate resources, and thereby work to coordinate economic activity. Markets expand as the world becomes increasingly integrated, and the coordinating role of the market price system becomes even more valuable as economies become more complex.

Given the price system's important coordinating role, this alternative approach to policy making argues that policy frameworks that improve or foster the workings of the price system should be adopted. Instead of emphasizing macro-imbalances, economic stabilization, and the coordination of centralized policy making, government should promote the institutional framework that enables the market price system to function most effectively in an increasingly integrated world. The market price system's performance can be improved by establishing "rules of the game." Governmental policy should set out certain standards, property rights, and legal frameworks that foster the workings of the market price system. The international harmonization of these "rules of the game" can be facilitated by appropriate governmental policies in other countries.

Key elements of this approach involve international agreements removing restrictions hindering the international mobility of commodities, services, capital, and labor, as well as promoting competition. Tariff and nontariff trade barriers, capital controls, and impediments to immigration should be minimized. Rules fostering uniform property rights (e.g., harmonious bankruptcy, patent, and contract law) should be established, and international agreements on common standards (e.g., accounting, measurement, and disclosure standards) should be adopted.

Price system proponents argue that the ill-defined "externalities" or "spillovers" purportedly resulting from decentralized policy making and emphasized by proponents of centralized policy making are neither the type of externalities signifying market failure nor those providing the rationale for macroeconomic policy coordination.[16] Vaubel (1983), for example, argues that these effects do not result from market failure but from market interdependence; they are the "pecuniary externalities" rather than the "technological externalities" detailed by Viner (1931). Proponents of the centralized view confuse pecuniary and technological externalities; pecuniary externalities are *not* incompatible with Pareto optimality in competitive equilibrium and thus should not concern policy makers.[17] Nonetheless, some proponents of the decentralized view concede that policy coordination may be necessary in circumstances where Pareto-relevant technological international externalities appear relevant (e.g., for establishing property rights, certain standards, and rules of conduct in international trade policy) (Vaubel 1983, 12).

This price-system perspective has very important implications for regulatory policy, fiscal policy, and monetary policy. Regulatory policy is viewed not as a vehicle for discretion or for centralized control, but for establishment of international standards and the like to foster the workings of the price system. Of course, deregulation and reduction of burdensome regulation are still important, but establishing the rules of the game is essential.

Establishing international standards fostering the workings of the price system is an important element of these rules of the game. Standards can foster trade and exchange by reducing uncertainty and the costs of acquiring information and knowledge about product quality or particular sellers. Uniform standards that define units of measure for weight, length, temperature, time, or value serve as a form of information provision and reduce uncertainty and information costs. Standards for specifications, definitions, dimensions, classifications, or grades serve as additional examples. And accounting standards and rules for disclosure also perform this function, enabling agents better comparability. They conserve information, reduce waste, promote interchangeability, and facilitate trade. In short, with global integration and expanding markets, standards and uniform rules enable market participants to engage in exchange without having to know or verify certain facts and information about particular sellers or products. Establishing certain international standards and rules, therefore, is a form of international policy coordination that can promote the workings of markets and the price system (Kindleberger 1988; Grundfest 1990; Coles 1949). Other forms of international regulatory coordination also are compatible with this perspective. Rules for property rights in clearing and settlement, disclosure rules which avoid duplication and filing burdens, and certain common international rules for the regulation of various financial markets also serve as relevant examples.

But standardization and uniform regulation can be overdone; regulation can be undesirable if it prevents regulatory innovation and experimentation, fosters or institutionalizes cartel powers and the rents of regulators, or prevents competition. Regulatory and institutional competition is often desirable and diversity in regulation may be beneficial when it fosters regulatory experimentation, innovation, and adaptability.[18] Such competition may promote harmonization of efficient regulation and enable markets to serve as a disciplinary force on institutional development. Competition of this type does not lead to an underprovision of regulation or public services (Siebert 1990). And such competition is fully compatible with (and depends on) the efficient functioning of the market price system.

Similarly, the coordination of fiscal policy takes an entirely different form in this alternative approach to policy coordination. Specifically, fiscal policy is neither a discretionary policy instrument nor something to be implemented by manipulating budget deficits to stabilize the business cycle or manage aggregate demand. Indeed, proponents of this alternative position view budget deficits and their influence on aggregate demand as inappropriate, misleading guides to changes in fiscal policy.

Rather, longer-term fiscal tax and spending rules (fiscal constitutions) should be established to promote long-term growth and budgetary control. Both spending programs and taxes should be selected and fashioned to minimize their distorting effects on the price system. Lowering tax rates or levels of government spending likely work to minimize price-system distortions.[19] Thus, longer-term aggregate supply considerations receive prominent attention of fiscal policy rather than the short-term aggregate demand focus of the Keynesian perspective.

Proponents of this alternative view interpret the coordination of fiscal policy as the harmonization of taxes, tax statutes, and sometimes government spending rather than budget deficits. Moreover, harmonization often results not from decisions of centralized tax authorities but from tax competition. Multiple taxing authorities and tax competition are disciplinary devices which, if promoted judiciously, can aid in harmonizing market-compatible tax and spending policies. But contrary to some opinion, tax competition yields neither an underprovision of public goods[20] nor complete equalization of tax or spending rates.[21] [Complete equalization of taxes is undesirable since differing tastes and preferences will always exist for some non-tradable public goods. And differing tax rates do not necessarily distort the price system; tax diversity does not imply inefficiency and is perfectly acceptable as long as it is compatible with neutrality.[22] Logic suggests that equality of tax rates may be appropriate for some goods and services (e.g., taxes on tradable/mobile goods or services), but not for others (e.g., taxes on non-tradable/immobile goods or services).]

Proponents of this alternative perspective do not interpret monetary policy as a discretionary policy instrument used in a policy mix geared to stabilizing the business cycle. Instead, existing central banks adopt rules or strategies to achieve price-level stability.[23] Some favor establishing (monetary or price-based) rules directly promoting price stability; others support instituting international monetary standards involving fixed exchange rates with secure, credible monetary anchors.[24]

Both approaches promote the workings of the price system; both attempt to establish a predictable, stable money so that (relative) price movements reflect changes in supplies and demands rather than uncertainty premiums or changes in inflationary expectations. In short, price-level stability enables the price system to perform its all-important information and knowledge disseminating function while keeping the value of the monetary unit constant.

Supporters of well-anchored, fixed exchange-rate international monetary standards contend that such regimes not only produce price stability but also remove both excessive volatility and overshooting of exchange rates. In doing so, such standards minimize the variability and dispersion of many other prices, and so further improve the workings of the price system.

An important theme common to the regulatory, fiscal, and monetary policies of this alternative approach relates to its promotion of the price system to coordinate economic activity. Government can adopt policies that foster the working of the price system rather than substituting for it. Throughout, decentralized private decision makers are seen as better able to use existing disbursed information and decentralized knowledge than are the centralized public decision makers. Market prices and not aggregated accounting data are the "raw data" actively employed by these decentralized decision makers.

Some Historical Evidence

A number of empirical studies have attempted to quantify the effects of Keynesian macroeconomic policy coordination of the type described earlier.[25] While subject to a number of qualifications, these studies generally find the benefits of macro-policy coordination quantitatively quite small.[26] Little hard evidence, then, supports discretionary macroeconomic policy coordination, particularly of the type emphasizing fiscal policy as a key tool to manage aggregate demand. A number of studies have also examined historical episodes when policy coordination efforts occurred. Most studies of the interwar period concede that discretionary monetary policy coordination did occur in the 1920s among central banks attempting to reconstruct and maintain an international gold standard. Central bankers such as Montague Norman and Benjamin Strong were key architects of this monetary policy coordination. And such coordination is generally considered to have been beneficial—at least for a limited period prior to the 1930s. Coordination of fiscal policy, however, was not part of this effort, largely because of very different perceptions as to its proper role prior to the "Keynesian Revolution."[27]

Similarly, several studies of macro policy making in the post–Bretton Woods era have detailed macroeconomic policy coordination efforts. One episode involving attempts to coordinate key components of a macroeconomic policy mix and receiving a good deal of attention is the Bonn Summit of 1978. Heralded as a paradigmatic case of international policy cooperation in some quarters, it included no monetary policy commitments (Bryant and Hodgkinson 1989, 2). While its key commitments were implemented, many of the agreed-upon policy initiatives were in place only a relatively short time and have subsequently received critical review (Putnam and Henning 1989; Holtham 1989). Similarly, several extensive studies review dollar management between the 1985 Plaza Accord and the 1987 Louvre Agreement or, more generally, the G-7 coordination process after the Plaza Accord.[28] Some aspects of macro-policy coordination efforts were arguably quite successful during portions of this period. But other elements of the period's coordination efforts were unsatisfactory, and effective active coordination did not persist.[29]

In short, researchers have identified only a few, limited episodes of successful macro-policy coordination involving discretionary decision making of the type outlined previously. In these cases, central authorities found it advantageous to temporarily join coordination efforts, but they did not persist when their self-interests conflicted with continued policy coordination goals. Accordingly, as the situation (and participants) changed, the effectiveness of policy coordination ended.

This lack of success can be attributed to a number of formidable obstacles, including (1) differing policy objectives among governments; (2) disagreements as to how economies work and interact; (3) political and constitutional constraints on the bargaining process; and (4) important incentives of participants to renege on their agreements.[30]

First, bargaining governments often have differing policy objectives that may reflect differing circumstances such as differing degrees of economic openness, different perceptions as to the costs of policy coordination, or different views as to the trade-offs between, say, price stability and economic growth or between domestic versus international policy goals.

Second, governments can disagree as to how economies work, how they interact, and how they are structured. Even countries with identical policy objectives may disagree as to the expected effects of a given policy change or as to the relationship of means to ends. In practice, some G-7 governments have quite different perceptions as to the role and workings of fiscal policy as well as to the key determinants of exchange rates.

Third, political or constitutional constraints often confound the international coordination bargaining process. Different agencies may control different aspects of policy in different countries. Sometimes international bargaining is possible only after domestic policy bargaining has ended. For example, the U.S. Treasury secretary controls neither fiscal policy nor monetary policy. And policies pertaining to exchange-rate management may be controlled by different (sometimes multiple) agencies in different countries, often complicating the negotiation of international agreements.

Finally, governments may have important incentives to renege on bargains made in a discretionary manner. The self-interest of bargainers as well as the problem of "time inconsistency" may sometimes create important incentives to cheat on policy agreements. These considerations are particularly relevant to secret agreements or vague commitments made with reference to multiple policy indicators where bargainers are not accountable and agreements are difficult to enforce. The desire to maintain autonomy or the freedom to conduct independent policy without being committed to future action sometimes also makes governments prone to renege on bargains to coordinate policy.

For all these reasons there has been little, if any, success for discretionary, centralized policy coordination of the type described earlier.

Microeconomic, Rules-Based Policy Coordination

Whereas evidence of successful macroeconomic discretionary policy coordination is scarce, evidence of successful microeconomic-structural, rules-based policy coordination is widespread. Examples of competitively-driven policy harmonization (e.g., tax and regulatory harmonization) are also readily evident. Indeed, several highly respected economists even suggest that such microeconomic, rules-based (constitutional) policy coordination may be the only type of policy coordination that can persist over time.[31] Examples of the successful implementation of this rule-based form of policy coordination are provided in the following paragraphs.

The General Agreement on Tariffs and Trade (GATT)

Policy coordination efforts to reduce tariffs are one of the major success stories of post-World War II international economic cooperation. GATT, negotiated in a series of eight multilateral "rounds" since 1947, when tariffs on manufactured goods ranged from 30 to 60 percent, has reduced tariffs to an average of 4 to 8 percent (Finger 1991, 125; Bhagwati 1988, 4; Dam 1970, 56). Most economists concur that GATT clearly played a major role in fostering world economic growth in the 1950s and 1960s (Lepage 1989, 15). Coordination of tariff policy under the aegis of GATT is a rules-based form of policy coordination in which countries establish rules of the game. [The General Agreement, after all, is a set of legal rules (Dam 1970, xiii).] These rules involve removing impediments to commodity mobility and distortions to prices, thus allowing the price system to better coordinate activity and decentralized decision makers to better use dispersed, decentralized knowledge and information. While many problems remain with GATT (Jackson 1989, 303), most economists agree that this rules-based form of international policy coordination has achieved considerable success.

Bretton Woods

The Bretton Woods system was a monetary regime involving a rule-based standard. The agreement established fixed (albeit adjustable) exchange rates, thereby effectively committing participating countries to common (coordinated) monetary policies and ensuring that price levels moved together.[32] The system was based on the dollar with a non-circulating gold base or "anchor"—in other words, gold theoretically anchored the system. The agreement established (1) a common international monetary standard of value serving to measure changes in the value of money, and (2) rules of the game for monetary authorities. In short, the system created institutional rules under which the price system could better function and decentralized decision makers could make better use of decentralized information and dispersed knowledge.

While not without well-known defects, the Bretton Woods system performed remarkably well.[33] Compared to post–Bretton Woods monetary arrangements, for example:

1. The volatility of both nominal and real exchange rates was substantially smaller under Bretton Woods (McKinnon 1990, 5; Giavazzi and Giovannini 1989, 54). Moreover, no exchange rate overshooting occurred.

2. The volatility of commodity prices was significantly lower under Bretton Woods (Keleher 1991).

3. On average, levels and volatility of inflation were significantly lower under Bretton Woods.[34] And inflation in various countries moved together rather than diverging.[35]

4. The levels and volatility of both short- and long-term interest rates were lower under Bretton Woods (McKinnon 1990, 6, 8, 9; McKinnon and Robinson 1989).

In short, the evidence suggests that the Bretton Woods system allowed the price system to function more effectively than under alternative monetary regimes. Bretton Woods, a rule-based international monetary standard that fostered the coordination of national monetary policies, not only promoted an effectively functioning price system but also fostered the expansion of both trade and economic growth. Importantly, it enabled decentralized decision makers to use decentralized information and dispersed knowledge so as to better coordinate economic activity.

The European Monetary System (EMS)

Like Bretton Woods, the EMS is a rules-based international monetary agreement involving exchange-rate bands that promote the coordination of monetary policy. The EMS, which operates with a German anchor, has been associated with a decline in the variability of nominal and real exchange rates among its members. (This reduced variability has become more evident in recent years.)[36] Inflation differentials and the dispersion of inflation have decreased among EMS members (Russo and Tullio 1988, 48). And both (nominal) short-term and long-term interest rates have converged among EMS countries relative to non-EMS countries (ibid., 50). Consequently, the performance of the price system likely has improved within the EMS. This system, still evolving since its creation in 1979, has nevertheless been deemed quite successful by many analysts. In short, the EMS provides another example of a successful rules-based coordination of monetary policy (Giavazzi and Giovannini 1989, 191).

The U.S. Constitution

The U.S. Constitution is yet another example of a successful and lasting rules-based coordination of economic policy making. Recognizing the many coordination failures under the Articles of Confederation, state representatives met in Philadelphia in 1787 and agreed to a number of formal policy rules laid out in the Constitution that ensured the gains of economic integration.[37] In effect, these representatives agreed to coordinate important elements of economic policy making. The Constitution created the largest free trade area in the world at the time (McDonald 1985, 260; 1982, 58); eliminated restrictions to the mobility of capital, labor, and commodities across states; and established important property rights, standards, and a common currency area. These rules of the game fostered exchange and allowed the market price system to coordinate economic activity and the activity of decentralized decision makers.

More specifically, the Constitution established uniform property rights in the form of (a) uniform Federal taxation throughout the states (Article I, section 8); (b) uniform bankruptcy, contract, and patent laws (Article I, section 8); and (c) uniform legal tender codes (Article I, section 8). It created congressional power to establish uniform standards of weights and measures (Article I, section 8), and standards by which to regulate the value of money (Article I, section 8). The Constitution prohibited state governments from coining money (Article I, section 10)—thereby effectively creating a common currency area; prohibited protectionist legislation among the states; prohibited interstate barriers to trade (Article I, section 9); and prohibited "locally preferred" regulation of commerce. In short, the Constitution allows the market price system to coordinate economic activity and enables decentralized decision makers to best utilize dispersed information and knowledge.

Other International Agreements

Other cases of successful, rules-based policy agreements can be cited, including Greenwich Mean Time, the metric system, and Morse Code. And international agreements such as BIS bank capital standards, the Law of The Sea Treaty, international public health agreements, and nonproliferation treaties serve as additional examples of rule-based agreements that coordinate various aspects of policy making.

Tax and Regulatory Harmonization

As indicated above, removing impediments to the mobility of commodities, capital, and labor promotes the harmonization of certain aspects of fiscal and regulatory policy. Tax harmonization often results not from centralized edict, but from competition among decentralized tax authorities when factors and products are mobile. Such competition may even foster efficient fiscal arrangements as emphasized by Tiebout (1956). Indeed, whereas virtually no examples of the successful coordination of Keynesian fiscal policies exist, there are many examples of tax harmonization produced by decentralized tax competition, described as a "micro-structural coordination approach" to policy coordination in previous sections.

The uncoordinated, widespread individual and corporate tax rate reductions and tax reform experienced during the 1980s in both developed and underdeveloped countries provide an example (Boskin and McLure 1990, 11; Tanzi and Bovenberg 1990, 173–75). These reductions followed neither a coordinated plan nor a centralized international agreement. Rather, they resulted from the pressures of competition unleashed by the mobility of capital, labor, and commodities.

Following the introduction of a nearly uniform VAT, a degree of harmonization of taxation has also occurred within the EEC. For example, some harmonization has occurred among product taxes as well as among capital gains and corporate income taxation (Cnossen 1987, 45, 48, 49; Giovannini and Hines 1991, 175–76). Indeed, Micossi (1988) has shown that European authorities are becoming quite sympathetic to the approach of removing barriers to mobility and fostering competition to promote integration and tax harmonization.

A degree of tax harmonization has also occurred among states in the United States, as Eichengreen (1990) has ably demonstrated. While a high degree of factor and product mobility creates pressures for tax harmonization, significant tax differences remain among the states: tax harmonization does not imply tax equalization. Nonetheless, the variability of state tax rates in the United States is about 40 percent less than in the EEC (Eichengreen 1990, 164).

Summary and Conclusions

Deregulation of financial institutions, revolutions in telecommunications and information processing, and the global integration of financial markets have transformed the environment in which public policy makers operate. These changes have spawned recommendations for the international coordination of economic policy making.

Two different approaches to the coordination of policy making have materialized. One promotes the coordination of discretionary macroeconomic stabilization policies among centralized decision makers. The other emphasizes microeconomic-structural policies and promotes certain policy rules, standards, and legal conventions. Once these "rules of the game" are in place, market price signals can work both to coordinate economic activity and to enable decentralized, dispersed information to be utilized most effectively.

There is little, if any, evidence of lasting successes of the former approach to policy coordination, particularly of the coordination of deficit-based fiscal stabilization policy. A number of successes—and virtually the only examples of persistent successful international policy coordination—characterize the rules-based or structural form of policy coordination. For successful international policy coordination, policy makers should employ this latter, rules-based form of coordination.

Notes

1. See, for example, Dermine (1990), Cooper (1986), Folkerts-Landau and Mathieson (1988), Germany and Morton (1985), and Khoury (1990).
2. See, for example, Khoury (1990), Cargill and Garcia (1985), Folkerts-Landau (1990, 419–20), and Dermine (1990).
3. See, for example, Khoury (1990); Cargill and Garcia (1985); Dermine (1990); and Kaufman, Mote, and Rosenblum (1984).
4. See, for example, Grundfest (1990, 364–65); Eichengreen (1990); Folkerts-Landau (1990, 419–20); and Micossi (1988).
5. See, for example, Cooper (1986); Frenkel, Goldstein, and Masson (1990); Fischer (1988); Frenkel (1983); Frenkel (1986); and Branson, Frenkel, and Goldstein (1990, 12).
6. Frenkel and Goldstein (1991, 11); Goldstein, Mathieson, and Lane (1991, 7–11).
7. Goldstein, Mathieson, and Lane (1991, 7); see Frenkel (1991) for a summary of the evidence.
8. See, for example, Goldstein, Mathieson, and Lane (1991,25–27; Johnson and Keleher (1992, chapter 2).
9. See, for example, Frenkel, Goldstein, and Masson (1990, 10–11). These authors point out that in a Mundell-Fleming model, a domestic monetary expansion can cause contraction abroad.
10. As suggested by Frenkel and Razin (1987, 568), "The Mundell-Fleming model is still the 'work horse' of traditional open economy macroeconomics." This approach is also sometimes characterized as a saving-investment balance approach to the analysis of international economic interaction.
11. For more recent discussion of the assignment problem, see Swoboda (1990) and Levin (1979). For earlier discussions see Sohman (1969) and Cooper (1969).
12. Since these models posit important decision-making roles for highly centralized organizations, international organizations charged with duties relating to policy coordination (such as the IMF or World Bank) fully embrace this approach.
13. See, for example, Frenkel and Razin (1987, 573). Some simulation models provide results supporting this view. See Frenkel, Goldstein, and Masson (1989); Bryant, Helliwell, and Hooper (1989); McKibbin and Sachs (1989); Taylor (1989); and Bryant et al (1988).
14. Note that treasury securities and finance ministers by their very nature tend to focus on budgetary data and tax revenues as key policy tools.
15. Economists (implicitly or explicitly) endorsing this approach include Vaubel (1983, 1985); McLure (1986); Cnossen (1987, 1990); Salin (1989, 1990, 1991); Siebert (1990); Siebert and Koop (1990); Tiebout (1956); Hayek (1948); Sinn (1990a,b,c); Hansson (1990); and others.
16. See, for example, the several writings of Salin, Vauble (1983), Lal (1990), Siebert and Koop (1990).
17. Vaubel (1983, 10, 12). See also Vaubel (1985, 230–31); Lal (1990, 12–13, 17, 39–40); and Siebert and Koop (1990, 450).

18. See, for example, Harraf (1988, 438); Grundfest (1990); Fischel (1989); Siebert and Koop (1990); Scott (1977); and Folkerts-Landau (1990).
19. See Barth, Keleher, and Russek (1990) for a discussion of the forms of government spending that promote economic growth.
20. See, for example, Siebert (1990) and McLure (1986). Encouraging competition in subsidies, however, can be dangerous (Harraf 1988, 438).
21. See Cnossen (1990, 216–18) for a discussion of why tax equality is not desirable.
22. See, for example, Salin (1990, 216–18); Cnossen (1990, 1987). Notably, statutory tax rates are often imperfect indicators since different degrees of tax enforcement or different definitions of relevant tax bases inevitably exist.
23. Some economists sympathetic to this approach advocate changing current institutional arrangements by establishing a competitive money system. See, for example, the several works of Vaubel, Salin, and Hayek.
24. One such regime would employ market price indicators to achieve price stability (Keleher 1990).
25. See the short review of this literature provided in Currie, Holtham, and Hallett (1989, especially 25–27).
26. Persistent economic shocks and policy makers' credibility can appreciably increase the value of coordination. See, for example, Currie, Levine, and Vidalis (1987); and Gomel, Saccomanni, and Vona (1990, 16–18).
27. For studies of the interwar period, see Dam (1982, 51–54); Eichengreen (1985).
28. See, for example, Destler and Henning (1989); Dobson (1991); Funabashi (1988); and Gomel, Saccomanni, and Vona (1990).
29. For example, whereas protectionist pressures were contained (in part) due to these coordination efforts, binding policy commitments were not adopted.
30. See, for example, Cooper (1985a); Frankel (1990); Frenkel, Goldstein, and Masson (1990); Kenen (1990); Horne and Masson (1988).
31. See, for example, Cooper (1985a, 1226–28; 1985b, 369, 371; 1989, 241); Fratianni and Pattison (1991, 101); Gomel, Saccomanni, and Vona (1990, 31); and Tabellini (1990, 264). Tabellini concludes:

> International policy coordination can be either "good" or "bad." But it is more likely to be good if it takes the form of cooperation around general rules of conduct that are conceived to be binding for current and future governments alike. This form of cooperation is most likely to solve the time inconsistency of policy as well as the political distortions that originate from alternating governments. Conversely, international cooperation is more likely to be bad if it takes the form of coalitions between two or more sovereign governments on some discretionary policy action. This kind of agreement fails to correct the possible lack of economic or political commitment technologies. And thus it can induce the policymakers to choose the socially inefficient policies.

32. For a discussion of how price levels move together under fixed-exchange rate systems, see Keleher (1988).
33. The defects of Bretton Woods included the unwillingness of the United States to lose gold or to accept either balance of payments discipline or the global discipline of gold. See Mundell (1982, 8).
34. See, for example, McKinnon and Robinson (1989), table 3, table 5.
35. Ibid., fig. 6.
36. See, for example, Russo and Tullio (1988, 48); Guitian (1988, 11).
37. For a discussion of these failures, see McDonald (1985, 154–57).

References

Barth, James R., Robert E. Keleher, and Frank Russek. 1990. "The Scale of Government and Economic Activity." *The Southern Business and Economic Journal* 13, 3 (April): 142–83.

Bhagwati, Jagdish. 1988. *Protectionism.* Cambridge, MA: MIT Press.

Booth, Sherman F. 1960. *Standardization Activities in the United States.* Washington, DC: GPO.

Boskin, Michael J., and Charles E. McLure, Jr. 1990. *World Tax Reform.* San Francisco, CA: ICS Press.

Branson, William H., Jacob A. Frenkel, and Morris Goldstein, eds. 1990. *International Policy Coordination and Exchange Rate Fluctuations.* Chicago: University of Chicago Press.

Brennan, Geoffrey, and James M. Buchanan. 1980. *The Power to Tax: Analytical Foundations of a Fiscal Constitution.* Cambridge: Cambridge University Press.

Bryant, Ralph C., John F. Helliwell, and Peter Hooper. 1989. "Domestic and Cross-Border Consequences of U.S. Macroeconomic Policies." In *Macroeconomic Policies in an Interdependent World,* edited by Bryant et al. Washington, DC: IMF.

Bryant, Ralph C., Dale W. Henderson, Gerald Holtham, Peter Hooper, and Steven A. Symansky, eds. 1988. *Empirical Macroeconomics for Interdependent Economies.* Washington, DC: Brookings.

Bryant, Ralph C., and Edith Hodgkinson. 1989. "Problems of International Cooperation." In *Can Nations Agree?* Washington, DC: Brookings.

Buiter, Willem H., and Richard C. Marston. 1986. *International Economic Policy Coordination.* Cambridge: Cambridge University Press.

Cargill, Thomas F., and Gillian G. Garcia. 1985. *Financial Reform in the 1980s.* Stanford, CA: Hoover University Press.

Carraro, Carlo, Didier Laussel, Mark Salmon, and Antoine Soubeyran, eds. 1991. *International Economic Policy Coordination.* Oxford: Blackwell.

Cnossen, Sijbren. 1990. "On the Direction of Tax Harmonization in the European Community." In *Reforming Capital Income Taxation,* edited by H. Siebert. Boulder, CO: Westview Press.

Cnossen, Sijbren, ed. 1987. *Tax Coordination in the European Community.* Deventer, The Netherlands: Kluwer.

Coles, Jessie V. 1949. *Standards and Labels for Consumer Goods.* New York: Ronald Press.

Cooper, Kerry, and Donald R. Fraser. 1986. *Banking Deregulation and the New Competition on Financial Services.* Cambridge, MA: Ballinger Publishing Co.

Cooper, Richard N. 1969. "Comment: 'The Assignment Problem.'" In *Monetary Problems of the International Economy,* edited by Robert A. Mundell and Alexander K. Swoboda. Chicago: University of Chicago Press.

———. 1985a. "Economic Interdependence and Coordination of Economic Policies." In *Handbook of International Economics,* edited by Ronald W. Jones and Peter B. Kenen. Vol. 2. New York: North Holland.

———. 1985b. "Panel Discussion: The Prospects for International Policy Coordination." In *International Economic Policy Coordination,* edited by Willem H. Buiter and Richard C. Marston. Cambridge: Cambridge University Press.

———. 1986. "The United States as an Open Economy." In *How Open Is the U.S. Economy?,* edited by R. W. Hafer. Lexington, MA: Lexington Books.

Cooper, Richard N., Barry Eichengreen, Gerald Holtham, Robert D. Putnam, and G. Randall Henning. 1989. *Can Nations Agree?* Washington, DC: Brookings.

Currie, David A., Gerald Holtham, and Andrew Hughes Hallett. 1989. "The Theory and Practice of International Policy Coordination: Does Coordination Pay?" In *Macroeconomic Policies in an Interdependent World*, edited by Ralph Bryant et al. Washington, DC: IMF.

Currie, David A., Paul Levine, and Nic Vidalis. 1987. "Cooperative and Noncooperative Rules for Monetary and Fiscal Policy in an Empirical Two-bloc Model." In *Global Macroeconomics: Policy Conflict and Cooperation*, edited by Ralph Bryant and Richard Porters. London: MacMillan.

Dam, Kenneth W. 1970. *The GATT: Law and the International Economic Organization*. Chicago: University of Chicago Press.

————. 1982. *The Rules of the Game*. Chicago: University of Chicago Press.

Dermine, Jean. 1990. *European Banking in the 1990s*. London: Basil Blackwell.

Destler, I. M., and C. Randall Henning. 1989. *Dollar Politics: Exchange Rate Policymaking in the United States*. Washington, DC: Institute for International Economics.

Dobson, Wendy. 1991. *Economic Policy Coordination: Requiem or Prologue*. Washington: Institute for International Economics.

Eichengreen, Barry. 1985. "International Policy Coordination in Historical Perspective: A View from the Interwar Years." In *International Economic Policy Coordination*, edited by Willem H. Buiter and Richard C. Marston. Cambridge: Cambridge University Press.

————. 1990. "One Money for Europe? Lessons from the U.S. Currency Union." *Economic Policy* (April).

Finger, Michael J. 1991. "The GATT as an International Discipline Over Trade Restrictions: A Public Choice Approach." In *The Political Economy of International Organizations*, edited by Roland Vaubel and Thomas D. Willett. Boulder, CO: Westview Press.

Fischel, Daniel R. 1989. "Should One Agency Regulate Financial Markets?" In *Black Monday and the Future of Financial Markets*. Homewood, IL: Dow-Jones Irwin, Inc.

Fischer, Stanley. 1988. "International Macroeconomic Policy Coordination." In *International Economic Cooperation*, edited by Martin Feldstein. Chicago: University of Chicago Press.

Folkerts-Landau, David. 1990. "The Case for International Coordination of Financial Policy." In *International Policy Coordination and Exchange Rate Fluctuations*, edited by William H. Branson, Jacob A. Frenkel, and Morris Goldstein. Chicago: University of Chicago Press.

Folkerts-Landau, David, and Donald J. Mathieson. 1988. "Innovation, Institutional Changes, and Regulatory Response in International Financial Markets." In *Restructuring Banking and Financial Services in America*, edited by William S. Haraf and Rose Marie Kushmeider. Washington, DC: American Enterprise Institute.

Frankel, Jeffrey A. 1990. "Obstacles to Coordination, and a Consideration of Two Proposals to Overcome Them: International Nominal Targeting (INT) and the Hosomi Fund." In *International Policy Coordination and Exchange Rate Fluctuations*, edited by William Branson et al. Chicago: University of Chicago Press.

————. 1991. "Quantifying International Capital Mobility in the 1980's" In *National Saving and Economic Performance*, edited by Douglas Bernheim and John Shoven. Chicago: University of Chicago Press.

Fratianni, Michele, and John Pattison. 1991. "International Institutions and the Market for Information." In *The Political Economy of International Organizations*, edited by Roland Vaubel and Thomas D. Willett. Boulder, CO: Westview Press.

Frenkel, Jacob A. 1986. "International Interdependence and the Constraints on Macroeconomic Policies." *Weltwirtschlaftiches Archiv.* 122, 4.

————. 1983. "International Liquidity and Monetary Control" In *International Money and Credit: The Policy Roles*, edited by George M. Von Furstenberg. Washington, DC: IMF.

Frenkel, Jacob A., and Morris Goldstein. 1991. "The Macroeconomic Policy Implications of Currency Zones." Paper prepared for symposium sponsored by the Federal Reserve Bank of Kansas City. Jackson Hole, WY. 22–24 August.

Frenkel, Jacob A., Morris Goldstein, and Paul R. Masson. 1989. "Simulating the Effects of Some Simple Coordinated Versus Uncoordinated Policy Rules." In *Macroeconomic Policies in an Interdependent World*, edited by Bryant et al. Washington, DC: IMF.

————. 1990. "The Rationale for, and Effects of, International Economic Policy Coordination." In *International Policy Coordination and Exchange Rate Fluctuation*, edited by Branson et al. Chicago: University of Chicago Press.

Frenkel, Jacob A., and Assaf Razin. 1987. "The Mundell-Fleming Model A Quarter Century Later." *IMF Staff Papers* 34 (December): 567–720.

Funabashi, Yoichi. 1988. *Managing the Dollar: From the Plaza to the Louvre.* Washington, DC: Institute for International Economics.

Germany, David J., and John E. Morton. 1985. "Financial Innovation and Deregulation in Foreign Industrial Countries." *Federal Reserve Bulletin* 71 (October): 743–53.

Giavazzi, Francesco, and Alberto Giovannini. 1989. *Limiting Exchange Rate Flexibility: The European Monetary System.* Cambridge, MA: MIT Press.

Ghosh, Atish R., and Paul Masson. 1988. "International Policy Coordination in a World With Model Uncertainty." *IMF Staff Papers* 35 (June): 230–58.

————. 1991. "Model Uncertainty, Learning, and the Gains From Coordination." *American Economic Review* 81, 3 (June): 465–79.

Giovannini, Alberto, and James R. Hines, Jr. 1991."Capital Flight and Tax Competition: Are There Viable Solutions to Both Problems?" In *European Financial Integration*, edited by Alberto Giovannini and Colin Mayer. Cambridge: Cambridge University Press.

Giovannini, Alberto, and Colin Mayer. 1991. "Introduction." In *European Financial Integration*, edited by Alberto Giovannini and Colin Mayer. Cambridge: Cambridge University Press.

Goldstein, Morris, Donald J. Mathieson, and Timothy Lane. 1991. *Determinants and Systemic Consequences of International Capital Flows.* Occasional Paper No. 77. Washington, DC: IMF.

Goldwin, Robert A., and William A. Schambra, eds. 1982. *How Capitalistic is the Constitution?* Washington, DC: American Enterprise Institute.

Gomel, G., F. Saccomanni, and S. Vona. 1990. "The Experience with Economic Policy Coordination: The Tripolar and European Dimensions." *Temi di Discussione.* Banca D' Italia. 140. Luglio.

Grundfest, Joseph A. 1990. "Internationalization of the World's Securities Markets: Economic Causes and Regulatory Consequences." *Journal of Financial Services Research* 4, 4 (December): 349–78.

Guitian, Manuel. 1988. "The European Monetary System: A Balance Between Rules and Discretion." In *Policy Coordination in the European Monetary System.* Occasional Paper No. 61 (September). Washington, DC: IMF.

Hansson, Göte. 1990. *Harmonization and International Trade.* New York: Routledge.

Haraf, William S. 1988. "Principle Policy Conclusions and Recommendations of the Financial Services Regulation Project." In *Restructuring Banking and Financial Services in America*, edited by William S. Haraf and Rose Marie Kushmeider. Washington, DC: American Enterprise Institute.

Haraf, William S., and Rose Marie Kushmeider, eds. 1988. *Restructuring Banking and Financial Services in America*. Washington, DC: American Enterprise Institute.

Harriman, Norman F. 1928. *Standards and Standardization*. New York: McGraw-Hill.

Hayek, Friedrich A. 1948. "The Economic Conditions of Interstate Federalism." In *Individualism and Economic Order*. Chicago: Henry Regnery.

Hemenway, David. 1975. *Industrywide Voluntary Product Standards*. Cambridge, MA: Ballinger.

Holtham, Gerald. 1989. "German Macroeconomic Policy and the 1978 Bonn Summit." In *Can Nations Agree?* Washington, DC: Brookings.

Horne, Jocelyn, and Paul R. Masson. 1988. "Scope and Limits of International Economic Cooperation and Policy Coordination." *IMF Staff Papers* 35 (June): 259–96.

Jackson, John H. 1989. *The World Trading System: Law and Policy of International Economic Relations*. Cambridge, MA: MIT Press.

Johnson, Manuel, and Robert E. Keleher. 1992. *Monetary Policy: A Market Price Approach*. Cambridge: Cambridge University Press.

Kaufman, George G., Larry R. Mote, and Harvey Rosenblum. 1984. "Consequences of Deregulation for Commercial Banking." *Staff Memoranda* SM 84-3 (May).

Keleher, Robert E. 1991. "Commodity Prices: Rationale and Evidence as to Their Use as an Indicator for Monetary Policy." unpublished manuscript.

———. 1988. "Price Level Changes and the Adjustment Process Under Fixed Exchange Rates." *CATO Journal* 8, 2 (Fall): 385–92.

———. 1990. "The Use of Market Price Data in the Formulation of Monetary Policy." *Business Economics* 25, 3 (July): 36–40.

Kenen, Peter B. 1990. "The Coordination of Macroeconomic Policies" In *International Policy Coordination and Exchange Rate Fluctuations*, edited by Branson et al. Chicago: University of Chicago Press.

Khoury, Sarkis J. 1990. *The Deregulation of the World Financial Markets*. New York: Quorum Books.

Kindleberger, Charles P. 1988. "Standards as Public, Collective and Private Goods." In *The International Economic Order, Essays on Financial Crisis and International Public Goods*, edited by Kindleberger. Cambridge, MA: MIT Press.

Lal, Deepak. 1990. *The Limits of International Cooperation*. London: Institute of Economic Affairs.

Lepage, Henri. 1989. "Countering the Climate of Growing Protectionism: The Need for Free Trade." In *Towards Free Trade Between Nations*, edited by John Nieuwenhuysen. Oxford: Oxford University Press.

Levin, Jay. 1979. "The International Assignment of Stabilization Problems Under Fixed and Flexible Exchange Rates." *Journal of International Economics* 1.

McDonald, Forrest. 1982. "The Constitution and Hamiltonian Capitalism." In *How Capitalistic Is the Constitution?*, edited by Robert A. Goldwin and William A. Schambra. Washington, DC: American Enterprise Institute.

———. 1985. *Novus Ordo Seclorum: The Intellectual Origins of the Constitution*. Lawrence: University Press of Kansas.

McKibbin, Warwick J., and Jeffrey D. Sachs. 1989. "Implications of Policy Rules for the World Economy." In *Macroeconomic Policies in an Interdependent World*, edited by Bryant et al. Washington, DC: IMF.

McKinnon, Ronald I. 1990. "Interest Rate Volatility and Exchange Risk: New Rules for a Common Monetary Standard." *Contemporary Policy Issues* 8 (April).

McKinnon, Ronald I., and David Robinson. "Dollar Devaluation, Interest Rate Volatility, and the Duration of Investment." In *Economic Growth and the Commercialization of New Technologies*, edited by R. Landau and N. Rosenberg.

McLure, Charles E. 1986. "Tax Competition: Is What's Good for the Private Goose also Good for the Public Gander?" *National Tax Journal* 39: 341–48.

Micossi, Stefano. 1988. "The Single European Market: Finance." *Banca Nazionale Del Lavoro* 165 (June).

Mishkin, Frederic S. 1990. "Financial Innovation and Current Trends in U.S. Financial Markets." Working Paper Series, National Bureau of Economic Research. Working Paper No. 3323 (April).

Mundell, Robert A. 1982. "The Case for a Managed International Gold Standard." In *The International Monetary System: Choices for the Future*, edited by Michael B. Connolly. New York: Praeger.

National Industrial Conference Board. 1929. *Industrial Standardization*. New York: National Industrial Conference Board.

Oates, Wallace E., and Robert M. Schwab. 1988. "Economic Competition Among Jurisdictions: Efficiency Enhancing or Distortion Inducing?" *Journal of Public Economics* 35, 3 (April).

Pelkmans, Jacques. 1990. "Regulation and the Single Market: An Economic Perspective." In *The Competition of the Internal Market*, edited by H. Siebert. Boulder, CO: Westview Press.

———. 1986. "The New Approach to Harmonization and Standardization." In *Cementing the Internal Market*, edited by Rita Beuter and Jacques Pelkmans. Maastricht, The Netherlands: European Institute of Public Administration.

Persson, Torsen, and Guido Tabellini. 1990. "The Politics of 1992: Fiscal Policy and European Integration." NBER Working Paper No. 3460 (October).

Putnam, Robert D., and C. Randall Henning. 1989. "The Bonn Summit of 1978: A Case Study in Coordination." In *Can Nations Agree?* Washington, DC: Brookings.

Razin, Assaf. 1991. "Vanishing Tax on Capital Income on the Open Economy." Seminar paper presented at International Monetary Fund, 6 August.

Razin, Assaf, and Efraim Sadka. 1990. "Capital Market Integration: Issues of International Taxation." NBER Working Paper No. 3821 (March).

———. 1989. "International Tax Competition and Gains From Tax Harmonization." NBER Working Paper No. 3152 (October).

Rogoff, Kenneth. 1985. "Can International Monetary Policy Cooperation Be Counter Productive?" *Journal of International Economics* 18: 199–217.

Russo, Massimo, and Giuseppe Tullio. 1988. "Monetary Coordination Within the European Monetary System: Is there a Rule?" In *Policy Coordination in the European Monetary System*. Occasional Paper No. 61 (September). Washington, DC: IMF.

Salin, Pascal. 1991. "A Single Market Without Tax Harmonization." Paper presented at the Annual Meeting of the European Public Choice Society. Beaune. April.

———. 1990. "Comment on Vito Tanzi and A. Lans Bovenberg, 'Is There a Need for Harmonizing Capital Income Taxes Within EC Countries?'" In *Reforming Capital Income Taxation*, edited by H. Siebert. Boulder, CO: Westview Press.

———. 1989. "The Case Against Tax Harmonization." Report prepared for the Conference on "Global Disequilibrium." Montreal: McGill University. May.

Scitovsky, Tibor. 1954. "Two Concepts of External Economies." *Journal of Political Economy* 62: 70–82.

———. 1950. "Ignorance as a Source of Oligopoly Power" *American Economic Review* 40, 2 (May).

Scott, Kenneth E. 1977. "The Dual Banking System: A Model of Competition in Regulation." *Stanford Law Review* 30, 1 (November): 1–49.

Siebert, Horst, ed. 1990. *The Completion of the Internal Market*. Boulder, CO: Westview Press.

———. 1990. "The Harmonization Issue in Europe: Prior Agreement or a Competitive Process?" In *The Completion of the Internal Market*, edited by H. Siebert. Boulder, CO: Westview Press.

Siebert, Horst, and Michael J. Koop. 1990. "Institutional Competition: A Concept for Europe?" Aussenwirtschaft, 45, Heft IV, Grüsch, Rüegger, S., Jahrgang, 439–62.

Sinn, Hans-Werner. 1990. "Tax Harmonization and Tax Competition in Europe." NBER Working Paper No. 3248 (January).

Sinn, Stefan. 1990a. "Comment on Assaf Razin and Efraim Sadka, 'Capital Market Integration: Issues of International Taxation.'" *Reforming Capital Income Taxation*. Boulder, CO: Westview Press.

———. 1990b. "The Taming of Leviathan: Competition among Governments." Keil Working Papers No. 433 (August). The Keil Institute of World Economics.

Smith, Clifford W., Jr. 1990. "Globalization of Financial Markets." Carnegie-Rochester Public Policy Conference, 20–21 April.

Sohmen, Egon. 1969. "The Assignment Problem." In *The Monetary Problems of the International Economy*, edited by Robert A. Mundell and Alexander K. Swoboda. Chicago: University of Chicago Press.

Soule, George. 1934. "Standardization." In *Encyclopedia of the Social Sciences*. Vol. 14: 319–22. New York: MacMillan.

Swoboda, Alexander K. 1990. "Financial Integration and International Monetary Arrangements." In *The Evolution of the International Monetary System*, edited by Yoshiro Suzuki, Junichi Miyake, and Mitsuake Okabe. Tokyo: University of Tokyo Press.

Tabellini, Guido. 1990. "Domestic Politics and the International Coordination of Fiscal Policies." *Journal of International Economies* 28: 245–65.

Tanzi, Vito, and A. Lans Bovenberg. 1990. "Is There a Need for Harmonizing Capital Income Taxes Within EC Countries?" In *Reforming Capital Income Taxation*, edited by H. Siebert. Boulder, CO: Westview Press.

Taylor, John B. 1989. "Policy Analysis With a Multicountry Model." In *Macroeconomic Policies in an Interdependent World*, edited by Bryant et al. Washington, DC: IMF.

Tiebout, Charles M. 1956. "A Pure Theory of Local Expenditures." *Journal of Political Economy* 64, 5 (October): 416–23.

Vaubel, Roland. 1983. "Coordination or Competition Among National Macroeconomic Policies?" In *Reflections on a Troubled World Economy*, edited by Fritz Machlup, Gerhard Fels, and Hubertus Müller-Groeling. London: Trade Policy Research Centre.

———. 1985. "International Collusion or Competition for Macroeconomic Policy Coordination? A Restatement." *Recherches Economiques de Louvain* 51, 3–4 (Decembre).

Viner, Jacob. 1931. "Cost Curves and Supply Curves." *Zeitschrift für National Ökonomie* 3: 23–46.

Watson, M., R. Kincaid, C. Atkinson, E. Kalter, and D. Folkerts-Landau. 1986. *International Capital Markets, Developments and Prospects*. Washington, DC: IMF.

Wilson, John Douglas. 1987. "Trade, Capital Mobility, and Tax Competition." *Journal of Political Economy* 95, 4 (August).

III

Foundations for Monetary and Banking Reform

10

The Political Economy Of Discretionary Monetary Policy: A Public Choice Analysis Of Proposals For Reform

Richard C. K. Burdekin, Jilleen R. Westbrook and Thomas D. Willett

Elected politicians typically have an incentive to support expansionary policies that boost the incumbent's political standing by temporarily lowering both interest rates and unemployment. However, a great deal of empirical evidence suggests that, over time, higher rates of monetary expansion merely result in higher interest rates and prices without any sustained employment gains. These differences between short-run and long-run economic relationships are crucial to the substantial inflationary bias that has operated in the postwar period. While the 1980s and early 1990s registered considerable progress in reducing inflation in many countries, we cannot safely assume that such restraint will be continued over the coming decades. We feel that there is a need for major institutional reforms to safeguard against the re-emergence of inflationary excesses.

Traditionally, the most popular types of proposed institutional reforms have taken relatively simple forms such as a return to a gold standard or the adoption of a simple Friedman monetary rule. Strong systems of this type often raise substantial problems, however. For example, the development of a balance of payments disequilibrium

An earlier version of this paper was presented at the 1992 meetings of the Western Economic Association in San Francisco, California, 9–13 July. The authors thank Paul Evans, King Banaian, and the editors for helpful comments and suggestions.

under a gold standard or a substantial shift in velocity under a simple monetary rule could subject the domestic economy to substantial inflationary or deflationary pressures. Moreover, even though proposals for more complicated monetary rules or constraint systems are popular in the academic world, such proposals do not appear to have generated much support in public policy circles.

On the other hand, two softer types of institutional reforms—granting greater independence for central banks and using exchange rate pegging as part of anti-inflationary policy strategies—have attracted considerable public interest in recent years. This paper reviews recent experiences with these two approaches and critically evaluates them as possible bases for future monetary reform efforts. Such considerations are quite relevant, not only for reform of the Federal Reserve System in the United States, but also for other countries including the prospective members of an European Monetary Union (EMU), the emerging market-orientated economies of Eastern Europe and the former Soviet Union, and for many developing countries adopting market-based stabilization plans.

Inflationary Biases and Constitutional Rules

Sources of Inflationary Bias

The general trend of macroeconomic research findings over the past decade has been to undermine the case for discretionary national monetary policy making. This, of course, weakens the argument against the adoption of fixed rules for monetary policy. One important aspect of recent research has been the combination of theoretical and empirical analysis that has undercut earlier beliefs that lower unemployment could be bought with higher inflation over the long run—as well as emphasizing the uncertainty costs of higher inflation (Fischer 1993; Burdekin et al. 1994; Barro 1995; Burdekin, Salamun, and Willett 1995). While the strongest version of new classical economic theory went further in arguing that monetary policy would be ineffective even in the short run, the latest generation of empirical studies suggests that changes in monetary policies typically still have significant real effects on economic variables, at least over the shorter term.

Much stronger than the case against discretionary national monetary policy making made by the policy ineffectiveness theories of the New Classical school is the critique developed in recent years from a public choice perspective. The argument here is not that policy is ineffective, but that substantial pressures exist that make it difficult for monetary authorities to pursue sensible long-run economic goals. The short time horizon that pervades the political process creates pressures for short-run maximization that often run counter to the requirements for promoting long-run economic stability—and efforts to hold interest rates and unemployment rates below sustainable levels are often considered to be a particularly important source of inflation and macroeconomic instability (Willett 1988; Mayer 1990).

The evidence of politically-induced inflationary biases is not completely airtight. Reasonable people can differ about its importance; but our own research and reading of the literature convinces us that these biases pose a major problem. While public reactions to the rampant inflationary excesses of the 1970s have constrained such political tendencies in recent years, there is a substantial danger of their reemergence in the future. In particular, to the extent that politicians trade off the short-run benefits of inflation against the long-run costs, it remains likely that, as the onset of recession and rising unemployment raises the benefits of surprise inflation, there will be mounting pressure for faster rates of monetary expansion. The weakening of the U.S. economy at the beginning of the 1990s is a case in point. Following repeated urging by Treasury Secretary Nicholas Brady and Bush's chief economic adviser, Michael Boskin, successive interest rate reductions by the Federal Reserve pushed the discount rate down to 3 percent by July 1992, down from 7 percent in 1990 and below the level reached during the 1973 energy crisis.[1]

Certainly, it is difficult to argue with Bernholz's (1986, 477) characterization that the "present age of discretionary monetary policies, which began in 1914, has turned out to be an age of permanent inflation. Inflation rates have ranged from low and moderate to hyperinflationary, but have scarcely anywhere and mainly only during the Great Depression been absent." However, there is considerable disagreement as to what can, or should, be done to rectify this situation.

Problems with Simple Rules

The two most popular types of proposals for new monetary institutions have been a return to a gold standard or the adoption of a constant growth rate rule for the domestic money supply. Unfortunately, however, all such institutional rules that would be tight enough to make a major contribution toward restraining inflationary biases typically run a serious risk of restricting the economy's ability to adjust to exogenous shocks. For example, the maintenance of a rigid zero inflation rule would require the monetary authority to *reduce* the rate of monetary expansion in the face of a negative supply shock, thereby exacerbating the adverse effects on output and employment levels. As argued by Mayer and Willett (1988), all these proposals for simple and easily enforceable monetary constitutions also rest on quite strong assumptions about the stability of particular sets of demand and supply curves in the economy and the instability of others. Thus, arguments for systems based on fixed exchange rates tend to assume stability in demand and supply in the foreign exchange market but variability in the demand for and supply of money, while Milton Friedman's case for a fixed rate of money growth and flexible exchange rates rests on just the opposite set of assumptions.[2]

In principle, we do not believe it is wise to adopt constitutional-type proposals that rely on the correctness of any particular set of economic assumptions that are the subject of serious debate among leading economic scholars. The empirical evidence suggests that over the time frames relevant for constitutional-type analysis, there will be significant demand and/or supply shifts in all of the relevant markets. Thus, while we believe that there is a need for new constitutional-type arrangements to constrain inflationary biases, none of the most popular strong proposals for such arrangements seems very satisfactory (cf. Neumann 1991a).

Various refinements to meet these problems have been proposed, but all share the problem of being more complicated and hence less politically salable. Representative proposals include those of Meltzer (1984), which allows for a response to trend changes in velocity; McCallum (1987), whose "rule" also allows for a response to trend changes in output; and Willett (1987), who proposes a two-part rule approach. Each of these proposals remains subject to the trade-off between the gains from increased flexibility and the danger that "permitting amendments opens the Pandora-box of policy abuse" (Neumann 1991b, 182).[3]

This judgment raises a second type of problem, one that has been too little emphasized in the recent literature on the political economy of monetary constitutions—although Kane (1982, 1988) remains an important exception. While public choice or political economy analysis explains the need for institutions to restrain inflationary biases, the same logic suggests that there will likely be considerable political and bureaucratic opposition to the adoption of such reforms. Of course, we observe enough desirable constitutional reforms to know that the task is not always impossible; but the study of the political economy of substantive constitutional reforms suggests that combinations of conditions which make such reforms feasible are not common occurrences. Typically, underlying developments must generate sufficient demand for reform from political leaders and/or the general public; and, to be effective over the longer term, the reforms must have sufficient teeth to change significantly the constraints (or incentives) that affect bureaucratic and political actions after the initial period of high intensity outside monitoring has passed (Goodman 1991).

Other Strategies for Overcoming Inflationary Biases

Recently, the debate on constitutional reform has shifted in the direction of redefining the goals of monetary policy without requiring the drastic revision in operating procedures required by the approaches discussed above. In the United States, Representative Stephen L. Neal proposed legislation in 1989 (introduced as H.J. Res. 409) that would instruct the Federal Reserve to lower the inflation rate to zero within five years. While this bill ultimately "died" in the House, it generated quite widespread support within the Federal Reserve System (see, for example, Black 1990; Hoskins 1991). Detractors, however, argued that such a policy would impose considerable transition costs. Moreover, implementation of alternative—and less costly—policy measures, such as deregulating interest rates on commercial demand deposits, could reduce the potential welfare gains from the zero-inflation rule (Aiyagiri 1990, 1991). In general, different judgments about the benefits of eliminating the uncertainty surrounding future central bank policy and future inflation rates continue to support diametrically opposed viewpoints on this question. Similar debate was ignited in Canada by Bank of Canada Governor John Crow's 1988 announcement that the primary objective of Canadian monetary policy was to be the attainment of price-level stability (Freedman 1991; Siklos 1997).

While neither the United States nor Canada has yet taken any concrete steps towards a mandatory zero inflation objective, New Zealand in 1990 became the first country to impose a legally binding operational commitment to price stability on its central bank. Under Section 8 of the *Reserve Bank of New Zealand Act 1989*, which took effect in

February 1990, the "primary function of the Bank is to formulate and implement monetary policy directed to the economic objective of achieving and maintaining stability in the general level of prices." The initial Policy Targets Agreement, signed by the Minister of Finance and the Governor of the Reserve Bank, committed the Reserve Bank to attaining price stability—as reflected in annual increases in the Consumer Price Index (CPI) that are restricted to the 0–2 percent range— by the end of 1993.[4]

The renewed emphasis on anti-inflation policies in the 1980s under the European Monetary System (EMS) has also focused attention on the monetary discipline required of member central banks. In particular, there have been growing demands for greater central bank independence from politically-responsive government policy. For example, in Italy in 1981 steps were taken to reduce the influence of fiscal deficits on monetary policy (Epstein and Schor 1989). Moreover, it has been agreed in the Maastricht Treaty that the new European currency under EMU is to be managed by a central bank designed to have a good deal of political independence—with price stability as its primary goal. Concern with establishing an independent central bank has also characterized much of the discussion of central bank reform in Eastern Europe and the former Soviet Union (Willett et al. 1995).

Another type of monetary policy regime that has received considerable attention is the use of exchange rate pegging as part of an anti-inflation strategy. The success of the members of the EMS in achieving lower inflation rates over the 1980s had a substantial impact on public perceptions of the possible advantages of exchange-rate pegging. In the academic community theoretical developments in the analysis of credibility have reinforced this interest in exchange-rate pegging as an anti-inflationary commitment device. The use of exchange-rate pegging has also been a major ingredient of stabilization efforts in many developing countries and some Eastern European countries.

Both central bank independence and exchange-rate pegging strategies have had their critics. In the United States there have been periodic attempts by Members of Congress to reduce the independence of the Federal Reserve. Such efforts have received support from a number of leading academic economists spanning the political spectrum from Milton Friedman to Lester Thurow. Likewise, many economists have warned that excessive use of exchange-rate pegging could recreate the types of distortions that led to the breakdown of the Bretton Woods regime of adjustable pegged exchange rates. Similarly, it has been suggested that the anti-inflation properties of the EMS have been substantially exaggerated (see, for example, Fratianni and von Hagen 1990, 1992).

In the following sections, we critically evaluate these two approaches to reducing the inflationary bias of discretionary monetary policy.

Exchange-Rate Pegging

Fixed exchange rates are often advocated as an anti-inflationary device that constrains a country's ability to inflate. In the absence of capital controls, any attempt to increase the domestic inflation rate above the inflation rate prevailing in the other member countries will result in a loss of reserves that forces the inflation rate back down. Recognition of this constraint mechanism would in turn discipline wage demands and make noninflationary monetary policy easier to develop. The much higher inflation rates in the decade following the break-down of the Bretton Woods pegged rate system, as compared with the preceding decade, are often cited as evidence of this discipline argument (Barro 1982).

Modern analysis suggests, however, that the issue is not so clear-cut. One must distinguish between temporarily pegged and more permanently fixed exchange rates and consider the mechanics by which monetary policies react to balance of payments developments. One must also examine the determination of the growth of aggregate monetary expansion. For example, while the dollar retained some aspects of gold convertibility until 1971, developments in U.S. gold holdings played little if any role in the determinants of the U.S. money supply during the postwar period. Nor for that matter did the U.S. balance of payments.[5] Indeed, the pressures that led to the acceleration of worldwide inflation during the 1970s developed under the pegged exchange rates of the 1960s.

More recent analysis of the impact of the exchange rate regime on the costs and benefits of inflation has focused on credibility, or reputational, effects. The successful anti-inflation programs of members of the EMS during the 1980s contributed to the popularity of the argument that, by tying one's hands through the adoption of pegged exchange rates, governments would enjoy credibility gains, thereby shifting short-run inflation-unemployment relationships in a favorable manner and reducing the cost of disinflation. The empirical evidence for such credibility effects is weak at best, however. The industrial

countries outside of the EMS disinflated at least as successfully as the
EMS members and often seemed to enjoy reduced unemployment costs
(Collins 1988; De Grauwe 1989; Fratianni and von Hagen 1990).
Disinflation also generally proceeded at a more rapid pace outside of
the EMS. This latter result may be due in part to the role of exchange
rate appreciation in lowering import prices and hence speeding up the
decline in inflation (Arndt, Sweeney, and Willett 1985).

Giavazzi and Pagano (1988) have propounded the view that the EMS
had an anti-inflationary effect through increasing the cost of generating inflationary surprises. However, during the early days of the EMS,
parity adjustments were fairly frequent; and it is very doubtful that
these adjustments were entirely unanticipated at the time. Even though
devaluations became less frequent as the idea of "one Europe" increased
in popularity during the late 1980s, the behavior of interest rates suggested that the pegs between many of the EMS countries *still* fell short
of being completely credible (Giovannini 1990; Weber 1991).

Given that government announcements of anti-inflationary policy
intentions have often not been realized, it would be surprising if markets were not skeptical of policy strategies that depend on the
government's willingness to incur substantial costs in the future (e.g.,
to defend fixed parities). At the very least, the success of exchange rate
pegging is likely to be tied to the specific economic and political conditions in those countries. (See Burdekin, Westbrook and Willett 1994,
for some empirical evidence on the impact of political events on the
credibility of the peg among the EMS countries.)

Moreover, the credibility of an announced policy of defending a
particular parity should be greater, the lower are the costs of defending
the parity, and the greater are the costs of abandoning the parity. Some
of these costs may be purely political. For example, it seems likely that
the foreign policy cost of a parity adjustment by an EMS country is
considerably higher today than it was a decade ago. Standard economic
considerations are also likely to matter. The theory of optimum currency areas implies that the most crucial criteria for currency union are
size and openness (Tower and Willett 1976). Generally, the smaller the
economy, the less likely it is to support a viable independent currency
of its own. While some of the traditional optimum currency area analysis
was based on simple Keynesian models which do not appear relevant
to modern analysis, these major conclusions still hold over a wide set
of models (Wihlborg and Willett 1991).

An attractive option for countries with small open economies who
wish to enjoy the benefits of credible fixed exchange rates without

giving up the seigniorage from local currency issues is the adoption of a currency board that allows expansion of domestic currency only to the extent that the board has 100 percent backing in the form of foreign exchange reserves. Estonia adopted such a regime in 1992. Some recent advocates have been unaware of the theory of optimum currency areas, however, and have advocated currency boards for large as well as small countries (see Hanke and Schuler 1991; Hanke, Jonung and Schuler 1993).

Pegged rates have recently become popular not only in Western Europe but also amongst the developing economies of Latin America and the newly market-orientated economies of Central and Eastern Europe. The experiences of the countries that have adopted exchange-rate pegs is by no means universally favorable, however. While countries such as Bolivia and (until 1994) Mexico appear to have successfully used a dollar exchange-rate peg as part of their stabilization packages, similar measures adopted in 1979 in Chile failed to eliminate the inflationary trend. Furthermore, the exchange-rate pegs adopted by Poland and the former Yugoslavia led to substantial appreciations of the real exchange rate that hurt international competitiveness. By mid-1991 Yugoslavia had abandoned the fixed rate, and Poland had devalued the zloty by about 17 percent and switched from a dollar peg to a currency basket (Kolodko, Gotz-Kozierkiewicz, and Skrzeszewska-Paczek 1992; Burdekin, Nelson, and Willett 1997).

Such experiences certainly lend little support to the view that exchange-rate pegging *alone* can stop or prevent inflation. Pegging the exchange rate is, after all, a price control measure that treats the symptom, rather than the cause, of inflation.[6] If other fundamental features of the economy such as large budget deficits and other pressures for monetary expansion remain unchanged, the inflationary pressure will, at best, be only temporarily suppressed. Indeed, Edwards' (1991) comparison of the Mexican and Chilean stabilization attempts suggests that breaking inflationary inertia requires: (1) fiscal discipline or reform; (2) price liberalization or monetary reform; and (3) ending the indexation of contracts—particularly labor-market contracts—to inflation, since backward indexation leads to inertia. The Mexican reform process included all three of these components, as well as anchoring the peso to the dollar, while the Chilean exchange-rate-based reform only included the first two.[7]

Where a reasonable level of the exchange rate can be chosen and there are no major real shocks that shift equilibrium real exchange rates, then exchange-rate pegging may be an attractive option. Where either of these considerations fails to be met, however, pegging efforts may generate financial instability and/or severe economic hardships for the domestic economy. This suggests that a pegging strategy is particularly problematic for high-inflation countries attempting to disinflate because it would be extremely difficult to forecast the level of the equilibrium exchange rate at which domestic prices would become stabilized. If set too high, the resulting overvalued currency would likely stimulate speculative runs on the currency. On the other hand, if one errs on the side of making sure that the domestic currency is undervalued, the resulting balance of payments surplus could force domestic monetary expansion and provoke inflation. Some have argued that this describes the case of Poland's initial large devaluation.

Even when domestic inflation is relatively low, real shocks may put huge strains on pegged exchange rate regimes. The 1992 crisis in the EMS, which resulted in Italy, Spain, and the United Kingdom being forced to allow their currencies to depreciate, is a case in point. Indeed, Italy and the United Kingdom were forced out of the exchange rate system in September 1992, when intervention by their respective central banks proved unable to staunch the massive speculation against the lira and the pound sterling at the time.

For these reasons, exchange-rate pegging is not a good general strategy. A better approach, we believe, is to focus on adopting monetary constitutions that give central banks the *incentive* to deliver a monetary policy consistent with price stability. That is, rather than relying on a rigid rule that is unlikely to fit even the briefest range of future contingencies, Germany and Switzerland allow their central banks discretion to adjust the particular operating strategies used in pursuing the goal of price stability. The absence of a firm exchange rate target certainly has not prevented Switzerland from enjoying one of the lowest inflation rates in the post-Bretton Woods era. Indeed, the inflation performance of Switzerland was demonstrably better during the post-1973 floating exchange rate period than it was in last five years of the Bretton Woods system.[8] Moreover, while a ranking of countries according to the degree of fixity of their exchange rates would encompass an enormous range in inflation performance at each level, we show below that a ranking by degree of central bank independence reveals a striking correlation with the respective countries' inflation record. Even though exchange rate management may be a fruitful tool in guiding the transition to a stable price environment, we should not lose sight of the fact that it is only a tool, not an end in itself.

Central Bank Independence

A major theme of recent research on U.S. monetary policy has been the role that political pressures play in the behavior of the "independent" Federal Reserve (Willett 1988; Mayer 1990). While this literature by itself would seem to reduce the attractiveness of central bank independence as a bulwark against inflationary pressures, a number of comparative studies have presented strong evidence that increased central bank independence is consistently associated with lower inflation rates. This literature also suggests that there are a number of important dimensions to central bank independence. On the basis of comparative institutional analysis, the Federal Reserve is not as independent as the German or Swiss central banks; and this is reflected in comparative inflation rates. The United States has recorded inflation rates well below the average of industrial countries—most of whom have dependent central banks—but has typically had inflation rates higher than Germany and Switzerland. The implication is that the United States, as well as most other countries, might stand to benefit from increasing the degree of central bank independence.

In a well-known effort to rank central banks according to their degree of legal independence, Parkin and Bade (1978) distinguish Germany, Switzerland, and the United States as countries where the central bank has the statutory right to formulate monetary policy without any provision for direct government override. Within this class of "independent" central banks, Germany and Switzerland are ranked ahead of the United States because of the reduced role played by the government in appointing members of the bank's governing body in the former two countries.[9]

Subsequent rankings of central bank independence have generally supported the autonomous position of the German, Swiss, and U.S. central banks (see, for example, Epstein and Schor 1986; Grilli, Masciandaro, and Tabellini 1991).[10] In Burdekin and Willett (1991) we do, however, argue that a strong case can also be made for viewing Austria as possessing an independent central bank based on the Austrian National Bank's freedom from government veto power coupled with the fact that a significant minority of the bank's policy board are nongovernment appointees (see also Hochreiter, 1990). As shown in table 10.1, our ranking of central banks has Germany and Switzerland at the top because of their high degree of independence both in policy formulation and in the appointment of top officials, while Austria and

TABLE 10.1
Central Bank Independence and Inflation

Country	Institutional Features			Inflation Record		
	Statutory Policy Independence	Proportion of Government Appointees on Policy Board	Legislated Objectives	Overall Ranking (3 point scale)[a]	Average Inflation Rate 1960–89	Inflation Variability 1960–89
Australia	No	100 percent	P/X/E	1	6.9 percent	17.5 percent
Belgium	No	100 percent	—	1	4.9	10.2
Canada	No	100 percent	P/X/E	1	5.5	11.1
France	No	12/13	—	1	6.7	13.5
Italy	No	100 percent	—	1	9.1	36.7
Japan	No	100 percent	—	1	5.7	19.8
Netherlands	No	100 percent	P/X	1	4.7	8.4
New Zealand	No	100 percent	P[b]	1	8.9	28.3
Sweden	No	100 percent	—	1	6.8	9.4
United Kingdom	No	100 percent	—	1	7.9	31.0
Average: Category 1	—	—	—	—	6.7	18.6
Austria	Yes	8/14	P/X	2	4.4	4.4
United States	Yes	7/12	P/E/R[c]	2	5.0	11.0
Average: Category 2	—	—	—	—	4.7	7.7
Germany	Yes	10/21	P	3	3.8	5.1
Switzerland	Yes	2/10	P/X/E	3	3.4	3.6
Average: Category 3	—	—	—	—	3.6	4.4

Key: P = Price stability objective; X = Exchange rate objective
E = Full employment objective; R = Interest rate objective
Notes: a The higher the score, the higher the degree of independence
b In effect only from February 1, 1990 (1989 Reserve Bank of New Zealand Act).
c Objectives stipulated in the 1977 Federal Reserve Reform Act. Previously, the System had been required simply to "furnish an elastic currency."

the United States are placed in a second category.[11] The central banks of the remaining countries are classified as being politically dependent on government.

The ordering of central banks in table 10.1 receives support from the recent classification provided by Cukierman, Webb, and Neyapti (1992). Their ranking of central banks by average legal independence has Germany, Switzerland, Austria, and the United States ranked first, second, third, and fifth, respectively. (Denmark, which is not included in our sample, is ranked fourth—narrowly ahead of the United States.) Moreover, the inflation record of the fourteen countries listed in table 10.1 affirms the link between central bank autonomy and price stability for the industrialized nations (see also Banaian, Laney, and Willett 1983; Alesina 1988; Banaian et al. 1988; Burdekin and Laney 1988; Cukierman, Webb, and Neyapti 1992; Havrilesky and Granato 1993; Banaian, Burdekin, and Willett 1995).[12] Over the 1960–89 period, inflation (as measured by the rate of growth of consumer prices) averages 3.6 percent in Germany and Switzerland, while inflation in Austria and the United States averages 4.7 percent, and the other ten countries with more politically dependent central banks average 6.7 percent. Inflation variability is also higher for the less independent central banks, ranging from 4.4 percent for Germany and Switzerland to 18.6 percent for the ten non-independent central banks.[13]

Inspection of the list of mandated central bank policy objectives in table 10.1 further reveals that, while all independent central banks have an official price stability objective, the existence of this objective has not, for example, prevented Australia from experiencing one of the highest inflation rates in the sample at 6.9 percent. Thus, merely having a price stability objective "on the books" does not seem to confer any guarantee that price stability will actually be achieved—particularly where the price stability objective is specified only as one of several competing goals. Prior to the 1989 Act, for example, the Reserve Bank of New Zealand was called upon to promote the highest level of production and trade and full employment, as well as to maintain a stable price level! Archer's (1992, 7–8) critique of these arrangements may have relevance for other nations as well:

> "No attention was paid in the legislative framework to relative priorities amongst these objectives; to the coordination of multiple instruments wielded by the range of government agencies accorded overlapping objective sets; to the implications of non-trivial information costs for the optimal design of policy; or to the establishment of an accountability framework that focused the attention of individual bureaucrats."

At the same time, New Zealand has now become a highly valuable testing ground within which to gauge the impact of a clearly defined price stability goal that is backed up by some political muscle. It is still too early to judge whether the 1989 Act will permanently free the Reserve Bank from the political pressures lying behind the high inflation rates previously experienced in New Zealand. Nevertheless, the initial results have been promising, and the annual CPI inflation rate actually fell below 1 percent in the first quarter of 1992 as compared to 7.6 percent in June 1990.

Certainly, the New Zealand case should continue to receive attention as an important constitutional experiment. The combination of a firm "bottom line" coupled with flexibility in how to meet the mandated target perhaps also bears comparison with Leijonhufvud's proposal that Congress should legislate a maximum rate of monetary base growth (Leijonhufvud 1986, 42). Under this rule, "while the authorities would retain short-term discretion as long as they are below the ceiling, the possibility that U.S. monetary policy might come to follow a long sequence of predominantly inflationary moves is eliminated." However, as with the zero inflation rule, there remains the problem of both setting an appropriate tolerance range and monitoring the central bank's compliance.

We take the view that, at a minimum, such rules can only succeed if they are part of a widespread change in the relationship between dependent central banks and their governments. That is, the government must cede its power to manipulate the money supply through the central bank in a manner that is seen as being hard, if not impossible, to reverse. The New Zealand case seems to fit these requirements, at least to the extent that any shift from the price stability objective by the government would require a formal Order in Council that would have to be published and laid before Parliament (*Reserve Bank of New Zealand Act 1989*, 8–9). Thus, any deviation in policy would be immediately apparent, thereby reducing the likelihood of such a reversal occurring.

In addition to the role of clearly specified and enforceable inflation targets, recent literature on reform of the Federal Reserve and the design of an independent central bank for the proposed EMU has suggested a number of possible institutional arrangements that could contribute to greater central bank independence. Noticing the tendency for regional bank presidents to take stronger anti-inflationary stands than members of the Federal Reserve Board in the United States, Burdekin and Willett (1991) have proposed that all regional bank presidents be given votes on the Federal Open Market Committee, thus placing them in a majority. Other suggestions have included the establishment of longer terms for central bank policy makers and removal of the possibility of reappointment as methods of reducing susceptibility to political pressures (see the analysis and references in Neumann

1991a; and Fratianni and von Hagen 1992). We believe that such proposals deserve careful consideration.

Conclusion

We have argued that political pressures generate powerful incentives for inflation. There is a strong case for the adoption of institutional arrangements designed to counter such pressures. Unfortunately, the most commonly discussed types of reform, such as the return to a gold standard or the adoption of a simple money growth rule appear problematic in all but the most special cases.

In recent years two other options—exchange-rate pegging and the creation of greater central bank independence—have attracted increased attention. Most of our paper has been devoted to the evaluation of these options. We find that the prospective credibility effects of exchange-rate pegging has been substantially exaggerated in much of the recent literature. We conclude that, while exchange-rate pegging may be a useful complement to domestic policy measures as part of an anti-inflationary strategy, exchange-rate pegging by itself is unlikely to have a sustained impact on a nation's inflation performance. There appears to be much stronger evidence in favor of central bank independence. Thus, even for countries for which exchange rate pegging may be sensible, the introduction of substantial central bank independence would, at the very least, be a useful complement.

It is true that simple comparisons of the differences in inflation rates between countries classified as having dependent versus independent central banks almost certainly overstate the likely benefits of transferring institutional arrangements from one country to another. After all, the factors that led countries like Germany and Switzerland to adopt independent central banks are also likely to have contributed to lower propensities to inflate under a wide range of institutional arrangements. Institutions do matter, however. In our judgement, the analysis of various possible institutional innovations to help protect central bankers from political pressures and increase their incentives to achieve price stability should be at the top of the research agenda for monetary reformers.

Notes

1. The discount rate was eventually raised in 1994 in the face of strong economic growth. Long-term interest rates remained relatively high, perhaps reflecting continuing fears about future inflation performance.

2. The two sets of proposals also differ in the sense that fixed exchange rates only offer a target for monetary policy through fixing a single relative price, while the Friedman money growth rule is itself a policy.

3. See Judd and Motley (1991) for an assessment of the empirical performance of nominal feedback rules. A useful critique of the merits of such rules is provided by Phelps (1991).

4. Inflation was already in the required range by the first quarter of 1992.

5. For empirical evidence on these issues, see Briggs et al. (1988).

6. Unless the country in question is very small and the rate of inflation is effectively determined by the price of foreign goods (as with Luxembourg, for example).

7. See Bruno (1991) for further analysis of the efficacy of exchange-rate pegging by high-inflation countries. Note, however, that even the Mexican peg could not be sustained after 1994, collapsing amidst non-sustainable real exchange rate appreciation and loss of reserves.

8. While the Swiss National Bank continued to react to movements in the exchange rate between the Swiss franc and Deutsche mark, the freedom from the constraints imposed by the Bretton Woods regime enabled the authorities to focus more directly on the price stability objective (see Burdekin 1987, for further details of the Swiss case).

9. Although Bade and Parkin (1987) later added Japan to the group of countries they considered to possess statutorily independent central banks, this reclassification hardly seems appropriate given that Article 47 of the Bank of Japan Law empowers the government to summarily dismiss the central bank governors. See Burdekin and Willett (1991, 626–29) for additional discussion of the Japanese case.

10. Grilli, Masciandaro, and Tabellini (1991) also classify Canada and the Netherlands as countries possessing politically autonomous central banks. But these cases are vulnerable to the criticism that in each one there is explicit provision for the minister of finance to issue directives to the bank (on this point, see Burdekin, Wihlborg, and Willett 1992).

11. The distinction between categories 2 and 3 lies in the government's ability to appoint a majority of the bank's governing board in the "category 2 countries" of Austria and the United States. In Germany and Switzerland only a minority of the governing board are direct government appointees. (See Burdekin and Willett 1991, for further details of the data used to compile Table 10.1.)

12. An important element in achieving any such long-run reductions in the rate of inflation concerns the central bank's ability to resist pressures to monetize government budget deficits. For extended analysis on this topic, see Burdekin and Wohar (1990) and Burdekin and Langdana (1992).

13. At the same time, the superior inflation performance of the more autonomous central banks has not come at the expense of lower rates of economic growth (Grilli, Masciandaro, and Tabellini 1991; Alesina and Summers 1993).

References

Aiyagiri, S. Rao. 1990. "Deflating the Case for Zero Inflation." *Federal Reserve Bank of Minneapolis Quarterly Review* 14 (Summer): 2–11.

———. 1991. "Response to a Defense of Zero Inflation." *Federal Reserve Bank of Minneapolis Quarterly Review* 15 (Spring): 21–24.

Alesina, Alberto. 1988. "Macroeconomics and Politics." In *NBER Macroeconomics Annual 1988*, edited by Stanley Fischer. Cambridge, MA: MIT Press.

Alesina, Alberto, and Lawrence H. Summers. 1993. "Central Bank Independence and Macroeconomic Performance: Some Comparative Evidence." *Journal of Money, Credit, and Banking* 25 (May): 151–62.

Archer, David J. 1992. "Organizing a Central Bank to Control Inflation: The Case of New Zealand." Paper presented at the 1992 meetings of the Western Economic Association in San Francisco, California, 9–13 July.

Arndt, Sven W., Richard J. Sweeney, and Thomas D. Willett. 1985. *Exchange Rates, Trade and the U.S. Economy*. Cambridge, MA: Ballinger Publishing Company.

Bade, Robin, and Michael Parkin. 1987. "Central Bank Laws and Monetary Policy." Mimeo, Department of Economics, University of Western Ontario.

Banaian, King, Richard C.K. Burdekin, and Thomas D. Willett. 1995. "On the Political Economy of Central Bank Independence." In *Monetarism and the Methodology of Economics: Essays in Honour of Thomas Mayer*, edited by Kevin D. Hoover and Steven M. Sheffrin. Brookfield, VT: Edward Elgar.

Banaian, King, Leroy O. Laney, and Thomas D. Willett. 1983. "Central Bank Independence: An International Comparison." *Economic Review*. March: 1–13. Dallas: Federal Reserve Bank of Dallas.

Banaian, King, Leroy O. Laney, John McArthur, and Thomas D. Willett. 1988. "Subordinating the Fed to Political Authorities Will Not Control Inflationary Tendencies." In *Political Business Cycles*, edited by Thomas D. Willett. Durham, NC: Duke University Press.

Barro, Robert J. 1982. "United States Inflation and the Choice of Monetary Standard." In *Inflation: Causes and Effects*, edited by Robert E. Hall. Chicago: University of Chicago Press.

———. 1995. "Inflation and Economic Growth." *Bank of England Quarterly Bulletin* 35 (May): 166–76.

Bernholz, Peter. 1986. "The Implementation and Maintenance of a Monetary Constitution." *Cato Journal* 6 (Fall): 477–511.

Black, Robert P. 1990. "In Support of Price Stability." *Economic Review* 76 (January/February): 3–6. Richmond: Federal Reserve Bank of Richmond.

Briggs, John, D. B. Christensen, Pamela Martin, and Thomas D. Willett. 1988. "The Decline of Gold as a Source of U.S. Monetary Discipline." In *Political Business Cycles*, edited by Thomas D. Willett. Durham, NC: Duke University Press

Bruno, Michael. 1991. "High Inflation and the Nominal Anchors of an Open Economy." *Essays in International Finance* 183 (June). Princeton, NJ: Princeton University Press.

Burdekin, Richard C. K. 1987. "Swiss Monetary Policy: Central Bank Independence and Stabilization Goals." *Kredit und Kapital* 20: 454–66.

Burdekin, Richard C. K., and Leroy O. Laney. 1988. "Fiscal Policymaking and the Central Bank Institutional Constraint." *Kyklos* 41: 647–62.

Burdekin, Richard C. K., and Farrokh K. Langdana. 1992. *Budget Deficits and Economic Performance*. London: Routledge.

Burdekin, Richard C. K., and Thomas D. Willett. 1991. "Central Bank Reform: The Federal Reserve in International Perspective." *Public Budgeting and Financial Management* 3: 619–49.

Burdekin, Richard C. K., and Mark E. Wohar. 1990. "Monetary Institutions, Budget Deficits and Inflation: Empirical Results for Eight Countries." *European Journal of Political Economy* 6: 531–51.

Burdekin, Richard C.K., Heidi Nelson, and Thomas D. Willett. 1997. "Central European Exchange Rate Policy and Inflation." In *Exchange Rate Policies for Emerging Market Economies*, edited by Richard J. Sweeney, Clas Wihlborg, and Thomas J. Willett. Boulder, CO: Westview Press.

Burdekin, Richard C. K., Suyono Salamun, and Thomas D. Willett. 1995. "The High Costs of Monetary Instability." In *Establishing Monetary Stability in Emerging Market Economies,* edited by Thomas D. Willett, Richard C. K. Burdekin, Richard J. Sweeney, and Clas Wihlborg. Boulder, CO: Westview Press.

Burdekin, Richard C. K., Jilleen R. Westbrook, and Thomas D. Willett. 1994. "Exchange Rate Pegging as a Disinflation Strategy: Evidence from the European Monetary System." In *Varieties of Monetary Reforms: Lessons and Experiences on the Road to Monetary Union,* edited by Pierre L. Siklos. Boston: Kluwer Academic Publishers.

Burdekin, Richard C. K., Clas G. Wihlborg, and Thomas D. Willett. 1992. "A Monetary Constitution Case for an Independent European Central Bank." *World Economy* 15 (March): 231–49.

Burdekin, Richard C. K., Thomas Goodwin, Suyono Salamun, and Thomas D. Willett. 1994. "The Effects of Inflation on Economic Growth in Industrial and Developing Countries: Is There a Difference?" *Applied Economics Letters* 1 (October): 175–77.

Collins, Susan M. 1988. "Inflation and the European Monetary System." In *The European Monetary System,* edited by Francesco Giavazzi et al. New York: Cambridge University Press.

Cukierman, Alex, Steven B. Webb, and Bilin Neyapti. 1992. "Measuring the Independence of Central Banks and Its Effect on Policy Outcomes." *World Bank Economic Review* 6 (September): 353–98.

De Grauwe, Paul. 1989. "Disinflation in the EMS and in the Non-EMS Countries. What Have We Learned?" *Empirica* 16: 161–76.

Edwards, Sebastian. 1991. "Stabilization and Liberalization Policies in Central and Eastern Europe: Lessons from Latin America." Working Paper prepared for the IRIS-IPR conference on Eastern European Reform, Prague, Czechoslovakia, 24–26 March.

Epstein, Gerald A., and Juliet B. Schor. 1986. "The Political Economy of Central Banking." Discussion Paper No. 1281 (July). Harvard Institute of Economic Research.

———. 1989. "The Divorce of the Banca d'Italia and the Italian Treasury: A Case Study of Central Bank Independence." In *State, Market, and Social Regulation: New Perspectives on Italy,* edited by Peter Lange and Marino Regini. New York: Cambridge University Press.

Fischer, Stanley. 1993. "The Role of Macroeconomic Factors in Growth." *Journal of Monetary Economics* 32 (December): 485–512.

Fratianni, Michele, and Jürgen von Hagen. 1990. "The European Monetary System Ten Years After." *Carnegie-Rochester Conference Series on Public Policy* 32 (Spring): 173–241.

———. 1992. *The European Monetary System and European Monetary Union.* Boulder, CO: Westview Press.

Freedman, Charles. 1991. "The Goal of Price Stability: The Debate in Canada." *Journal of Money, Credit, and Banking* 23 (August): 613–18.

Giavazzi, Francesco, and Marco Pagano. 1988. "The Advantage of Tying One's Hands: EMS Discipline and Central Bank Credibility." *European Economic Review* 32 (June): 1055–82.

Giovannini, Alberto. 1990. "European Monetary Reform: Progress and Prospects." *Brookings Papers on Economic Activity* No. 2: 217–91.

Goodman, John B. 1991. "The Politics of Central Bank Independence." *Comparative Politics* 23 (April): 329–49.

Grilli, Vittorio, Donato Masciandaro, and Guido Tabellini. 1991. "Political and Monetary Institutions and Public Financial Policies in the Industrial Countries." *Economic Policy* 13 (October): 341–92.

Hanke, Steve H., and Kurt Schuler. 1991. "Ruble Reform: A Lesson from Keynes." *Cato Journal* 10 (Winter): 655–66.

Hanke, Steve H., Lars Jonung, and Kurt Schuler. 1993. *Russian Currency and Finance: A Currency Board Approach to Reform.* London: Routledge.

Havrilesky, Thomas, and James Granato. 1993. "Determinants of Inflationary Performance: Corporatist Structures vs. Central Bank Autonomy." *Public Choice* 76 (July): 249–61.

Hochreiter, Eduard. 1990. "The Austrian National Bank Act: What Does It Say About Monetary Policy?" *Konjunkturpolitik* 36: 245–56.

Hoskins, W. Lee. 1991. "Defending Zero Inflation: All for Naught." *Federal Reserve Bank of Minneapolis Quarterly Review* 15 (Spring): 16–20.

Judd, John P., and Brian Motley. 1991. "Nominal Feedback Rules for Monetary Policy." *Economic Review.* Summer: 3–17. San Francisco: Federal Reserve Bank of San Francisco.

Kane, Edward J. 1982. "External Pressure and the Operations of the Fed." In *Political Economy of International and Domestic Monetary Relations*, edited by Raymond E. Lombra and Willard E. Witte. Ames: Iowa State University Press.

———. 1988. "Fedbashing and the Role of Monetary Arrangements in Managing Political Stress." In *Political Business Cycles*, edited by Thomas D. Willett. Durham, NC: Duke University Press.

Kolodko, Grzegorz W., Danuta Gotz-Kozierkiewicz, and Elzbieta Skrzeszewska-Paczek. 1992. *Hyperinflation and Stabilization in Postsocialist Economies.* Boston: Kluwer Academic Publishers.

Leijonhufvud, Axel. 1986. "Rules with Some Discretion." In *Alternative Monetary Regimes*, edited by Colin D. Campbell and William R. Dougan. Baltimore: Johns Hopkins University Press.

Mayer, Thomas, ed. 1990. *The Political Economy of American Monetary Policy.* New York: Cambridge University Press.

Mayer, Thomas, and Thomas D. Willett. 1988. "Evaluating Proposals for Fundamental Monetary Reform." In *Political Business Cycles*, edited by Thomas D. Willett. Durham, NC: Duke University Press.

McCallum, Bennett T. 1987. "The Case for Rules in the Conduct of Monetary Policy: A Concrete Example." *Economic Review* 73 (September-October): 10–18. Richmond: Federal Reserve Bank of Richmond.

Meltzer, Allan H. 1984. "Overview." In *Price Stability and Public Policy.* A Symposium Sponsored by the Federal Reserve Bank of Kansas City, Missouri.

Neumann, Manfred J. M. 1991a. "Precommitment by Central Bank Independence." *Open Economies Review* 2: 95–112.

———. 1991b. "Commentary." In *Monetary Policy on the 75th Anniversary of the Federal Reserve System: Proceedings of the Fourteenth Annual Economic Policy Conference of the Federal Reserve Bank of St. Louis*, edited by Michael T. Belongia. Boston: Kluwer Academic Publishers.

Parkin, Michael, and Robin Bade. 1978. "Central Bank Laws and Monetary Policies: A Preliminary Investigation." In *The Australian Monetary System in the 1970s*, edited by Michael G. Porter. Clayton, Australia: Monash University.

Phelps, Edmund S. 1991. "Precommitment to Rules in Monetary Policy." In *Monetary Policy on the 75th Anniversary of the Federal Reserve System: Proceedings of the Fourteenth Annual Economic Policy Conference of the Federal Reserve Bank of St. Louis*, edited by Michael T. Belongia. Boston: Kluwer Academic Publishers.

Reserve Bank of New Zealand Act 1989. 1990. Wellington, New Zealand: Government Printer.

Siklos, Pierre L. 1997. "Charting a Future for the Bank of Canada: Inflation Targets and the Balance between Autonomy and Accountability." In *Where We Go from*

Here: Inflation Targets and Cananda's Monetary Policy, edited by David Laidler. Toronto, Canada: C.D. Howe Institute.

Tower, Edward, and Thomas D. Willett. 1976. *The Theory of Optimum Currency Areas and Exchange Rate Flexibility*. Special Papers in International Economics No. 11 (May). Princeton, NJ: Princeton University Press.

Weber, Axel. 1991. "Reputation and Credibility in the European Monetary System." *Economic Policy* 12 (April): 57–102.

Wihlborg, Clas G., and Thomas D. Willett. 1991. "Optimal Currency Areas Revisited on the Transition Path to a Currency Union." In *Financial Regulation and Monetary Arrangements after 1992*, edited by Clas G. Wihlborg, Michele Fratianni, and Thomas D. Willett. Amsterdam: North-Holland.

Willett, Thomas D. 1987. "A New Monetary Constitution." In *The Search for Stable Money: Essays on Monetary Reform*, edited by James A. Dorn and Anna J. Schwartz. Chicago: University of Chicago Press.

———, ed. 1988. *Political Business Cycles: The Political Economy of Money, Inflation, and Unemployment*. Durham, NC: Duke University Press.

Willett, Thomas D., Richard C.K. Burdekin, Richard J. Sweeney, and Clas Wihlborg, eds. 1995. *Establishing Monetary Stability in Emerging Market Economies*. Boulder, CO: Westview Press.

11

The Misguided Drive toward European Monetary Union

Kevin Dowd

One of the ironies of recent years is that while central planning was being thrown out in Central and Eastern Europe in favor of reforms to introduce freer markets, the countries of the European Community (EC) in Western Europe have been going in the opposite direction in a misguided effort to establish the basis of a dirigiste super-state. There are certain political factors behind this drive (e.g., the desire of the French political establishment to restrain Germany), but there are also ideological factors as well. The political establishments in European countries are strongly attached to corporatist and paternalist views of the state. Most European politicians and civil servants see a strong state as necessary to protect "their" citizens, whom they regard as unable to look after themselves. This paternalism in domestic policy goes hand-in-hand with a mercantilistic view of the world, which sees the world economy primarily in terms of mutually antagonistic trading blocs in a state of near permanent trade war with one another. According to this view, Europe must overcome its divisions and establish itself as a homogenous bloc to be able to deal effectively with its primary trading rivals in North America and the Far East. This "Fortress Europe" mentality has been associated with the promotion of an artificial sense of European nationalism whose principal characteristic is animosity to the United States and Japan. This manufactured "European national-

The author thanks Charles Goodhart, Paul Mizen, Dick Timberlake, and most especially, Bernard Connolly of the European Commission for helpful comments and corrections. The views expressed here are the author's sole responsibility.

ism" is then used to (try to) bolster the internal cohesion of the European trading bloc, and the trading bloc is to be transformed into an economic superpower that can match (i.e., take on) the United States or Japan.

If this vision of Europe is to be implemented, its proponents argue that the powers of the current EC would need to be considerably strengthened. That, in a nutshell, is what the Maastricht Treaty of 1991 is all about. The current executive, the Council of Ministers, and the European Parliament are to be transformed into a federal government; and that government is to have more resources and greater autonomy from the various national member governments. The Brussels bureaucracy is therefore to have a bigger budget—a much bigger one, in fact—and the power to enforce "broad economic guidelines" on member governments to "coordinate" their economic policies. Its supporters also insist that the new European state must have the various other trappings of sovereignty, including in particular its own currency. If it is to have its own currency, they go on to argue, it should have its own central bank as well, and, by implication, its own monetary policy. The separate national currencies that exist at present should therefore be replaced by a new common currency; and the various national central banks should be replaced by, or to be more precise, become a part of, a new European central bank, the European System of Central Banks (ESCB).

This chapter assesses the monetary aspects of the Maastricht plan.[1] It suggests that the attempt to establish a monetary union in Europe is driven primarily by political or ideological considerations—and questionable ones at that—and its supporters have made very little effort to defend it on economic grounds. The whole plan presupposes, for example, that the benefits of a single currency outweigh the costs of adopting one, and yet there has been very little attempt to assess the costs to establish that that is the case.[2] The costs of switching to a single currency might well exceed whatever benefits there would be in having one. Indeed, given that they have not established that Europe is an optimal currency area, no one can be confident that adopting a single currency would be worthwhile even if the switching costs were all zero, which they clearly are not. Furthermore, even if one granted that the EC was in some sense an "optimal currency area" and that the benefits of monetary union outweighed the costs of adopting one, it still would not follow that the new common currency should be provided by a new central bank or, for that matter, by any of the existing

ones. Once again, no real case has been made in favor of the chosen
option (i.e., in this case, a new central bank), let alone a convincing
one. What we have is fundamentally a political program driven by
political considerations (i.e., by a very dubious "vision" of Europe).
What minimal attempts there have been to defend the economic rationality of the program have been little more than window dressing.[3]

The Nature and Development of the EC

I shall now begin with some background information and then proceed to look at the proposed monetary arrangements in more detail.
The original European Economic Community (EEC) was an extension
of the earlier European Coal and Steel Community which had been
founded in 1952 as a joint cartel between France and Germany to gov-
ern their coal and steel industries. The "success" of this arrangement
led to the establishment of EEC itself in 1957, with the six founder
member states being France, Germany, Italy, Holland, Belgium, and
Luxembourg. The earlier cartels were now extended to cover various
other industries, including in particular agriculture, and the members
of the EC were to maintain a common external tariff against nonmem-
ber states. Following earlier European precedents, these cartels were
used to promote producer rather than consumer interests, and they were
set up in response to lobbying from the producer groups concerned.
Prices were usually pegged above (and sometimes well above) world
market levels, and large amounts of money were poured into these
industries to maintain them.[4] Once these privileges were granted, of
course, it became very difficult to claw them back, and the producers
concerned have been very successful in preventing attempts to reduce
their subsidies or open their markets to free competition. Ever since
the EC was founded, political economy in the EC was essentially the
political economy of the producer lobby.

For many years European producer lobbies were effectively able to
prevent any significant move toward free trade with the EEC, which
thus remained a common market in name only. European producer lobbies were also very effective in hindering the periodic GATT talks designed to move the world economy toward free trade. Since the early
1980s, they have also been very successful in promoting European
protectionism in various guises; and the activities have brought repeated conflict with the EC's major trading partners, especially the
United States and Japan. It is in large part thanks to them, and to some

extent their counterparts in other countries, that the world economy in June 1993 stood on the brink of a major trade war. A certain school of thought in the EC establishment in Brussels has always wanted to make the EC into a federal superstate and has therefore sought conflict with other countries, the United States especially, to create the pressures within Europe that would lead to unification. The deterioration of the climate of world trade since the early 1980s gave them the opportunity they sought, and a vicious circle developed in which trade problems led to more lobbying and increasingly confrontational trade negotiations; they in turn created further disputes and a worsened climate of world trade. This process in the meantime created the external "enemies" the Brussels establishment wanted, and the latter could then use the threats posed by these enemies to promote the internal policies they really desired.

The development of the EC was also significantly influenced by overtly political factors. The old EEC was originally built on a bilateral axis between France and Germany. At that time, there were three significant powers in Western Europe—the United Kingdom, France, and Germany—and the United Kingdom had chosen to stay out of the EC when it was first set up. Of the other two countries, France saw itself as the leading country in Western Europe, but with its bigger population and rapid postwar recovery it was also clear that Germany was, if not stronger at the time, then likely to become so in the future. For the third time within a century, French politicians once again faced the familiar specter of superior German power and the problem of how to contain it. Their response was to take over the driver's seat of EC policy and remain there for as long as the Germans allowed them. The Germans for their part were still anxious to live down the recent past, and therefore had no real objection to the French "vision" of Europe.

The Franco-German axis remained the basis of the EC for many years; and even when Britain joined in 1973, the French and Germans were together able to ensure that British influence remained little more than marginal. However, by the mid-1980s, the Germans were increasingly inclined to put their own national interests first, and it was clear that the new German assertiveness was gradually tilting the balance of power away from France. The French political establishment—the French government and parts of the European Commission (i.e., civil service), including in particular its president, Jacques Delors—therefore became increasingly concerned that they would lose their position of influence. If they could not contain Germany indefinitely, they concluded that they needed to erect a federal superstructure above her; and they set about to persuade German politicians to accept this superstructure while they still had the influence to do so. A federal Europe was thus a good way to assuage the old French fear of the growing German "threat."

There were also the problems of the Exchange Rate Mechanism (ERM) and the German Bundesbank's dominance of it. The ERM had been set up in 1979 as a vehicle for producing European union in the face of Bundesbank opposition. However, the Bundesbank succeeded in subverting this political aim and managed to use the ERM for much of the 1980s to provide a zone of exchange rate stability in Europe. The combination of the Bundesbank's relatively conservative monetary policies and the obligation of other central banks to defend their exchange rates within the ERM had helped to reduce inflation in countries such as France and Italy whose central banks had previously pursued more inflationary policies. Despite these benefits, the Bundesbank's dominance within the ERM was widely disliked among politicians in other countries, especially in France and to some extent in the U.K., who saw in it sinister overtones of German hegemony in Europe.[5] Much the same group of politicians also resented what they regarded as the excessively conservative monetary policies followed by the Bundesbank. Despite the fact that Bundesbank policies had helped to keep inflation relatively low in Germany and other ERM countries, there were always those who wanted more expansionary monetary policies (i.e., more inflation) to "stimulate" the economy and who deeply resented the unwillingness of the German central bankers to provide it. What was needed, they argued, was to replace the current dominance of the Bundesbank by a more amenable European central bank that did not share the Bundesbank's "obsession" with inflation. Resentment of the Bundesbank and what it was held to imply combined with the desires of the Euro-federalists who wanted their own central bank for their own reasons.

The Delors Plan

In June 1988 Delors persuaded the heads of government at their summit in Hanover to establish a committee, under his chairmanship, which would put together a program to implement this vision of Europe. Its report the next year set out a detailed plan for a federal European superstate. There was to be a radical centralization of fiscal powers

and a massive increase in the resources channeled through the EC itself (i.e., the Brussels bureaucracy). The separate European central
banks were also to be merged into a new supranational central bank
modeled on the Federal Reserve System, and the existing European
currencies were to be merged into one. As a preliminary step, Britain,
Spain, Portugal and Greece were to join the ERM from which they had
hitherto abstained. Member governments then agreed at their Rome
summit in December 1990 to hold a further intergovernmental conference to agree upon a new treaty to amend the Treaty of Rome on which
the original EEC had been founded.[6] The Rome summit also added the
idea of a new "Social Chapter" which would impose (idealized) northern European standards of minimum wages and work conditions
throughout the Community.[7]

One might have thought that such an ambitious plan would be mer-
ited a lengthy debate and a mature consideration of possible alternatives. Instead, other options were ignored and the Delors Committee
produced their plan with such speed that one can only suppose that
they already knew what they were going to say before they started. As
Professor Charles Goodhart of the London School of Economics wrote,
the Delors Report

> reads as if its authors were convinced that there is only one currently feasible
> strategy for the coming phases of European monetary unification: this is a federal
> strategy, a Hamiltonian strategy, to transfer increasing powers to a federal centre
> of the United States of Europe. *No alternative is even considered.* (Goodhart 1989,
> 24, emphasis added)

The plan was to be accepted in total and implemented according to
a tight and rigid timetable. There was also no willingness to engage in
open debate even after the documents had been produced, and those
who criticized the plan were usually ignored or dismissed as "bad"
Europeans who stood in the way of "progress."

Eleven of the twelve member governments promptly accepted the
plan in principle, with only the British government rejecting it. As an
alternative, the British government suggested that European currencies be allowed to compete with each other; but what they meant by
currency competition was never made clear, and the British proposal
was never taken seriously by the supporters of the Delors Plan. In any
case, the British government soon dropped their competing currencies
proposal for a proposed new parallel currency, the "hard ecu," that
would compete alongside the existing currencies and be pegged by the

other member governments. The British government continued to face intense pressure to fall into line. The pressure had its effect and, already weakened by domestic problems, Thatcher felt obliged to make concessions—the most significant of which was sterling's entry into the ERM in October 1990.[8]

The Maastricht Treaty

The heads of government met to hammer out the new treaty at their Maastricht summit in December 1991. In the meantime, Margaret Thatcher had been replaced as British prime minister by John Major, who did not share his predecessor's Euro-skepticism. The British government's position thus softened, and the way was now open for agreement between all member governments. The resulting Maastricht Treaty incorporated the key features of the Delors Plan, but the British were to be allowed to opt out of stage three of EMU and the Social Chapter.

The Treaty sets out the basic objectives of the new European Central Bank (ECB), which I shall discuss presently, as well as its structure and governance. The ECB is to be a federal central bank modeled on the Federal Reserve System in the United States. Existing national central banks will then become branches of the ECB with a status analogous to that of the individual Federal Reserve Banks within the Federal Reserve System. There is to be an Executive Board with six members to run the ECB on a day-to-day basis, and the activities of the board are to be overseen by a Bank Governing Council consisting of board members and the governors of the existing central banks. The Treaty is unclear on how the ECB should operate and what its broader powers and responsibilities should be (e.g., over prudential issues),[9] but it ordered the establishment of a European Monetary Institute (EMI) to consider these issues and make appropriate preparations.[10]

The Treaty also sets out a timetable to implement the reforms, the most important feature of which is that the final stage (i.e., stage three, which covers the irrevocable fixing of exchange rates and the actual transition to the common ecu currency) should begin no later than 1 January 1999. In order to reduce transition problems in the run-up to monetary union, the Treaty also sets out "convergence criteria" that should be met before any currency is admitted into the final system of fixed-exchange rate systems prior to the start of stage three. These criteria are meant to ensure that individual governments' fiscal policies are in a sufficiently healthy state, that inflation and interest rates are relatively low, and that the currency concerned has a stable position within the ERM.[11] Finally, the Treaty obliges member governments other than the British to pass legislation to make their central banks formally independent, if they are not so already, and there are certain provisions relating to specific countries (e.g., the article allowing Britain to opt out of the Social Chapter and the single currency).

Having been agreed upon, the Treaty had to be ratified by each individual member state. It was not open to further negotiation, and it was only valid if ratified by every member state. With characteristic hubris, the framers of the Treaty saw the ratification process as little more than a formality. No contingency was made for its rejection by any individual member state. As with the Delors Plan, European governments had no intention of engaging in serious debate with skeptics, and each government was concerned only to ensure that the Treaty was ratified back home with the minimum of political inconvenience.

The "Commitment" to Price Stability

The Maastricht Treaty emphasizes that the primary, indeed overriding, objective of the ECB's monetary policy should be to maintain price stability, but it provides little concrete assurance that price stability would actually be achieved. It appears to be reassuring at first sight: Article 2 of the Protocol on the Statute of the ECSB states the Bank's "primary objective...shall be to maintain price stability." The Bank would pursue other objectives as well, but only if they are consistent with price stability. In the words of the same article, the Bank should "support the general economic policies [and] the objectives of the Community," but these other objectives should only be pursued "without prejudice to" price stability.

Unfortunately, these clauses are undermined by the fact that the Treaty neither defines what it means by "price stability,"[12] nor gives a date by which price stability, whatever it is, is to be achieved. If price stability is not defined, it becomes very difficult, if not impossible, to assess objectively whether it has been achieved or not. The objective of price stability then becomes operationally meaningless, and the central bank can always claim to have achieved it in its periodic reports. As Goodhart (1992, 32) says,

> such Reports are occasions for the expressions of ex-post justification of whatever, for good or ill, those in authority have chosen to do. Without a clear defini-

tion of price stability, and preferably some incentive in the form of bonus payments for achieving that outcome, there is no firm basis for accountability. The ECB's report is bound to state that their actions were consistent, as they saw best, with the achievement of price stability over the appropriate horizon. Most Central Bank reports have made that claim year after year for decades!...The failure to define price stability provides...a system constructed by, with and for Central Bankers, to give them an easier life. It is neither necessary nor desirable.

The ECB's commitment to price stability is also undermined in other ways. Article 109(1) allows the EC's Council of Ministers (i.e., the EC's political executive) to make formal agreements on exchange rates with non-EC currencies. And while it has an obligation to "consult" with the ECB,[13] it has no obligation to accept the ECB's view (i.e., the ECB has no veto).[14] The council could therefore impose its will against the wishes of the Bank, subject only to the requirement that it go through the formality of consultation with it. The problem, of course, is that a system of exchange rates negotiated by the politicians may not be consistent with price stability; and the power of the politicians to impose an exchange rate system on the ECB would allow the politicians to override the Bank's commitment to price stability, even if we had a clear idea of what price stability actually meant. If the political heads of the EC were to fix the exchange rate of the ecu with the U.S. dollar, for example, and if the Federal Reserve were to pursue an inflationary policy, then there would be a real danger that the EC would end up importing U.S. inflation. However committed it might be to price stability, there would be little or nothing the ECB could do about it.

The Failure to Safeguard the ECB's "Independence"

The ECB's commitment to price stability is also undermined in other ways. An important issue in any central bank constitution is the relationship of the central bank to the political authorities, and in particular the extent of the central bank's independence from political interference. There are good reasons to expect that the political authorities will be more inclined than central bankers to resort to inflation—they usually have shorter horizons, they have an incentive to use short-term monetary policy to engineer preelection booms, and so on—and the empirical evidence strongly suggests that more independent central banks deliver lower inflation rates (see the chapter by Burdekin, Westbrook, and Willett in this volume). If the ECB is to be expected to deliver stable prices, it needs to be completely independent of political authorities.

Once again, the treaty provides only superficial reassurances at best. Admittedly, Article 7 of the Protocol on the Statutes of the ECB and Article 7 of the Treaty explicitly state that the ECB should be independent of the political authorities; and other articles reinforce this independence by stipulating that members of the Bank's Board and Council are to have long and (in the case of the members of the executive board) nonrenewable terms of office (e.g., Articles 11 and 109a of the Treaty). Furthermore, Article 104(1) of the treaty prohibits loans by the ECB or national central banks to Community institutions or member governments, a stipulation that would appear at first sight to protect the Bank by prohibiting predatory government demands for cheap credit. But the problem is that this prohibition of loans to government is then immediately qualified in Article 104a(1), which states that it only applies to credit that cannot be justified on "prudential considerations." Since "prudential considerations" have not been defined, we cannot be sure of the circumstances where this exception applies; and we cannot therefore be sure in practice whether loans to governments are actually prohibited or not.

To make matters worse, Article 104a(1) is not the only loophole in the prohibition of loans to governments, nor even the most serious one. Article 103a(2) states that European Community institutions can extend financial assistance if a government is "in difficulties or is seriously threatened with severe difficulties caused by exceptional circumstances beyond its control," and the Treaty makes it clear that the ECB would be regarded as a "Community institution." In other words, despite the prohibition against central bank loans to member governments in Article 104(1), Article 103a(2) implies that the ECB *can* provide such loans by virtue of its status as a Community institution. The ECB would therefore be allowed to make loans to member governments despite the prohibition against doing so! What that means in practice is that when a national government is faced with acute fiscal crisis brought on by its own policies, the Community need only declare that the crisis is an exceptional circumstance beyond the control of the governments concerned—the veracity or plausibility of the announcement does not matter—and it can authorize the ECB bailout. Any idea that the ECB would be protected against predatory government demands for credit is an illusion.

Worse still, the same article actually *encourages* member governments to pursue irresponsible fiscal policies. A government that pursues sound policies and keeps its fiscal house in order receives nothing, but one that spends itself into a corner gets a handout. Such incentives undermine fiscal prudence and create the very fiscal problems supporters of the Treaty claim they want to avoid. A rational fiscal federalism would have put the responsibility for fiscal policies firmly where it belongs, on the member governments themselves, and would not have encouraged them to play irresponsible fiscal games at other people's expense. The reader might recall, for example, how New York City only began to sort out its financial problems in the mid-1970s when President Ford told New York to go to hell. While hope of a federal bailout still persisted, no one in New York had any incentive to take responsibility for the difficult decisions that had to be made to sort out the fiscal mess. Genuine reform could only begin when it was clear that there would be no federal assistance and New York would have to resolve its own problems. Similarly, Europeans cannot expect individual member governments to adopt the unpopular policies needed to restore their fiscal health if their governments think that Community institutions will bail them out. The Community cannot realistically hope to avoid fiscal irresponsibility if it provides rewards for it. If there is a demand for fiscal irresponsibility, the supply will rise to meet it.[15]

The Regulatory Powers of the ECB

The Treaty is very unclear on the regulatory powers and modus operandi of the ECB. It takes the view that most of these issues should be settled later, and leaves it to the EMI to submit appropriate recommendations by a date no later than 31 December 1996.[16] What the Treaty actually says on these issues is also unclear and, to put it kindly, open to different interpretations. Thus, Article 2 of the Protocol of the ECB states, reasonably enough, that the ECB "shall act in accordance with the principle of an open market economy with free competition, favouring an efficient allocation of resources." The content of Article 2 is undermined, however, by the fact that the Treaty sidesteps the issue of what an efficient open market economy with free competition actually implies. It undermines it further by implying the issue is to be settled in practice by the appropriate authorities, which in effect means the authorities can do whatever they like.

Article 2 also sidesteps various other awkward issues. How, for example, can the ECB act in "accordance with the principle of an open market economy with free competition" in an economy that is not open—recall the EC's protection policies, for instance—and does not have free competition and would have even less competition under the Social Chapter? Whatever force Article 2 might have is undermined even further by other articles, in particular by Article 20 of the Protocol which effectively allows the ECB to do whatever it wants anyway.[17] Similarly, Article 104(6) of the Treaty allows the Bank to assume (unspecified) "specific tasks concerning...the prudential supervision of credit institutions," though the Council must be unanimous and the ECB must act on a recommendation from the EC Commission and with the approval of the European Parliament. The floodgates thus seem to be open to the ECB acquiring whatever regulatory powers the appropriate authorities feel it should have. Also worrying is Article 32.4 of the Protocol which allows the ECB "in exceptional circumstances" to indemnify national central banks for losses that can be attributed as arising from ECB policies, a bailout clause that creates a potentially serious moral-hazard problem between the ECB and its various national branches.

And even when the Treaty purports to give indication of the ECB's future prudential role, it usually does so in a vague and confusing manner. Perhaps the best example of this confusion arises with the (normally) straightforward questions of reserve requirements on commercial banks. Are central banks to be allowed to impose reserve requirements or not? There is much to be said for their abolition, and Article 104a of the treaty appears to call for them to be abolished in stage two (i.e., the intermediate stage) except as required for "prudential considerations." Leaving aside the issue that "prudential considerations" are undefined, Article 19 of the Protocol of the Treaty then does an about-turn and states that the ECB and national central banks will be allowed to impose reserve requirements in stage three "in pursuance of monetary policy objectives." The reader might also recall from the previous paragraph how Article 20 of the Protocol effectively allows the ECB to do whatever it wants anyway.

Having given up their reserve requirements in Stage Two, the German and Italian central banks could therefore reimpose them again. There is, however, a catch. The reserve requirements imposed in Article 19 were subject to the provisions of Article 2 of the Protocol mentioned a little earlier requiring that the ECB "act in accordance with the principle of an open market economy with free competition" and promote economic efficiency. Even leaving aside the broader issues that arise from this Protocol article, many monetary economists would argue that reserve requirements are neither consistent with free markets nor with efficient resource allocation, so we might perhaps be tempted to conclude that reserve requirements are meant to be banned after all. But then again, Article 2 of the Protocols is itself subject to Article 3a of the Treaty which talks vaguely about the policy objectives of the Community and member governments, and there is a clear implication that these objectives could override free competition and the efficient allocation of resources if the appropriate authorities were inclined to do so (e.g., by following whatever policies they want and simply claiming that they are consistent with free competition and economic efficiency). In any case, as the advocate of reserve requirements might argue, why include Article 19 at all if reserve requirements were meant to be eliminated?

We therefore have one article of the Protocol that appears to prohibit reserve requirements subject to the prudential caveat, an article in the Treaty that appears to allow them, but subject only to the provisions of a second Protocol article, a reasonable reading of which would suggest that those conditions could not be met. But that article is itself subject to the provisions of two other Protocol articles suggesting that reserve requirements might be allowed after all. To make the issue even more confusing, there is also the unclear legal question of whether the Treaty article prohibiting non-prudential reserve requirements overrides, or is overridden by, the two Protocol articles that appear to allow them. Where all this leaves reserve requirements in the end is, to say the least, unclear.

Confusion over Legal Tender and the Note Issue

When the British government had set out its "competing currencies" proposal in late 1990, the supporters of the Delors Plan had been quick to dismiss it, not unreasonably, on the grounds that it appeared to imply that each currency should be legal tender in every other country. Yet, having dismissed the British proposal, the authors of the Maastricht Treaty then incorporated legal tender provisions into it that could produce the very outcome they earlier ridiculed. The key Article 105a(1) states that the notes authorized by the ECB should "have the status of legal tender within the Community." This article seems to imply, for example, that a German newsagent could be confronted by customers who insisted on paying for their newspapers in drachmas, and he would have no legal right to refuse. The same of course goes for those who insisted on paying in escudos, or liras, or Irish pounds. Not only had the German government signed away the Deutschemark which is due to be eliminated by 1999, along with all other national currencies, but it also accepted that the ECB could make all the other national currencies legal tender in Germany in the meantime.[18] What applies to the German newsagent also applies to his counterparts elsewhere in the Community.

There are also serious problems with the transition to a single currency. As Goodhart (1992, 22) points out, stage three of the Maastricht Plan appears to involve two substages: the irrevocable fixing of exchange rates and the adoption of a single currency. Most historical currency changes usually involved relatively straightforward changes in currency units (e.g., the deletion of zeros). One of the few exceptions was the decimalization of the U.K. currency in the early 1970s, in which the pound was retained as the basic currency unit but its subsidiary units—shillings and pence—were converted into new pence, with one new penny being equal to 2.4 old ones. As Goodhart says, U.K. decimalization "took some five years, or so, to plan and involved considerable redesign of school-books, vending machines," and so on, but the fractions involved would be "child's play" compared with the "seven, or so, figure decimals in which each currency's parity with the ecu is presently stated." One possible way round this problem would be to have a final realignment of ERM currencies to facilitate post-conversion calculations, but such realignments then run into Article 109f of the Treaty which requires that currencies entering the "final union" should not have devalued against any other member currencies over the past two years.[19] Member currencies *might* be able to have a suitable realignment and then wait two years, assuming that they could maintain their exchange rates for that period, but failing that

> the conversion fractions (decimals) will be barbarous indeed. How are people to react when their goods worth 10 Dm suddenly become 4.91 ecu? The confusion among the old and the educationally subnormal will be horrendous. It is not good enough to suggest that we can all cope by carrying around pocket calculators with us for a few weeks. The problems will be intense even if the conversion fractions are user friendly, more so if they are not. (Goodhart 1992, 23)

Goodhart goes on to suggest that this transition would probably need about three years to plan and three more years to complete. He concludes that suggestions that the transition could be made rapidly seem to be "very wide of the mark" (ibid., 24). The authors of the Delors Report and the Maastricht Treaty give no indication of having thought through these issues, or of having any real idea of what the resource or psychic costs of the transition to a single currency would be.[20]

The Collapse of the Treaty

The Danish Referendum and its Aftermath

It turned out that ratifying the Maastricht Treaty was not the straight-forward formality that member governments had anticipated. Different governments were left free to seek ratification according to the traditions and political systems of their different countries. Two of them, Denmark and Ireland, chose to put the treaty to a popular vote. The first of these votes, the Danish referendum, took place in June 1992; but the anti-Treaty sentiment in Denmark was stronger than anticipated and the Danish people rejected the Treaty. Given that the Treaty had to be ratified by all member governments, the Danish result meant that the treaty was legally dead. Yet, rather than accept this outcome, the reaction among member governments was that the ratification process should continue as if nothing untoward had happened. The French government promptly announced that France would hold a referendum, too, on the illogical grounds that a French "yes" vote would somehow put the ratification process back on track. There were also some who suggested that the Danish government should simply hold as many referenda as it took until the Danish people produced the "right" answer, the underlying argument presumably being that the Danes were to be allowed to accept the Treaty but not to reject it. It was also disturbing that a member of the European Court (i.e., the body responsible for interpreting the Treaty) went so far as to declare that Denmark should leave the Community if it would not ratify the Treaty.[21] Not unreasonably, the Danish prime minister felt that he could not call a second referendum on the same question and this option was dismissed. The Danish government were still keen to ratify the Treaty, of course, so they initially took the view that they could only call a second vote if the Treaty were revised to take account of certain concerns expressed in Denmark during the referendum campaign, conveniently ignoring the point that the Treaty was drawn up on a take-it-or-leave-it basis and had no mechanism for revisions. Strictly speaking, the option of putting a revised Maastricht Treaty to the Danish people did not legally exist.

Nonetheless, the member governments were not to be put off. The ratification process continued, and some of the cracks were papered over at the Edinburgh summit of December 1992. This meeting produced a "declaration"—a worthless piece of paper with no legal standing whatever—announcing that, while the Treaty remained unchanged, Denmark would not be bound by the provisions on EMU, common citizenship of the European union, and common defense and security issues. The Danish government took this legally meaningless "declaration" as an excuse to re-present the same Maastricht Treaty, completely unaltered, for a second referendum. Despite this obvious sleight-of-hand, and despite the fact that a few weeks after Edinburgh the Danish prime minister was forced to resign when it became clear that he had been lying to the Danish parliament, the result of the first— that is to say, legitimate—referendum was overturned by the second referendum in May 1993. This new result followed a campaign in which the Danish public had been blackmailed and browbeaten, and opponents of the Treaty were systematically denied the opportunity to confront the advocates of the Treaty in the media.

Even apart from the fact that it helped the Danish government to get the Treaty ratified, the meaningless Edinburgh declaration came with a very high price tag. The four poorest countries—Ireland, Greece, Spain, and Portugal—used the threat of blocking the declaration to get large increases in the already large handouts they were getting from the EC. To make it appear that the EC budget would nonetheless balance, and thus disguise their blackmail, the weaker countries acquiesced in what all must have regarded as a hopelessly overoptimistic forecast, made by the EC Commission, of EC growth in 1993. (And once the agreement was reached, the commission shamelessly revised its growth forecasts down to more realistic levels.) By the spring of 1993, it was clear that a major budgetary crisis was brewing.

At the time of writing in June 1993, there were only two countries left which had not yet ratified the Treaty, Britain and Germany. There was considerable opposition within Britain to the Maastricht Treaty, and though the British government ruled out a referendum and had the qualified support of the major opposition parties within Parliament, it had great difficulty steering the Maastricht bill through Parliament because of divisions within the Conservative Party itself. Rather than risk further (and possible fatal) divisions within its own party, the government may well be forced in the end to capitulate to demands for a popular vote, and the people might well vote to reject the treaty. There is also considerable opposition to the Treaty in Germany, and it is more than likely there will be problems ratifying the treaty there as well.

The Crisis in the ERM

There were also other problems. The financial markets had never been convinced of the merits of the Treaty, or that individual member governments were prepared to make the sacrifices to their own individual autonomy that the unification process required. These doubts came to a head with the crisis in the ERM in September 1992. The ERM was to play a pivotal role in the unification process. Once sterling joined the ERM (which it did in October 1990), monetary policies were to converge and exchange rates at some point were to become irrevocably fixed. Only when that was done could the new single currency be introduced and the monetary unification process be completed. The ERM was therefore to provide the jumping-off point for monetary unification, and it was essential that it operate smoothly and build up the credibility in the market that the transition process required. Yet at the same time, it was clear in the market that certain governments—the British and Italian governments especially—were reluctant to pay the price that maintaining their exchange rates within the ERM bands entailed. Britain was in a severe recession, for example, and the British government refused to raise domestic interest rates to a level that would reassure the markets that it was serious when it said that the ERM was the centerpiece of its macroeconomic policy. There were doubts about the Italian government's commitment as well, and it was widely believed that the ERM would collapse altogether if the French people voted in their referendum on 20 September to reject the treaty.

The obvious course of action in the marketplace was to bet against the weaker currencies that stood to be devalued, and speculative sales of the weaker currencies soon became unstoppable. The first victim was the lira, but sterling and the peseta soon followed. Sterling and the lira were "temporarily" suspended from the ERM, and the peseta was devalued. Their governments' macroeconomic policies had been torn in shreds. The British government had seen the "centerpiece" of its macroeconomic policy destroyed and most of its foreign exchange reserves wiped out in a few hours in a futile attempt to defend the pound.[22] While the government continued to pay lip service to the principle of ERM membership, it made it clear Britain was in no hurry to return to the system. In any case, it was patently clear that having blown whatever credibility the government might have had, it would have found it very difficult to maintain any new set of exchange rate bounds even if it had the stomach to try.[23] The pressure then intensified on the French franc, despite the vote that narrowly endorsed the Maastricht Treaty. The ERM was thus very lucky to have survived at all, let alone to have provided the jumping-off point for monetary unification that Maastricht required of it. Stage One (i.e., the accession of Britain to the ERM) had been reversed with a vengeance, Italy was no longer a member of the ERM, and neither of the governments of these countries was in any position to contemplate renewed attempts to join the ERM within the foreseeable future. It would take years for the ERM to recover to the point where it was before, so even if the Maastricht Treaty had been ratified by all member governments, there is no way the ERM could accommodate the hurried timetable that Maastricht seeks to impose on it.

It is much more likely, in fact, that the ERM will shrink further. There have been two subsequent devaluations of the peseta and the escudo, and one of the Irish pound. It is still very doubtful that Spain and Portugal can remain within the ERM, and it looks as though they will only remain within it if the mark becomes so weak that it no longer imposes any serious constraint on their central banks' inflationary policies. (In that case, of course, the ERM would appear to have no rationale whatever.) It is also quite possible that much the same incompatibility between the ERM and preferred domestic monetary policy would lead France to pull out as well, in which case the ERM will simply collapse to a Deutsche Mark bloc consisting of Germany and a small number of minor countries.

Any idea that the ERM can somehow "grow" into a fully fledged monetary unification must therefore be dismissed as fanciful. All that saved the ERM in the short-run was the insistence of the German government that the (nominally independent) Bundesbank should do whatever was necessary to support it, even if that meant the abandonment of the Bundesbank's own monetary targets and the violation of the Bundesbank's much-vaunted "independence." (It was therefore not surprising to hear the Bundesbank president, Schlesinger, saying later in the year that the ERM had become an engine of inflation.) By mid-1993 the incompatibility of the ERM with fiscal responsibility made it quite clear that no EC country except Luxembourg could meet the Treaty's fiscal convergence criteria in time for the first 1997 deadline. The Belgian and French governments were already talking about relaxing the convergence requirements—a clear indication that once constraints start to bite, member governments will generally respond, not by changing their policies and submitting to the discipline the constraints are there to provide, but by simply removing the constraints.

Some Final Observations

The proponents of a common European currency and a European central bank have never seriously tried to argue the case for them, and the discussion that has taken place makes it very clear that they advocate these objectives for primarily political or ideological reasons that are themselves more or less taken for granted. But even if one were sympathetic to the idea of a common currency and a continental central bank, it would still be difficult to argue that the Maastricht Treaty provided a sensible way to achieve them. One obvious problem is that the Treaty and its protocols are often so vague and even self-contradictory that one often cannot make sense of what they are trying to say. Frequently, some objective or prohibition is stated clearly enough in one article, but then that article is contradicted or overridden by some other article, which in turn is qualified or contradicted by other articles, and so on. Even if one starts off thinking that the Treaty is saying something definite, the more one reads, the more mystified one becomes, and one ends up doubting that the Treaty says anything definite at all.[24]

There are also deeper problems. Even if one accepts that the Treaty makes certain definite points (e.g., that the ECB should be "committed to price stability"), these points are frequently too vague to be operationally meaningful. If the ECB is committed to price stability, for example, we need to know what "price stability" actually means so that we can tell whether or not it has been achieved. If objectives or powers are not clearly defined, or appear to contradict each other, then certain questions naturally arise: Who should judge what the objectives or allowable powers actually are? Who should judge how conflicts between objectives should be reconciled? Who should judge how far the objectives have been achieved or whether allowable powers have been exceeded? *Quis custodiet ipsos custodes?*

The Treaty largely dodges these issues, and we are left with the distinct impression that the "guardians" will be left to guard themselves. The central bankers will sometimes have to report to the politicians, and the central bankers will sometimes write progress reports on the policies pursued by the politicians, but by and large the appropriate authorities will simply exercise their judgment as they see fit (i.e., they will do as they want) and that will be the end of the matter.[25]

Furthermore, even if we as "outside" observers knew what certain objectives actually meant, or what powers certain bodies had, and could therefore infer whether those objectives had been met or those powers appropriately used, the Treaty provides us with no sanction to apply in the case of failure to achieve those objectives or in the case of misuse of power by the bodies concerned. If the ECB chose to inflate, there would be very little that private citizens could do about it. The bodies concerned would only be accountable to political authorities, and only the latter could apply sanctions against them. Since the political authorities would normally have the most to gain from the ECB inflating or giving "prohibited" loans to governments, we can hardly expect the politicians to want to discipline the ECB. Indeed, on the basis of past experiences, it would probably be the politicians who pressured the ECB into following such policies in the first place![26]

In short, the recent effort to establish a European Federal Reserve System is a classic case study of the fatal conceit of would-be central planners who have the supreme arrogance to think that they can impose their "will" on peoples and markets alike in total disregard of any notions of economic rationality or even common sense.

Notes

1. The chapter focuses on one particular plan for European monetary union and does not discuss wider issues such as whether any form of EMU would be economically desirable or sensible. For a good discussion of the latter question, the reader should refer to Connolly and Kröger (1993).
2. It is relatively obvious, in fact, that the adoption of a new common currency as called for in the Maastricht Treaty *must* be economically suboptimal. The costs to individuals of switching currencies are clearly greater than zero. If we wish to minimize these switching costs, we should all adopt whatever existing currency is most widely used. We should therefore presumably adopt the deutschmark which would at least save the German people the costs of switching. Why then did the Maastricht Treaty not suggest that we all adopt the mark (or maybe one of the other existing currencies)? The answer, of course, is obvious: it would have been politically inexpedient to do so. Throughout the Treaty, and the discussions surrounding it, economic rationality takes second place to considerations of political expediency. It is therefore disingenuous, to put it mildly, for supporters of the Treaty to claim that it makes economic sense.
3. See, for example, Minford, Rastogi, and Hughes-Hallett's (1991) devastating econometric critique of the spurious arguments in the EC Commission's propaganda tract, "One Market, One Money" (EC, 1990).
4. The best known example, the Common Agricultural Policy (CAP), was set up in response to pressure from the powerful agricultural lobby, which was especially strong in France. Ever since it was set up, the CAP has managed to swallow up a very large proportion of the EEC's total budget while simultaneously maintaining food prices in Europe at about twice world levels.

5. The spirit of goodwill toward other Europeans only goes so far. It is amusing, too, how little it takes for self-styled "pro-European" politicians to reveal their true colors and give vent to traditional national jealousies. The British and the French have never got on, the Irish dislike the British, the Dutch dislike the Belgians, the Belgians dislike each other, everyone dislikes the Germans, and so on. The new European "spirit" is fine so long as we can carry on hating each other in our time-honored ways.

6. Significantly, Mitterand and Kohl also prompted the heads of government to agree on a parallel intergovernmental conference on political union. The prompting for this second conference came apparently out of the blue, though one suspects that the key advocates of a federal Europe—Delors, Mitterand, and Kohl—had intended such a conference all along.

7. In the process, the Social Chapter would also price many European workers out of their jobs, especially in the poorer countries. As far as I can tell, the main impetus behind the Social Chapter was the desire of labor union in northern Europe, especially in Germany, to have some protection against cheaper labor from the poorer countries; the Social Chapter provides that protection by making the cost of labor in those other countries artificially high. In return for agreeing to the Social Chapter, the governments of the poorer countries were compensated by a large rise in the EC's regional and structural adjustment funds. The German unions get their protection, the other governments get a bailout, and only the workers and the taxpayers lose out. For more on the problems the Social Charter would cause, see Tony Sampson's "The Anti-Social Charter" (1992).

8. The British government was by no means alone in having misgivings about the Delors Plan. Barely was the ink dry, when the president of the Bundesbank, Karl Otto Pöhl—himself one of the plan's signatories—was voicing misgivings about its inflationary potential. There was clearly very strong feeling within the Bundesbank against the plan. An editorial in the London *Financial Times* in December 1991 quoted an unnamed Bundesbank official as saying that the plan was a "criminal act"—the same phrase used by the Nazis to describe the Versailles Treaty of 1919—which the Bundesbank intended to sabotage by maintaining a tight monetary policy that would undermine the ERM by making it difficult for other currencies to maintain their ERM bands. How far the German government shared this view in private was not clear, but in public they professed to support the plan and dismissed British and Bundesbank reservations about it. My own feeling is that they were not particularly enthusiastic about it, but Chancellor Kohl was quite happy to let others—Margaret Thatcher in particular—go out on a limb and take the flak for opposing it. There must be serious doubts how far the German people would go along with the Plan, and it is surely significant that Germany still hasn't ratified the Maastricht Treaty yet. That of course did not stop Kohl from lecturing the British and the Danish governments for holding things up because of their tardiness in ratifying the Treaty.

9. Not surprisingly, perhaps, a number of awkward issues were swept under the rug. One of these is the site of the ECB's headquarters, which, as Goodhart (1992, 12–20) points out, is an important issue because it has various implications for the conduct of open market operations and other aspects of monetary policy. Article 37 of the ECB Protocol required that this issue be resolved by the heads of governments by the end of 1992, but as far as one can tell, they have barely begun to discuss it. The fact that heads of government feel free to ignore awkward Treaty requirements in cases like this is not reassuring. If they can ignore one Treaty requirement when it suits them, what is to stop them from ignoring others as well? Indeed, what then is the point of having any Treaty requirements

at all? Instead of facing up to these issues, the response of the EC establishment was to look for scapegoats. In April 1993 the chairman of the Committee of EC Central Bank Governors blamed the delay in agreeing on a site for the ECB's headquarters on British and Danish delays in ratifying the Treaty. The fact that Germany still had not ratified the Treaty was conveniently ignored.

10. The underlying principle of the Treaty again seems to be that one should avoid straightforward ways of going about tasks when more complicated and confusing ways are available. While the EMI is supposed to prepare the way to Stage three, Article 109(b) of the Treaty also orders the EC's Monetary Committee, which becomes its Economic and Finance Committee, to examine the financial and monetary situation in each country. "Once Stage 3 has begun," writes Goodhart dryly, "the Monetary Committee is to be transmogrified into an Economic and Financial Committee" which will continue much the same function, but "it is not at all clear to me how the dividing lines for its remit and responsibilities are to be drawn relative to the EMI/E[S]CB on the monetary side, or the Commission on the economic side, or what the specific purpose of its establishment is perceived to be..." (Goodhart 1992, 10). It is in fact very likely that the Economic and Financial Committee would in practice become a forum for deciding Community economic policy, contrary to the letter (though not the underlying intention) of Maastricht, and do so in a way that would be completely unaccountable to any electorate.

11. These criteria are another example of the Maastricht Treaty's penchant for deliberate obfuscation. At first sight they seem clear enough: government deficits should be no more than 3 percent of GDP; the annual CPI inflation rate should be no more than 1.5 times higher than that of the average of the three lowest inflation countries over the preceding year; average long-term interest rates should be no more than 2 percent above the average of the lowest three countries for the previous year; and the exchange rate should be in the narrow band of the ERM and should not have been devalued or suffered serious downward pressure within the last two years. However, the government deficit criterion is then qualified to allow higher deficits on an undefined "temporary" or "exceptional" basis. Does this qualification allow for deficits to be greater than 3 percent of GDP as part of a counter-cyclical fiscal policy? Does it allow Germany to have a greater deficit to pay for unification costs? No one knows. Similarly, the debt-GDP ceiling is qualified to allow a higher ratio than 60 percent, but only if it is not too far above 60 percent and is falling at a "satisfactory" rate. What does this mean? Again, no one knows. Taken at face value, every single EC country except Luxembourg would fail these criteria (and Luxembourg does not matter anyway because it does not have its own currency). As Goodhart (1992, 7) points out, Belgium, Denmark, and Eire clearly fail to meet the fiscal criteria, and it must now be doubtful whether Britain or Germany can meet them either. Since long-term interest rates incorporate expectations of long-term inflation, the interest rate criterion can presumably only be satisfied if expected long-term inflation rates are roughly the same as expected long-term inflation in the "best three" countries. That in turn seems to presuppose, dubiously, that the governments or central banks concerned have solved their own credibility problems, an important problem in view of the near collapse of the ERM in September 1992. The exchange rate criterion also implies that governments have solved their credibility problems, but it also runs into the problem, discussed further in the text below, that it makes it difficult to readjust parities to reduce accounting costs in the transition to the single currency. The process of deciding whether countries have met these criteria also promises to be interesting. The bodies responsible for deciding

whether they have been satisfied would be the European Commission and the EMI. Since one cannot expect the Commission to make an objective report and the Bundesbank representative on the EMI is likely to insist on a strict interpretation of the criteria, there is a good chance of a major clash between these two bodies.

12. The most obvious definition of price stability is that a particular price index should show zero growth over time and have a small variance around that long-term trend. But two problems arise. First, even if one accepts this definition, we still do not know how small the variance must be, and lack of precision on this point leaves scope for a central bank to argue that the variance is small enough to satisfy the price stability criterion regardless of whatever value it actually takes. Second, there are many economists who interpret "stability" primarily in terms of "predictability," and this line of interpretation leaves one free to argue that prices are stable if only they are predictable. Leaving aside the question of how predictable prices might then need to be, what matters in that case is not the inflation rate, but its predictability, and one no longer has any reason to prefer low or zero inflation to high inflation, other things being equal. It seems to me that these difficulties make the Treaty's undefined notion of price stability so vague as to be almost useless.

13. Strictly speaking, to reach a formal exchange rate agreement with a non-EC country, the Council of Ministers must act unanimously, consult the European Parliament, and either act on an ECB recommendation or on a recommendation of the EC Commission after having consulted ECB. Hence, if the ECB is opposed to such an agreement, all the council needs to do to override the bank is get the commission to make the recommendation, act unanimously, and go through the formality of consulting the ECB and the European Parliament.

14. The central bankers who signed the Delors Report were naive in the extreme in thinking that politicians such as Delors would construct a European superstate and then hand over the running of monetary policy to them. Mitterand made this point very clear during the French referendum campaign on the Maastricht Treaty in the fall of 1992. His comments enraged the Bundesbank and did much to precipitate the virtual collapse of the ERM in September. The sincerity of European political establishments of all parties on this issue was typified by remarks made during the recent French parliamentary elections by Eduard Balladur, now French prime minister, when he spoke of the need for the greater independence of the Bank of France "*at least in statutes*" (my italics).

15. The Community's record to date on this issue is very poor. Two "balance of payments" loans have already been made to Greece, and one to Italy, but these were no more than politically-inspired bailouts. The EC did insist on "conditionality," but only for form's sake. No well-informed observer ever took its conditionality terms seriously.

16. A large number of issues remain to be resolved. Apart from the siting of the headquarters of the ECB itself, decisions have to be made about where and how to carry out open market operations, foreign exchange operations, and so on. The modi operandi of ECB last-resort discount operations also need sorting out, and there will almost certainly need to be a great deal of accommodating institutional change. Goodhart (1992,12–25) has an excellent discussion of these and other related issues. He also makes the point (ibid., 18–19) that the ECB will be under considerable pressure to unify the EC payments system, if only to smooth out the effects of its own policies on financial markets. But it would take years, first to plan, then to carry out, the unification of the EC payments system. The appropriate authorities give little indication of having begun to think about these issues.

17. Article 20 specifies that, provided it gets at least a two-thirds majority of cast votes, "The Governing Council may...decide upon such other operational methods of monetary control as it sees fit."

18. One presumes that the German government was not aware of what it was doing. Conceivably, perhaps, lawyers could subsequently try to claw back this concession by claiming that it was not what the agreement really meant. The legal tender question and hundreds like it that result from the member governments' attempts to outsmart their electorates and each other will then have to be decided by the European court. The chaos that resulted from undecided property issues in the former East Germany will then be as nothing compared to resulting chaos in the Community itself.

19. As usual with the Maastricht Treaty, these provisions are much more complicated than they appear at first sight. The two-year no-alignment rule is a condition for the European Council to give a country the green light to go forward to stage three, but the Treaty apparently does not rule out a realignment between the decision to go forward to stage three and the actual implementation of stage three. Apart from raising the issue of conversion rates, this loophole also raises the prospect of a final devaluation to repudiate government debt in real terms just before entering stage three. The markets would presumably anticipate such an attempt, however, and interest rates would rise accordingly.

20. There are other problems relating to the currency issue. The Protocol makes provision for seignorage receipts to be shared out among central banks, but what do the latter do with them? If they are truly independent, they would presumably keep them or at least decide how much to keep and how much to pass on to their government. But then who holds them accountable for their use of seignorage funds, and how can such accountability be reconciled with their independence?

21. This pronouncement is all the more disturbing in that it clearly violates the Treaty of Rome, which the Court is also responsible for interpreting—and does so in highly political, centralizing manner. European citizens and member governments would clearly be unwise to rely on the Court to uphold their rights.

22. To describe the British government's handling of the crisis as inept hardly does the word justice. The week before the crisis erupted, there had been much pressure on the Bundesbank to lower German interest rates. To its credit, the Bundesbank resisted that pressure, refusing to make cuts beyond a token of one-quarter percentage point. It was clear at the time that if it wanted to maintain its ERM parities, the British government should have responded by raising British interest rates to reassure the markets, but that it refused to do. The speculative pressure then built up extremely quickly; and when the government woke up to the danger, it responded by a series of panicky interest rate hikes. On the morning of 16 September, it announced that interest rates were to be raised by 2 percent and then by an additional 3 percent. By then it was too late, and the government suspended sterling from the ERM in the afternoon and canceled the interest rate hikes. Interest rate policy had been altered three times within a few hours, a vast amount of money had been lost in the foreign exchange markets, the centerpiece of British macroeconomic policy had been destroyed, and so confident was the government that this could not happen that the U.K. Treasury had not even prepared a contingency plan on which the government could fall back. The next day, even the government had no clear idea what its policy was. Nonetheless, John Major steadfastly rejected calls from those who demanded that the Chancellor of the Exchequer, Norman Lamont, should resign. Instead, he defended the Chancellor and his policies, announced that he personally took full responsibility (and ignored the implication that he should resign himself),

and carried on as if he could not understand what all the fuss was about. Lamont enjoyed his fullest confidence, Major repeatedly declared, and he had no intention of replacing him. He was still protesting his confidence in Lamont even as he sacked him in May 1993.

23. The suspension of sterling from the ERM also had another interesting consequence. Rather than take responsibility himself, Norman Lamont simply blamed the Germans—in particular, the Council of the Bundesbank—for not reducing interest by more in the week before the crisis erupted. Instead of being laughed out of court, Lamont's claims were then picked up by that section of the U.K. establishment that still has not forgiven Germany for the Second World War, and the British public were treated to an unending barrage of anti-German sentiment. The German government was not impressed, naturally enough, and the German Chancellor responded in kind with a torrent of anti-British abuse. It was not a good week for Anglo-German relations, and the exchange of opinions did no credit to either side. The Irish finance minister adopted much the same approach when Eire was forced to devalue within the ERM three months or so later. Like Lamont, he blamed the Germans for their interest rate policies; but he also managed, somehow, to blame the British as well. It never ceases to amuse me how quickly the facade of being a "European" is dropped in circumstances like these and the people involved give way to old-fashioned nationalist sentiment of a very crude kind.

24. It seems to me that this mystification is partly deliberate, since it enables supporters of the Treaty to quote selectively from it to reassure critics that their particular concerns have been met. For example, the articles on price stability can be quoted to reassure those who worry about the inflationary potential of the new central bank. Supporters of the Treaty can then give the impression that the Treaty is a rational document that takes all proper concerns into account; meanwhile, they can conveniently ignore the qualifications, contradictions, and other problems that only become apparent when one looks at the Treaty more closely.

25. The reader might recall, for example, how heads of government simply ignored Article 37 of the Treaty which required them to agree by the end of 1992 on where the EMI should be headquartered. If the authorities can blatantly ignore Treaty requirements, they can effectively do what they like.

26. Furthermore, there is no sanction that the voters of a particular country can apply against the Council of Ministers. Voters in the Community's member states can never change the Community's "government." It is, after all, the lack of such governmental accountability in countries such as Belgium and Italy that has led to debt/GDP ratios of well over 100 percent—and the near inevitability of future inflation. The Maastricht Treaty imposes Belgian and Italian (i.e., no) accountability on the Community as a whole, and we must expect similar results.

References

Connolly, Bernard, and Jurgen Kröger. 1993. "Economic Convergence in the Integrating Community Economy and the Role of Economic Policies." *Recherches Économiques de Louvain* 59 (1–2): 37–63.

European Commission. 1990. "One Market, One Money—An Evaluation of the Potential Benefits and Costs of Forming an Economic and Monetary Union." *European Economy* 44 (October).

Goodhart, Charles A. E. 1989. "The Delors Report: Was Lawson's Reaction Justifiable?" Special Paper Series No. 15. London School of Economics Financial Markets Group.

————. 1992. "The ECSB After Maastricht." Special Paper Series No. 44. London School of Economics Financial Markets Group.

Minford, Patrick, Anupam Rastogi, and Andrew Hughes-Hallett. 1991. "The Price of EMU." Paper prepared for the Konstana Seminar on Monetary Theory and Policy.

Sampson, Anthony A. 1992. "The Anti-Social Charter: A Theoretical Analysis of Choice of Wages and Hours Worked in a Right to Manage Model." Salford Papers in Economics 92–11. Department of Economics, University of Salford.

12

Monetary Nationalism Reconsidered

Lawrence H. White

The rational choice would seem to lie between either a system of "free banking," which not only gives all banks the right of note issue and at the same time makes it necessary for them to rely on their own reserves, but also leaves them free to choose their field of operation and their correspondents without regard to national boundaries, and on the other hand, an international central bank.

—F. A. Hayek (1937, 77)

International monetary regimes come in two basic types: those based on various independent national base moneys, and those based on a unified international base money. Regimes of the unified type can differ in at least two dimensions. First, there may be distinct national deposit-transfer and currency systems variously regulated by national governments, that is, national "inside moneys." Hayek in 1937 called the doctrine behind this option "monetary nationalism." Alternatively, checkable deposits and banknotes denominated in international money may be provided by private banks operating transnationally. The latter option allows international inside moneys. Second, a common international base money can emerge from the free acceptance in various nations of a common base money supplied apolitically (for example, a commodity money such as gold). Joined to transnational banking, the result is international free banking: a global payment system with a single monetary standard, regulated by market institutions, not dependent on any national or supranational government. Alternatively, an international money can be created by an international central bank. The choice between these alternatives is the "rational choice" Hayek describes in the epigraph above: international free banking or an international central bank.

This essay explores these distinctions and the practical differences associated with them. As a vehicle for doing so, it critically reconstructs the arguments of Hayek's 1937 book *Monetary Nationalism and International Stability*, a largely neglected work on the topic by one of this century's leading economists.[1] Hayek set out to dissect the policy doctrine he labeled "monetary nationalism" in a series of lectures subsequently published as a slim volume. At that time, monetary nationalism was a leading belief system in the world of economic policy ideas and an incipient trend in the world of realpolitik.

Hayek (1937, 4) defined "monetary nationalism" as "the doctrine that a country's share in the world's supply of money should *not* be left to be determined by the same principles and the same mechanism as those which determine the relative amounts of money in its different regions or localities." In other words, the stock of money within national boundaries is not to be freely altered by movements of money through interlocal payment systems. Money is not to cross national borders, at least not in the same guises that it circulates domestically. It is characteristic of a regime of monetary nationalism that a currency's sphere of circulation is coextensive with the borders of the nation whose central bank issues it.

With the breakdown of the Bretton Woods and stopgap Smithsonian systems in 1971 and 1973, full-blown monetary nationalism became the status quo in both the realm of policy and the realm of ideas. Today its dominance is qualified by the European Monetary System (EMS) and the movement toward a European Central Bank. Still, the quantity of basic money in each major nation remains controlled by the national monetary authority within its borders, there being no international money that flows across borders from the banks of one nation to the banks of another.[2] Until the movement toward a European Central Bank began, few thought seriously of questioning this state of affairs. The central debating point had instead been the degree to which national monetary authorities should coordinate their policies.

Full-blown monetary internationalism—the antithesis of monetary nationalism—entails a globally homogeneous monetary system. Hayek (1937, 4) spoke in this regard of a "truly International Monetary System...where the whole world possessed a homogeneous currency such as obtains within separate countries and where its flow between regions was left to be determined by the results of the action of all individuals." In such a system, ordinary money (including deposits as well as currency) crosses national borders freely to settle international payments. Money can flow among regions without hindrance, regardless of whether the regions are part of the same nation-state.

In the world of a globally homogeneous monetary system, there are no national monetary authorities who control national monetary aggregates. There is, indeed, little point in even compiling statistical records of national monetary aggregates, no more point than there would be today in compiling separate monetary aggregates for each of the fifty United States. Such an effort would be inconsequential (not to mention its practical difficulties), because it would be unreliable for prediction of regional economic activity. Dollar holders stand ready to make purchases from vendors anywhere in the dollar region, not only within their home states. Tracking of the aggregates could not be used in an effort at their control. To anticipate a point we will return to later, control of the national money stock in a globally homogeneous monetary system is not necessary for desirable macroeconomic performance, nor would people have reason to feel that it was necessary. Money flows from nation to nation would be no more a cause for macroeconomic concern than flows within national boundaries.

In the choice between the two routes to a truly international monetary system, Hayek in 1937 expressed a preference for an international central bank over international free banking. This is surprising given the outlook on economic policy for which he was well known, a classical liberal appreciation for the profound limitations of government activism.[3]

The language Hayek used is even more surprising in light of his more recent (1973, 1988) critiques of "constructivist rationalism" in social thought. In the 1937 lectures, he spoke (74) of "the ideal" of "a rationally regulated world monetary system," and commented (93) that "a really rational monetary policy could be carried out only by an international monetary authority, or at any rate by the closest cooperation of the national authorities and with the common aim of making the circulation of each country behave as nearly as possible as if it were part of an intelligently regulated international system." His preference for such a system is implicit in the following statement (93–94):

> [S]o long as an effective international monetary authority remains an utopian dream, any mechanical principle (such as the gold standard) which at least secures some conformity of monetary changes in the national area to what would happen under a truly international monetary system is far preferable to numerous independent and independently regulated national currencies. If it does not provide a really rational regulation of the quantity of money, it at any rate tends to make it behave on roughly foreseeable lines, which is of the greatest importance.

The final section of this report attempts to puzzle out (since he was less than fully explicit about it) what concrete policy would, in Hayek's 1937 view, represent "really rational regulation of the quantity of money," and to consider whether such a policy is in fact more desirable than the behavior of the quantity of money under an international free banking system. The purpose is not primarily to set the doctrine-historical record straight, but rather to analyze a live issue of monetary policy. Arguments for an international central bank have achieved political dominance in Europe today, and have been made in America by such economists as Richard N. Cooper (1988) and Ronald I. McKinnon (1988). It remains to be seen to what extent those sympathetic to Hayek's basic outlook on economic policy share a common cause with advocates of an international central bank.

This essay will not address directly the relative merits of a common international money as against numerous independent currencies with floating exchange rates. But the argument made below—that the major defects in the performance of the historical gold standard are remediable by allowing greater international integration of banking—may, if persuasive, remove some important misgivings about a common international money.

Purely Metallic Monetary Systems

Monetary internationalism is in several respects a matter of degree. The simplest example of a "truly" international system, to use Hayek's phrase (and something close to his example), would be a world of two countries where only uniform gold coins were used as money in both countries. The system's internationalism might be compromised if there were distinct national coinages; however, as Hayek (1937, 5) noted, nationalistic markings and denominations of coins would be irrelevant in practice if local mints would restrike foreign coins at a zero price and thereby allow unlimited interchanging of coins. A fully integrated currency system would then exist, with international movements of coins no more inhibited (unless transportation costs were discontinuously greater) than movements within each country.

Hayek's discussion here may be read as assuming that minting services are nationally monopolized by law. Regionally specific standard coins (and standard units of account) can be expected to emerge spontaneously in the early stages of a system with coinage provided entirely by competitive private mints (Selgin and White 1987). The process of market standardization of coins could conceivably follow national borders even without specific legal compulsion if such borders happened to correspond to boundaries of distinct linguistic, trade, or legal regions.[4]

With competitive mints, the price of coin restriking services will not be quite zero. What really matters for full integration, however, is zero-spread interchangeability (par acceptance) between the coins in trade. If this prevails, international currency flows will not be inhibited. The exchange rate between two coins will naturally correspond to their relative bullion contents. Coins of both denominations may even circulate widely in both countries. This is especially likely if the bullion content of one standard coin is a simple multiple of the other, so that the computational difficulties of dealing in both coins are minimal.

Mixed Currency Systems and the Historical Gold Standard

As Hayek emphasized at length (1937, 4–16), the historical world monetary system as organized under the gold standard prior to World War I fell far short of the ideal of true monetary internationalism—despite the global acceptance of gold. It is important to recognize this point because the macroeconomic problems associated with the historical system have wrongly been thought to be inherent to any system making use of a common international money. In fact, as Hayek argued, those problems were due to the system's failure to live up fully to the ideal of international money. Shortcomings appeared in two areas: (1) nonmetallic moneys gained circulation nationally but not internationally; and (2) the gold reserves held against bank-issued moneys came to be held by national central banks, rather than by transnational private banks.

In addition to gold, bank liabilities redeemable for gold (banknotes and checkable deposits) were generally accepted as media of exchange; indeed, they formed the bulk of the money supply in every commercially developed area. That a monetary system is "mixed" (as nineteenth-century writers characterized it) of coin, paper currency, and deposits is not itself a barrier to full international monetary integration. The circulation of a bank's notes and checks could easily be international if the bank had branch offices in more than one country. Because banks were legally constrained to operate only within national boundaries, however, the money they issued was effectively irredeemable abroad and did not circulate there. The banknotes and checks of a French bank, for example, did not function as money in England.[5] Thus, only a fraction of the stock of money in circulation (namely, the coins held by the public) plus bank reserves, which constituted only a fraction of monetary bank liabilities, served as international money.

The difference made by the national specificity of bank-issued moneys was twofold. First, it altered the equilibrium distribution of gold around the world. Second, and more importantly, in conjunction with the national pooling of reserves it altered the process through which a new equilibrium would be approached following a disturbance.

In any system with a basic money accepted internationally, the world stock of basic money comes to be distributed among various regions in accordance with the depth of demands to hold it by individuals and firms in those regions. For the sake of concreteness, let us assume for now that gold is accepted internationally as basic money, whatever the various national banking structures. In any international gold standard system, gold tends to flow in exchange for other goods into any area whose residents currently value it comparatively highly at the margin and thereby give it a comparatively high purchasing power (or, alternatively, whose residents experience an excess demand for gold). These gold flows are self-limiting, because the marginal value of gold falls for the recipients as more gold is gained and rises for the senders as more gold is lost.

In stock equilibrium the purchasing power of gold is everywhere the same (within the narrow limits set by transportation costs). The concepts of an equilibrating specie flow mechanism and an equilibrium distribution of basic money among the nations in accordance with the distribution of demand are well-known ideas emphasized by David Hume ([1752]1970) and David Ricardo ([1817]1971) in their respective analyses of the international gold standard.

The advent of bank-issued money naturally reduced the real demand for gold by providing a close substitute for some money-holding purposes. Where bank-issued money circulated locally or nationally, it provided a substitute more convenient than gold for most local or national payments. The global pattern of demand would not have been altered (though real demand would have been everywhere reduced) if in every nation at every date members of the public had regarded bank money as preferable to gold for exactly the same class of transactions (e.g., all but international transactions), if those transactions had constituted the same fraction of total transactions, and if banks had held identical fractional reserves of gold against their liabilities. In actuality these conditions did not hold, and deviations from them were not mutually offsetting (which would, of course, have been extremely unlikely).

The effect of the availability of banknotes and checkable deposits on the demand for gold by both the public and the banks clearly varied from nation to nation, as bank-mediated payment practices developed in different ways and at different paces.[6] These differences were due at least in part to the variety of legislated restrictions and regulations that produced the growth of banking systems along strictly national lines. Had international branch banking been allowed, and had banking been placed on the same regulatory footing in all nations, banking practices would not have varied so much from nation to nation. The global pattern of demand for gold and the equilibrium allocation of the stock were therefore different from what they would have been in the absence of monetary nationalism.

Contrasting International Payment Mechanisms

The national specificity of bank-issued money also altered importantly the process by which money flowed from one nation to another. The relevant benchmark here is a system of free international branch banking rather than the purely metallic international system considered above, for our focus is on the difference made by monetary nationalism, not by the existence of bank-issued money as such. We need to go beyond Hayek's treatment of "the function and mechanism of international flows of money" in his second lecture (1937, 17–34), where he contrasted the historical gold standard with a purely metallic system rather than with an international free banking system. His discussion did not clearly separate the difference made by bank-issued money from the differences made by national specificity of that money and by the existence of national reserve systems.

Hayek (1937, 10) made the important point that the development of bank-issued money "would have made little difference [for international monetary relations] if the banks had not developed in a way which led to their organization into banking 'systems' along national lines." He was not clear, however, concerning the characteristics of the relevant benchmark non-nationalistic banking system. He continued:

> Whether there existed only a system of comparatively small local unit banks, or whether there were numerous systems of branch banks which covered different areas freely overlapping and without respect to national boundaries, there would

be no reason why all the monetary transactions within a country should be more closely knit together than those in different countries.

Hayek's point here was that in neither case would all the inhabitants of a country become dependent on "the same amount of more liquid assets held for them collectively as a national reserve," as they did historically.

Contrary to Hayek, there *are* reasons to expect systems of "small local unit banks" to be knit together nationally. Local unit banking (certainly in the United States, and probably generally) represents not a free market outcome but the result of interventionist banking policies. Such policies are the work of national or subnational governments. No two governments are likely to pursue them in such a way that domestic banks may interact—in clearing systems, for instance— as easily with banks across the border as with other similarly regulated domestic banks. U.S. experience shows clearly that the development of a national reserve system is perfectly congenial with, and in several ways encouraged by, unit banking. The Federal Reserve System was in large part designed in deference to unit banking interests as a substitute for the management and interlocal allocation of reserves that in freer banking systems (such as Canada's) was conducted by the head offices of widely branched banks (see E. White 1983).

In effect, a policy of local unit banking—by drawing the lines a bank may not cross even more narrowly than does a policy of monetary nationalism, and thereby circumscribing to an even greater degree the circulation of bank-issued money—represents an even further regression from the ideal of a truly international monetary system. The relevant benchmark for assessing monetary nationalism is the second system Hayek mentions in the extract above, a system of free international branch banking.

To draw the most immediate but certainly not the most important contrast first, clearing and settlement mechanisms for individual payments differ between the systems of free international branch banking and of monetary nationalism. In the first system, but not in the second, it is possible for any particular international payment to involve two customers of the same bank, so the simple transfer of a claim on that bank settles the payment. In such a case no movement of reserve money from bank to bank is necessary. Bank-issued money can serve as international money. We may assume that regional unit-of-account differences would not persist, or would prove no obstacle given two-way par convertibility. A bank presumably would be indifferent to conversion of a dollar-denominated claim against it into a bullion-equivalent franc-denominated claim.

Now consider an international payment that involves an interbank transfer. Under either system a payment from a customer of domestic Bank X to a customer of foreign Bank Y means at the margin a loss of reserve money by Bank X and a gain by Bank Y. In the limiting case of fully integrated international branch banking, where all competing banks operate globally and all belong to a single global clearing system, all international payments would be cleared and settled in exactly the same manner as intranational payments. Bank X's reserve loss would become Bank Y's gain directly through the clearinghouse, with no third bank involved.

Under the monetary nationalism attending the historical gold standard, commercial banks seldom were allowed to branch abroad or to belong to multiple national clearing systems. Rather, correspondent arrangements linked pairs of banks in different nations. Two intermediary banks were thus typically needed for international clearing and settlement.

In the less pure case of partially integrated international branch banking, where some banks are internationally branched while others have limited range, and where distinct national clearinghouses therefore still exist, direct settlement can occur for checks and wire transfers against deposits in the internationally branched banks that belong to both the domestic and the relevant foreign clearing system. International banks can also, for a fee, perform the service of linking the two clearinghouses for the other banks. International Bank Z can transfer reserve money from its foreign branch to foreign Bank Y through the foreign clearinghouse in exchange for receiving matching reserves domestically from Bank X. In the section that follows, the case of partial integration will be neglected in order to focus on the cleaner contrast between full international banking integration and complete monetary nationalism.

Contrasting Adjustment Mechanisms

The primary concern in this contrast of monetary processes under the two systems is not with the settlement of individual transactions, but with how the systems as wholes would respond to large-scale disturbances to money supply or demand. Following Hayek's example, consider a shift in demand away from a particular product produced in Country A in favor of a product produced in Country B. The resulting gain in real income by workers and investors in the favored industry, and in turn by their trading partners as increased real spending spreads outward from the favored industry, will normally mean an increase in Country B's real money demand. The reverse process will spread from the disfavored industry in Country A.[7] Some further adjustment is needed to satisfy these shifts in money demand.

The regeneration of monetary equilibrium, given the above hypothesized shifts in money demand, calls for a redistribution of real money balances: an increase in the real quantity of money in Country B and a decrease in Country A. With a common money accepted in both countries and able to flow from one to the other, as characterizes both of the banking systems we are considering here, an actual transfer of some kind of money from A to B will constitute at least part of the equilibrating process that brings about the requisite changes in both countries.

Under a system of fully integrated international branch banking, the redistribution of money can be made completely in the same manner as a redistribution between two neighborhoods within a single country, namely, by what appear to be simple transfers of bank-issued money. Country B residents will accept payment for their net exports in banknotes and checks issued by Country A bank branches, because the same parent banks do business in their own country. The same brands of banknotes and checks are current in both countries. Country B bank branches will accept at par banknotes and checks issued by Country A bank branches. Transnational Banks X and Y find the liabilities issued by their Country A branches contracting in volume, while the liabilities issued by their Country B branches expand. No crisis arises for either bank. These transfers of bank-issued money are not the entire international story: they will be accompanied by small international movements of reserve money from A to B to the extent that the banks perceive marginal shifts in that direction in the prudent levels of their vault cash reserves at branches in the two countries.

The process of international redistribution of money may incidentally favor one bank over another. Country B residents may for whatever reason prefer to divide the additions to their balances among the various banks in proportions different from those chosen by the Country A residents who are reducing their balances. Perfect equality of proportions is indeed improbable. In the likely case of a slight change in the market shares of the various banks, there will be an interbank transfer of reserve money. Suppose that in the two countries put together, Bank X experiences a reduction in the volume of its monetary liabilities held by the public, whereas Bank Y on net gains deposits and enjoys greater circulation for its banknotes, and all other banks are unaffected in the aggregate. The result will be a net transfer of clearing reserves from X to Y. There is net "destruction" of X-money and "creation" of Y-money, to use the textbook terminology, though these events are more appropriately thought of in this case as instigating rather than resulting from the reserve flow.

The important point to be made is that these events involved with an interbank redistribution of money do not themselves constitute an international monetary redistribution, nor are they an essential part of the process of international adjustment discussed two paragraphs back. Under the assumption that both banks are multinational, the expansion of Bank Y's share of the market for bank-issued money at the expense of Bank X's share is not as such a movement of money from one nation to another. Bank moneys in the system we are hypothesizing are not nationally specific, but circulate globally. (If international circulation seems implausible, consider that Visa, MasterCard, and American Express are globally accepted today.)

Under the assumption of an international clearing system, the reserves held for clearing are not nationally specific either, so transfer of ownership of them from one multinational bank to another does not constitute an international transfer of reserve money. The process of interbank redistribution may create difficulties for the contracting bank, but interbank transfers as such do not create any of the macroeconomic problems associated with monetary contraction in a specific regional economy. While one bank is contracting, another is expanding alongside it. No banking system is losing reserves.

In a system with all bank moneys restricted to national circulation, by contrast, international monetary redistribution must take a route other than transfers of bank-issued money. Assuming that in both countries the bank-issued moneys are fractionally backed, the appropriate redistribution could not come about through a transfer of reserve money to the full amount of the warranted money stock changes (assuming the positive and negative changes in money demand to be equal in absolute value). Such a large transfer would lead the banks in Country B to expand their liabilities by a multiple of the reserves gained, and the reverse for the banks in Country A. Total money stock changes would then exceed the amounts appropriate for reestablishing monetary equilibrium.

The redistribution must, to paraphrase Hayek (1937, 17), be brought about partly by an actual transfer of reserve money from country to country, but largely by a contraction of the quantity of bank-issued money in one country and a corresponding expansion in the other. With nationally restricted rather than multinational banks, the redistribution of bank-issued money from one nation to another is unavoidably associated with redistribution from one set of banks to another nonintersecting set, and thereby with transfers of clearing reserves from one set of banks to another and from one nation to another. One banking system is contracting, and another is expanding, with potentially momentous macroeconomic consequences.

Contrasting Reserve-Holding Systems

This contrast between the mechanism of monetary redistribution that operated under the monetary nationalism prevailing during the classical gold standard era, and the mechanism that is available under a free international banking system, was sharpened by the historical development of what Walter Bagehot called the "one-reserve system of banking," or what Hayek (1937, 76) called "the organization of banking on the 'national reserve' principle." A single institution, the central bank, came to hold the entire gold reserve of a nation's banking system. This was not a natural development, but rather the result (not always deliberate) of banking legislation. In Britain, as Bagehot explained in his celebrated *Lombard Street* (1873, 99–100), it grew out of the legal privileges bestowed on the Bank of England. Until the 1830s,

> the Bank of England had among companies not only the exclusive privilege of note issue, but that of deposit banking too. It was in every sense the only *banking* company in London. With so many advantages over all competitors, it is quite natural that the Bank of England should have far outstripped them all. Inevitably it became *the* bank in London; all the other bankers grouped themselves round it, and lodged their reserve with it. Thus our *one*-reserve system of banking was not deliberately founded upon definite reasons; it was the gradual consequence of many singular events, and of an accumulation of legal privileges on a single bank...which no one would now defend.

Other nations in the later nineteenth and early twentieth centuries, taking Britain as their model, more deliberately fostered exclusive gold reserve holding by a central bank.

It is a central theme of Bagehot's book that, as he opens his concluding chapter (329), "the natural system of banking is that of many banks keeping their own cash reserve, with the penalty of failure before them if they neglect it," whereas England had through the privileges bestowed upon the Bank of England arrived at the system "of a single bank keeping the whole reserve under no effectual penalty of failure." Hayek's treatment of this aspect of the contrast between the natural banking system that would arise in the absence of legislative interference and the system that results from centralizing privileges is unfortunately muddied.

Hayek suggested (1937, 11) that the centralization of reserves is "only partly due to deliberate legislative interference" and is "partly due to less obvious institutional factors," such as "the fact that a country usually has one financial centre" where excess reserves can most readily be invested in liquid earning assets. He cited the United States prior to the founding of the Federal Reserve System as an example of a country where such a centralization of reserves took place "in spite of the absence of branch banking." He added that the tendency toward centralization "is considerably strengthened if instead of a system of small unit banks there are a few large joint stock banks with many branches; still more if the whole system is crowned by a single central bank, holder of the ultimate cash reserve."

Hayek's discussion here is problematic in several respects. The congregation of banks' head offices in a financial center, which can be expected to occur under a system of unrestricted branch banking, does not in fact represent centralization of reserves in the sense that Hayek (1937, 10) himself rightly insisted is relevant: it does not mean that "all the inhabitants of a country" become "dependent on the same amount of more liquid assets held for them collectively as a national reserve." Each of the many widely branched banks will hold its own distinct reserves. In the United States it was precisely the fact that banks from the hinterlands were legally barred from opening New York offices, and vice versa, that led country banks to deposit their reserves with city banks. Only as a result of such restriction-driven interbank deposits were reserves treated as a collective resource or common pool. Many separate banks counted on the availability of reserve funds that could not in fact be made available to them all in the event of simultaneous need. Country banks had to play preemptive strategies of claiming reserves before others could do so when even the possibility of a coming reserve stringency was perceived. Branch banking is an alternative to this treatment of reserves, not a "strengthening" of it. Much less is it a way station between unit banking and central banking.

Branch banking eliminates the problems of strategic behavior among independent claimants to a pool of reserves by bringing the various claimants within the same firm. Many branch banks rely on the same central pool of reserves, as did the several country banks who had deposits in the same city bank, but potential conflicts among the satellite banks are internalized by unitary ownership. In the terminology of industrial organization theory, vertical integration eliminates the problem of a potential for postcontractual opportunistic behavior between contracting firms (see Klein, Crawford, and Alchian 1978). In branch banking we have vertical integration between reserve-holding and reserve-claiming bank offices.

The industrial organization perspective is useful here because it enables us to see that central banking does not really solve the problem at hand, but instead perpetuates the division of responsibility between the reserve holder and the reserve claimants. Central banking changes only the form of the problem. Given that a central bank has the power to create new reserves for the domestic commercial banks,[8] its problem is not to ration a fixed stock of reserves when there are multiple independent banks laying claim, but to limit the creation of new reserves when they are sure to be called for by near-illiquid banks (and possibly by other claimants). Under a gold standard, such a limitation is needed to prevent an external drain from carrying away all of the central bank's gold reserves. In a fiat money system, the limitation is needed to prevent uncontrolled inflation.

In a passage separate from the last one quoted, Hayek (1937, 13) referred to what is essentially the problem of opportunistic claimants faced by a central bank on a gold standard:

> [T]he fundamental dilemma of all central banking policy has hardly ever been really faced: the only effective means by which a central bank can control an expansion of the generally used media of circulation is by making it clear in advance that it will not provide the cash (in the narrower sense) which will be required in consequence of such expansion, but at the same time it is recognized as the paramount duty of a central bank to provide that cash once the expansion of bank deposits has actually occurred and the public begins to demand that they should be converted into notes or gold.

Hayek's capsulization of it can easily be read as emphasizing the fact that this dilemma—the classic conflict between fighting external and internal drains placed in a dynamic context—is a case where conflicting strategic claims on the central bank's reserves arise. The dilemma arises from the central bank's inability, given a duty to fight internal drain, to credibly precommit itself not to create reserves. To borrow a term from the modern literature (Kydland and Prescott 1977), the central bank faces a time-consistency problem even under a gold standard regime. The head office of a branch banking firm has no such problem.

Contrasting Macroeconomic Effects

International redistributions of money under the one-national-reserve system are potentially momentous. The initial outflow means a loss of central-bank reserves. The central bank's reserves are typically too slender to allow the outflow to run its natural course unaided, that is, to allow the volume of central bank liabilities (which serve as reserves for the commercial banks) to shrink merely unit for unit with its reserves. The cumulative loss of international reserve money under that process would exhaust the central bank's reserves.

Thus, the central bank must artificially accelerate the process that curtails the net export of international reserve money. It can do so by (1) selling securities in its portfolio; (2) taking the route that Hayek (1937, 27) emphasized, "compelling people to repay loans," which likewise shrinks its portfolio; or (3) raising its discount rate in the manner of classical central-banking policy. Each of these measures contracts the national supplies of high-powered money and loanable funds, and temporarily raises short-term interest rates, with the dual effects of suppressing spending on imports (by suppressing spending generally) and attracting inflows of funds from abroad.

Hayek (1937, 28–30) emphasized that such a credit squeeze changes the allocational impact of the process of international monetary redistribution. The contraction in loans "will mean that the full force of the reduction of the money stream will have to fall on investment activity." The engineered rise in the interest rate will put it "above the equilibrium or 'natural' rate of interest" for a time. (Once the natural flow-limiting process acting through income and expenditure reductions—which continues to run its course—has progressed far enough, the credit squeeze becomes overkill and can be discontinued.) Investors "who would otherwise not have been affected by the change" are thus compelled "to give up money which they would have invested productively." Investment plans are disappointed, and a spell of unemployment of capital and complementary labor—a recession—results.

Those familiar with the business cycle theory of Hayek's *Prices and Production* (1935) will recognize this account as the inverse of the unsustainable Hayekian boom fueled by artificially low interest rates. The central point of this discussion, however, does not depend on the empirical importance of interest-rate-linked allocational effects in accounting for business cycle phenomena (about which many economists are skeptical). Within the framework of almost any monetary theory of business cycles, the central bank causes a disturbance when it engineers a contraction of the domestic money supply that outruns the cumulative reduction in money demand from the chain of income reductions set in motion by the real shift initially postulated.

Viewed in a monetary disequilibrium framework (see Yeager 1986), the critical feature of the external-drain-curtailing central-bank policy is that it creates an excess demand for money, which implies an excess supply of commodities and labor, and which instigates a recession. Alternatively viewed in a continual-market-clearing framework, the policy creates a negative price-level shock.[9] In either of these frameworks, we have "a disturbance which possesses all the characteristics of a purely monetary disturbance, namely that it induces changes...which...are not based on any corresponding change in the underlying real facts" of tastes, technology, or resources (Hayek 1937, 31).

As Hayek (1937, 33) emphasized, monetary disturbances of this sort are "defects inherent in the system of the collective holding of proportional [fractional] cash reserves for national areas, whatever the policy adopted by the central bank or the banking system," short of reserves being kept "large enough to allow them to vary by the full amount by which the total circulation of the country might possibly change." The national limitation of bank-issued money will inevitably mean that international flows of money are attended by money supply disturbances (unless the classical Currency Principle of 100 percent marginal gold reserve requirements, which would force the money supply to shrink precisely one-for-one with exports of gold, is applied to all forms of bank-issued money).

International redistributions of money within a system of fully integrated international branch banking would involve no such worrisome side effects. An interlocal money transfer, prompted, for example, by a change in spending patterns and relative money demands of the sort considered above, would reduce the quantity of money in one area and raise it in another. There is no reason to believe, however, that it would create a monetary disturbance in either place the way accelerated money destruction or creation within a national banking system does. The absence of disequilibration that Hayek (1937, 24) affirmed for interregional money flows under a purely metallic international monetary system holds also for an international branch banking system with bank-issued money.

As already discussed, the process of international money redistribution under global free banking is likely to (although it logically need not) involve a net expansion of monetary liabilities for some banks, a contraction for others, and a corresponding interbank reserve flow. The aggregate of all the contractions is much smaller in magnitude than it is under monetary nationalism, because the typical transnational bank will have inflows of money at some branches to offset at least partially the losses of its branches in the outflow region. The banks that contract on net may individually be forced to sell off marketable securities or actively call in loans in order to offset their losses of reserves.

This process does not mean a credit crunch for the region of net monetary outflow, however, nor the creation of an excess demand for money there. Even if bond and loan markets retain some regional specificity, no interest rate rise should be created by the actions of the contracting banks. Recall that the banks enjoying net expansion also have branches in the outflow region. Those banks will be in a position to buy an equivalent volume of securities and to extend loans to the borrowers turned away by the contracting banks. The profit motive will prompt them to take just such actions at the initially prevailing interest rate.

Alternatively, the expanding banks are in a position to lend reserves to the contracting banks to enable them to contract their assets at an optimizing pace not requiring hasty securities sales or calling in of loans. Being members of the same international clearing system or, in the case of partial integration, being linked by membership of at least some banks in multiple national clearing systems, the banks involved can be expected already to be regular players in an interbank reserve loan market (like the present-day Federal Funds market) that makes such loans extremely easy to arrange.

Taking the branches of net-contracting and net-expanding banks in the outflow region together, then, there is no reason for an exaggerated regional contraction of bank assets or monetary liabilities. Market forces will act to prevent any such occurrence. No excess demand for money will tend to afflict one nation while an excess supply crops up in another.

International integration of banking on a common monetary standard, furthermore, would promote the international integration of financial markets. International interest arbitrage would be even more complete than it is today, unburdened by exchange rate risk. Thus, an excess demand for loanable funds in one nation matched by an excess supply in another could not persist for any significant period. Interest rates would be less influenced by nationally distinct supply and demand conditions under international free banking than under a national reserve system.

To forestall possible misunderstanding, the argument advanced here does not involve the following two claims. First, it does not claim that all monetary disturbances are ruled out in a truly international monetary system. Exogenous region-to-region shifts in money demand can still occur, as the case discussed illustrates. The argument claims only that an international free banking system, unlike a system of national central banks, does not amplify such disturbances by adding money supply shocks to the process of adjustment. Interregional integration, whether across nations or across parts of a single nation, promotes the smoothest possible adjustment to interregional money demand shifts. Interregional shifts in the demand for dollars are presumably going on all the time within the United States as growth rates vary among parts of the country, but U.S. citizens hardly notice. Interregional monetary redistributions within an integrated banking system create no balance-of-payments crises.

Second, the argument here does not claim that the process of international monetary redistribution goes smoothly in an integrated system because each unit of money transferred necessarily reflects, and simultaneously relieves, excess supply of money in the sending country and excess demand in the recipient country. A shift in spending patterns of the type we have discussed may result in an outflow of money in the intermediate run greater than the final outflow, due to the "shock absorber" function of money balances. (This fact contributes to the difficulty a central bank faces in simply letting the outflow run its course.) Money balances may fall in the first country below the long-run desired level of money balances, and the reverse may happen in the second country, because individuals do not immediately decide upon or execute the changes in spending and income-earning activities necessary to reestablish the desired levels. A "long and variable lag" may transpire before the senders replenish excessively depleted balances and before the recipients dissipate an excess accumulation.

The gradualness of these adjustments is part and parcel of a process of economic coordination. Though in this sense there may be "overshooting" of national money stocks, no rationale emerges for a counteracting official policy. It is a demerit of the accelerated stanching of reserve flows that is characteristic of monetary nationalism that, as Hayek (1937, 29) put it,

> the transfer of only a fraction of the amount of money which would have been transferred under a purely metallic system, and the substitution of a multiple credit contraction for the rest, as it were, deprives the individuals in the country concerned of the possibility of delaying the adaptation by temporarily paying for an excess of imports in cash.

The international acceptance of bank-issued moneys, and the presence of branches of expanding banks even in the region from which money is flowing, furnishes the possibility of optimally gradual adaptation under a system of international free banking.

To put the argument of this section in a slightly different way, the process of international redistribution of money does not, with global branch banking, involve a deflationary process in one country and an inflationary process in another. For this reason, one is not compelled toward regarding independent national currencies with floating exchange rates as the best feasible option among international monetary arrangements, even upon accepting for an unalterable fact, as did Milton Friedman (1953, 171) in his classic essay "The Case for Flexible Exchange Rates," that "nations have been unwilling to allow [balance of payments] deficits to exert any deflationary effect."[10]

International Free Banking, or an International Central Bank?

The basic flaw underlying the doctrine of monetary nationalism, in Hayek's critical interpretation (1937, 35), is to be found in the premise "that the criteria of a good monetary policy which are applicable to a closed system are equally valid for a single country" within a network of global trade. This premise is false, whatever the criteria of good monetary policy might be.

The rational choice between alternative truly international monetary systems to which Hayek referred in this chapter's opening epigraph— the choice between free banking without regard to national borders and an international central bank—depends crucially on spelling out the criteria of good monetary policy and comparing the alternative systems' abilities to fulfill them. If indeed "there is no rational basis for the separate regulation of the quantity of money in a national area which remains a part of a wider economic system" (Hayek 1937, 73), is there yet a rational basis for the deliberate regulation of the quantity of money by a world central bank?

It should be noted that Hayek, unlike Cooper, McKinnon, and advocates of the European Central Bank project, did not endorse the establishment of a multinational fiat money, at least not until the political realities change. So long as contending national states and the temptations of inflationary finance continue to exist, the benefits of an international commodity money exceed its costs.

> On purely economic grounds it must be said that there are hardly any arguments which can be advanced for, and many serious objections which can be raised against, the use of gold as the international money. In a securely established world State with a government immune against the temptations of inflation it might be absurd to spend enormous effort in extracting gold out of the earth if cheap tokens would render the same service as gold with equal or greater efficiency. Yet in a world consisting of sovereign national States there seem to me to exist compelling political reasons why gold (or the precious metals) alone and no kind of artificial international currency, issued by some international authority, could be used successfully as the international money. (Hayek 1937, 74–75)

Hayek elaborated (1937, 75) that a suitable reserve money is one that "in all eventualities will remain universally acceptable in international transactions." The threat of war and other crises will loom "so long as there are separate sovereign States." Against such threats people will want to hold

> the one thing which by age-long custom civilized as well as uncivilized people are ready to accept—that is, since gold alone will serve one of the purposes for which stocks of money are held...and since to some extent gold will always be held for this purpose, there can be little doubt that it is the only sort of international standard which in the present world has any chance of surviving.

This is a powerful argument against proposals for an international fiat money issued by a coalition of central banks, because coalitions among national governments are notoriously fragile. It also suggests that there are natural obstacles to the market acceptance of a newfangled international money issued privately. Gold has the virtue of being no issuer's liability, and therefore of being independent of any issuer's solvency, probity, reputation, or political fortunes. Gold has a history that assures potential holders of its future acceptability.

Hayek's argument alerts us to the likelihood that so long as nations exist, gold is going to continue to be held in both official reserves and private portfolios, as we have indeed seen since its official demonetization in 1971. Given that the real demand to hold gold is going to persist under any fiat money regime, and may even grow (as the rise in gold's relative price since 1971 suggests has occurred) due to the uncertainty inherently surrounding fiat money, monetization of gold is not costly. One of the leading objections to the monetary use of gold—the additional resource cost it is supposed to entail by comparison to fiat money—rests on empirically false premises (Garrison 1985).

With the basic money of the world being furnished outside the banking system by gold mines and private mints, a world central bank could act on the quantity of money through the "money multiplier" that links the quantity of bank-issued money to the quantity of gold. Hayek's statements concerning the desirable characteristics of a monetary system suggest that he considered it desirable for a world central bank to act so as to offset changes that would otherwise raise or lower the multiplier. For each nation taken individually, he espoused the Currency Principle ideal (1937, 86, 90) that the money stock should change only one-for-one with flows of gold, "making the credit money provided by the private banks behave as a purely metallic circulation would behave under similar circumstances." Following that principle, changes in a money multiplier should be avoided for the global stock of money. Hayek's ideal of "really rational regulation of the quantity of money" may consist largely in this.

This interpretation is reinforced by reading the fourth lecture of Hayek's 1935 *Prices and Production*, in which a more explicit guide to "neutral" monetary policy is offered. Hayek argued there (108–11) that prima facie "the supply of money should be invariable" in the face of changes in production. Though changes in the quantity of money in an open economy serve an important function, that "of enabling the inhabitants to draw a larger or smaller share of the total product of the world," no such function is served by changes in the quantity of money in a closed economy. "An increase of its monetary circulation either for [an isolated] community or for the world as a whole [is] useless." The fact that changes in the quantity of money can come about through changes in a money multiplier, and the fact that the multiplier shows a well-known procyclical pattern, creates a role for the central bank (Hayek 1937, 117): it should contract its own high-powered liabilities to offset increases in the multiplier due to reductions in commercial bank reserve ratios during the upswing.

Hayek also argued that the central bank of a closed economy should, for the sake of monetary neutrality, vary the quantity of money reciprocally with movements in velocity, so as to keep constant "the volume of payments made during a period of time" (1937, 123); that is, the central bank ideally should follow a rule of keeping constant what the quantity equation denotes MV, the product of the money stock M and its velocity of circulation V. But he conceded (1937, 124–25) that this rule "can never be a practical maxim of currency policy," as it is impossible to translate into operational guidelines. Hence "the only practical maxim for monetary policy" is that the bank should not expand its liabilities either to allow for a boom or to combat a recession.

It is not possible to offer a thorough examination of various policy criteria here. George A. Selgin (1988, 1991) has discussed at some length the concept of monetary equilibrium and has argued that a free banking system is better equipped than a central banking system to maintain it.[11] Selgin does not deny that the ratio of bank-issued money to gold would vary in a free banking system, but argues that unregulated competition would tend to allow such variations only in response to changes in demand for bank-issued money, and thereby would promote equilibrating rather than disequilibrating adjustments. A central bank, by contrast, inherently lacks the knowledge necessary to simulate the competitive result.

Quite apart from the informational problems of central banks, anyone who shares Hayek's "practical" concern with counteracting central banks' tendency toward unwarranted expansions of the quantity of money may well find a free banking system to be the best practical alternative, given the temptations to which central banks are prone. A world central bank, and to a slightly lesser extent a pan-European central bank, would be a monopolist without any competitive discipline. It is difficult to imagine how effective incentives could be created for its managers to adhere to an ideal policy, or why its sponsoring governments would even want to tie its hands, since they would thereby limit its ability to serve their changing wants. If inflationary biases are as inherent to a multinational central bank sponsored by a consortium of nation-states as they are to the fiat-money-issuing central banks individually sponsored by those states, then the fundamental obstacle to a sound international monetary system is not so much monetary nationalism as it is monetary statism.

Notes

1. As Ruiz (1989) notes, Hayek (1978, 104 n. 1) has provided the following retrospective view of his own 1937 work: "It contains a series of lectures hastily and

badly written on a topic to which I had earlier committed myself but which I had to write when I was pre-occupied with other problems. I still believe that it contains important arguments against flexible exchange rates between national currencies which have never been adequately answered, but I am not surprised that few people appear ever to have read it."

2. An exception might be made here for the informal use of dollars and other foreign currencies, especially in financially repressed and high-inflation countries. The central bank's control over the quantity of money is of course constrained more or less tightly where it commits to a pegged exchange rate, as in the EMS, the West African franc zone, and in countries like Argentina which at the moment are pegged to the U.S. dollar.

3. Ruiz (1989) reminds us that Hayek endorsed central banking in *The Constitution of Liberty* (1960, chapter 21). But that endorsement may be viewed as acquiescence to the status quo, whereas advocacy of an international central bank in 1937 amounted to pushing for an expansion of state control over money.

4. The geographical domain of a legal system need not be coextensive with that of a nation-state. Nor vice-versa. On the history of non-nationalistic legal systems in Europe, see Berman (1983). On the history of private mints in the United States, see Kagin (1981).

5. An interesting exception that qualifies the rule was the circulation of Scottish banknotes in northern English counties during the early nineteenth century, despite the prohibition of cross-border branching. Because their circulation was limited to counties adjacent to the border, the episode actually illustrates the point that the area of circulation for a bank's liabilities is normally limited by the extent of its branch network (L. White 1984, 42).

6. The comparatively early spread of gold-economizing bank liabilities in Scotland, for example, allowed that country to export gold and silver in exchange for consumable and capital goods in the manner discussed at length by Adam Smith (1976, 292–98, 320–21).

7. Hayek (1937, 21–23) rightly pointed out that it can be misleading to leap from the hypothesized shift in product demands to reasoning in terms of aggregate shifts in real income, money demand, and money supply, and especially to movements in national price levels. The particular B residents whose incomes directly rise may spend some of their increased incomes on imports of certain goods from Country A, rather than simply increase the demand for the products of their B neighbors generally. The income losers in Country A may cut back on particular imports from Country B. There will generally be both winners and losers within each country from the relative price and income movements finally brought about by the sequence of spending adjustments prompted by the initial shift.

8. Even under the international gold standard, a central bank could create new reserves for the domestic banking system by issuing more of its own liabilities, at least in the short run before the price-specie-flow mechanism would begin to drain it of its own gold reserves and thereby force it to reverse course. It could ignore even that limit if it were prepared to suspend redeemability.

9. The hypothesis that markets continually clear, combined with the hypothesis (found in the "Iowa City" model of McCloskey and Zecher [1984, 124–25]) that the law of one price continually reigns internationally, would, however, seem to rule out the possibility that a national central bank could ever create a monetary disturbance. For criticism of the historical applicability of such a combination, see Friedman (1984).

10. One can, in similar fashion, make a case against independent national currencies by accepting as unalterable the fact that national governments have been unwill-

ing to allow rapid exchange rate appreciations (which cheapen imports) to exert any strongly negative effect on the position of domestic import-competing industries, but instead have moved to protectionism and exchange rate intervention. Hayek (1937, 65, 73–74) anticipated such a case.

11. For discussion of the Hayek and Selgin norms for monetary policy, see Ebeling 1991 and L. White 1991.

References

Bagehot, Walter. 1873. *Lombard Street: A Description of the Money Market.* London: Henry S. King.

Berman, Harold J. 1983. *Law and Revolution: The Formation of the Western Legal Tradition.* Cambridge, MA: Harvard University Press.

Cooper, Richard N. 1988. "Toward an International Commodity Standard?" *Cato Journal* 8 (Fall): 315–38.

Ebeling, Richard M. 1991. "Commentary: Stable Prices, Falling Prices, and Market-Determined Prices." In *Austrian Economics: Perspectives on the Past and Prospects for the Future,* edited by Richard M. Ebeling. Hillsdale, MI: Hillsdale College Press.

Friedman, Milton. 1953. *Essays in Positive Economics.* Chicago: University of Chicago Press.

———. 1984. "Comment [on McCloskey and Zecher 1984]." In *A Retrospective on the Classical Gold Standard, 1821–1931,* edited by Michael D. Bordo and Anna J. Schwartz. Chicago: University of Chicago Press.

Garrison, Roger. 1985. "The Costs of a Gold Standard." In *The Gold Standard: An Austrian Perspective,* edited by Llewellyn H. Rockwell. Lexington, MA: Lexington Books.

Hayek, F. A. [1935] 1967. *Prices and Production.* 2d ed. Reprint, New York: Augustus M. Kelley.

———. [1937] 1971. *Monetary Nationalism and International Stability.* Reprint, New York: Augustus M. Kelley.

———. 1960. *The Constitution of Liberty.* Chicago: University of Chicago Press.

———. 1973. *Law, Legislation, and Liberty.* Vol. 1. *Rules and Order.* Chicago: University of Chicago Press.

———. 1978. *The Denationalisation of Money.* 2d ed. London: Institute of Economic Affairs.

———. 1988. *The Fatal Conceit: The Errors of Socialism.* Vol. 1 of the Collected Works of F. A. Hayek, edited by W. W. Bartley III. London: Routledge.

Hume, David [1752] 1970. "Of the Balance of Trade." In *Writings on Economics,* edited by Eugene Rotwein. Madison, WI: University of Wisconsin Press.

Kagin, Donald H. 1981. *Private Gold Coins and Patterns of the United States.* New York: Arco.

Klein, Benjamin, Robert Crawford, and Armen Alchian. 1978. "Vertical Integration, Appropriable Rents, and the Competitive Contracting Process." *Journal of Law and Economics* 21 (October): 297–326.

Kydland, Finn E., and Edward C. Prescott. 1977. "Rules Rather than Discretion: The Inconsistency of Optimal Plans." *Journal of Political Economy* 85 (June): 473–91.

McCloskey, D. N., and J. Richard Zecher. 1984. "The Success of Purchasing-Power Parity: Historical Evidence and Its Implications for Macroeconomics." In *A Retrospective on the Classical Gold Standard, 1821–1931,* edited by Michael D. Bordo and Anna J. Schwartz. Chicago: University of Chicago Press.

McKinnon, Ronald I. 1988. "An International Gold Standard Without Gold." *Cato Journal* 8 (Fall): 351–73.

Ricardo, David [1817] 1971. *Principles of Political Economy and Taxation*. Edited by R.M. Hartwell. Harmondsworth: Penguin Books.

Ruiz, Jose Luis Garcia. 1989. "Comment on 'Monetary Nationalism Reconsidered.'" Unpublished manuscript. Universidad Complutense, Madrid.

Selgin, George A. 1988. *The Theory of Free Banking: Money Supply Under Competitive Note Issue*. Totowa, NJ: Rowman and Littlefield.

———. 1991. "Monetary Equilibrium and the 'Productivity Norm' of Price-Level Policy." In *Austrian Economics: Perspectives on the Past and Prospects for the Future*, edited by Richard M. Ebeling. Hillsdale, MI: Hilldale College Press.

Selgin, George A., and Lawrence H. White. 1987. "The Evolution of a Free Banking System." *Economic Inquiry* 25 (July): 439–57.

Smith, Adam. 1976. *An Inquiry into the Nature and Causes of the Wealth of Nations*, edited by R. H. Campbell, A. S. Skinner, and W. B. Todd. Oxford: Oxford University Press.

White, Eugene Nelson. 1983. *The Regulation and Reform of the American Banking System*. Princeton, NJ: Princeton University Press.

White, Lawrence H. 1984. *Free Banking in Britain: Theory, Experience, and Debate, 1800–45*. Cambridge: Cambridge University Press.

———. 1991. "Commentary: Norms for Monetary Policy." In *Austrian Economics: Perspectives on the Past and Prospects for the Future*, edited by Richard M. Ebeling. Hillsdale, MI: Hillsdale College Press.

Yeager, Leland B. 1986. "The Significance of Monetary Disequilibrium." *Cato Journal* 6 (Fall): 369–99.

———. 1997. "Hayek's Monetary Theory and Policy: A Critical Reconstruction." Unpublished manuscript, University of Georgia.

13

Currency Boards and Free Banking

Steve H. Hanke and Kurt Schuler

In this century, three types of monetary systems have predominated: central banking, free banking, and currency boards. Central banking is familiar to us all, because it is today the monetary system of almost every country. Free banking once existed in approximately seventy countries during the 1800s and the early 1900s (Dowd 1992a). Today there are no free banking systems, but free banking is enjoying an intellectual revival as a theoretical alternative to central banking, thanks to the work of economists such as Lawrence H. White, whose essay elsewhere in this volume describes free banking in more detail.

The currency board system, unlike free banking, is witnessing a real revival. Like free banking, the currency board system was once widespread: it has existed in approximately sixty-five countries. Unlike free banking, it still exists today in Hong Kong, Brunei, the Falkland Islands, Gibraltar, Argentina, Estonia, Lithuania, and (in greatly modified form) Singapore (Hanke and Schuler 1994). And if all goes according to plan, Bosnia and Bulgaria will have currency board systems in 1997. We think the currency board system is well suited for many countries today.

What Is a Currency Board?

A currency board is an institution that issues notes and coins convertible into an external "reserve" asset, such as a foreign currency or a commodity, on demand at a fixed exchange rate. It does not accept deposits. As reserves, a currency board holds high-quality, interest-bearing securities denominated in the reserve asset. A currency board's reserves are equal to 100 percent or slightly more of its notes and coins

403

in circulation, as set by law. The board generates profits (seignorage) from the difference between the interest earned on the securities that it holds and the expense of maintaining its note and coin circulation. It remits to its owner (historically, the government) all profits beyond what it needs to cover its expenses and to maintain its reserves at the level set by law. The currency board has no discretion in monetary policy. The central bank of the reserve-currency country (or, for a currency board whose reserve asset is a commodity, supply and demand in the commodity market) determines the supply of the reserve asset. The public's demand for notes and coins determines their circulation in the currency board system, and banks determine the supply of deposits (trying to keep this in accord with the public's demand by interpreting the meaning of changes in reserves). A currency board based on a foreign currency is much like using that currency directly, except that it captures for domestic benefit the seignorage that would otherwise accrue to the foreign issuer.

Commercial banks in a currency board system need not hold 100 percent reserves in reserve assets; only the currency board must hold reserves of 100 percent or more. Commercial banks in currency board systems have been typical fractional-reserve banks. Few currency board countries have imposed any legal reserve requirements on commercial banks. The currency board system therefore is not like the "Chicago Plan" of the 1930s, which would have required banks to hold 100 percent reserves in government bonds (Simons 1934; Fisher 1935), nor is it like Rothbard's (1962) plan for 100 percent gold-reserve banking. The currency board system seeks to ensure that the banking system remains solvent by allowing banks wide freedom to diversify risks, especially the freedom to establish branch networks. Also, a currency board does not act as a lender of last resort to commercial banks. The government may provide deposit insurance, but most governments of currency board countries have not done so; consequently, most currency board systems have lacked the element of moral hazard present in central banking systems, where the central bank's commitment to fund insolvent banks may be open-ended.

The duties of a currency board are confined to exchanging its notes and coins for the reserve asset at a fixed rate and to holding securities in sufficiently liquid form to ensure that it always can meet demands for redemption. Besides the usual reserve of 100 percent in securities denominated in the reserve asset, many currency boards have held an additional reserve of up to 10 percent to provide against losses in the value of the bonds they held.

Currency boards originally arose to replace free banking.[1] Banks in British colonies were prohibited from issuing more notes than the amount of their paid-in capital, so in some cases they would have been unable to fully satisfy increases in the demand for notes if rival banks failed. One solution would have been for colonial governments to repeal restrictions on note issue, but the British government would not have allowed it because the restrictions were a matter of imperial policy. Nor could the smaller colonies easily attract new banks to open and issue notes immediately. Under the circumstances, note issue by the colonial government seemed to be the only way out. Monopolizing note issue with the government would prevent bank failures from causing shortages of notes.

The Indian Ocean colony of Mauritius established the first currency board in 1849 after one of its note-issuing banks failed. Ceylon established a currency board in 1884, after a similar failure. The West African Currency Board, which opened in 1913, became a model for boards that followed because it was the first British colonial board to hold almost all its reserves in sterling-denominated securities. Previous British colonial boards had held large reserves of gold or silver coin, which paid no interest and reduced the seignorage that the boards generated. After the West African Currency Board, no new free banking systems were established in British colonies; and existing free banking systems, such as those of the Caribbean colonies and Rhodesia, were converted to currency board systems. Colonial governments abetted conversion because they were eager to gain seignorage as a source of revenue.

Although most currency boards have existed in British colonies or former colonies, there have been a number of currency boards elsewhere, including Argentina, the Philippines, Libya, and even Russia. The performance of the non-British and the British colonial currency boards was similar, suggesting that the currency board system itself rather than factors peculiar to British colonial administration were responsible for the success of the system. Most non-British currency boards used sterling assets as reserves, because sterling was the main currency for their international trade. A few boards used U.S. dollar assets or gold as reserve assets instead.

Currency board systems had excellent records. Only one currency board has ever devalued: the East Caribbean Currency Authority did so in 1976, not because it lacked adequate reserves, but because East Caribbean nations apparently wanted to improve their terms of trade. The currency boards of North Russia and Burma maintained fixed rates even during civil wars. Although the Japanese army overran Hong Kong and Malaya during World War II, their currency boards were able to resume their fixed exchange rates within months after the war because they had kept their assets safe in London.

Economic growth was satisfactory under currency board systems. British investment poured into colonies with currency boards because there was no exchange risk and because property rights were secure. It financed the rubber plantations and tin mines of Malaya, the cocoa and peanut plantations of West Africa, and the ports of Hong Kong and Singapore. Because sterling was one of the world's most stable currencies, at least until 1949, inflation rates were low in currency board systems. Fixed exchange rate with sterling, or with other relatively stable currencies such as the U.S. dollar, kept inflation low. Contrary to a frequently made theoretical criticism, in practice the currency board system did not stultify foreign capital investment.

Despite the success of currency boards, most countries replaced it with central banking in the 1950s and 1960s. Economic theory played some role: Keynesians expected wonderful results from discretionary monetary policy. But the main reasons for change were political. Politicians saw central banking as a way of manipulating the money supply to their own advantage. Newly independent nations attached great symbolic importance to central banks as supposed symbols of political maturity.

The Problem of Credibility

To be effective, a monetary system must be credible. Credibility means that people believe the institutions operating the monetary system will keep explicit promises to maintain convertibility or implicit promises not to depreciate the currency quickly. In the 1950s and 1960s, when most countries that had currency boards replaced them with central banks, economists did not appreciate the connection between credibility and policy rules. They supposed that a central bank could retain credibility despite a lack of rules to restrain its behavior. They neglected to consider that discretionary monetary policy can easily (or inevitably, according to Selgin [1988, 89–125]) become a destabilizing force in the economy.

The few central banks today that have a fair degree of credibility exist mainly in developed countries. Of those, the central banks that have caused the least inflation have been the most politically independent (Alesina 1989, 81). Most of the central banks that replaced currency boards have had little political independence and have performed abysmally, as have other central banks in less developed countries. For the ninety-nine nations that the World Bank classifies as low- and middle-income, average annual inflation was 16.7 percent from 1965 to 1980 and 53.7 percent from 1980 to 1989. Average annual growth in gross national product (GNP) per person for the same nations was 2.5 percent from 1965 to 1989, barely more than the average of 2.4 percent in high-income countries (World Bank 1991, 205). Hong Kong and Singapore, the main economies that still have currency boards, did much better, in part because their currency board systems provide them with relatively stable currencies. In Singapore, average annual growth in GNP per person was 7.0 percent from 1965 to 1989, and in Hong Kong it was 6.3 percent. Moreover, Hong Kong and Singapore maintained inflation rates that on average were as low as those of the high-income countries.

The poor performance of central banks explains why Paul Volcker, the former chairman of the U.S. Federal Reserve System, has expressed little hope that central banks in formerly communist nations can achieve full currency convertibility. Addressing central bankers in Jackson Hole, Wyoming, in 1990, Mr. Volcker noted that markets developed long before central banks, stressing that Eastern Europe and the USSR might actually retard their transition to markets by relying on central banks (Volcker 1990). Indeed, central banks are essentially a form of central planning, which is why Marx and Engels said in the *Communist Manifesto* that one of the steps for achieving communism was "Centralization of credit in the hands of the state, by means of a national bank with state capital and an exclusive monopoly" (Marx and Engels [1848] 1948, 30).

To gain credibility, central banks in less developed countries, including those in Eastern Europe and the former Soviet Union, must painstakingly establish good track records. (Governments in many of those countries have a long tradition of violating the spirit of the laws. Consequently, attempts to improve independence will probably fail. The discretionary powers of central banks will be too tempting a prize for politicians and bureaucrats to disregard.) The lack of credibility of official promises has already led many people in less developed countries to conduct their own unofficial monetary reform by dollarizing local markets. To a lesser extent, credibility is even a problem for central banks in many developed countries. Dollars and other relatively stable foreign currencies are the principal store of value in many less developed countries; in some countries they are even the unit of account and medium of exchange for large payments.

A central bank that is not credible must play against the public in a game that has no winners. Promises by the central bank to maintain currency stability, even by means of fixed exchange rates, are not credible. Prices continue to rise quickly because workers base their wage demands on the central bank's dismal past performance. State-owned enterprises and government ministries continue to run deficits, because they will correctly expect that the government will rescue them by forcing the central bank to print money, as has so often happened before. Workers and enterprises anticipate that this "soft budget constraint" will continue, and they behave accordingly.

If a central bank with severe credibility problems does establish and maintain currency stability, the consequences can be even worse than under continued inflation. Because the central bank lacks credibility, people will remain skeptical of it for years. To gain credibility, the central bank must keep its currency overvalued and keep real (inflation-adjusted) interest rates high, which may plunge the country into a depression. That is what happened in Yugoslavia, whose December 1989 currency reform was insufficiently credible. People correctly anticipated that the National Bank of Yugoslavia would not maintain the original fixed exchange rate, so real interest rates exceeded 30 percent per year because the rates contained a large devaluation risk premium (Hanke and Schuler 1991a, 9–10). Similarly, Argentina's March 1991 monetary reform installed a quasi-currency board, without a firm commitment to the present exchange rate of the Argentine peso with the U.S. dollar (cf. Hanke and Schuler 1991b, 8). As of August 1992, rates on peso loans remained higher than rates on dollar loans in Argentina, which reflected devaluation risk. In a monetary system with no devaluation risk and no barriers to capital movements, arbitrage tends to keep interest rates the same as they are in the country to whose currency the local currency is fixed.

One approach to the problem of credibility is to sidestep it by floating the exchange rate. But though a floating exchange rate balances supply and demand for domestic currency against foreign currency, it does not restrain the central bank's power to create credit. Instead, it often leads to a South American-style hyperinflation. Domestic political pressure groups that benefit from soft budget constraints favor renewed inflation rather than stable money and prices. As inflation mounts, prices become increasingly unreliable indicators for guiding economic activity and output falls. This is happening now in the former Soviet Union.

To really solve the problem of credibility under fixed exchange rates and the dangers of high inflation under floating exchange rates, less developed countries should replace their central banks.[2] The purpose of a central bank is to manipulate the money supply. Central banks have a bias towards inflation because in the short term inflation can increase seignorage and reduce the real burden of government debt. Promises by central banks to maintain a stable currency rarely have been binding; and even where supposedly binding, promises have not been enforceable.

Free banking systems were quite credible because they depoliticized the supply of money. Under free banking, governments gained little seignorage from inflation. Bank notes comprised most of the currency, and profits from issuing them accrued to banks instead of to governments. Since governments benefited little from inflation, legislatures and courts could fairly impartially enforce the promises of creditors, including the promises of free banks to redeem notes and deposits in gold or silver. Not all free banking systems were equally successful in limiting government involvement; some governments intervened to force the monetary system to accept unwanted government debt (Schuler 1992a, 29, 35; Schuler 1992b, 84–86). Overall, however, free banking systems more effectively depoliticized the money supply than central banking systems have done.

The currency board depoliticizes the supply of money not by leaving it exclusively to the private sector, but by requiring reserves in external assets of at least 100 percent against government note and coin issue. The orthodox currency board system does not permit "fiduciary" note and coin issue backed by domestic government securities, though some less orthodox currency boards did maintain a fiduciary issue. Limited fiduciary issue is theoretically compatible with an automatic, completely rule-bound monetary policy, but in practice, political pressure for further fiduciary issue is greater when fiduciary issue already exists. Fiduciary issue by currency boards speeded their conversion into central banks in Rhodesia and East Africa. Governments have exhibited a uniform tendency to loosen limits on fiduciary issue by central banks, leading eventually to depletion of reserves and devaluation; the Federal Reserve System, for instance, originally had strict limits on fiduciary issue, and today it issues a fiat currency.

How Currency Boards Can Lay
the Groundwork for Free Banking

Currency boards and free banking are similar in their intent to depoliticize the supply of money. The currency board system does so by subjecting government issue of money to strict rules, whereas free banking did so by eliminating or at least marginalizing government issue of money. Most currency boards have been monopoly issuers of notes and coins. However, some have issued in competition with free banks, and no necessary conflict exists between the currency board system and free banking.

The main obstacle to free banking is central banking. Central banks will not give up their accumulated monopoly powers without a fight. Despite the poor performance of most central banks, public opinion at present supports the idea of government monopoly in note and coin issue, largely because monopoly issue has existed for so long that most people cannot imagine how competitive note issue could work. (We invite anyone who doubts our claims to argue the case for free banking with anyone not already familiar with free banking.)

On the surface, the currency board system appears a little different from central banking, although appearances are deceiving. It is fairly easy to make people understand how the currency board system works and what advantages it offers over central banking. The currency board system commands respect even from central bankers (e.g., Hetzel 1990). It has also recently received encouragement in legislation: the U.S. Public Law 102–392, U.S. Statutes-at-Large, vol. 106, 1636, which directs the IMF to use the U.S. quota contribution to establish currency board systems in IMF member countries, if appropriate.

Even as a monopoly issuer, the currency board, especially in the form we propose, would be a giant step towards free banking. Advocates of free banking should support the currency board system at least as a way station towards competitive issue of currency. By depoliticizing the supply of money, the currency board system encourages the tendencies essential to a stable free banking system. It is thus especially well suited for Eastern Europe,[3] where banking until recently was a government monopoly.

The financial wreckage left by socialism will take some time to remove. Most government banks are in effect bankrupt because they accumulated large portfolios of bad loans. Many new "private" banks have state enterprises (whose finances are often shaky) as their largest stockholders, depositors, and borrowers. There is nothing inherently wrong with industrial-financial combines, provided that they impose no drain on taxpayers. However, many East European "private" banks are really just unofficial appendages of the government banking system; and they are engaging in the same behavior that bankrupted the government banks because they expect that the central bank will bail them out. Another defect of East European banking systems is that knowledge of Western-style accounting, risk analysis, and other skills necessary for running a bank in a market economy is low. We have encountered a number of East European bankers who do not even know how to prepare a proper balance sheet!

A developed financial system has enough strength to partly neutralize the effects of an unstable currency by means of indexation, floating interest rates, futures markets, and shorter maturities for loans. An underdeveloped financial system lacks such instruments, making it far more vulnerable to instability in the currency. It is crucial that during the transition to capitalism, the currency have unquestioned stability. No system of checking accounts and check clearing exists yet in much of Eastern Europe, so currency has a greater role in business and personal payments than it does in the West. An unstable currency would destroy the emerging links of monetary exchange that are replacing business relationships formerly linked through central planning. An unstable currency would also keep the financial system underdeveloped ("repressed"), because lenders would lack the confidence to make long-term loans.

Central banks in the region have already shown that they cannot provide stable currencies. Domestic banks probably cannot do so either: they lack capital and talent. Large foreign banks could issue currency just as they now issue travellers checks, but Eastern European governments will not let them. The currency board system is the solution. Currency boards could operate within national boundaries or could be international, as several British colonial currency boards were.

By issuing stable currencies, currency boards would promote the financial development of Eastern Europe, both by restoring incentives to save and by encouraging the transfer of capital and banking know-how that Eastern Europe needs. Currency boards linked to the U.S. dollar or German mark would eliminate exchange risk with major trading partners, facilitating trade. If property rights are secure, with trade would come investment, and with investment would come branch offices of foreign banks. Residents in currency board systems would have access to large pools of capital available at terms roughly comparable to those in the West. Foreign banks would also bring new financial techniques that would enable East European economies to mobilize domestic savings more efficiently. Competition would weed out weak banks, probably resulting in a few large, well-capitalized banks with nationwide branch networks and with ready access to international financial markets. Moral-hazard risks that currently plague East European banking systems would vanish, because there would be no central banks to guarantee deposits. (Governments could provide deposit insurance, though it would be unwise. Privately provided deposit insurance would be superior.)

In nations with repressed financial systems, currency boards can play a beneficial role even where free banking is allowed immediately. A currency board, operating as a competitive issuer, would ensure that at least one brand of currency would be stable, no matter what happened to the currencies issued by commercial banks. A sudden move to free banking with no currency board might be politically disastrous. A widely publicized failure by a note-issuing bank could permanently tarnish the idea of free banking, as it did in some cases that we mentioned above where free banking was replaced by the currency board system.

To be more realistic, it is probable that developing nations in Eastern Europe and elsewhere will not allow free banking for some years, if ever. At present, competitive issue of notes is too unfamiliar to be politically feasible. In the meantime, establishing currency boards would move their monetary system in the direction that advocates of free banking desire (cf. Hayek 1978, 20).

Replacing a Central Bank with a Currency Board

Places as diverse as North Russia, Palestine, Danzig, and the Philippines once replaced central banks with currency boards. The steps are simple. We have discussed the details elsewhere (Hanke and Schuler 1991d; Hanke, Jonung, and Schuler 1992, 80–83), so we shall just sketch the outline here. The steps that follow are for a socialist nation with a monopoly banking system, but with suitable modifications they can fit a nation that already has competing deposit banks. The first five steps should occur nearly simultaneously, if possible, and the entire sequence could be carried out within a few months if competently executed.

1. Delegate to other bodies all central banking functions that do not directly concern influencing the supply of money. The finance ministry can regulate bank practices and give advice on monetary affairs. Commercial banks themselves can manage the check clearing system, as they do in Canada. Commercial banks can also provide mutual deposit insurance protection, as they do in Germany and Switzerland.

2. *Abolish the central bank's power to increase the supply of money.* This requires the overall deposit credits of the central bank, although not individual credits, to be frozen at existing levels. Also, the supply of notes and coins should be frozen at existing levels. A government can budget deficits under a currency board system, but it cannot rely on a central bank to monetize government debt. To finance deficits, it must either borrow from the public or raise taxes. Government-owned banks or other enterprises that incur losses must be sold, declared bankrupt, or subsidized out of tax revenue. Hence, a currency board system imposes a "hard budget constraint" on government fiscal practices.

3. *Separate the central bank's commercial banking functions from its currency issue functions.* In many former socialist countries the central bank both is a "monobank" that both issues currency and lends to state enterprises. The commercial banking functions should be spun off into independent commercial banks and privatized.

4. *Make sure that commercial banks have adequate reserves.* In a monobank system, no distinction exists between reserves and other assets. To provide the commercial banks spun off from the monobank with some liquidity, it will be necessary to give them some reserves. The free reserves held by banks in developed countries rarely exceed 5 percent of deposit liabilities. In socialist countries, higher reserves will probably be necessary because the condition of banking technology is primitive. We suggest 10 percent reserves as a rule of thumb, realizing that in many cases bank deposits will have to be frozen or written off even for this high level of reserves to be adequate. As we said above, socialism has left many East European banks insolvent, and depositors may never be able to recover the full value of their deposits. While restructuring of the banks proceeds, it is vital that individuals and enterprises be allowed some use of their deposits to avoid costly cash-only settlement of payments and the ensuing temporary shortage of currency. Giving banks 10 percent reserves would complete the freeze of deposits.

5. *Convert liabilities of the central bank into currency board notes and coins.* After steps (3) and (4), the monobank's deposit liabilities will have been converted into deposit liabilities of the commercial banks spun off from it or into reserves of the commercial banks. After this

step, all that remains of the monobank are its note and coins issue, net worth (as liabilities), and its holdings of foreign exchange (as its main assets).

6. *Fix an exchange rate.* The government must now fix an exchange rate with a reserve asset (probably a foreign currency) and, simultaneously, make sure that the nascent currency board has external assets of at least 100 percent of notes and coins in circulation. If the existing exchange rate is somewhat credible, the government can use that rate for the currency board. If not, and if the economy is in such a crisis that an immediate solution is necessary, the government can set the exchange rate at the existing black-market rate. Doing so typically results in temporary undervaluation of the currency, choking imports (however unfortunately), and causing an export boom. We recommend against using calculations of purchasing power parity for setting the exchange rate, because they are notoriously unreliable.

Where the situation permits a more leisurely approach, the government can set the currency free for a brief "clean float." It should announce at the beginning of the float what reserve currency it intends to use and on what date it will fix the exchange rate. Expectations may be volatile, so the exchange rate will be only a rough guide to the "correct" exchange rate. Since the object of a currency reform such as we propose is to give market forces freer reign, however, there is no better guide than the floating market rate to indicate the roughly correct fixed rate.

7. *Ensure that foreign currency reserves equal 100 percent of note and coin circulation.* The currency board should begin with foreign currency reserves equal to 100 percent of its note and coin circulation. Allowing the board a fiduciary issue may subject it to pressure for further fiduciary issue and for mutation into a type of central bank. If existing government reserves of foreign currency reserves are inadequate for 100 percent backing, the government could increase the reserve ratio by selling state property. If reserves are still less than 100 percent, it will be necessary to borrow the difference from international agencies, foreign central banks, or foreign commercial banks.

8. *Open the board for business.* We have not yet discussed how costly a currency board system would be. It need not require enormous reserves at the start. In most countries that are prime candidates for the currency board system, the real supply of domestic currency is small. Years of high inflation and currency restrictions have induced people to hold real assets and hard foreign currency in preference to domestic financial assets and domestic currency. For instance, before the March

1991 reform that established a quasi-currency board system in Argentina, it was estimated that U.S. currency in circulation was equal to domestic currency plus deposits. In Eastern Europe, substitution out of domestic currencies has occurred to such an extent that at present market rates of exchange, the reserves necessary for currency board systems (100 percent reserves for notes and coins in circulation plus, say, 10 percent reserves for bank deposits) would range from $70 million in Albania to no more than $6 billion for Russia. As in Argentina, much of the supply of money in Eastern Europe does not appear in official statistics because it is held in foreign currency.

It may seem that a currency board country would need to run continual current account surpluses to enable the supply of domestic money supply to grow rapidly. As we said above, the currency board system does not rigidly link the supply of money to the current account balance. Hong Kong and Singapore have run current account deficits for decades at a time, yet massive foreign capital investment promoted by the currency board system enabled them to increase their domestic money supplies and to enjoy rapid economic growth.

A Currency Board as a Competitor to the Central Bank

Entrenched political forces that favor central banking may prevent a nation from abolishing the central bank outright. It may still be feasible to establish a currency board as the issuer of a parallel currency. In a parallel-currency system, the central bank can continue to function with its existing staff and its existing assets. The central bank currency will not have a fixed exchange rate with the currency board currency unless both use the same reserve asset. The currency board's notes and coins should be given equivalent legal tender status with those of the central bank. A parallel currency will give the central bank the choice of ceasing to depreciate its currency or withering away as people switch to using the currency board's currency.

Contrary to what one might expect, government revenue from seignorage under a parallel-currency system may *increase*. A currency board would give countries where dollarization is extensive the chance to capture some seignorage that it is now losing to the Federal Reserve System.

To start the currency board in such circumstances, people need an incentive to reverse the process of dollarization. The solution is to offer a small premium on foreign currency for a short period. During that period, the board would only accept foreign currency. For instance, after announcing a choice of reserve currency and an exchange rate, the board can offer to pay a premium of 2 percent on all hard currency offered to it within one week by citizens of the country. To prevent arbitrageurs from using its offer for pure speculative gain, the board could limit the amount converted per person and retain the right to revoke the premium at its discretion. After the offer expired, the board would only conduct exchanges at the previously announced exchange rate and would cease paying a premium. As long as there is some confidence in the board, it will easily be able to recoup the expense of the premium within a short time from the interest earned on reserve-currency assets. The board should secure a loan to ensure that it has 100 percent reserves from the start, but soon its interest income will enable it to repay the loan.

Rather than competing with a domestically issued currency, a parallel currency may complete with the Russian ruble in some former Soviet republics (see Schuler, Selgin, and Sinkey 1991; Hanke, Jonung, and Schuler 1992, 35–42). Unlike the case we just discussed, where the currency board begins with no reserve currency at all, the former Soviet republics have hard currency assets. For them, the steps for establishing a currency board as a parallel issuer are:

1. Fix an exchange rate with the reserve currency and issue no more currency than the board has reserves. The exchange rate merely determines the units in which the new currency is denominated. It has no other effect. The new currency and the old will circulate in parallel, at floating exchange rates. It will be a matter for individuals to decide if they want to continue to use the old currency or use the new currency. Presumably, the new currency will eventually almost drive the old currency out of circulation, because the new currency will be more stable; but the pace will be determined by the market. People will be able to exchange the two currencies at floating market exchange rates because another step in the reform is

2. Remove all foreign exchange restrictions.

3. Distribute the new currency according to some formula. The new currency could be given away on a per person or per household basis. Once it has been distributed, people will start depositing it in banks as savings and using it in payments, so there will be a dual system of bank accounts and prices in each currency, with the freedom to switch from one currency to the other at market rates of exchange. The government may require payment of taxes in the new currency, but it should allow private transactions to occur in whatever currency is agreeable to the parties involved. If the government wishes to switch its own payments and revenues into the new currency, it should make the conversion using the floating exchange rate. For instance, if the new currency—call it the gelt—has a fixed exchange rate equal to 0.5 German marks, and 0.5 marks trade at a floating exchange rate of 40 rubles on the day that the government makes the conversion, all payments of 40 rubles become payments of one gelt. Such a conversion leaves the real amount of payments unchanged; it simply redenominates them in a more stable currency.

Ways of Insulating the Currency Board from Political Pressure

Past currency boards were too easily converted into central banks. Future currency boards can avoid the same fate by combining elements that past boards used into a package of measures that will forestall attempts at government manipulation (Hanke, Jonung, and Schuler 1992, 47–51, 54-56).

We suggest that a majority of the currency board's directors be foreign nationals, chosen by private institutions in their home countries. They could be top managers from large West European, American, or Japanese banks. Important decisions should require a supermajority. The currency board should be incorporated in a safe-haven country such as Switzerland. It should be made clear that the board's assets belong to the board itself and are not subject to expropriation by the government. The currency board will be a semiprivate, nonprofit organization.

Competition with foreign currencies will improve the currency board's incentive to maintain the fixed exchange rate. Forced-tender laws, which compel people to accept payment in local currency, should be abolished. People should be able to make contracts in and to use any currency that they find mutually agreeable. In particular, reserve currency notes and coins should be allowed to circulate alongside the currency board's notes and coins. The board's currency could be made interchangeable with the reserve currency by redenominating (*not* revaluing) the local currency so that the exchange rate is 1-to-1.

A major source of dissatisfaction with past currency boards was that they had no organized procedure for abandoning unsatisfactory reserve currencies. A system of fixed exchange rates is only as good as the reserve asset to which it is linked. Most past currency boards were linked to sterling, which was a chronically weak currency in years of the Bretton Woods system. They devalued with sterling against the U.S. dollar in 1949, 1967, and 1971. Devaluation raised the cost of the foreign goods that the sterling-area countries needed for their economic development, such as the food that Hong Kong imported from China. Many nations that replaced currency boards with central banks hoped that doing so would remove the ball and chain that sterling had become. Ironically, in the years since, sterling has been more stable than most of the currencies in the former sterling area. None the less, the possibility that a currency board system may become tied to an unstable reserve asset needs to be addressed.

We suggest specifying trigger points for switching reserve assets. For example, a board linked to the U.S. dollar could be required to reset the exchange rate or to switch to a more stable reserve asset if annualized wholesale price inflation in the United States falls outside the range minus 5 percent to 25 percent for more than two years, or minus 10 percent to 50 percent for more than six months. The board's profits will help cushion any losses from switching reserve currencies.

It may also be advisable to specify trigger points in a similar fashion to prevent the domestic currency from appreciating or depreciating too fast in real terms against the currencies of major trading partners. (Chile, for example, suffered from linking its currency to the U.S. dollar in the early 1980s, just as the dollar began an enormous real appreciation against other currencies.) The point is that predetermined rules known to the public are better than the ad hoc responses to problems with the reserve asset that currency board systems have previously made.[4]

Currency Boards as Competitive Issuers

A more radical step to protect the currency board from political meddling would be to auction it to the private sector. The franchise to operate the currency board could be permanent or extend for a fixed term, at the end of which it would be auctioned again. The private purchaser of the currency board franchise should be willing to pay just enough to exhaust the monopoly profits of note issue (cf. Demsetz 1968). The franchise could be auctioned to multiple operators. Two or more private issuers could be given the right to issue notes, which would introduce limited competition among domestic issuers. The ultimate goal should be to open the field to unfettered competition, so that the currency board becomes one of a number of competing issuers. Banks should not be subject to any special reserve requirements for notes or coins, but should be allowed to issue notes and coins on the same basis as deposits. Historical precedents for such an arrangement exist. In British Caribbean colonies, bank notes circulated alongside currency board notes from the 1930s until the 1950s, when local governments outlawed bank note issue to gain more seignorage revenue for themselves. The notes of the North Russian currency board competed with the notes of other Russian governments.

Whether the currency board would continue to exist in the face of competition from banks would depend on whether consumers wished to continue holding its notes and coins. If not, its note and coin circulation would fall as that of banks gained circulation. The currency board could be subjected to a "sunset clause" requiring it to cease business when its market share of domestic note circulation fell below, say, 10 percent (Dowd 1993). Because the board would have 100 percent foreign assets, it would easily be able to meet demands to redeem its notes and coins. The board would disappear after having served as a bridge between central banking and free banking.

Bank-issued notes and coins could be convertible into the same reserve asset as those of the currency board or into a different reserve asset; they could even be fiat money. (Unlike government fiat money, fiat money issued by free banks would not be a forced legal tender.) Competitive issue would permit each consumer to pick his own monetary policy from the choices offered by the issuers, rather than imposing a single (and often widely undesired) standard on everyone. Competitive issue is an alternative and superior approach to the usual way of posing questions of the monetary standard or monetary policy as a debate over rules versus discretion for a monopoly issuer (White 1989). The history of competitive issue suggests that market forces usually lead to convergence on a single (widely desired) monetary standard. But there have been exceptions, most notably in China, where for several centuries of free banking until the 1920s, silver and copper were parallel standards, with floating exchange rates (Shiu 1991).

In many countries, the currency board system has been a transitional stage between free banking and central banking. The result of central banking has been high inflation and frequently economic ruin. The currency board system deserves another look, this time as a transitional system from central banking to free banking that is particularly appropriate for countries that lack the conditions for establishing free banking immediately.

Notes

1. The next few pages draw on Schuler (1992c).
2. The problem of credibility is not confined to central banks in developing countries, as continuing speculative pressure on the currencies of the European Monetary System shows. The problem of credibility is more severe in most developing countries than in developed ones, however. For a theoretical treatment of credibility, see Persson and Tabellini (1990).
3. We use this term in an extended sense to include all of the former Soviet Union.
4. It may be objected that trigger points will encourage destablizing speculation when they are close to being triggered. Speculation will occur, but it is incorrect to describe it as destabilizing. Destabilizing speculation occurs when the commitment to maintaining an exchange rate is in doubt. Under our proposal, the currency board will be following well-defined rules. Until a trigger point is reached, it is committed to maintaining the existing exchange rate; after a trigger point is reached, it has no commitment to the previous exchange rate.

References

Alesina, Alberto. 1989. "Politics and Business Cycles in Industrial Democracies." *Economic Policy* 8 (April): 57–98.

Demsetz, Harold. 1968. "Why Regulate Utilities?" *Journal of Law and Economics* 11, 1 (April): 55–65.

Dowd, Kevin, ed. 1992a. *The Experience of Free Banking*. London: Routledge.

———. 1993. "Money and Market: What Role for Government?" *Cato Journal* 12, 3: 557–76.

Gressel, Daniel. 1989. "Soviet Macroeconomic Imbalances During Perestroika." Unpublished manuscript. GT Capital Management, San Francisco.

Fisher, Irving. 1935. *100% Money*. New York: Adelphi Press.

Hanke, Steve H., Lars Jonung, and Kurt Schuler. 1992. *Monetary Reform for a Free Estonia: A Currency Board Solution*. Stockholm: SNS Förlag.

Hanke, Steve H., and Kurt Schuler. 1991a. *Monetary Reform and the Development of a Yugoslav Market Economy*. London: Centre for Research into Communist Economies.

———. 1991b. *Banco central o caja de conversion?* Buenos Aires: Fundacion Republica.

———. 1991c. "Ruble Reform: A Lesson from Keynes." *Cato Journal* 10, 3 (Winter): 655–66.

———. 1991d. "Currency Boards for Eastern Europe." Heritage Lectures No. 355. Washington, DC: Heritage Foundation.

———. 1994. *Currency Boards for Developing Countries*. San Francisco, CA: International Center for Economic Growth.

Hanke, Steve H., and Alan A. Walters. 1991. *Capital Markets and Development*. San Francisco: Institute for Contemporary Studies Press.

Hayek, F. A. 1978. *Denationalisation of Money—The Argument Refined: An Analysis of the Theory and Practice of Concurrent Currencies*. 2d ed. Hobart Special Paper No. 70. London: Institute of Economic Affairs.

Hetzel, Robert. 1990. "Free Enterprise and Central Banking in Formerly Communist Countries." *Federal Reserve Bank of Richmond Economic Review* 76, 3 (July): 13–19.

Marx, Karl, and Friedrich Engels. [1848] 1948. *The Communist Manifesto*. New York: International Publishers.

Persson, Torsten, and Guido Tabellini. 1990. *Macroeconomic Policy, Credibility and Politics*. Chur, Switzerland: Harwood Academic Publishers.

Rothbard, Murray N. 1962. "The Case for a 100 Percent Gold Dollar." In *In Search of a Monetary Constitution*, edited by Leland B. Yeager. Cambridge, MA: Harvard University Press.

Schuler, Kurt. 1992a. "Overview: The World History of Free Banking." In *The Experience of Free Banking*, edited by Kevin Dowd. London: Routledge.

————. 1992b. "Free Banking in Canada." In *The Experience of Free Banking*, edited by Kevin Dowd. London: Routledge.

————. 1992c. "Currency Boards." Ph.D. dissertation, George Mason University.

Schuler, Kurt, George Selgin, and Joseph Sinkey, Jr. 1991. "Replacing the Ruble in Lithuania: Real Change versus Pseudoreform." Cato Institute Policy Analysis No. 163 (28 October). Washington, DC: Cato Institute.

Selgin, George A. 1988. *The Theory of Free Banking: Money Supply under Competitive Note Issue*. Totowa, NJ: Rowman and Littlefield.

Shiu, M. C. 1991. "Free Banking in China." Unpublished manuscript, George Mason University.

Simons, Henry. 1934. *A Positive Program for Laissez Faire*. Chicago: University of Chicago Press.

Volcker, Paul. 1990. "The Role of Central Banks." In *Central Banking Issues in Emerging Market Economies: A Symposium Sponsored by the Federal Reserve Bank of Kansas City*. Kansas City: Federal Reserve Bank.

White, Lawrence H. 1989. "Free Banking as an Alternative Monetary System" and "Fix or Float? The International Monetary Dilemma." In *Competition and Currency: Essays on Free Banking and Money*. New York: New York University Press.

World Bank. 1991. *World Development Report 1991: The Challenge of Development*. Oxford: Oxford University Press.

About the Editors

Kevin Dowd is Research Fellow at the Independent Institute in Oakland, California, and Yorkshire Bank Professor of Financial Economics, Sheffield Hallam University. Professor Dowd received his Ph.D. in economics from the University of Sheffield. He is associate editor of *The Review of Policy Issues*, and his books include *Competition and Finance, Laissez-Faire Banking, Private Money,* and *The State and the Monetary System*. His articles have appeared in *Applied Economics, Canadian Journal of Economics, Economic Journal, Economic Modeling, Greek Economic Review, Journal of Economic Surveys, Journal of Macroeconomics, Journal of Money, Credit and Banking, Oxford Economic Papers, Scottish Journal of Political Economy, Southern Economic Journal* and *The World Economy*.

Richard H. Timberlake, Jr., is Research Fellow at the Independent Institute and professor of economics (retired) at the University of Georgia. Professor Timberlake received his Ph.D. in economics from the University of Chicago. He came to the University of Georgia in 1964 after teaching at several other colleges. He is a past vice president of the Southern Economic Association and has been several times a visiting scholar in the Research Department at the Federal Reserve Bank of Richmond. He is the author of several books: *Money, Banking and Central Banking,* 1965; *Money and Banking* (with Edward Selby), 1972; *The Origins of Central Banking in the United States,* 1978; *Gold, Greenbacks and the Constitution,* 1991; and *Monetary Policy in the United States, an Institutional and Intellectual History,* 1993. His many articles and reviews have been published in the *Review of Economics and Statistics; Journal of Finance; Journal of Political Economy; Southern Economic Journal; Journal of Economic History; Journal of Money, Credit, and Banking; Journal of Monetary Economics; American Economic Review; Kredit und Kapital; Cato Journal; History of Political Economy;* and others. He has also had articles in the *Wall Street Journal; Bankers' Magazine; National Review; Human Events;*

and other news media. He has contributed to professional encyclopedias: *Encyclopedia of American Business History and Biography; The New Palgrave Dictionary of Money and Finance;* and *Business Cycles and Depressions, An Encyclopedia.* He is currently working on a research project that reargues the major monetary decisions that have come before the Supreme Court.

About the Contributors

Richard C. K. Burdekin is associate professor of economics at Claremont McKenna College. Professor Burdekin received his Ph.D. in economics from the University of Houston and has served as assistant professor of economics at the University of Miami and Visiting Scholar at the Federal Reserve Bank of Dallas. His books include *Distributional Conflict and Inflation* (with P. Burkett), *Establishing Monetary Stability in Emerging Market Economies* (ed. with T. Willett, R. Sweeney, and C. Wihlborg), *Confidence, Credibility and Macroeconomic Policy* (with F. Langdana), and *Budget Deficits and Economic Performance* (with F. Langdana). A contributor to nine scholarly volumes, his articles and reviews have appeared in such journals as *Economic Inquiry, Economic Record, Explorations in Economic History, European Journal of Political Economy, Journal of International Money and Finance, Journal of Macroeconomics, Journal of Money, Credit and Banking, Public Choice, Review of Economics and Statistics,* and *World Economy.*

Thomas F. Cargill is professor of economics at the University of Nevada, having received his Ph.D. in economics from the University of California at Davis. Professor Cargill has been visiting scholar at the Bank of Japan, comptroller of the Currency, Federal Reserve Bank of San Francisco, Hoover Institution, and the Ministry of Japan. His books and monographs include *Financial Deregulation and Monetary Control* (with G. Garcia)*; Financial Reform in the 1980s* (with G. Garcia)*; The Transition of Finance in Japan and the United States* (with S. Royama)*; Money, the Financial System and Monetary Policy; Central Bank Independence and Regulatory Responsibilities;* and *The Political Economy of Japanese Monetary Policy* (with M. Hutchinson and T. Ito). Professor Cargill is the author or coauthor of over 100 articles and reviews in such scholarly journals as the *American Economic Review, Applied Economics, Econometrica, Economic Inquiry, History of Political Economy, International Economic Review, Journal of Finance* and *Journal of Money, Credit and Banking.*

David Glasner is staff economist with the Bureau of Economics at the Federal Trade Commission. Having received his Ph.D. in economics from the University of California at Los Angeles, he has been assistant professor of economics at Marquette University and visiting assistant professor of economics at New York University, and he has taught at California State University at Long Beach and the University of California at Riverside. The author of the books, *Politics, Prices and Petroleum* and *Free Banking and Monetary Reform*, he is the editor of the *Business Cycles and Depressions: An Encyclopedia*, and his articles have appeared in *Antitrust Law Bulletin, Commentary, Encounter, Freeman, History of Economics Society Bulletin, History of Political Economy, The Independent Review, Intercollegiate Review, International Review of Law and Economics, Michigan Quarterly Review, National Review, New Leader, Newsweek, The New York Times, Southern Economic Journal, This World,* and *The Wall Street Journal.*

Steve H. Hanke is professor of applied economics at Johns Hopkins University. He is also vice chairman of the Friedberg Mercantile Group, President of the Toronto Trust-Argentina in Buenos Aires, and President of FCMI NZ Financial Corporation, Ltd., Auckland, New Zealand. A columnist for *Forbes*, he is a member of the steering committee of the G7 Council, Fellow at the World Economic Forum in Geneva, and member of the board of governors at the Philadelphia Stock Exchange. Professor Hanke has served as senior economist on President Reagan's Council of Economic Advisors, economic advisor to the vice president of Yugoslavia, state counselor on monetary and financial issues for the Republic of Lithuania, advisor to the minister of economy of the Republic of Argentina, and advisor to the president of Bulgaria. He is the author of the books, *Alternative Monetary Regimes for Jamaica, Capital Markets and Development, Currency Boards for Developing Countries, Juntas Monetarias para Paises en Desarollo, Privatization and Development, Prospects for Privatization* and *Russian Currency and Finance.*

Robert E. Keleher is chief macroeconomist at the Joint Economic Committee. He has also served as chief economist at Johnson Smick International, associate director of the G7 Council, special monetary advisor to the vice chairman of the Federal Reserve System, senior macroeconomist to the Council of Economic Advisors, and senior financial officer at the Federal Reserve Bank of Atlanta. Dr. Keleher received his Ph.D. in economics from Indiana University. He is the author of the books, *Monetary Policy* (with M. Johnson) and *The Mon-*

etary Approach to the Balance of Payments, Exchange Rates and World Inflation (with T. Humphrey). A contributor to numerous scholarly volumes, Dr. Keleher is the author of articles in such publications as *Bankers' Magazine, Business Economics, Contemporary Policy Issues, Economic Impact, Economic Journal, International Economy, Money Manager, Public Budgeting and Financial Management, Southern Business and Economic Journal,* and *The World of Banking*.

Merton H. Miller received the Nobel Memorial Prize in Economic Science in 1990, and he is the Robert R. McCormick Distinguished Service Professor Emeritus, Graduate School of Business, University of Chicago. A Fellow of the Econometric Society and American Academy of Arts and Sciences, Distinguished Fellow of the American Economic Association, and Senior Fellow of the American Association of Financial Engineers, Professor Miller is past president of the American Finance Association. His books include *Auditing Management Games and Accounting Education, Essays in Applied Price Theory, Essays in Economic Semantics, Financial Innovations and Market Volatility, Macroeconomics,* and *The Theory of Finance*. Professor Miller is the author of over sixty articles and reviews in scholarly journals, and he is the recipient of honorary degrees from De Paul University, Suffolk University, Universidad Nacional de Educacion a Distancia (Spain), University of Illinois (Chicago), University of Karlsruhe (Germany), University of Leuven (Belgium), and University of Rochester.

Alan Reynolds is director of economic research for the Hudson Institute. He has been research director for the National Commission on Economic Growth and Tax Reform and director of economic research at the Hudson Institute, chief economist with Polyconomics, senior economist at Argus Research, and vice president of First National Bank of Chicago where he was editor of *First Chicago World Report*. A member of President Reagan's Transition Team on Tax Policy, he has been an advisor on tax reform to the Finance Ministry of Canada. Mr. Reynolds is a frequent contributor to *The Wall Street Journal, Forbes, Fortune, Harvard Business Review, Policy Review, National Review* and *The Washington Times*.

Kenneth J. Robinson is senior economist and policy advisor at the Federal Reserve Bank of Dallas, having joined the bank in 1986 specializing in macroeconomics and money and banking. Dr. Robinson received his Ph.D. in economics from Ohio State University.

Murray N. Rothbard was the S. J. Hall Distinguished Professor of Economics at the University of Nevada at Las Vegas until his death in

1995. The recipient of the Richard M. Weaver Prize for Scholarly Letters, he received his Ph.D. in economics from Columbia University, and he served as instructor at City College of New York, senior analyst for the William Volker Fund, associate of the University Seminar in the History of Legal and Political Thought at Columbia University, consultant to the U.S. Commission on Gold, and professor of economics at New York Polytechnic Institute. Founding editor of the *Journal of Libertarian Studies* and the *Review of Austrian Economics*, Professor Rothbard contributed to over thirty scholarly volumes and his articles and reviews appeared in such scholarly journals as the *American Economic Review, American Political Science Review, Journal of Economic Literature* and *Journal of the History of Ideas*, as well as in such publications as *The New York Times, National Review, Los Angeles Times* and *Washington Post*. Among his many books are *America's Great Depression, Austrian Perspectives on the History of Economic Thought, The Case Against the Fed, The Case for a 100% Gold Dollar, Conceived in Liberty, The Ethics of Liberty, For a New Liberty, Man, Economy and State, The Mystery of Banking, A New History of Leviathan* (ed. with R. Radosh), *The Panic of 1819, Power and Market*, and *What Has Government Done to Our Money?*

Kurt A. Schuler is an independent consultant specializing in money and banking. Previously, he was a post-doctoral Fellow at the Johns Hopkins University in Baltimore, where he was Dr. Hanke's assistant. Dr. Schuler's most recent book is, *Should Developing Countries Have Central Banks?* (1996).

Genie D. Short is vice president of the Federal Reserve Bank of Dallas where she oversees the Financial Industry Studies Department and the monitoring of the Mexican banking system. A contributor to numerous scholarly volumes on banking and financial policy, Dr. Short received her Ph.D. in economics from the University of Virginia, and she has served as planning officer at Southeast Banking Corporation and economist at the Federal Reserve Bank of New York. Having also taught at the University of Miami, her articles have appeared in such scholarly journals as the *Consumer Finance Law Quarterly, Financial Industry Studies, Journal of Commercial Bank Lending, Journal of Money, Credit and Banking*, and *North American Journal of Economics and Finance*, as well as in such publications as *Bankers Magazine, Euromoney, Financial Industry Issues, Money Manager* and *The Wall Street Journal*.

Frank van Dun is senior lecturer in the Philosophy of Law at the University of Maastricht, The Netherlands, and the University of Ghent,

Belgium. Dr. van Dun received his Ph.D. in the philosophy of law and legal theory from the University of Ghent, and he has been a research fellow at the National Foundation for Scientific Research in Brussels. His books include *Natural Law and the Right to Tax*, *The Fundamental Principle of Law*, and *Utopian Paradoxes* (with H. Crombag), and his articles and reviews have been published in *Logique et Analyse* and numerous other scholarly journals.

Jilleen R. Westbrook is assistant professor of economics at Temple University, having received her Ph.D. in economics from Claremont Graduate School. Professor Westbrook has taught at Scripps College, Pfitzer College, Fresno Pacific College, and the University of California at Davis. Her articles have appeared in such journals as *Applied Economics* and *Economic Inquiry*, and she is a contributor to the volumes, *Economics Slamdunk*, *Economics USA*, *Exchange Rate Policies for Emerging Market Economies*, and *Varieties of Monetary Reform*.

Lawrence H. White is associate professor of economics at the University of Georgia. Professor White received his Ph.D. in economics from the University of California at Los Angeles. A contributor to twenty scholarly volumes, he is the co-editor (with M. Rizzo) of the book series, *The Foundations of the Market Economy*. His books and monographs include *African Finance, Competition and Currency, The Crisis in American Banking, Democratick Editorials: Essays in Jacksonian Political Economy, Do We Need a Reserve Bank?, Free Banking* and *Free Banking in Britain*. His articles and reviews have appeared in *American Economic Review, Business History Review, Economic Inquiry, Economica, History of Political Economy, Journal of Economic Literature, Journal of Monetary Economics, Journal of Money, Credit and Banking* and *Journal of Post Keynesian Economics*.

Thomas D. Willett is Horton Professor of Economics at Claremont Graduate School and Claremont McKenna College and Director of the Claremont Institute for Economic Policy Studies. Having received his Ph.D. in economics from the University of Virginia, he has served as deputy assistant secretary of the Treasury for International Affairs, director of international monetary research at the U.S. Treasury, and senior staff economist at the Council of Economic Advisors. He has also taught at Cornell University and Harvard University. The author of over 200 scholarly articles and reviews, he is co-editor of *Economic Inquiry* and editor of the book series, *The Political Economy of Global Interdependence*. Among Professor Willett's twenty-five scholarly books and monographs are *Challenges to a Liberal International Eco-*

nomic Order (edited with G. Haberler), *The Economic Approach to Public Policy* (edited with R. Amacher and R. Tollison), *Exchange Rate Policies for Emerging Market Economies* (ed. with R. Sweeney and C. Wihlborg), *Financial Regulation and Monetary Arrangements After 1992* (ed. with C. Wihlborg and M. Fratianni), *Floating Exchange Rates and International Monetary Reform, The International Monetary System* (ed. with L. Officer), *The Internationalization of the American Economy* (ed. with J. Finger), *International Trade Policies* (ed. with J. Odell), *Monetary Policy for a Volatile Global Economy* (ed. with W. Haraf), *Political Business Cycles, Presidential Measures on Balance of Payments Control* (with G. Haberler), and *Reaganomics* (edited with W. Stubblebine).

Leland B. Yeager is the Ludwig von Mises Distinguished Professor Emeritus of Economics at Auburn University and the Paul Goodloe McIntire Professor of Economics Emeritus at the University of Virginia. He received his Ph.D. in economics from Columbia University, and he has also taught at George Mason University, New York University, Southern Methodist University, Texas A&M University, University of California at Los Angeles, and University of Maryland. Professor Yeager has served as president of the Southern Economic Association, Atlantic Economic Society, Interlingua Institute, and Union Mundial pro Interlingua. He is the author or editor of fourteen books and monographs, including *In Search of a Monetary Constitution, International Monetary Relations, Trade Policy and the Price System* (with D. Tuerck), and *The Fluttering Veil*. The author of over 100 articles and reviews in scholarly journals, he is a contributor to forty volumes as well as to the *Compton Encyclopedia* and *The New Palgrave: A Dictionary of Economics*.

Index